COMPARATIVE EDUCATION, TERRORISM AND HUMAN SECURITY

COMPARATIVE EDUCATION, TERRORISM AND HUMAN SECURITY: FROM CRITICAL PEDAGOGY TO PEACE BUILDING?

Edited by
Wayne Nelles

First published 2003 by
PALGRAVE MACMILLAN™
175 Fifth Avenue, New York, N.Y. 10010 and
Houndmills, Basingstoke, Hampshire, England RG21 6XS
Companies and representatives throughout the world

PALGRAVE MACMILLAN is the global academic imprint of the Palgrave Macmillan division of St. Martin's Press, LLC and of Palgrave Macmillan Ltd. Macmillan® is a registered trademark in the United States, United Kingdom and other countries. Palgrave is a registered trademark in the European Union and other countries.

ISBN 1–4039–6415–7 hardback

Library of Congress Cataloging-in-Publication Data
    Comparative education, terrorism, and human security: from critical pedagogy to peacebuilding?/edited by Wayne Nelles.
        p. cm.
    Includes bibliographical references and index.
    ISBN 1–4039–6415–7 (hardcover)
      1. Comparative education. 2. Critical pedagogy. 3. Politics and education.
    4. Interdisciplinary approach in education. I. Nelles, Wayne C.

    LB43.C683 2003
    370.9—dc21   2003050900

A catalogue record for this book is available from the British Library.

Design by Newgen Imaging Systems (P) Ltd., Chennai, India.

First edition: December, 2003
10 9 8 7 6 5 4 3 2 1

Printed in the United States of America.

CONTENTS

NOTES ON CONTRIBUTORS

ANDI BAKTI is a research fellow (2002–2003) at the International Institute for Asian Studies (IIAS) at Leiden University (The Netherlands) and was assistant professor at the Department of Pacific and Asian Studies, University of Victoria (Canada). He completed his doctoral dissertation in international communication and development studies through a joint Ph.D. (Université du Québec à Montréal, Concordia University, and Université de Montréal) on "Communication, Islam, and Development in Indonesia." He was Fellow of the Social Sciences and Humanities Research Council of Canada as well as Fellow of the *Fonds pour la formation de chercheurs et l'aide à la recherche* (FCAR, Quebec Government Research Foundation). He is a former lecturer of the Alauddin Institute, Indonesia, and is actively involved in security issues with the Canadian Consortium on Asia Pacific Security (CANCAPS), as well as with issues of good governance, civil society, decentralization, in Southeast Asia.

MATTHEW CANNON B.A. (Syracuse University 1994), Ph.D. (University of Limerick 2001), is originally from New York. In 2002 he received an award from the European Union Committee of the Regions for his study of the role of local governments in the formation of the Transmanche Euroregion across the English Channel. His research interests include cross-border cooperation, policing and developments in the role of local government. He cofounded the *University of Limerick Political & Economic Review*, now known as *Perspectives*, edited the journal for two years. Dr. Cannon is the programme director for the Irish Peace Institute, a nongovernmental organization that works to promote peace and reconciliation on the island of Ireland through programs of education, research and outreach.

SHENG YAO CHENG is a doctoral candidate in Comparative and International Education at the University of California, Los Angeles (UCLA). He is also a research coordinator at the Center for International and Development Education (CIDE). His dissertation and research centers on educational policy analysis with an emphasis on aboriginal education reform in Taiwan and the United States. His research interests are in the areas of comparative and international education, policy analysis and the politics of identity among minority and marginalized groups. His M.A. thesis was later published into a book on education in Hong Kong during its transition from the United Kingdom to China. He has also conducted extensive research on higher education in China, Singapore and The Netherlands. He was also a founding member of the Paulo Freire Institute at UCLA.

CASANDRA CULCER is a doctoral student in Higher Education at the University of Toledo, OH. From 1993 to 1999 she worked as a referent for international relations at the University of Bucharest, Romania, and as a member of the EAIE (European Association for International Education), of the EUPRIO (European Universities Public Relations and Information Officers) and of the AMU (University Managers Association in Romania). She was involved in international programs launched by the European Commission such as Socrates and Tempus, as well as in various other forms of international academic cooperation. Since 1999 she has been pursuing her Ph.D. in the United States.

MARK GINSBURG is Professor of Comparative Sociology of Education and Co-Director of the Institute for International Studies in Education at the University of Pittsburgh (Pennsylvania, U.S.A). He previously was a faculty member at the University of Aston (Birmingham, England) and the University of Houston (Texas, U.S.A), and has lectured in China, Cuba, Egypt, Korea, Norway, Mexico and South Africa. His publications include: *Contradictions in Teacher Education and Society* (1988), *Understanding Educational Reform in Global Context* (1991), *The Politics of Educators' Work and Lives* (1995), *The Political Dimension in Teacher Education* (1995), *Cuba in the Special Period: Cuban Perspectives* (1997) and *Limitations and Possibilities of Dialogue among Researchers, Policy Makers, and Practitioners* (2003, forthcoming).

BUDD HALL Ph.D., is currently Dean of the Faculty of Education at the University of Victoria. Budd was formerly Professor and Chair of Adult Education at the University of Toronto (1991–2001) and Secretary-General of the International Council for Adult Education (1978–1991). He is a founder of the participatory research movement, which he initiated while working in Tanzania during the early 1970s. He has published extensively in both academic and social movement publications. His book *Voices of Change: Participatory Research in Canada and the United States* (1993) has been widely used as a text in North American universities. His most recent book, edited with Dr. George Sefa Dei, is *Indigenous Knowledges in Global Perspectives: Multiple Readings of the World* (2000). Social movement learning is the term that most fully describes his intellectual location. He is also a poet.

W. JAMES JACOB is a doctoral candidate in Comparative and International Education at the University of California, Los Angeles. He is also research coordinator at the Center for International and Development Education (CIDE). His work focuses on program evaluation in developing countries with an emphasis on East Africa and China. He coordinated a national unit-cost study on private secondary education in Uganda from 2000 to 2001. From 2001 to 2003, he was the principal investigator of a sub-Saharan African HIV/AIDS education research program for Laubach Literacy International, the world's oldest and largest literacy organization, and simultaneously directed a national HIV/AIDS education evaluation for the Uganda Ministry of Education and Sports. He is currently conducting a study on the influences of the market on higher education in China.

Mark S. Johnson trained in Soviet studies and history with a M.A. and Ph.D. from Columbia University (1995) and the Harriman Institute. His current position is in history and educational studies at Colorado College. He has worked as a policy analyst and evaluator of international assistance programs for various U.S. government agencies and private foundations in Eastern Europe, Russia, the Caucasus and Central Asia, and has conducted field research relevant to this chapter in Georgia, Azerbaijan, Kazakhstan and the Kyrgyz Republic. He has numerous publications, and is currently writing a textbook, *Education in World History* (under contract with Routledge).

Robert Krech is an independent consultant based in Washington, DC working in the area of peace education and child rights. His recent research in Sierra Leone examined NGO programing for the reintegration of former child combatants. He holds an M.A. in Education from the Ontario Institute for Studies in Education at the University of Toronto, Canada.

John Marciano is Professor Emeritus of Social–Historical Foundations of Education at the State University of New York at Cortland. An activist, teacher and scholar, he is coauthor of *Teaching the Vietnam War* (with William L. Griffen, 1979), and author of *Civic Illiteracy and Education: The Battle for the Hearts and Minds of American Youth* (1997).

Stuart McAninch is Associate Professor in the division of Urban Leadership and Policy Studies in Education at the University of Missouri, Kansas City, where he teaches undergraduate and graduate courses on the social and historical foundations of American education. He has authored or coauthored articles published in *Educational Foundations, Educational Studies, Educational Theory, and Theory and Research in Social Education*, as well as chapters that have appeared in several books.

Nagwa Megahed is an Assistant Faculty of Social and Philosophical Foundations of Education at Ain Shams University (Cairo, Egypt). She is currently a Doctoral Candidate at the Administrative and Policy Studies Department, School of Education, University of Pittsburgh (Pennsylvania, U.S.A). She worked as Graduate Student Researcher at the Institute for International Studies in Education (University of Pittsburgh) on projects related to educational reform and teacher education. Her presentations and publications include: *Understanding Islam and the Arab Culture (2001), Secondary Education Reforms in Egypt: Rectifying Inequality of Educational and Employment Opportunities (2002), Voices of Teachers in Academic and Vocational Schools in Egypt (2002).*

Richard Maclure is an Associate Professor and former Acting Dean in the Faculty of Education, University of Ottawa. He has a doctorate from

Stanford University. His current research program focuses on policy issues pertaining to at-risk children in Africa and Latin America. He is currently involved in a two-year CIDA-sponsored research project focusing on the experiences of child soldiers in Sierra Leone and their reintegration into community environments that are themselves undergoing processes of social reconstruction. An action-research project that is being conducted collaboratively with two NGOs in Sierra Leone, the study has been designed to facilitate local programs as well as to enhance broader policy perspectives related to the rehabilitation of child soldiers. Prior to this project, in 2000 Professor Maclure also coordinated a participatory evaluation of an NGO-sponsored rapid education project for displaced children in Freetown.

SHAHRZAD MOJAB, Associate Professor, teaches at the Department of Adult Education, Community Development and Counseling Psychology, The Ontario Institute for Studies in Education at the University of Toronto. Her speciality includes: educational policy studies with focus on policies affecting the academic life of marginalized groups in universities; comparative and international adult education policy; adult education, globalization and learning. Her publications include, among others, articles and book chapters on skilling and de-skilling of immigrant women; adult education and the construction of civil society, women, violence and learning and feminism, globalization and nationalism. She is the editor of a book titled *Women of A Non State Nation: The Kurds* (2001) and the coeditor of *Of Property and Propriety: The Role of Gender and Class in Imperialism and Nationalism* (2001). She also was the editor of *Convergence*, the journal of the International Council of Adult Education.

JORGE NEF is Professor of Politics, International Development and Rural Extension Studies at the University of Guelph. A graduate of the University of Chile and a Ph.D. in Political Science, he has been a Visiting Professor in Canadian and foreign universities. He was Vice-President of the Chilean College of Public Administrators and president of the Canadian Association of Latin American and Caribbean Studies (CALACS), and has been the recipient of various teaching awards. He was Editor of the *Canadian Journal of Latin American and Caribbean Studies* (CJLACS) and has written numerous books and monographs, edited collections and journal articles or book contributions. His most recent book *Human Security and Mutual Vulnerability* appeared in 1999. He has worked with national and international development agencies in Latin America and the Pacific. He has been the Director of the School of Government, Public Administration and Political Science at the University of Chile.

WAYNE NELLES is Senior Associate with the Sustainable Development Research Initiative at the University of British Columbia where he also received his Ph.D. He was program director of SDRI's International Internship Program from 1996 to 2000 and served on boards of professional associations including the Canadian Consortium on Asia Pacific

Security and Canadian Association for Development Studies. He has a special fondness for both the Balkans and Mongolia where he has worked. His research on education, youth, sustainability and security issues has been published in: *Asian Perspective; BC Historical News; Canadian and International Education, Canadian Journal of Development Studies; Higher Education in Europe; International Journal (of the CIIA); International Journal of Canadian Studies; International Politics; Learning Quarterly; Our Schools–Our Selves* and the *UNESCO Encyclopedia of Life Support Systems.* He was awarded a 2002 Canadian Department of Foreign Affairs and International Trade Human Security Fellowship allowing him to edit the present book.

HEIDI ROSS is Professor of Educational Studies and Robert Ho Fellow in Chinese Studies at Colgate University. She has recently served as President of the Comparative and International Education Society and is an executive board member of the World Council of Comparative Education Societies. She publishes widely on girls' education, gender, social class formation and secondary schooling in China. Her publications include *China Learns English* (1993), *The Ethnographic Eye* (2000), and numerous articles and reviews in *The China Education Forum, China Information, Chinese Education and Society, Comparative Education Review, Compare, History of Education Quarterly, Journal of Asian Studies, Journal of Thought, Journal of Women and Gender Studies* and *McGill Journal of Education.*

1

INTRODUCTION

Wayne Nelles

This book attempts to stimulate fresh academic and policy debate on education and security relationships. It includes critical assessments of American issues as well as selected national and regional case studies with theoretical, cross-disciplinary and comparative analyses to illustrate broader themes. The studies presented could lead to other comparative education research, illuminating links to terrorism, school-based violence, and conflict or security issues more broadly. In short the volume offers a range of empirical, theoretical, qualitative, analytical and policy-oriented reflections on how education reproduces, and may help mitigate or prevent, political violence or future wars. It provides new contexts, analysis and lessons that could stimulate relevant education policy, administrative and curricular reforms.

This book by no means claims to be comprehensive or conclusive. But it points to a new interdisciplinary research agenda linking human security and critical pedagogy discourse. These issues have mostly been ignored by scholars, teachers and field practitioners so the book could be of general interest for those seeking to better understand the role education plays in international affairs. It could be used as a graduate textbook in Comparative and International Education (CIE), International Relations (IR), Security Studies, and Peace and Conflict Studies (PCS), and peace education or violence prevention programs, as well as for those specializing in International Development Studies (IDS) or study of education aid or technical assistance programs. It may also have broader value, for educational professional organizations, aid agencies, government departments and voluntary associations with interests in education, counterterrorism, international development, peace building and security. Two theoretical premises inform most contributions. The first is that universal, global "human security" for all persons ought to be a principal moral goal for all governments and their citizens, not a narrowly conceived or poorly justified "national security" that protects state power or personal interests of privileged elite. A second is an emphasis on nonviolent means for achieving personal or national security, preventing unnecessary violence or military conflicts, and building peace (preferably *before*, but also after wars) through education.

The thematic focus for this volume is partly as a response to the events of September 11, 2001 ("9/11") in the United States, an attack in which Americans and scores of other nationals suffered tragic losses. It does not dispute that the United States remains vulnerable or that it has a right to its security and sovereignty, but several chapters here challenge public or official analyses about that threat, and violent American responses. This is not a book only about American issues or suffering and its problematic and narrow notion of "security." However, its 9/11 retaliation through a "war on terrorism" cannot be ignored since there is hardly a nation or person on earth unaffected, by the American response and its further projection of moral and military power with problematic outcomes. As such the book is partly about intellectually deconstructing and pragmatically responding to recent events. It explores some educational implications behind developments, in terms of domestic teaching or curricular challenges for the United States. But it goes beyond American concerns and perspectives.

This book does not attempt to "justify" or promote terrorism, criminal behavior, political violence and religious extremism by any definition or through any form. Anticipating the book's critics it is not about "appeasement," or being "soft on terrorism." Military strategists or hawks might (wrongly) argue this about nonviolent or nonmilitary perspectives explored here. Rather, this book links education, security and international relations research with critical pedagogy analysis to better understand how all forms of violence (diplomatic bullying and institutionalized militarism among them), including terrorism (and war, as its big brother or "cousin") are reproduced through education. It is also about alternatives or mitigating strategies for countering political violence through nonmilitary security cooperation and peace building.

There are two interrelated challenges discussed. First are the pedagogical dilemmas and imperatives for schools, teacher training institutions, the media, communities and nation-states generally in the way domestic populations are informed or educated about their own country's foreign policies and international relations. This covers a range of formal or informal learning institutions or processes. Several chapters point to problematic concerns, including the need for domestic reforms in American education. Second are impacts or outcomes of various types of teaching or learning on international relations, and roles of education in domestic or political violence and civil or international wars. Generally this book brings new scholarship contributing to critical pedagogy, preventive diplomacy and nonmilitary security cooperation including theory or practice about educational aid and peace building for meeting basic needs and responding to terrorism.

The idea for this book evolved from sessions at the 2002 Annual Conference of the Comparative and International Education Society (CIES) in Orlando as well as related panels later at the 2002 American Educational Studies Association (AESA) meetings in Pittsburgh. Professor Mark Ginsburg and Ph.D. candidate, Nagwa Megahed, organized a panel called "Education, Religion, Human Security, and Terrorism in the Global Context before and after September 11, 2001." Palgrave-Macmillan expressed interest in the theme and the panel nominated me to follow-up. My approach was not to focus on American and 9/11 issues alone but to involve a wider group of scholars and themes in a comparative and cross-disciplinary project through a "Call for Papers," recruiting potential contributors among education, security and development scholars or professionals. What you are reading is a selection of papers submitted.

All books are informed by biography. The emphasis here on a "human security" approach to education, conflict and terrorism evolved from my long-standing interest as a Canadian working on related issues. My earliest experiences included adolescent crisis counseling intervention, mental health and street youth work using violence and conflict prevention techniques. I then worked among various NGOs, and participated in United Nations debates and other conferences as well as coordinated interfaith cooperation and multicultural education activities from the mid-1980s on. I linked some of this work to Comparative and International Education research while managing an international internship program at the University of British Columbia. This combination of domestic social work, international policy dialogue and university administration revealed to me a substantial amount of largely disconnected disciplinary analysis and policy, or curricular reforms surrounding education, socialization processes, youth violence, peace, security and development. Fortuitous circumstances allowed me to do more systematic research, including a 2002 Canadian government-funded Human Security Fellowship award allowing me to study such themes more closely.[1]

Not every contributor may view such issues in precisely the same way, but I starkly contrast human security-oriented versus national security approaches for responding to terrorist violence. I develop some of these ideas in my own chapter (chapter 2), but generally suggest we need to better problematize education-related issues. I note one principal concern—the need to better support personal, individual and economic security over elite, state-centric and military-led models of security. While the book examines some specific 9/11 issues and implications it is also attempts to engage a wider, more diverse community of discourse and practice. Each author approaches their topic uniquely. At the same time they are united by some understanding of and commitment to a critical pedagogy analysis or a human security paradigm that questions the militarization of educational discourse and emphasizes nonmilitary solutions to preventing violent conflict or war. They explore educational issues or mechanisms that could help build and sustain long-term peace.

The authors represented in this book are a diverse group. They have studied in or are now based at universities or research institutes around the world. They bring these different national, political and religious experiences to bear on the chapters presented. Our contributors have secular, Jewish, Muslim and Christian heritages and were born in, or have worked in countries as diverse as Canada, Chile, Egypt, Indonesia, Iran, Kenya, Romania,

Taiwan, Tanzania, Uganda and the United States. Some discuss American issues while others explore different education systems and present case studies or comparative analyses discussing East Africa, Iraqi-Kurdistan, Northern Ireland, Sierre Leone and Central Asia. In sum this unique, eclectic group of scholars analyzes and pragmatically responds to a complex set of interrelated challenges linking education, conflict, terrorism and security from local or domestic concerns to international policies and aid programs.

Part I of the book begins by exploring conceptual issues and theoretical challenges more closely. My own chapter (chapter 2) examines some empirical, theoretical, analytical and policy-oriented issues for better understanding education, terrorism and security linkages, while exploring how education may help mitigate or prevent political violence or future wars and build or sustain security. It reviews related literature and policy debates among education and international relations scholars focusing on recent human security discourse to illustrate tensions, trends and potential including future research needs. Heidi Ross (chapter 3) presents a thoughtful analysis of "relational" thinking in education as a means to build more authentic understandings of, and connections with, others to better appreciate vulnerability, overcome differences and increase personal security. She introduces a feminist critical pedagogy to bear on the challenge, offering a healthy skepticism of the Freire tradition. For a contrasting, but complementary, perspective Jorge Nef (chapter 4) presents a theoretical and biographically rich view of what he calls the "pedagogy of violence." His analysis is based on experiences as a student of Paulo Friere in 1960s Chile, and that country's own 9/11—an illegal American-backed overthrow of Allende's government on September 11, 1973, with his subsequent research and teaching about terrorism issues. Nef, now a Canadian, has since become an internationally recognized scholar of human security. For this book he offers a unique insight into the educational reproduction of political violence.

Part II examines the United States through domestic responses to 9/11, how American students and policy makers are educated to view the world, and perspectives of those international students adapting. Casandra Culcer, herself a Ph.D. student from Romania studying in the United States, offers an introduction to related debates (chapter 5) with a small qualitative study of Middle Eastern male student experiences after 9/11. She explores the problematic climate of "suspicion" facing these men, and although not all face physical danger as a result, she suggests this may still cause psychological harm. John Marciano, building on his own recent book on a related theme, offers a critique of American "civic illiteracy" (chapter 6) that reproduces a dominant-elite and "chosen people" view of patriotism, militarism and terrorism who do not seriously question U.S. government foreign policy. He argues this undermines thoughtful and active citizenship, examining media and policy debates about "teaching 9/11" or its "lessons" to illustrate. Stuart McAnich (chapter 7) presents an interesting organizational case study of the American Council of Trustees and Alumni (ACTA) and how it has sought to support patriotism and political correctness while curtailing academic freedom after 9/11. He further explores some problematic issues arising, including support from some of the nation's most powerful intellectual and political leaders, who have misrepresented scholarly critiques of American foreign, military and security policies. He concludes that the ACTA and their supporters are driven by political ideology, propaganda and media sound bytes to control the production and dissemination of knowledge.

Part III explores other national perspectives or analytical assessments through specific case studies from Europe, Asia, Africa and the Middle East. Some indirectly have American connections or implications, but they are intended as unique assessments in their own right. Andi Bakti's exploration of Indonesian religious learning groups (chapter 8) should be of obvious interest in the wake of 9/11 and especially the September 2002 Bali bombings that killed over 200 mostly Australian tourists. He does not examine that event, but his timely chapter uniquely explores some historical, political and economic contexts for religious study groups in Indonesia. His analysis, based on a related Ph.D. thesis and recent field work, offers some unique insights to Indonesian Islamic views of security, and may help us to question some Western concepts of terrorism. Matt Cannon (chapter 9) presents a similarly useful case study of how education has reproduced violence and terrorism in Northern Ireland, in the context of imperialism, colonialism and religious differences. Equally important he discusses how education has been central to process of future conflict management, violence prevention and building human security. His study points to broader lessons for approaching education in other conflict zones. Robert Kretch and Richard Maclure (chapter 10) offer insights from Sierre Leone demonstrating how problematically education failed to bring socioeconomic development after decolonization while power and corruption brought more suffering and war, including recruitment of child soldiers with poor education and employment prospects. Based on field work they discuss endemic problems, psycho-social challenges, peace-building and national reconstruction efforts with education at the core. They demonstrate that although it is difficult to understand all issues, education is central to Sierre Leone's long-term human security. Shahrzad Mojab and Budd Hall offer another timely case study (chapter 11), of Iraqi-Kurdistan, where the university has been central to the Kurdish struggle to build a "non-state nation." Canadian universities entered into knowledge partnerships, collaborative research and technical assistance amidst a very problematic geopolitical climate in "Kurdistan," which although still technically part of Iraq, culturally overlaps with Turkey, Iraq, Iran and Syria. They discuss theoretical and pragmatic issues arising, poorly supported postwar reconstruction efforts following the previous conflict, and raise concerns about the new American-led war over Iraq while questioning the international community's seriousness in support for authentic education for state building.

Part IV more systematically explores comparative, regional and religious perspectives on education, terrorism and security. Mark Ginsburg and Nagwa Megahed compare Egyptian and Muslim views (chapter 12), as well as a scholarly American and personal Jewish perspective, on terrorism and Islam with implications for pre- and post-9/11 education. They explore what this may mean for pre-service and in-service teacher training and social foundations of education courses. They approach this from multiple perspectives and a critical pedagogy framework. Similarly Sheng Yao Cheng and W. James Jacob (chapter 13) offer another comparative analysis of perspectives from East Africa (Kenya, Tanzania and Uganda) Taiwan and the United States after 9/11. The East African comparison has particular value for obvious reasons since both Kenyan and Tanzanian citizens (not Americans) mostly suffered in 1998 from terrorist attacks on U.S. embassies there but the issues raised in their chapter are important for other citizens and educators; since the aftermath these have been virtually ignored amidst the current American-centric "war on terrorism." The authors offer a useful comparative analysis of national perspectives on those attacks and peace-education alternatives. The chapter by Mark Johnson (chapter 14) offers a unique insight into the politics of education aid and technical assistance in Central Asia after 9/11. Based on field experience as a consultant and participation in recent Washington debates over new policies and programs Johnson raises concerns about increased education aid to the region, suggesting more work is needed to monitor developments.

In sum the contributors to this book cover a wide range of theoretical, geographic, national and personal perspectives. No particular chapter or book could thoroughly assess all issues, but some basic research (theoretical, empirical, case study-oriented and comparative) begins to problematize violence, terrorism and security in domestic and international education policies or programs. The book brings critical pedagogy, development research and comparative foreign policy analysis to explain trends within, or between different countries while offering some practical domestic, foreign and aid policy implications that could lead to more constructive, nonviolent, nonmilitary interventions domestically and abroad. The book should also contribute to more debate about better understanding and responding creatively, nonviolently and nonmilitarily to terrorism and security concerns through education. It is hoped this volume will also stimulate new research and pragmatic cooperation, perhaps even lead to a broader, international collaborative research project on related themes among a diverse academic, policy and professional community.

NOTES

1. I am grateful for the funding and flexibility of the Canadian Consortium on Human Security (CCHS) and its Fellowship program as well as the University of Victoria's Centre for Global Studies and its Director Dr. Gordon Smith as my host. Most of my 2002 program and field research (which I continue) was meant to focus on education and human security issues in Southeast Europe, especially Kosovo. However, CCHS Fellowship director, Dr. Brian Job, allowed me to pursue related issues arising in the post-9/11 world. My argument here in no way

represents the official views or policies of the Canadian government, or its Department of Foreign Affairs and International Trade (DFAIT), that provides CCHS funding. The government of Canada from the late 1990s on has promoted a human security agenda, some linking education, child protection and global security issues. But whereas I believe Canada has offered this among other innovative and useful models for peacekeeping, multilateralism and development cooperation over the past few decades, it has problematically supported more economic integration and military alignment with the United States, while Canadian business leaders and right-wing or neoliberal policies have supported this. The educational implications of such continentalization and globalization for Canada have yet to be well studied. Nonetheless, the critical pedagogy and human security emphasis of the book—focusing on nonmilitary and multilateral means to prevent violent conflict, terrorism or war—is typically Canadian in objective and tone. There is no Canadian case study presented in this volume but I am pursuing such work separately.

I

Theoretical Issues

2

THEORETICAL ISSUES AND PRAGMATIC CHALLENGES FOR EDUCATION, TERRORISM AND SECURITY RESEARCH

Wayne Nelles

PROBLEMATIZING TERRORISM, EDUCATION AND SECURITY DEBATES

This chapter seeks to problematize education, terrorism, violence and security issues and relationships through various theoretical and disciplinary perspectives in the context of the American "war on terrorism" after the September 11, 2001 attacks on the United States (hereafter referred to as "9/11"). However, it focuses not only on American issues, perspectives or definitions of "war" or "terrorism" or "security" or suffering and tragedy alone. It stresses universal, global and human security through critical pedagogy and comparative perspectives while highlighting future research possibilities.

Terrorism has a long history but there are no universally accepted definitions. The notion grew out of Robespierre's "Reign of Terror," or the terror "system" in the Revolutionary era (1793–1794) in France, but later evolved to describe wider or more specific uses, including criminal or political purposes.[1] Generally, terrorism is "a policy intended to strike with terror those against whom it is adopted; the employment of methods of intimidation; the fact of terrorizing or condition of being terrorized." A "terrorist" is "any one who attempts to further his views by a system of coercive intimidation."[2] "Terrorism" is typically referred to as the systematic, calculated or strategic (not incidental, random or isolated) practice of spreading fear, unrest and instability in a targeted area, or defined generically as:

> The use of violent and intimidating acts, especially for political ends. Terrorism has been used most commonly by revolutionary groups, whose objective is the overthrow of a particular state authority, and by nationalist groups seeking national self-determination.[3]

Problematically, though, American definitions and designations have overwhelmingly prevailed in academic or policy discourse while the United States has long exempted itself as a state sponsor of terror or alleged terrorist groups, even though it funded or trained many.[4] Despite a substantial academic terrorism literature after 1968 much has been seriously criticized for poor empirical grounding, with at least 80 percent mostly "narrative, condemnatory, and prescriptive" as one group of security researchers recently argued.[5] Aside from political purposes there is also no shortage of explanations including psychological, societal, economic or ecological causes with many variations. But formal education and social learning processes that lead to terrorism, or other forms of violence are an explanatory subset not well studied.

Beyond documenting or explaining trends about particular politically motivated incidents, types or identified groups, terrorism is a culturally relative and "socially constructed" moral concept that gained specific, legitimated meanings over time.[6] Western, especially American and state-centric, definitions and categories have dominated policy discourse and much popular literature. Political scientists and so-called security experts through an emerging "industry" have emphasized (not surprisingly) terrorism as a political act against governments or innocent civilians, separate from other forms of violence.[7] Some distinguish between localized "terrorism" and "war" by "guerrillas" or government armies.[8] But mere use of the word describes little since governments have often used the terrorism label to denounce opponents who may use violence as a last resort counter-response to state repression or international wars. Of late ordinary citizens and the media have also used the term indiscriminately, labeling people they (or their governments) view as "terrorists," resulting in illegal vigilante justice, more human rights abuses, and as an excuse for crushing democratic pluralism or political dissent in scores of countries with changes to many domestic laws to satisfy American demands.[9] So any narrowing or rigid precision advocated by many IR security scholars, or adopting definitions or labels of particular governments, obscures such nonpolitical analyses and contexts. It discourages cross-disciplinary or comparative analyses and nonmilitary responses. It also obfuscates many socioeconomic (including education-related) factors, giving rise to or sustaining political violence.

Just as Western political scientists and U.S. government or policy analysts, have dominated definitions of terrorism, they also influenced notions of international or interstate relations and "national security" mostly conceived as military security. Some chapters in this book challenge such discourses by examining terrorism and education through a human security lens. Scholars and diplomats over the past two decades have advocated "common security" or "comprehensive security" concepts (although largely marginalized or undermined) that paralleled military-dominated or national security approaches. The "human security" notion incorporated many such alternative themes as UN officials, IR scholars, and development specialists reconceptualized global power relations and a sought a "peace dividend" after the

Cold War. The United Nations Development Programme (UNDP) introduced the human security concept in its 1994 *Human Development Report* (*HDR*).[10] Other than threats from conventional or nuclear wars, it viewed new challenges as economic security, food security, health security, environmental security, personal security, community security and political security.

The *HDR* addressed both "freedom from want" (meeting basic needs) as well as "freedom from fear" (personal or human rights protection). IR or security scholars and political scientists largely ignored UNDP-related work, until some governments took political leadership, advancing the human security concept to operationalize security and protection for individuals rather than state-centric, national security alone. Canada recently introduced foreign policy changes, focusing on "freedom from fear"[11] while initiating modest related multilateral cooperation. Canada and Norway launched a "Human Security Network" (HSN) of foreign ministers including Chile, Ireland, the Netherlands, Switzerland, Austria, Slovenia, Jordan and Thailand. Countering terrorism and political violence is one human security challenge identified. In the wake of 9/11, the HSN specifically committed to "address growing sources of global insecurity, remedy its symptoms and prevent the recurrence of threats...including those aimed at eradicating terrorism."[12] The HSN also included education among other "personal protective considerations" in a list of issues and activities.[13] Governments such as Japan led the establishment of an international Commission on Human Security, which so far has mainly discussed education as a development or personal security challenge.[14]

But human security concepts and policies raise many new dilemmas for governments, as well as unintended consequences. For example, Canada under then foreign minister, Lloyd Axworthy, launched an International Commission on Intervention and State Sovereignty (ICISS) largely in response to public criticism and diplomatic fall-out from the controversial 1999 North Atlantic Treaty Organization (NATO)–Kosovo war that raised important issues about the "responsibility to protect" innocent civilians against human rights abuses. The ICISS Cochair Gareth Evans, stressed the right or responsibility of countries to intervene where human rights appeared at risk was a "troubling and difficult" issue for the international policy agenda.[15] The Commission stressed: "prevention is the single most important dimension of the responsibility to protect: prevention options should always be exhausted before intervention is contemplated, and more commitment and resources must be devoted to it." However, after 9/11 major powers such as the United States used its Kosovo "success" to justify (not prevent) future military interventions for more dubious reasons. An American Defense Policy Board member pointing to Kosovo has even argued historians would view an Iraq war and its "liberation" as another in just a few good examples of "humanitarian intervention."[16]

The implications for understanding education and terrorism relationships have not been well researched. Study of education's role in violent conflict has been limited,[17] and not well integrated in human security literature.[18]

Related research has been the mostly post–Cold War study and policy dialogue on "education in emergencies," conflict zones and failed states.[19] Other agency and scholarly work has examined "post-conflict reconstruction" following civil or international wars, where education is an essential element in reconstruction or aid programs to help create long-term security and stability in new or reformed states.[20] The crises educators respond to are often results of local terror or civil and international war, requiring rapid responses from aid agencies that deliver education programs working parallel to (or in tension with) foreign militaries. But such issues raise particular "learning" challenges for governments and humanitarian agencies in how best to evaluate success, or in appropriate civil–military relations.[21]

Some work has examined how education reinforced ethnic divisions leading to war in Europe.[22] But it is often not clear how one distinguishes between "terrorism," ethnic or criminal violence, or civil and international war with concepts or activities used differently by accused or accuser, alleged or real. And while wars may officially end, violence or interethnic conflicts that fueled them may not. Terrorism and security concerns are linked to broader challenges such as community building, democratization, conflict mediation or resolution, preventing war and building or sustaining civil society or regional and international peace generally. More scholarly analysis, comparative and case study work including field evaluations are needed to assess specific concepts or types of implementation involving education. Some chapters in this volume (Indonesia, Iraqi-Kurdistan, Northern Ireland and Sierra Leone) offer relevant studies. Some complementary new work is also ongoing elsewhere.[23]

One important situation, however, gave rise to many theoretical debates or policy issues about human security. Although the 1999 NATO–Kosovo war was justified to protect innocent civilians against human rights abuses, Albanian "terrorism" was a principal measure that the West supported against Milosevic and the Serbs. NATO backed the Kosovo Liberation Army (KLA), which one American diplomat described as a terrorist organization encouraging Milosevic to counter Albanian violence.[24] Militarization of this conflict undermined a 1996 "Education Accord" between Belgrade and Pristina, which gave Albanians rights suppressed by Serbs. After the conflict, aid agencies promoted education to help achieve and sustain regional peace under a "*Stability Pact.*"[25] Yet political violence and organized crime still destabilizes the region through former KLA members. An unresolved territorial dispute still fuels violence, while ethnic divisions reinforced by education hamper reconstruction and regional stability.[26]

What lessons arise? The Kosovo military intervention avoided serious questions about the conflict's causes and solutions, especially its "terrorist" roots while educational concerns were at the heart of the dispute. Intervention also problematically militarized the human security concept while educational issues were mostly ignored.[27] Now there is more division and inconsistency among governments leading global human security and terrorism debates. Canada, for example, offered military support with ground troops to Afghanistan for America's "war on terrorism," itself a controversial issue among Canadians. Jordan, a traditional American ally, is a HSN member. But at the United Nations a few weeks after 9/11, Jordan's representative said use of force was legitimate and "justified in cases of self-defence and when used against foreign occupiers to achieve self-determination."[28] This implied support for the Palestinian cause as a liberation movement, which Israel and the United States view as a "terrorist" problem. Yet reconciling the need to counter violence of all kinds with concerns of social movements seeking liberation from what they view as oppression is imperative.

Understanding the role of education in this conflicting and explosive mix of differing objectives and perspectives remains important. Scholars writing about "nontraditional" security issues in recent years noted education among the least expected, but clearly important foci of attention. As Hayes and Sands argue:

> One, final and perhaps surprising, security area is education. Opening schools and getting children (particularly teenagers) off the streets reduces one source of potential instability, and frees their parents to go to work. School attendance also gives children hope for the future and provides them an alternative to joining factional militias.[29]

This theme has since been echoed among activists and policy makers seeking to provide alternatives. Chapter 10 in this volume examines related issues for Sierre Leone. Other human security work has focused specifically on children in armed conflict, or child soldiers and "war-affected children," more broadly.[30] Children have been both victims and progenitors of local and international violence or "terrorism." But any systematic analysis of such education and human security issues cannot ignore global historical developments or institutional structures and relationships, or international agencies and power politics governing national governments or the world system. Here Galtung's notion of "structural violence" is useful.[31] Structural violence can include systems, mechanisms or processes that reproduce "social injustice," through uneven distribution of resources affected by unequal local or international power relationships. Discussing its educational relevance Brock-Utne argues peace is "the absence of all types of violence." The idea includes:

> micro-structures, everyday life violence like street-killings, incest and wife-battering as well as direct violence on a larger scale, on the macro-level as in wars. Within peace research the absence of direct violence is often termed negative peace. Peace also includes the absence of what we call indirect or structural violence. This is a type of violence which may also kill but at a slower pace . . .[32]

Without offering a rigid definition then, I build on complementary work. I adopt a working notion of human security that stresses violence prevention and nonmilitary solutions to conflict or human rights abuses while responding to injustices that create unmet basic needs. This combines two principal imperatives—"freedom from fear" and "freedom from want"—emphasized differently by numerous theorists or governments, involving a complex set of challenges and response tools according to particular circumstances. They could simultaneously involve traditional security measures or mechanisms from police and peacekeeping to even military intervention, but only as a last resort emergency protection measure. More broadly it can include examining how educational aid can lead to greater personal advancement, better jobs, social equity and recognition of human rights or help avoid violent conflict.

The role of politicized "educational empowerment" strategies in strengthening national or social liberation movements in response to structural violence or local and international state-sponsored terror also needs closer study. It is impossible here to do justice to the theory, adaptations and critiques of related ideas. However, among Freire's widely discussed concepts is "conscientization," a process of "learning to perceive social, political and economic contradictions, and to take action against the oppressive elements of reality."[33] Conscientization can evolve as a "pedagogy of the oppressed, which is the pedagogy of people engaged in the fight for their own liberation." It is a "humanitarian" and "libertarian pedagogy"[34] that challenges violence of oppressors and exploiters. Here I am not justifying violence in any form, but it is imperative that educators and policy makers address this issue directly. Paulo Freire's literacy and popular education work has already inspired many revolutionary or resistance activities. Literacy and popular education in 1980s El Salvador, for example, aided guerrilla warriors (which the Reagan administration labeled "terrorists" then killed them through covert and military operations).[35] The question of how education researchers should intellectually deconstruct (through critical pedagogy) or pragmatically respond (technically and nonviolently) to allegations of terrorism or counterresponses remains legitimate and pressing, especially amidst America's unending, global "war on terrorism."

AMERICAN EDUCATION, PUBLIC DIPLOMACY AND NATIONAL SECURITY IN LIGHT OF 9/11

For education scholars the new "Bush Doctrine" raises particular concerns. Outlined in the 2002 *National Security Strategy* (*NSS*) it epitomizes American faith in hegemonic military force, and preemptive use of it, as its principal source of its own security. Moreover, the *NSS* noted problems of failed states producing terrorism, while committing to increase development aid by 50 percent and "emphasize education."[36] New work is needed to examine implications for post-9/11 American and other Western aid programs. Johnson's discussion on Central Asia (chapter 14) in light of 9/11 begins to explore related questions in one region. While positive results could arise from new education aid, many countries could be adversely affected by American or other national interests. Meanwhile, after 9/11 the American administration initiated a foreign-student tracking system resulting in arrests and jailing, for even the most benign infractions, such as not attending all planned classes.[37] New research is needed on immediate and long-term implications for international students. Culcer (chapter 5) offers some insight into one aspect of this for Middle Eastern men on American campuses.

Beyond the broader international dimensions, policy debates or changes in aid regimes, so far much public discussion on education has been negative, especially by conservative Christian or Jewish scholars and an uncritical media offering little context, pointing to the Islamic "threat" at home or abroad, with accusations of biased teaching among university professors and research institutes. Some further worried about inviting more foreign students to the United States or allowing Muslim charities on campuses.[38] Others raised concerns about anti-Semitism, but lumped valid critiques with opposition to teaching courses on Islam and Middle East Studies scholarship with a "postcolonial studies paradigm," or "postmodern," or leftist theoretical discourse about race, gender, class that criticizes Israeli or U.S. policies.[39] Some critiques are racist in tone while advocating violent solutions (e.g, through more political support and military aid to Israel) to perceived problems. A closer study of such groups might be a focus for future critical pedagogy research. Many schools, campuses and preservice training or in-service teacher resource units reworked teaching or curricula to adapt, to aid the "war" against terrorism,[40] but often offering little critical or systematic thinking about causes or contexts for the 9/11 attacks. Or if a violent military response (instead of a criminal justice approach) to "fight" is effective or appropriate.

Clearly the education issue has not been ignored, but much debate has focused on failings of Islamic culture or education and what to do to "eliminate" terrorism or about "winning hearts and minds" to change behaviors of suicide bombers.[41] Some editorials placed America squarely against the (mostly Islamic) world stressing patriotism, nationalism and military service as solutions to terrorism.[42] Support for the military increased in schools and on college campuses with only minor controversy.[43] There was a significant rise of interest in the school teaching profession after 9/11 and new status came to academic posts previously of little interest, intellectually marginalized and poorly funded.[44] The idea that 9/11 was a "teachable moment"[45] grew. But the U.S. Department of Education discouraged critical thinking about foreign policy issues.[46] A Bush commencement speech at West Point supported American military leadership while the influential *Educational Testing Service* backing the president's remarks boasted of experience in 180 countries including a full page ad in *The Economist*, suggesting educational aid and more U.S. overseas student advising center support would help fight terrorism.[47] How this implicates the already contentious privatization and testing agenda that American companies want to globalize through exporting institutions and services would be another useful subject of research.

Controversy arose over specific programs. Some media offered support for the National Security Education Program (NSEP) including a *New York Times Magazine* story with a sidebar, "Study Abroad, Save the Nation," discussing foreign language preparation through federal funds. But critics raised concerns about students perceived as spies. A group of academics

initiated a boycott campaign expressing concern over the integrity of the
NSEP and its aims or potential impacts and dangers for individuals involved.
Concerns arose over questionable purposes and continued abuses of the
1991 Security Education Act.[48] After 9/11, more support for military education and training assistance also problematically followed.[49] Moreover,
foreign policy initiatives also influenced other governments and their
publics' perceptions of terrorism and war to view the United States as a
benign or benevolent international actor. This has been a central purpose of
American "public diplomacy" which, although connected to international
educational and foreign policy debates, has been poorly studied.[50]

America's 2002 pledge to reenter the United Nations Educational,
Scientific and Cultural Organization (UNESCO), partly as a counterterrorism strategy, is also noteworthy.[51] President Bush, problematically, made this
announcement to join the world's premiere peace education organization
while simultaneously making an advance war declaration on Iraq. Given
America's dubious past, its rekindled UNESCO relationship with new
American education aid pledges to fight terrorism, require more research
and monitoring. Not since the early 1960s was there hope for distinguish-
ing between and "information approach" that promoted American foreign
policies abroad, and what its first secretary of state for education called the
"educational and cultural approach... to foster *mutual* understanding and
to benefit both parties to the exchange."[52] But the United States never took
the latter seriously, during and after Vietnam. Under Reagan it withdrew
from UNESCO in 1984 while also directly attacking its communications
and literacy programs thereby undermining the institution. Discussing this
and related developments elsewhere I have argued that:

> America's UNESCO departure was its most symbolic counter-statement to a
> mutual understanding or "educational" approach described by Coombs...By
> leaving UNESCO the United States reinforced unilateralism as a solution to
> its problems while it weakened the institution, and avoided the more difficult
> challenge of building a multilateral democracy. It also reflected the American
> inability to reconcile a conflict between an informational, PYSOPS-oriented,
> propagandist and unilateral public diplomacy agenda to a more legitimate,
> cooperative, critical thinking and peace-building oriented educational
> approach that UNESCO ideally represented. America after leaving UNESCO
> invested in more sophisticated frameworks for public diplomacy and greater
> military spending to justify a covert war in Central America during the 1980s,
> the Kosovo war in the 1990s, and most recently to informationally and mili-
> tarily target the Islamic world after 9/11.[53]

My study concluded that while the United States claims its public diplomacy to be an instrument of "truth projection" and a means to "educate"
or "inform" international publics and diplomats, it has long been "pseudo-
educational" serving American-led globalization while reinforcing U.S.
power and cultural–economic–military advantage over weaker or vulnerable
states as well as potential adversaries. Moreover, it is exemplary of a narrow,

distorted, military-oriented national security approach that undermines nonviolent, nonmilitary, human security-led alternatives.

CRITICAL PEDAGOGY IMPLICATIONS OF 9/11

Before 9/11, some scholars were critical about American education's role especially as a means for reinforcing "whiteness" as an invisible culture of "terror" dominating and demonizing "others" who are different. McLaren suggested the need for a more "critical multiculturalism" in response to dominant meaning systems that reinforce Western imperialism and patriarchy.[54] What are the post-9/11 implications? Some new questions are worth asking. Does the American white "culture of terror" also exist as an oppressive force exported abroad? Does this help explain some "terrorism" or "blowback" against the United States?[55] Is, for example, the American "war on terrorism" (with civil liberty violations or racial profiling domestically and targeting mostly Muslim nations abroad) partly a racist, mostly Judeo-Christian inspired, neo-imperial project, adversely contributing to more violence and an unnecessary "war of civilizations," religious conflict or "clash of cultures?"

Some post-9/11 academic reflections on related issues for American education has begun, with debates on classroom or preservice teaching and learning issues, hinting at "political socialization" challenges.[56] Education journal literature on 9/11 and terrorism emerged.[57] Websites offered resource materials on teaching September 11 through a liberal-oriented approach compatible with a critical pedagogy perspective.[58] Giroux among leading scholars hoped to stimulate educator-thinking about the role public schools could play in a new discourse about militarism, consumerism and racism. He stressed the need to "rearticulate a notion of the social" not just with respect to 9/11 and terrorism, but with a continued critique of market-based philosophy. He argued this has undermined "the promise of democracy, the meaning of critical citizenship and the importance of public engagement." This, after 9/11, has meant even greater "militarization of visual and public space."[59] McLaren discussed the need to reinforce that critical and revolutionary pedagogy "takes a strong stand against terrorism," which is never justified.[60] He also argued the attacks were not the result of American foreign policy, but acknowledges the Central Intelligence Agency (CIA) helped train, fund and arm Afghans during the Cold War. McLaren said the more correct analysis is that this terrorism was the result of "reactionary religious fundamentalism...called Islamism."

Giroux's response, while a critique of the American body politic with deference to the need for national security, focused abstractly on the need for strengthening the democratization agenda and pedagogy of resistance to neoliberalism and militarization. This book builds on similar ideas beyond theory or American contexts alone. McLaren's explanation asserts that 9/11 and continued attacks are a form of intolerable "Islamic fascism" that must be eliminated by all means (presumably the military if necessary). However, defining this as mainly an Islamic problem tackled through an even more violent military response, does not resolve fundamental questions about how or why, and the role of agency, including global relationships and contexts. It also does not address the serious problem of militarism, especially projected through American foreign policy. This is an important issue raised by other critical pedagogy analyses and educational evaluations, including some chapters in this volume.

More specifically although there are questions about details, education and training systems were clearly contributing causes of terrorism originating in Afghanistan and Pakistan. Even before 9/11 madrasas and Pakistan's Islamic culture were part of the terrorism, security and foreign policy debate. After the 1998 African Embassy bombings, the Americans attacked selected targets in Pakistan and South Asia.[61] Foreign policy scholars identified madrasas as "schools of hate," growing partly because the youth lacked other employment and educational opportunities some students became "terrorists" inflaming the Kashmir conflict.[62] After 9/11 education was front-page news in Western newspapers. Some stories focused on terrorist "training camps" offering a "curriculum of ruthless sabotage."[63] Others highlighted Pakistan's madrasa schools.[64] Although debate followed about function and funding, clearly much terrorism in Afghanistan grew out of aggressive American ideological and military intervention to oust the Soviets in the 1980s. Beyond training camps, the CIA and the United States Agency for International Development (USAID) worked with the University of Nebraska to support at least 13 million anti-Soviet textbooks and a national curriculum using violent images and militant fundamentalist Islamic teachings.[65] Security analysts have only begun to examine recent national issues for Pakistan with regional and global implications.[66]

Education also figured prominently in other international debates. Because most 9/11 hijackers were Saudis, the American media and government attacked the Saudi education system as progenitors of religious extremism or terrorism.[67] *New York Times* columnist Thomas Friedman said accusingly "another country's faulty education software can destroy all of Wall Street," and that several thousand American children had no parents because of radical Islamists educated in Saudi schools.[68] In response, but hardly covered in American media, Arabs replied. Some accused Americans of a double standard concerning support of democracy or human rights and the inadequacies of their education system creating hatred or humiliation of others while sowing arrogance and conceit.[69] Saudi Foreign Minister Prince Saud Al-Faisal acknowledged that they must educate their people, to the dangers of al-Qaeda but also said: "people are bombarded by dramatic images of Palestinian homes destroyed by the Israeli Army or children killed. These images are not broadcast by the schools but by CNN, by the BBC or by French television." He argued "the Palestinian cause is exploited by extremists...It is neither our educational programs nor our policies... which motivate these youths."[70] The higher education minister, Al-Anqari, also rejected Western critiques of Saudi religious extremism in education saying:

> Can an entire education system be blamed if a few of these students are charged with carrying out terrorist activities?...If the system is blamed, then the educational system in the US need to be overhauled too, because recurrent violence is reported from schools there with students going on indiscriminate killing sprees.[71]

This was an obvious reference to the problem of school violence in the United States, the most well known being the 1999 Columbine massacre. Space does not permit an assessment of Friedman's or the Saudi's claims or even the more problematic and vexing relationship between Saudi Arabia and Pakistan through aid to madrasa religious schools, resulting in similar calls for reform there.[72] The even deeper and more complex, unresolved Israel–Palestinian conflict—with American foreign policy interests largely backing Israel—influencing the education–terrorism–security debate, also needs more careful analysis.[73] This issue has in turn strongly affected the stability of the entire Middle East, but especially after 9/11 the insecurity of many Western nations allied with America's "war on terrorism," and while the United States (claiming it was a "preemptive" counterterrorism strategy) planned to invade Iraq. Bakti's case study in this volume, while not focusing on this particular debate, examines relevant issues for Indonesia but may help us better understand educational and learning processes in other regions or countries. Beyond this book such developments within and beyond the Middle East and Islamic world require more serious and systematic comparative research to examine causes and long-term implications for education (especially the capacity for doing authentic diplomacy, peace building and human security work).

EDUCATION, CULTURE AND SOCIALIZATION FOR OR AGAINST TERROR AND VIOLENCE

Few would doubt education's importance in shaping individual lives and its role in transmitting culture or molding beliefs and behavior. But there is still much we do not understand about how or why violence occurs under specific circumstances or education's role in mitigating and preventing personal or political violence. Relationships between individual and local, school-based violence in Western countries are rarely examined with respect to international trends or relationships. For example, what relevance do school violence prevention or moral education, multicultural, or peace studies or exchange programs in Western countries have on approaching the problem of international terrorism? Has there been any substantive progress over the past few decades? Are these failed projects? Or is there simply more to do? If so what and how? Does America's "war on terrorism" or its interpretation by other nations help or hinder education for violence prevention? How can objectives, progress, learning processes and cause–effect relationships better be defined and measured?

These bodies of education research have been mostly disconnected. The literature on violence prevention in the United States has grown due to increased incidents of bullying, gun violence or other threats including dramatic and escalating instances of "school-yard terrorism" represented by very public bloody massacres.[74] Explanations abound. Personal/psychological, social, economic, religious, racial, political and other factors can play a role but need to be dis-aggregated and examined in particular cases. Moreover, studies ought to include insights based on decades of research on the origins of aggression and violent behavior generally, among children or youth in schools particularly, and should incorporate findings of criminology and social psychology.[75] Curricular, administrative or policy responses to be effective need to based on research, so far poorly or insufficiently done, or in not easily accessible or well-coordinated sources.[76] Studies of aggression point to other issues needing closer investigation.[77] Violent behavior may be learned in families, schools or in social and religious groups, then institutionalized among adults—translated into behaviors, government policies, international disputes or military actions and war. Violence may be "normalized" or "systemic" through administrative, institutional, military training, media, cultural, family and gender or racially biased means.[78] Violent aggression among youth in its most extreme form, homicide, may be the result of harm done to them, whether child abuse, neglect or media exposure encouraging violence as a means for problem-solving.[79]

But new questions might be asked. For example, what are the actual or possible effects of a more powerful country dominating or forcing another nation, or some of its peoples to adopt certain customs over others? Or is it possible to learn from domestic studies on violence and violent crime, especially in the United States? The National Commission on the Causes and Prevention of Violence launched by President Lyndon Johnson in 1968 is a useful starting point. Its report[80] warned about more places of "terror and widespread crime" in American cities if problems of poverty, racism and economic injustices were not better addressed. Using the word "terror" to describe local fear and intimidation in American or other cities might be better connected to discussions of international "terrorism" with parallel causes or solutions. Part of the Commission's thesis was that violence arose from failures to address needs of the abused, unemployed, educationally denied, underclass, many exercising their frustration, anger and power through gangs and criminal behavior.

Three decades later a new study assessing related developments, in light of recent school massacres argued, "America's failure to reduce endemic fear and violence over the long run is paralleled by its failure to establish justice." It argued the Commission reporting in1969 was right, more "dramatically than anyone could then have expected." The Eisenhower Foundation, noting international comparisons stressed American rates of violence were "*much higher*" than other industrialized nations, while prisons had become "a substitute for effective public policies on crime, drugs, mental illness, housing, poverty and employment." The 1999 Report recommended greater funding to reduce crime (through scientifically proven methods replicating what works) while at the same time "improve educational performance and help develop children, youth and young adults in positive directions." But it stressed education as a key factor in reducing violence.[81]

What can we learn from related violence prevention research either related to schools or human security more broadly, not just in the United States but internationally? What are the implications for the "war on terrorism?" What does research on bullying say about what others can learn about impacts of military force or threats? Recent polls may indicate some issues of concern. Some suggest many people in other nations, even close neighbors and traditional allies who offered Americans considerable compassion and comfort after 9/11, increasingly saw the United States as a nationally self-absorbed bully. Resentment has also increased about the U.S. abuse of military or economic power, flouting of international law or obligations, its seeing only American lives (and not others) as important, and America's inability to understand why other people are concerned or angry.[82] In such light America's new national security agenda contributes to perceptions of less universal human or global security for others, while anti-Americanism may fuel more popular sentiments that create more terrorism.

One issue particularly deserving further analysis is the argument that some "get tough" approaches fail to create safe environments while coercive strategies interrupt learning resulting in resistance and mistrust.[83] Empirical studies suggest certain forms of moral education—in one case about the UN Convention on the Rights of the Child—can make a positive difference in mitigating violence. Such efforts can improve self-esteem, how children view or support rights of others, and create a climate less conducive to bullying while encouraging greater acceptance of minorities.[84] What does this say about the most powerful nation on earth refusing to adhere to many international Conventions, including those supporting educational or children's rights, or the lack of accountability of its political and military leaders when rights are transgressed? Moreover, researchers studying bullying have recently argued that the arrogantly coercive approach the Bush administration took against the United Nations to invade Iraq (with or without international approval) demonstrated to children that aggressive violence, or threats of it through military action, was a legitimate (even most appropriate) approach to resolving problems, whether on school-grounds, in families or international affairs.[85]

CONCLUSION

Some chapters in this book begin related arguments or present useful case studies on various dimensions of education, terrorism and security while offering American as well as international and comparative perspectives on such issues. More work especially linking domestic education, social and economic reforms with international foreign policy, aid regimes and conflict management, postwar reconstruction or violence prevention programs is needed. There is much education, security, counterterrorism and development scholars can learn from more systematic research on such issues. This might include more comprehensive assessments of historical developments or policy trends. Studies of education-related field programs among aid workers and peace-building specialists to better understand impacts and outcomes would also be useful. This book begins related theoretical and pragmatic work.

NOTES

1. "French Revolution," *A Dictionary of World History* (Oxford University Press, 2000). *Oxford Reference Online*, posted at http://www.oxfordreference.com; and Walter Laqueur, *A History of Terrorism* (New Brunswick, USA/London, UK: Transaction Publishers), p. 6.
2. J. A. Simpson and E. S. C. Wiener, "Terror," "Terrorism" and "Terrorist" in *Oxford English Dictionary* 2nd Edition (Oxford: Oxford Clarendon Press, 1989), pp. 820–21.
3. Oxford University Press, "Terrorism," in *A Dictionary of World History* (Oxford University Press, 2000). *Oxford Reference Online*, posted at www.oxfordreference.com.
4. For this, and a broader critique, see Edward Herman and Gerry O'Sullivan, *The "Terrorism" Industry: The Experts and Institutions that Shape Our View of Terror* (New York: Pantheon Books, 1989), p. 47. The United States has kept statistics on terrorist incidents, states and groups as it defines them, issuing an annual *Patterns of Global Terrorism Report* posted at http://www.state.gov/s/ct/rls/pgtrpt since the early1980s.
5. The quote is from a 1988 "state of the art" article on empirical research by Robert Gurr referred to as a continuing trend in: Katja Haaversen-W. Skkolberg and Brynjar Lia, "Facts and Fiction in Theories of Terrorism: A Review of Research Literature on Causes of Terrorism," paper presented to *International Studies Association 2003 Conference*, Portland, Oregon (February 25–March 1, 2003).
6. For a brief discussion on this issue building on Berger and Luckman's classic work in the sociology of knowledge see Grant Wardlaw, *Political Terrorism: Theory, Tactics, and Counter-Measures, Second Edition Revised and Extended* (Cambridge: Cambridge University Press, 1989), pp. 5–6.
7. Herman and O'Sullivan, *The "Terrorism" Industry*, pp. 98–99.
8. Graham Evans and Jeffrey Newnham, "Guerrilla Warfare" and "Terrorism," *Penguin Dictionary of International Relations* (London: Penguin Books, 1998), pp. 214–15, 530–31.
9. For links to a damning 558-page report see Human Rights Watch, "New Survey Documents Global Repression: U.S. Human Rights Leadership Faulted," *Human Rights News* (January 14, 2003), posted at: http://www.hrw.org/press/2003/01/wr2003.htm. Also see Peter Maass, "Dirty War: How America's friends really fight terrorism," *The New Republic* (November 11, 2002), pp. 18–21.

10. UNDP, *Human Development Report 1994* (New York/Oxford: United Nations Development Programme/Oxford University Press), pp. 22–24.

11. Canada was one of the first countries to redefine human security through a new foreign policy. See Department of Foreign Affairs and International Trade (DFAIT), "Freedom From Fear: Canada's Foreign Policy for Human Security" (Ottawa: DFAIT, July 2000), posted at http://www.humansecurity.gc.ca/Freedom_from_Fear-e.pdf.

12. "Statement by the Human Security Network Concerning the Terrorist Attacks in the United States of America, 11 September 2001," *Human Security Network* (November 12, 2001), posted at: http://www.humansecuritynetwork.org/Terror_Statement-e.asp.

13. Knut Vollebaek, "*A Perspective on Human Security*," Chairman's (Norwegian Minister of Foreign Affairs) Conference Summary, Lysøen, Norway, Department of Foreign Affairs and International Trade, Government of Canada (May 20, 1999). This and related documents are available online at http://www.humansecuritynetwork.org.

14. See Amartya Sen, "Basic Education and Human Security," Kolata (January 2–4, 2002). This was a background paper prepared for the Commission on Human Security's India workshop, posted at http://www.humansecurity-chs.org.

15. DFAIT, Canada. "Axworthy Launches International Commission on Intervention and State sovereignty," press release, September 14, 2000, No. 233 located at: http://www.iciss-ciise.gc.ca/. The ICISS reported to the United Nations in late 2001. See *The Responsibility to Protect: Report of the International Commission on Intervention and State Sovereignty* (December 2001), posted at http://www.iciss-ciise.gc.ca/Report-English.asp.

16. Remarks made by guest, Professor Ruth Wegwood, also a lawyer and member of "Committee for the Liberation of Iraq" discussed on the program "Case for or Against War on Iraq," *Counterspin, CBC Newsworld* (January 8, 2002).

17. Exceptions are: David Hamburg, "Education for Conflict Resolution" (New York: Carnegie Commission on Preventing Deadly Conflict, 1995), posted at http://www.ccpdc.org/pubs/ed/edfr.htm; and David Hamburg, "Preventing Contemporary Intergroup Violence, Education for Conflict Resolution," New York: Carnegie Commission on Preventing Deadly Conflict, December 1999), posted at http://www.ccpdc.org/pubs/ham/hamfr.htm. For related and emerging research also see Mohammed Bedjaoui, "Preventive Diplomacy: Development, Education and Human Rights," in Kevin M. Cahill, ed., *Preventive Diplomacy: Stopping Wars Before They Start* (New York: Basic Books, 1996), pp. 35–60; and "Political Violence and Education," *Current Issues in Comparative Education*, Special Issue, (November 15, 2000) an online journal published by Teachers' College, Columbia University, posted at http://www.tc.columbia.edu/cice/content2.htm.

18. For a mostly theoretical piece from an education scholar, not a security researcher, see Christopher Williams, "Education and Human Survival: The Relevance of the Global Security Framework to International Education," *International Review of Education*, Vol. 46, Nos. 3–4 (2000), pp. 183–203.

19. See UNESCO, Emergency Educational Assistance Unit (ED/EFA/AEU), *Education in Situations of Emergency and Crisis* (Paris: UNESCO, October 1999). Collaborative efforts and research documentation through the Global Information Networks in Education (GINIE) project, reflects international collaboration. Note their website: http://www.ginie.org for details. Other

collaboration is evident through the Paris, UNESCO-housed Inter-Agency Network for Education in Emergencies (INEE).

20. Sobhi Tawil, ed., *Final Report and Case Studies of the Workshop Educational Destruction and Reconstruction in Disrupted Societies, 15–16 May 1997*, Geneva (Geneva: International Bureau of Education, 1997).

21. I have discussed such issues elsewhere in Wayne Nelles, "*Review of Humanitarian Action: Improving Performance through Improved Learning, ALNAP Annual Review 2002.* London, ANLAP/Overseas Development Institute, 2002," *Canadian Journal of Development Studies* (in press).

22. David Coulby and Crispin Jones, *Education and Warfare in Europe* (Burlington, VT and Basingstoke, UK: Ashgate Publishing Limited, 2001).

23. Some work building on Tawil, *Final Report and Case Studies* looks promising. See new comparative work on Bosnia-Herzegovina, Guatemala, Rwanda, Northern Ireland, Lebanon, Mozambique and Sri Lanka, part of a UNESCO-IBE related project called: "Curriculum Change and Social Cohesion in Conflict-Affected Societies" discussed in the IBE Newsletter, *Educational Innovation and Innovation*, No. 112 (December 2002), pp. 2–6.

24. Lenard J. Cohen, *Serpent in the Bosom: The Rise and Fall of Slobodan Milosevic* (Boulder: Westview Press, 2001), pp. 236–37.

25. *Stability Pact for South Eastern Europe, Cologne*, June 10, 1999, posted at www.stabilitypact.org. On education implications note: *Stability Pact*, "Task Force Education and Youth of the Enhanced Graz Process Stability Pact, Working Table 1, Democratisation and Human Rights" at www.stabilitypact.org outlining aid commitments and programs with links to other documents and peace-building activities after 1999.

26. See The Independent International Commission on Kosovo, *The Kosovo Report: Conflict, International Response, Lessons Learned* (Oxford: Oxford University Press, 2000), p. 125. Also see Alissa J Rubin, "Police Have Hands Full in Kosovo: Organized crime threatens stability of province, leading U.N. to bolster its operation," *Los Angeles Times* (August 13, 2002), posted at http://www.latimes.com; and Reuters, "Car bomb rocks Kosovo capital," *SwissInfo* (December 14, 2002), posted at http://www.swissinfo.org/sen/Swissinfo.html?siteSect=143&sid=1517282.

27. I discuss education in more detail on p. 468 of Wayne Nelles, "Canada's Human Security Agenda in Kosovo and Beyond: Military Intervention versus Conflict Prevention," *International Journal*, Vol. 57, No. 3 (Summer 2002), pp. 459–79, amidst a wider critique of the militarization of the human security concept. For a wider critique also see Wayne Nelles, "Will Education Serve War or Human Security?" *University Affairs*, a monthly magazine published by Association of Universities and Colleges of Canada, Editorial (November 2002), p. 39.

28. United Nations, "Assembly Hears Call for Definition of Terrorism—Fifty-sixth General Assembly GA/9925 Plenary 3 October 2001," (October 3, 2001), posted at http://www.un.org/News/Press/docs/2001/GA9925.doc.htm.

29. Quoted from p. 827 of Brad C. Hayes and Jeffrey I Sands, "Non-Traditional Military Responses to End Wars: Considerations for Policymakers," *Millennium: Journal of International Studies* (1997), pp. 819–44.

30. For background see Graca Machel, *The Impact of War on Children* (Vancouver: University of British Columbia Press, 2001). For documents, links and resource

materials see the International Conference on War-Affected Children, held September 10–17, 2000, and its website www.waraffectedchildren.gc.ca.

31. Johan Galtung, "Violence, Peace and Peace Research," *Journal of Peace Research*, Vol. 6, No. 3 (1969), pp. 167–91.

32. Birgut Brock-Utne, "Educating All for Positive Peace: Education for Positive Peace or Oppression?" *International Journal of Educational Development*, Vol. 15, No. 3 (1995), pp. 321–31.

33. Paulo Friere, *Pedagogy of the Oppressed*, translated by Myra Ramos (New York: Continuum International Publishing Group, 1993/2000, reissued from the 1970 original), p. 17.

34. Ibid., pp. 35–36.

35. Hammond, John L., *Fighting to Learn: Popular Education and Guerrilla War in El Salvador* (New Brunswick/New Jersey/London: Rutgers University Press, 1998).

36. White House, *National Security Strategy of the United States of America* (September 17, 2002), posted at http://www.whitehouse.gov/nsc/nssall.html.

37. Generally see Suzanne Gamboa, "U.S. to Track Foreign Students," *National Post* (May 11, 2002), p. A14. For recent implications see Canadian Press, "Foreign Students Jailed in Colorado for Cutting College Course Hours," *Canadian Press* (December 27, 2002).

38. There is far too much material to survey here, and indeed this would be an interesting subject for a unique research project. But for tone see Steven Emerson, *American Jihad: The Terrorists Living Among Us* (New York: The Free Press, 2002), especially chapter 6, "Jihad in the Academy," pp. 109–25. Also note Ben Shapiro, "Terrorists at our Universities," *TownHall.com* (September 19, 2002), posted at http://www.campus-watch.org/article/id/122; Leslie Carbone, "Terror's Academic Sympathizers," *FrontPage Magazine* (December 9, 2002), posted at http://www.campus-watch.org/article/id/384; and Pat Collins, "Jihad on Campus," *National Review Online* (June 6, 2002), posted www.nationalreview.com/comment/comment-collins060602.asp.

39. Daniel Pipes and Jonathan Schanzer, "Extremists on Campus," *New York Post* (June 25, 2002), posted at http://www.campus-watch.org/article/id/16; Campus Watch, "Esposito: Apologist for Militant Islam," *FrontPage Magazine*, (September 3, 2002), posted at http://www.campus-watch.org/article/id/78. One book, particularly reviled by these critics, revised several times since 1992 is John L. Espisito, *The Islamic Threat: Myth or Reality? Third Edition* (New York: Oxford University Press, 1999).

40. Eyal Press, "It's a Volatile Complex World: Today's Undergraduates Want to Understand it. Are Today's Universities Prepared to Teach Them?" *The New York Times, Education Life*. Special Issue on "Lessons of a New Reality" (November 11, 2001), pp. 20–22, 35. Also note especially the long-running NYT banner heading "A Nation Challenged," which for this day was subtitled "Studying Terrorism and Fighting it." The story was Karen W. Arenson, "Campuses Across America Are Adding 'Sept. 11 101' to Curriculums," *The New York Times* (February 12, 2002), p. A13.

41. Rick Bragg "Shaping Young Islamic Hearts and Minds," *The New York Times* (October 14, 2001), pp. A1, B10; and Philip Smucker and Michael Satchell, "Hearts and Minds: In Pakistan's religious schools, Tomorrow's Holy Warriors are Prepped for Conflict," *U.S. New & World Report* (October 15, 2001), pp. 28–29.

42. William J. Bennett, "Teaching September 11," *The Wall Street Journal* (September 10, 2002), p. A12. Also note the American Federation of Teachers public policy statement on national pride and patriotism by its President: Sandra Feldman, "Where we Stand -Turning Point," *The New York Times* (November 4, 2001), p. 5.

43. On trends see David W. Chen, "On College Campuses, Students See Military With New Set of Eyes: Even at the Most Liberal Colleges a New Respect for Armed Forces," *The New York Times* (November 26, 2001), p. A15. On debates see Tom Kim, "Recruiters' Access to Schools Draws Controversy," *Education Week On the Web* (December 5, 2001), posted at http://www.edweek.org/ew/newstory.cfm?slug=14recruit.h21.

44. Abby Goodnough, "More Applicants Answer the Call for Teaching Jobs," *The New York Times* (February 11, 2002), pp. A1, 21; and Robin Wilson, "Interest in the Islamic World Produces Academic Jobs in U.S." *Chronicle of Higher Education* (March 1, 2002), pp. A10–12.

45. National Council for the Social Studies. "Teachable moments," (n.d.), posted at http://www.socialstudies.org/resources/moments/. Michael Simpson, ed., "Teaching About Tragedy," Special Issue *Social Education, The Official journal of National Council for the Social Studies,* Vol. 65, No. 6 (October 2001), posted at http://www.socialstudies.org/resources/moments/. Chapters volume by McAnich and Marciano offer useful critiques on related issues.

46. U.S. Department of Education, "Helping Children Understand the Terrorist Attacks," (accessed March 21, 2002, page last modified), posted at http://www.ed.gov/inits/september11/index.html.

47. Kurt M. Landgraf, "International Education: The Best Defense Against Terrorism," *Educational Testing Service* (July 11, 2002 web update). This *Economist* ad was also posted at http://www.ets.org/search97cgi/s97_cgi.

48. Margaret Talbot "Other Woes," *The New York Times Magazine* (November 18, 2001), pp. 23–24; Sara Hebel, "National-Security Concerns Spur Congressional Interest in Language Programs," *The Chronicle of Higher Education*, Vol. 48, No. 27 (March 15, 2002), p. A26; and Anne Marie Borrego, "Scholars Revive Boycott of U.S. Grants to Promote Language Training," *The Chronicle of Higher Education* (August 16, 2002), pp. A25–26.

49. Harshest criticism has long come from School of the Americas Watch (SOAW), which monitors American-supported military training activities. See SOAW, "Frequently Asked Questions," posted at http://www.soaw.org/faq.html. For wider background and critique see Lora Lumpe, *U.S. Foreign Military Training: Global Reach, Global Power, and Oversight Issues*, Special Report, for Foreign Policy In Focus (May 2002), posted at http://www.fpif.org/papers/miltrain/index.html.

50. For one dated commentary see Beverly Lindsay, "Integrating International Education and Public Diplomacy: Creative Partnerships or Indigenous Propaganda," *Comparative Education Review*, Vol. 33, No. 4 (November 1989), pp. 423–36.

51. George W. Bush, "President's Remarks at the United Nations General Assembly," *White House, Office of the Press Secretary* (September 12, 2002) posted at http://www.whitehouse.gov/news/releases/2002/09/20020912-1.html.

52. Phillip Coombs, *The Fourth Dimension of Foreign Policy: Educational and Cultural Affairs* (New York: Harper and Row, 1964), pp. 122–23.

53. Wayne Nelles, "American Public Diplomacy as Pseudo-Education: A Problematic National Security and Counter-terrorism Instrument,"

International Politics: A Journal of Transnational Issues and Global Problems, (In Press).

54. Peter McLaren, *Critical Pedagogy and Predatory Culture: Oppositional Politics in a PostModern Era* (London/New York: Routledge, 1995), p. 132.

55. For background to some cause–effect linkages for American foreign policy see Chalmers Johnson, *Blowback: The Costs and Consequences of American Empire* (New York: Henry Holt and Company, 2000).

56. Note professional associations speaking to the issue. See the special issues of *Social Education: The Official Journal of National Council for the Social Studies*, Vol. 66, No. 2 (March 2002); and "September 11 and the Academic Profession: A Symposium," *ACADEME: Bulletin of the American Association of University Professors*, Vol. 88, No. 1 (January–February 2002), pp. 18–23.

57. See Michael Berson "A Counter-Response to Terrorism: The Hope and Promise of Our Nation's Youth," *Theory & Research in Social Education* (Winter 2002), pp. 142–44; and Carole L Hahn, "Implications of September 11 for Political Socialization, Research," *Theory & Research in Social Education* (Winter 2002), pp. 158–62 and other articles in this issue. Elsewhere see: Teachers' College Record, "A TCR Special Issue Education and September 11th," *Teachers' College Record (TCRecord.org)* (13 September 2002), posted at http://www.tcrecord.org. Also note the call for papers (February 1, 2002) for a "Special Issue on the Attacks of September 11th" forthcoming in *Educational Studies*, the journal of the American Educational Studies Association.

58. *War, Terrorism and Our Classroom*, a special report published by *Rethinking Schools Online: An Urban Educational Resource*, posted at http://www.rethinkingschools.org/special_reports/sept11/index.shtml.

59. From p. 1148 in H. A. Giroux, "Democracy, Freedom, and Justice after September 11th: Rethinking the Role of Educators and the Politics of Schooling," *The Teachers College Record*, Vol. 104, No. 6 (March 2002), pp. 1138–162.

60. The quotes are from pp. 13–15 of Lucia Coral Aguirre Munoz, "The Globalization of Capital, Critical Pedagogy, and the Aftermath of September 11th: An Interview with Peter McLaren," *Multicultural Education*, Vol. 10, No. 1 (Fall 2000), pp. 7–27.

61. Reported in Robert Marquand, "US Missiles Struck Graduates of Pakistani Islamic Schools," *Christian Science Monitor* (August 28–September 3, 1998), pp. 1, 10.

62. Jessica Stern, "Pakistan's Jihad Culture," *Foreign Affairs*, Vol. 79, No. 6. (2000), pp. 115–26.

63. Ha, Tu Thanh, "Camps Offer Curriculum of Ruthless Sabotage," *The Globe and Mail* (October 9, 2001), p. A14. There are also a plethora of related stories (some pre-9/11) such as: John Cooley, *Unholy Wars: Afghanistan, America and International Terrorism*, New Edition (London: Pluto Press, 1999/2000) especially, chapter 5, "Recruiters, Trainers, Trainees and Assorted Spooks," pp. 81–106; and post-9/11 also see Kathy Gannon, "Lesson for Terror Found at Camp," *The Globe and Mail* (January 4, 2002), p. A6.

64. Peter Fritsch, "Religious Schools in Pakistan Fill Void—And Spawn Warriors," *The Wall Street Journal* (October 2, 2001), pp. A1, 14; and Frontline, "Analysis: Madrassahs" *Frontline/PBS Television* (2002). Background to documentary is posted at http://www.pbs.org/wgbh/pages/frontline/shows/saudi/analyses/madrassas.html.

65. Joe Stephens and David B. Ottaway, "From the U.S. and The ABCs of Jihad: Violent Soviet-Era Textbooks Complicate Efforts to Educate Afghan Children," *The Guardian Weekly* (March 28–April 3 2002), p. 32.

66. International Crisis Group, *Pakistan: Madrasas, Extremism and the Military*, ICG Asia Report # 36 (Islamabad/Brussels: International Crisis Group 29 July 2002), posted at http://www.intl-crisis-group.org.

67. Neil MacFarquhar, "Anti-Western and Extremist Views Pervade Saudi Schools," *The New York Times* (October 19, 2001), pp. B1, 3.

68. Thomas Friedman, "Dear Saudi Arabia," *The New York Times* (December 12, 2001), p. A31.

69. Abdul Aziz Ghazzawi, "Makkah Imam Slams Western Arrogance," *Arab News* (January 5, 2002), posted at www.arabnews.com.

70. Staff writer. "Saudis Duped into Al-Qaeda: Prince Saud," *Arab News* (January 27, 2002), posted at www.arabnews.com.

71. Staff writer. "Anqari Rejects Attacks on Curriculum as Unfounded, " *Arab News* (February 7, 2002), posted at www.arabnews.com.

72. Some media reports highlighted the issue such as Fritsch. "Religious Schools in Pakistan," pp. A1, 14. But so far the most useful (although limited) assessment of the broader issue beyond Saudi connections alone is International Crisis Group, *Pakistan.*

73. This too deserves separate and serious treatment beyond this Introduction. For, example, Israeli discriminatory practices against Palestinians is one factor. See Human Rights Watch, "Israeli Schools Separate, Not Equal: Palestinian Arab Citizens Face Discrimination in Access to Education," *Press Release, Human Rights Watch* (December 5, 2001), posted at http://www.hrw.org/press/2001/12/SecondClass1205.htm. Also note media reports blaming Palestinians. See Matthew Kalman, "School Books Omit Israel," *The National Post* (November 24, 2001), p. A9; and Jeff Sallot, "Palestinian Mothers Teach Hate, Katsav says" *The Globe and Mail* (March 8, 2002), p. A5.

74. This is my term. I do not review related empirical evidence or trend literature, but suffice it to say many scholars argue that in the West, especially the United States, school-based violence has increased dramatically over some decades for various reasons. For background see Matthew W. Greene, *Learning about School Violence: Lessons for Educators, Parents, Students, and Communities* (New York: Peter Lang, 2001).

75. For background see "Culture of Violence," Panel Discussion, *Abstracts for Royal Society of Canada and Canadian Society for Studies in Education* (May 25, 2000), held at 2001 Congress of Social Sciences and Humanities (Laval University, Quebec City).

76. Marc Posner, "Research Raises Troubling Questions About Violence Prevention Programs," in Phillip Harris, ed., *Violence and the Schools: A Collection* (Palatine, Illinois: IRI/Skylight Publishing, 1994), pp. 117–24; and Richard Van Acker, "School-Based Programs for the Prevention and Treatment of Aggression and Violence: Why aren't they more effective?" in Lyndal M. Bullock and Robert A. Gable, *Perspectives on School Aggression and Violence: Highlights from the Working Forum on Children and Youth Who Have Aggressive and Violent Behaviors* (Tampa: Council For Children with Behavioral Disorders, 1995), pp. 9–17.

77. R. E. Tremblay, "The Development of Aggressive Behavior During Childhood: What Have We Learned in the Past Century?" *International Journal of Behavioral Development*, Vol. 24, No. 2 (2000), pp. 129–41; L. Pagani. B Boulerice, F. Vitaro and R. E. Tremblay, "Effects of Poverty on Academic Failure and Delinquency in Boys: A Change and Process Model Approach," *Journal of Child Psychology and Psychiatry*, Vol. 40, No. 8 (1999), pp. 1209–219.

78. Note David W. Johnson and Roger T. Johnson, *Reducing School Violence Through Conflict Resolution* (Alexandria, Virginia: Association for Supervision and Curriculum Development, 1995), pp. 3–4; and Juanita Ross Epp and Alisa M. Watkinson, eds., *Systemic Violence in Education: Promise Broken* (New York: State University of New York Press, 1997). On military training, especially see Joanna Bourke, *An Intimate History of Killing: Face-to-Face Killing in Twentieth Century Warfare* (London, Granta Books, 1999), particularly chapter 3, "Training Men to Kill," pp. 69–102.

79. Katherine D. Kelly and Mark Totten, *When Children Kill: A Social-Psychological Study of Youth Homicide* (Peterborough, Ontario: Broadview Press, 2002).

80. U.S. Government, National Commission on the Causes and Prevention of Violence, *To Establish Justice, To Insure Domestic Tranquility* (Washington, DC: U.S. Government Printing Office, 1969).

81. The Milton S. Eisenhower Foundation, *To Establish Justice, to Insure Domestic Tranquility: A Thirty Year Update of the National Commission on the Causes and Prevention of Violence* (Washington, DC: The Milton S. Eisenhower Foundation, 1999), posted at http://www.eisenhowerfoundation.org/aboutus/fr_publications.html.

82. Even Canada's former foreign minister has been blunt and outspoken. See Lloyd Axworthy, "Stop the U.S. Foul Play," *The Globe and Mail* (July 17, 2002), p. A13. More generally see Norma Greenaway, "Most See U.S. as a 'Bully,' Survey Finds: Canadians Conflicted About How Much Support to Show Americans," *The Ottawa Citizen* (December 28, 2002), posted at www.canada.com. Among recent stories note a Pew Trust poll of 44 countries in Richard Morin, "World Taking a Darker View of U.S. Motives," *The Guardian Weekly* (December 12–18, 2002), p. 27.

83. Pedro A Noguera, "Preventing and Producing Violence: A Critical Analysis of Responses to School Violence," *Harvard Educational Review*, Vol. 65, No. 2 (Summer 1995), pp. 189–212.

84. Katherin Covell and R. Brian Howe, "Moral Education through the 3 Rs: Rights, Respect and Responsibility," *Journal of Moral Education*, Vol. 30, No. 1 (2001), pp. 29–41.

85. Larry Pynn, "U.S. Bully Tactics Send Wrong Message to Youth: Study—UVic Researcher Says Young People Believe Aggression is Okay," *The Vancouver Sun* (February 21, 2003), p. A3.

3

Rethinking Human Vulnerability, Security, and Connection through Relational Theorizing

Heidi Ross

Educators, more than most other social actors (and more than they and others are often willing to recognize), are faced with heavy responsibilities in the era of globalization. A formidable concern for all progressive educators will be to defend those principles that make real democracy possible—a sense of solidarity and constant efforts toward the reduction of social inequalities....[1]

The Case for Relational Theorizing

In this volume we have been asked to consider how educators and scholars ought to intellectually deconstruct or pragmatically respond to America's "war on terrorism." This challenge requires that we engage in ethical reflection, perhaps even that we become political philosophers. To this end, I consider the relevance of relational theorizing to understanding human vulnerability, security, and alliance across difference.[2] I am motivated by perennial questions that have been raised with renewed urgency since September 11, 2001. What accounts for the ease with which we dehumanize each other? What allows us to see each other as human beings? Can universities nurture those abilities that critical theorists demand we nurture—"the ability to seriously interrogate the world, the capacity to imagine and re-envision a world free from the pain and disfigurement of domination and exploitation?"[3]

Henry Giroux, whose pedagogy of opposition is rooted, as I understand it, in a sort of reflexive reason, has written that September 11 revealed the need for an "alternative space for critical reflection," a space for educators to "set an example for creating the conditions for reasoned debate and dialogue."[4] I argue reasoned debate and dialogue alone cannot sustain alternative spaces for critical reflection. They cannot succeed unaided, because without the authenticity of emotional response reasoned debate and dialogue remain too weak to counter the media-saturated identity discourses our students and we use to determine our allegiances and our alliances.

Recognition that human understanding and communication "is not located in the heady realm of abstraction but centered in the earthy, emotion-infused world of human interaction"[5] provides the subtext of a number of educators' responses to September 11. Michael Apple, for instance, has encouraged us to attend closely to the personal, phenomenological ways we experience our responsibilities to our students, our professions, and our values regarding social change and justice.[6] Watching many of my students deny or struggle feebly with the possibility that human empathy might stand up to violence, I have turned to relational theorizing to consider our collective responses to September 11 and to seek alternative metaphors for conceptualizing "the way lives mesh, transmitting direction and power."[7]

Schools the world over provide precious few resources for helping students and teachers explore the complex interplay of external forces/structures and embodied emotions/reason that cuts and heals the bonds of human empathy and connection. Consequently, relational theorizing is relevant to the lives of educators and students positioned on all sides of the world's power hierarchies, not only to those who write from historical and social positions of relative strength. Relational thinking might hold all of us more accountable for the ethical compromise that difference and distance allow us to make as we accede to concepts like impersonal justice, collateral damage, and just wars.

Those who find structure and critical reason submerged by agency and naïve emotion in relational theorizing miss an important analytical opportunity. Relational theorizing, as I note later, can deal with power and structure by helping us conceptualize how human beings construct, find meaning from, and fear difference. Relational theorizing can help us understand how hegemony is created, how hegemony operates "through difference, rather than overcoming difference."[8]

Elsewhere I have outlined how "genres" of relational theorizing illuminate questions regarding human identity and connection.[9] What I mean by relational theorizing includes perspectives on knowing and acting primarily although by no means exclusively rooted in feminist approaches to the study of education, human relationship, and development. These approaches tend to be critical of rational choice perspectives on human motivation and encourage being in relationship through inclusive, multilateral, and generative approaches to power and respect.

For many feminist relational theorists the moral self is historically situated and "particularized."[10] Never is "knowledge of individual others a straightforwardly empirical matter requiring no particular moral stance toward the person."[11] Likewise, never is "oppression that is the ostensible cause of a conflict (say, ethnic or national oppression)" seen in isolation from "another cross-cutting one: the gender regime."[12] From this perspective, we might envision a war on terrorism as a continuum of preventing (or engendering) violence from household to street to battlefield to refugee camp. Women in domestic shelters have a particular view, indeed, on homeland security.

In what ways might relational thinking further our understanding of human vulnerability, security, and alliance? Relational theorizing can foreground "the combustible element of moral imperative"[13] that guides some of the world's most vigorous advocates of human rights, "ethical globalization," and "development as freedom." Relational theorizing can enrich critical pedagogy by taking the emotional core of human identity seriously, by expanding our understanding of interconnectedness, by critically evaluating how citizen subjects become subjected through surveillance and security measures promoted to protect their freedom.

Relational theorizing can also provide a promising lens through which to examine the paradox inherent in terrorism. In partnering deep passion and commitment with indiscriminate (and sometimes impersonal) violence, terrorism simultaneously embodies human connection and disconnection. Because a primary objective of relational theorizing is understanding and defining human connection, it can illuminate the alienation and urge to violence that provide "terror" its meaning and direction. Relational theorizing can also bring into sharp relief the human illusion and arrogance of invulnerability. Finally, relational theorizing neither underestimates the challenges of nor gives up on the possibilities for achieving transcultural understanding and communication.

In light of its promise, the relevance of relational theorizing to the field of comparative and international education is surprisingly underexamined, even though over a decade has passed since Vandra Masemann cautioned, "our conceptions of ways of knowing have limited and restricted the very definition of comparative education that we have taught students and used in our own research...."[14] Relational theorizing can inspire comparative visions that eschew "poststructuralist fracturing,"[15] that are instead, "holistic, context dependent, and integrative."[16] Recently, comparative educators have been chastised for not theorizing with sufficient rigor economic, technological, cultural, and educational relationships in the context of globalization.[17] Because the power of relational theorizing to illuminate the processes of globalization has not been deliberated in the literature, this chapter also includes a beginning attempt to do so.

Challenging Difference, Agency, and Power

The arrangements we choose to make for our interactions with each other, the structures and processes we create for our organizations, shape the way we deal with identities. A creative handling of difference is central to democratic process, and democracy disposes toward nonessentializing conceptualizations of identity.[18]

Throughout this essay, I pay particular attention to how relational theorizing confronts difference, agency, and power. This theme provides a kind of subtext for the essay and speaks to two central misinterpretations or concerns regarding relational theorizing.

Much relational theorizing is situated in or influenced by an "ethics of care" (morality grounded in relationships). The most influential relational theorist in educational studies is Carol Gilligan, whose path-breaking work in developing a voice-centered method of psychological inquiry "described morality based on the recognition of needs, relation, and response."[19] Gilligan's significant contributions to moral theorizing are a reconceptualization of identity to include experiences of interconnection and an expansion of "the moral domain by the inclusion of responsibility and care in relationships."[20]

Although Gilligan and relational ethicists like Nel Noddings, Larry Blum, and Rita Manning disagree on the extent and conditions of our "capacity for sympathetic identification with others,"[21] together they address the human being's moral task "of getting oneself to attend to the reality of other persons."[22] Relational theorists working from an ethics of care reassert into moral theory that which had been theorized away in impartialist approaches to ethics: compassion, empathy, and the importance of moral responsiveness and perception.

Because relational ethics assigns a high value to "imaginatively reconstructing someone's condition out of concern for her good,"[23] relational theorizing is occasionally criticized for pursuing a naïve or misleading dream of harmony and community. On the contrary, one hallmark of relational theorizing is that it treats difference as "a bridge to relationality."[24] Its overarching stance toward tolerance is skepticism, especially when tolerance is conceptualized strategically to "skate over difference and division."[25] It reminds us, "We cannot cure our estrangements and the suspicion they bring with them by ignoring difference or by imposing similarity."[26] If, as bell hooks puts it, human beings "do not need to eradicate difference to feel solidarity,"[27] then an ethics of care requires simultaneously finding ways of being in relationship and working against a politics of certainty, simultaneously recognizing the need for and the need to transcend our differences.

The ethics of care associated with relational theorizing also seems to be responsible for why relational theorizing is criticized for ignoring structural inequalities or for limiting its vision of justice and its scope of action to the therapeutic, to the agency of individuals. The point is not without merit. Nel Noddings has remarked that relational theorizing, at least as it is articulated through caring, puts priority on "creating, maintaining, and enhancing positive relations—not on decision making in moments of high moral conflict, nor on justification."[28] I agree that relational theorizing implies refraining from the rush to judgment, the rush to proclaim one form of violence justified and another abhorrent, the rush to declare one form of control necessary to democracy or stability and another deleterious to human rights.

Nevertheless, education scholars increasingly mobilize relational theorizing to understand effective policy-making and sustainable educational reform.[29] In fact, the authors of a recent study on reforming educational cultures identify relational knowing as the catalyst for action, precisely because it clarifies the resources and structures necessary for the establishment of critical relationships.[30] They are not alone in concluding that critical political action is sprung from feelings forged in committed relationship. Patricia Hill Collins, for example, writes, "When feelings are involved—when individuals feel as opposed to think they are committed—and when those feelings are infused with self-reflexive truths as well as some sort of moral authority, actions become fully politicized."[31]

Relational theorizing from postcolonial perspectives is particularly persuasive in showing us that the spatial politics of difference, what Adrienne Rich first called the politics of location, is central to both resisting as well as maintaining power. Relational theorists who write from ecological perspectives are likewise unflinching in their structural analysis, and highly critical of the sly postmodern habit of maintaining "analytical distance from power."[32] Relational theorizing successfully articulates the "dynamic dissonance"[33] of the human being's place in the world, and reveals how seductive words like community "hide inequalities."[34] In this context, relational theorizing could inform critical caring responses to all forms of oppression, to anyone (or any group) who promotes death and violence as an act of democracy, retaliation, cultural purity, retribution, faith, or peace. In the following, I consider how such critical perspectives might advance our understanding of human vulnerability, human security, and alliance.

RELATIONAL THEORIZING, CRITICAL PEDAGOGY, AND ALTERNATIVE VISIONS OF HUMAN VULNERABILITY, SECURITY, AND ALLIANCE

Rethinking Human Vulnerability and Security

> In the final analysis, human security is a child who did not die, a disease that did not spread, a job that was not cut, an ethnic tension that did not explode in violence, a dissident who was not silenced.[35]

"Vulnerability" and "security" are both inflated and distorted in public discourse. We are vulnerable to poverty, credit fraud, pathogens, terrorist attacks, to the downside of globalization. In a nod to the realization that terms like "empowerment" can glibly understate structural barriers to human "flourishing," it has now become common in development circles to equate development with the reduction of vulnerability.[36] To be vulnerable is to be victimized. From our resulting sense of precariousness, we have responded by erecting firewalls and subscribing to dangerous notions of preemptive violence that are designed to isolate and secure our positions from others, but in reality obliterate our capacities and responsibilities to interact with others.

Relational theorizing represents a poignantly timely critique of power characterized by invulnerability, that is the perceived ability to not to have to respond to human need, not to have to learn from others, the perceived ability to refrain from listening to or acting with others, the perceived ability to be unilateral. Such power is as delusional in a multicultural age as it is dangerous. From the perspective of relational theorizing, vulnerability is inevitable. To be vulnerable implies humility and risk, and openness to the unknown, a prerequisite for learning and communicating in a multicultural world.

Many educators on U.S. campuses have recalled that immediately after September 11, 2001 they engaged in what we might call a pedagogy of vulnerability. Students joined teachers and peers in un-graded, open-ended conversations to share not only what was on their minds but also what was in their hearts. To accommodate these conversations universities dislodged teaching schedules, if only for a day or two. Teachers admitted vulnerability, stating in public forums that students could on occasion comfort them. Classrooms became spaces in which caring and feeling as well as cognition were validated. By taking seriously the labor of collaboration, by engaging in what Nel Noddings has called the challenge to care in school, universities called a brief moratorium, if you will, on banking education.

According to the *Oxford English Dictionary* vulnerability has over time meant having the power to wound as well as being susceptible to wounding. Likewise, security ambiguously connotes both safety from and control over. Vulnerability and security cut both ways, and I believe the educational implications are clear. Exploring the complex and intertwined personal, symbolic, and structural violence and "unfreedoms" that breed and flow from terrorism requires relational intelligence and vigilance, a responsibility of being, a "curriculum for relational knowing."

That phrase, the subtitle of *Ecology, Spirituality, and Education*, captures Riley-Taylor's desire to confront alienation and separation from life in all its forms through "awakening praxis."[37] Her argument resonates with relational theorizing anchored in ecological thinking that might enlighten our understanding of human vulnerability and security. Ecological thinking represents the most radical form of relational theorizing, renegotiating not only the space between us but also who "us" is (the human and nonhuman world). Empathy in ecological thinking extends from an expansive sense of self in relationship, and its devaluation "is another form of destroying not just our selves but our intergenerational and interspecies environment."[38]

C. A. Bowers, for example, holds that current educational systems perpetuate "the most extreme expressions of modern consciousness, with devastating consequences for the environment."[39] Bower's conclusion that "moral relationships should meet the test of contributing to the long term sustainability of ecosystems,"[40] might provide an intriguing angle from which to analyze the "people-centered, not threat centered" definition of human security developed by individuals such as Gro Harlem Brundtland, former prime minister of Norway and director-general of the World Health Organization (WHO), Mary Robinson, former president of Ireland and UN high commissioner, and Sadako Ogata and Amartya Sen, cochairs of the Commission on Human Security. The Commission defines human security as the safeguarding of "the vital core of all human lives from critical pervasive threats, in a way that is consistent with long-term human fulfillment.[41] Conceptualizations of security as defined by the vital interests of human beings rather than of the state are long overdue—and still virtually absent from mainstream political and media deliberations. Yet treating people as the end of security also runs the risk of minimizing the sustained ecological interconnectedness upon which human well-being ultimately rests.

Relational Theorizing and Critical Pedagogy

Wayne Nelles has encouraged us to consider what role "educational empowerment" strategies, particularly Paolo Freire's notion of conscientization, might play in fostering critical education. Relational theorizing has an edgy relationship with liberation pedagogies. In an influential article published over a decade ago on "Freire and a Feminist Pedagogy of Difference,"[42] Kathleen Weiler raised pointed questions about the implied "universalism" in liberation theories, and called upon critical educators to frame the goals of justice "more specifically in the context of historically defined struggles."[43] In succeeding years, relational theorists have expanded Weiler's critique. In a recent example Michalinos Zembylas and Megan Boler fault critical literacy for being heavily rational and cognitivist, and lacking in its recognition of the "powerful *emotional* component that cannot be displaced simply through smarter critical reflection."[44] Their alternative "pedagogy of discomfort" identifies the contradictions and "emotionally-embedded investments that underlie ideologies such as nationalism and patriotism," and attempts to assist "students develop an emotional and intellectual stance of openness toward difference."[45]

Relational theorists who write from perspectives rooted in and inspired by indigenous or local knowledge pose tougher questions about "Freirean rescue missions."[46] Their wariness of the "colonialist subtexts" underlying many attempts at coalition building across borders by liberation and critical theorists are shared by a number of relational theorists who have attempted to build a more complex vision of liberation pedagogy that validates difference, challenges universal claims to truth, seeks to create social transformation in a world of shifting and uncertain meanings, and examines closely the interrelationship between structure and agency. These diverse theorists, from Chandra Mohanty to Trinh Minh Hah to Patricia Hill Collins, share the project of reconceptualizing agency not as self-assertion or mastery but as creating and sustaining relationships for change. These relationships are conceptualized as being enacted among and between individuals whose different group "standpoints" provide them with varying levels of power and advantage.[47] It is particularly in illuminating hierarchy, that is different levels of power, that relational theorizing, with its insistence on viewing change as embedded in particular historical moments, is so powerful.

The most pointed critics of liberation theories are educators like C. A. Bowers writing from environmental or deep ecology perspectives. They describe Freirean principles as "pre-ecological," based on "an individually-centered way of understanding intelligence, creativity, and moral judgment" that exemplifies the "cultural roots of ecological crisis."[48] Bower's alternative "pedagogy of the oppressor" simplifies the subtle theorizing of

Freire and Maxine Greene. Yet he is correct that the assertive individual is very present in liberation theories, and this ontological foundation of emancipatory education may indeed be reactionary in the face of environmental degradation and inequality.

Wolfgang Sachs examines this possibility with characteristic clarity and suggests that empowerment and agency rerooted in regenerative qualities of learning, sensitivity, goodness, and compassion would have the advantage of being impossible to co-opt.[49] The "complementarity between individual agency and social arrangements" implied by this vision of social–ecological action is central to relational theorizing. So is the conclusion that "to counter the problems that we face, we have to see individual freedom as a social commitment."[50] Recognizing relationship and freedom as mutually reinforcing broadens our view of the difficult human meetings that must animate critical pedagogy. It reminds us that, "Individual freedom is quintessentially a social product."[51]

Relational Theorizing and Human Alliance

> What the events of September 11 should have made clear, among many other things, is that the public still matters.[52]

Relational theorizing also plays a prominent role in ongoing attempts to reconceptualize the public and "challenge democracy" in the context of globalization.[53] In an engaging article on "imagining citizenship," Kathleen Knight Abowitz explores the tensions and commonalities between Martha Nussbaum's vision of cosmopolitanism and Walter Feinberg's program for civic education and concludes they share "the insistence on imagining the cultural other as the key step in building civic identity."[54] Abowitz' examination of the basis for cosmopolitanism is similar to Dale Snauweart's notion of "cosmopolitan democracy" that would assist human beings transcend national, communal, cultural, and civilizational boundaries.[55] Drawing on an ethic of care and an ethic of justice, both authors argue that democracy can no longer be conceived of as just a nation-state phenomenon but rather must be considered a transnational one.

I fear that in expanding our understanding of human vulnerability, security, and alliance cosmopolitan democracy does not go far enough in confronting difference. "Agonistic democracy," on the other hand, affirms that a democratic space

> has to afford an optimal distance between differences, small enough for mutual knowledge, for dispelling myths, but big enough for comfort... It has to be strong enough to prevent implosion, a collapse of differences into rape, silencing or annihilation. But it also has to be flexible enough to permit differences to change their form and significance, and for increased intimacy as and when the quality of relationships allow of it.[56]

Cynthia Cockburn's vision of democratic relationship and space is inspired by her attempts to understand how women form voluntary alliances to communicate across religious and ethnic spaces that have been violently politicized by nationalism and war. I was drawn back to her argument after September 11, recalling the question with which Cockburn begins, "we need to know more about how peace is done...how ordinary people arrange to fill the space between their national differences with words in place of bullets."[57]

Cockburn argues that if an alliance is to thrive it must confront the question of how people make democracy out of difference. She calls this process transversal politics, which rejects "the immobilizing contradiction in which we often find ourselves: between a dangerous belief in universal sisterhood and a relativist stress on difference that dooms us to division and fragmentation."[58] Cockburn concludes that people make alliances work by "holding together difference whose negotiation is never complete, and is not expected to be so...This is the crux of an alliance: a creative structuring of a relational space between collectivities marked by problematic differences."[59] Cockburn's insight is similar to the conclusion Zembylas and Boler draw from their attempt to develop a pedagogy of discomfort to push "the individual to think and feel far beyond the personal and understand how the individual is situated in a globalized history."[60]

Few scholars write as eloquently about the necessity to envision difference as a resource rather than a threat as Mary Catherine Bateson. In her analysis of living with strangers, she reminds us that our interactions with other human beings must by necessity proceed without complete knowledge. "Because it is not possible to stand aside from participation until we know what we are doing, it is essential to find styles of acting that accept ambiguity and allow for learning along the way."[61]

Open-minded humility, respect for others, and encumbered agency are central to the cultivation of what Bateson calls "peripheral vision," a sort of everyday participant observation that "depends on rejecting...the belief that questions of meaning have unitary answers."[62] Bateson's description of being present to context and other people reminds me very much of what Maxine Greene has called wide-awakeness and what Nel Noddings has called engrossment, a full receptivity to the other. Their relational theorizing increases our awareness of the powerful bond between presence and care, an awareness that is "newly necessary today. Men and women confronting change are never fully prepared for the demands of the moment, but they are strengthened to meet uncertainty if they can claim a history of improvisation and a habit of reflection."[63]

As I have noted throughout this essay, relational theorizing underscores that facilitating relationship through critical, caring reflection implies a reconceptualization of difference and diversity. Anthropologist Clifford Geertz has remarked that we need what Charles Taylor called "deep diversity," a "plurality of ways of belonging and being, that yet can draw from it a sense of connectedness, a connectedness that is neither comprehensive nor uniform, primal nor changeless, but nonetheless real."[64] "What unity there is, and identity, is going to have to be negotiated, produced out of

difference."[65] Relational theorizing has contributed a rich body of scholarship to help us reconceptualize identity toward this end, providing us with
a vocabulary of difference that does not alienate.

BREAKING THE PROPHYLAXIS OF SILENCE: TOWARD A PRAXIS OF DIALOGIC CIVILITY

> If we really do believe that all human beings are created equal and endowed
> with certain inalienable rights, we are morally required to think about what that
> conception requires us to do with and for the rest of the world.... [I]f we fail
> to educate children to cross those [national] boundaries in their minds and
> imaginations, we are tacitly giving them the message that we don't really mean
> what we say. We say that respect should be accorded to humanity as such, but
> we really mean that Americans as such are worthy of special respect. And that,
> I think, is a story that Americans have told for far too long.[66]

Recently, a colleague of mine used the phrase "prophylaxis of silence" to
describe the ubiquitous use of the term "political correctness" on college
campuses. The term provides distance, he suggested, shielding us from
things we'd rather not confront directly. By admitting care, risk, discomfort,
emotion, and vulnerability into educational discourse, relational theorizing
replaces a cherished prophylaxis of silence with an uncompromising call for
reconceptualizing the possibilities and the limits to interpersonal and transcultural understanding and action. Eschewing grand narratives and impossible
dreams of universal collective identity, relational theorizing provides guidance
for walking the fragile line between hope and unreflective cynicism.[67]

In their search for a relational ethic to ground civil dialogue, Arnett and
Arneson argue that three central metaphors have shaped human understanding of communication. The dominant communicative metaphor of the
agrarian age was place. Communication in the industrial era was imagined
through the metaphor of self. The prominent metaphor for the postmodern
era or information age is narrative. Arnett and Arneson hope to displace the
cynicism of our cacophonous narratives through a "dialogue of civility" that
might keep the conversation going across diversity.[68] Dialogic civility in this
sense is one of the key missions of education in a multicultural age. It "offers
a minimal basis for a public narrative" (with a small n), "a background set
of assumptions agreed upon enough for people to act."[69] At the same time,
dialogue "is not meant for the ethereal, but for those willing to walk with
others through the mud of everyday life.... Dialogue begins when we act
out of our situatedness, not when we respond from a position of unrealistic
hope."[70]

What relational theorizing leaves us as a resource for praxis, then, is situated hope. "Hope does not require ignorance of limitations and problems
any more than it needs the erasure of ambiguities and complexities to be
kept alive and generative."[71] Relational theories allow us to work against
"the dangers of routine cynicism,"[72] as well as our "lethal beliefs in the
proper name, home, blood, land,"[73] and speak to the future.

Negotiating, not negating the distances that separate us by persistent attention and care is the work we have before us as human beings seeking multiple alliances of dignity and equality. Deliberative examination of the vital connections between ourselves and others is what is missing from education—and what is necessary to our task of reimagining global education and meeting "broken covenants head on, not denying their brokenness."[74] Bateson has written, "multiple small spheres of personal experience both echo and enable events shared more widely."[75] What is missing from education is the nurturing environment, imbued with a "spirit of respectful listening,"[76] that would support those enabling connections between our small spheres of personal experience and the wider world—that is, the caring environment that could help us to remain vigilant about the impulse to dominate and to enable us to listen to and live with strangers.

NOTES

1. Nelly P. Stromquist, *Education in a Globalized World, The Connectivity of Economic Power, Technology, and Knowledge* (Lanham: Rowman and Littlefield Publishers, Inc, 2002), p. 187.

2. This chapter borrows from and extends ideas I developed in an address presented on March 8, 2002 at the annual meeting of the Comparative and International Education Society. In this address, I outline eleven "genre" of relational theorizing. See Heidi Ross, "The Space Between Us: The Relevance of Relational Theory to Re-imaging Comparative Education." *Comparative Education Review* 46:4 (November 2002), pp. 407–32.

3. H. Svi Schapiro, "Empowerment," in David A. Gabbard, ed., *Knowledge and Power in the Global Economy, Politics and the Rhetoric of School Reform* (Mahwah, N.J.: Erlbaum, 2000), pp. 103–10; quote on p. 23.

4. Henry A. Giroux, "Democracy, Freedom, and Justice after September 11th: Rethinking the Role of Educators and the Politics of Schooling," TCRecord.org (2002), content ID 10871, available at http://www.tcrecord.org/content.asp?contentid=10871, paragraphs 3, 8; last accessed November 15, 2002.

5. Rita C. Manning, *Speaking from the Heart: A Feminist Perspective on Ethics* (Lanham: Rowman and Littlefield, 1992), p. xii.

6. Michael Apple. "Patriotism, Pedagogy, and Freedom: On the Educational Meanings of September 11." *Teachers College Record* Vol. 103, No. 2 (2001), pp. 240–66, http://www.tcrecord.org, ID number: 10724, date accessed: 1/7/2003.

7. Leslie Rebecca Bloom, *Under the Sign of Hope: Feminist Methodology and Narrative Interpretation* (Albany, N.Y.: SUNY Press, 1998), p. 246.

8. Stuart Hall, "Fantasy, Identity, Politics," in Erica Carter, James Donald, and Judith Squires, eds., *Cultural Remix: Theories and Politics of the Popular* (London: Lawrence and Wishart, 1995), pp. 63–69; quote on p. 69.

9. See note 2.

10. Lawrence A. Blum, *Moral Perception and Particularity* (Cambridge: Cambridge University Press, 1994), p. 217.

11. Blum, *Moral Perception*, p. 218.

12. Cynthia Cockburn, *The Space Between Us: Negotiating Gender and National Identities in Conflict* (London: Zed, 1998), p. 8.

13. Deborah Valenze, "Passionate Politician," *Women's Review of Books* 20:5 (February 2003), pp. 4–5; quote on p. 4.
14. Vandra Masemann, "Ways of Knowing: Implications for Comparative Education," *Comparative Education Review* 34 (November 1990), pp. 465–73; quote on p. 465.
15. Lois Weis, "Foreword," in *The Cultural Production of the Educated Person: Critical Ethnographies of Schooling and Local Practice*, Bradley Levinson, Douglas E. Foley, and Dorothy C. Holland, eds. (Albany, N.Y.: SUNY Press, 1996), p. x.
16. Masemann, "Ways of Knowing," p. 471.
17. Stromquist, *Education in a Globalized World*, p. viii.
18. Cockburn, *The Space Between Us*, p. 214.
19. Nel Noddings, *The Challenge to Care in Schools* (New York: Teachers College Press, 1992), p. 21.
20. Carol Gilligan, *In a Different Voice* (Cambridge, Mass.: Harvard University Press, 1982), p. 17.
21. Manning, *Speaking from the Heart*, p. 67.
22. Ibid., p.12.
23. Blum, *Moral Perception*, pp. 175–76.
24. Elaine Riley-Taylor, *Ecology, Spirituality, and Education, Curriculum for Relational Knowing* (New York: Peter Lang, 2002), p. 128.
25. Cockburn, *The Space Between Us*, p. 9. A nice illustration is Haithe Anderson's recent exploration of the limits of "tolerance" in liberal pluralism and multiculturalism traditions. See "On the Limits of Liberalism and Multiculturalism," *Teachers College Record*, date published: 8/12/2002, http://www.tcrecord.org, ID Number: 11009.
26. Mary Catherine Bateson, *Full Circles, Overlapping Lives: Culture and Generation in Transition* (New York: Random House, 2000), p. 13.
27. bell hooks, *Feminist Theory from Margin to Center*, 2nd ed. (Cambridge, Mass.: South End, 2000), p. 67.
28. Nel Noddings, *Educating Moral People: A Caring Alternative to Character Education* (New York: Teachers College Press, 2002), p. 21.
29. See Mark B. Ginsburg and Jorge M. Gorostiaga, "Relationships Between Theorists/Researchers and Policy Makers/Practioners: Rethinking the Two-Cultures Thesis and the Possibility of Dialogue," *Comparative Education Review* 45:2 (May 2001), pp. 173–96.
30. Margaret A. Gallego, Sandra Hollingsworth, and David A. Whitenack, "Relational Knowing in the Reform of Educational Cultures: Gallego, Hollingsworth, Whitenack, et al," *Teachers College Record* Vol. 103, No. 2 (2001), pp. 240–66 http://www.tcrecord.org, ID number: 10724, date accessed: 2/8/2003.
31. Patricia Hill Collins, *Fighting Words: Black Women and the Search for Justice* (Minneapolis: University of Minnesota Press, 1998), p. 244.
32. Stromquist, *Education in a Globalized World*, p. 34.
33. Bateson, *Full Circles*, p. 30.
34. Cockburn, *The Space Between Us*, p. 44.
35. Sabina Alkire, Commission on Human Security, *Conceptual Framework for Human Security, Excerpt: Working Definition and Executive Summary*, February 16, 2002, p. 6, http://www.humansecurity-chs.org/doc/frame.html.

36. See Numa Markee, "Language in Development: Questions of Theory, Questions of Practice," *TESOL Quarterly*, Vol. 36, No. 3 (Autumn 2002), http://www.tesol.org/pubs/magz/tq/v36/toc36-03.html.
37. See note 23.
38. Sandra Steingraber, *Having Faith: An Ecologist's Journey to Motherhood* (Cambridge, Mass.: Perseus, 2001), p. 13.
39. See C. A. Bowers, *The Culture of Denial, Why the Environmental Movement Needs a Strategy for Reforming Universities and Public Schools* (Albany: SUNY Press, 1997), p. 84 and Bowers, *Educating for an Ecologically Sustainable Culture, Rethinking Moral Education, Creativity, Intelligence, and other Modern Orthodoxies* (Albany: SUNY Press, 1995).
40. Bowers, *The Culture of Denial*, p. 51.
41. Alkire, *Conceptual Framework*, p. 1.
42. Kathleen Weiler, "Freire and a Feminist Pedagogy of Difference," *Harvard Educational Review* Vol. 61, No. 4 (November 1991), pp. 449–74 reprinted in Christine A. Woyshner and Holly S. Gelfond, eds., *Minding Women, Reshaping the Educational Realm* (Cambridge: Harvard Educational Review Reprint Series No. 30, 1998), pp. 117–45.
43. Ibid., pp. 119–20.
44. Michalinos Zembylas and Megan Boler, "On the Spirit of Patriotism: Challenges of a 'Pedagogy of Discomfort,'" *Teachers College Record*, date published: 8/12/2002 http://www.tcrecord.org, ID number: 11007, date accessed: 2/8/2003.
45. Ibid.
46. Phyllis Robinson, "Whose Oppression is This?: The Cultivation of Compassionate Action in Dissolving the Dualistic Barrier" talk presented at Beyond Freire: Furthering the Spirituality Dialogue, Exploring Paulo Freire's Theory and the Spiritual in Social Justice Practice in the 21st Century, Smith College, October 26–27, 2000.
47. Collins, *Fighting Words*, p. 5.
48. Bowers, *The Culture of Denial*, pp. 86–87.
49. Wolfgang Sachs, *The Development Dictionary: A Guide to Knowledge as Power* (New York: Zed, 1992), p. 129.
50. Amartya Sen, *Development as Freedom* (New York: Alfred A. Knopf, 1999), p. xii.
51. Ibid., p. 31.
52. Nadine Dolby and Nicholas C. Burbules, "Education and September 11: An Introduction," *Teachers College Record*, date published: 7/28/2002, http://www.tcrecord.org, ID number: 10997, date accessed: 2/8/2003.
53. See Madeleine Arnot and Jo-Anne Dillabough, *Challenging Democracy, International Perspectives on Gender, Education and Citizenship* (New York: Routledge/Falmer, 2000).
54. Kathleen Knight Abowitz, "Imagining Citizenship: Cosmopolitanism or Patriotism?" *Teachers College Record*, date published: 8/12/2002, http://www.tcrecord.org, ID number: 11008, date accessed: 2/8/2003.
55. Dale Snauwaert, "Cosmopolitan Democracy and Democratic Education," *Current Issues in Comparative Education* 1 (December 18, 2001), p. 1.
56. Cockburn, *The Space Between Us*, p. 224.
57. Ibid., p. 1.
58. Ibid., p. 8.

59. Ibid., pp. 14, 211.
60. Zembylas and Boler "On the Spirit of Patriotism."
61. Mary Catherine Bateson, *Peripheral Visions: Learning along the Way* (New York: HarperCollins, 1994), pp. 234–35.
62. Ibid., pp. 7–8.
63. Ibid., p. 6.
64. Clifford Geertz, *Available Light, Anthropological Reflections on Philosophical Topics* (Princeton: Princeton University Press, 2000), p. 224.
65. Ibid., pp. 226–27.
66. Martha Nussbaum, *For Love of Country?* (Boston: Beacon Press, 2002), p. 18, quoted in Zembylas and Boler.
67. See Julia Wood's preface to Ronald C. Arnett and Pat Arneson, *Dialogic Civility in a Cynical Age, Community, Hope, and Interpersonal Relationships* (Albany: SUNY Press, 1999), p. xi.
68. See ibid., pp. 296, 303.
69. Ibid., p. 55.
70. Ibid., p. 32.
71. Leslie Rebecca Bloom, *Under the Sign of Hope: Feminist Methodology and Narrative Interpretation* (Albany, N.Y.: SUNY Press, 1998), p. 153.
72. Arnett and Arneson, *Dialogic Civility*, p. 281.
73. Cockburn, *The Space Between Us*, p.229.
74. Ibid., p. 303.
75. Mary Catherine Bateson, *With a Daughter's Eye: A Memoir of Margaret Mead and Gregory Bateson* (New York: Morrow, 1984), p. ii.
76. Ruth Hayhoe and Julia Pan, eds., *Knowledge Across Cultures: A Contribution to Dialogue Among Civilizations* (Hong Kong: Comparative Education Research Centre, The University of Hong Kong, 2001), pp. 20–21.

4

Terrorism and the Pedagogy of Violence: A Critical Analysis

Jorge Nef

Preamble

This essay studies the relationships between terrorism and the culture of violence from an interpretative, phenomenological, and standpoint perspective.[1] The span of its narrative covers nearly three decades. The conceptual framework used is centered on the notions of human security and mutual vulnerability. Such an approach posits that in an integrated system the security of the whole, including its stronger components is contingent upon its weakest links.[2] The human security construct offers a vantage point to look at the connections and dynamics between micro and macro scales, historical and structural factors, and the multiple flows and feedbacks between integrated global cores and their respective peripheries.

Historical Narrative

Our narrative begins with a date: September 11, 1973. That day, as a result of a bloody and unprecedented military coup, a long democratic tradition in Chile came to a sudden end. The perpetrators had done the unthinkable: the government palace had been bombed to rubble, the President killed, scores of civilians had been murdered.[3] All this had happened with the encouragement and active involvement of the Nixon administration.[4] In the months to follow, tens of thousands were imprisoned, tortured, or exiled.[5] The military dictatorship imposed in the country ushered in an equally unprecedented reign of repression on its way to implant what much later would constitute, and be hailed as, the first induced experiment of the "New World Order."[6]

Violence as an Object of Reflection

For many Chileans who were not supporters of the deposed and democratically elected socialist government, but who shared deep republican traditions and were proud of civility and democracy, the events were traumatic. How could it be that a reputedly law-abiding military establishment was able to perpetrate atrocious acts so discontinuous with the country's values and civic culture? How could violence be used to change established values and institutions so radically? I set myself to explore this intriguing and painful riddle. As a student of complex organizations, I had already spent considerable time researching, explaining, and trying to understand the values and behaviors of the "armed bureaucrats"[7] in the pre-coup period. Yet, until that time, I had allowed my wishful thinking to cloud the disturbing findings of my research. The orgy of violence of 1973 revealed what should have been obvious from the beginning of my study, namely that extreme, violent social behavior is, caeteris paribus, a function of a pedagogy of violence:[8] the systematic induction into a culture[9] where the destruction of life and abuse are prime directives. Moreover, this culture functions in a context—economic, political, social, and historical—and expresses itself in institutional forms, patterns of behavior and learning processes. The result of this reassessment was a 1974 article[10] that addressed the nature of training, ideology, and state terrorism.[11] Almost by drift I found myself shifting my research focus, from the social psychology to the largely unexplored social pathology of organization, especially the issue of repression and violence in institutional, "noncriminal" contexts.

In 1979 I received an invitation to participate in a forthcoming conference on terrorism sponsored by the Atlantic Council of Canada (ACC) and prepare a working paper to complement the presentation of the main guest speaker, Professor Ned Lebow[12] of the U.S. Naval Academy. In the following months I did intensive library research that provided me with numerous ideas, information, and conjectures.[13] Though this was my first formal engagement with the field, my earlier study of the politics of repression had brought forward some of the very same issues I encountered in the literature, especially with regards to theories of violence, social change, conflict, and social psychology.[14] My previous background and research were useful in giving me a head start, and providing me with a unique critical perspective.[15]

Several generalizations emerged from by my broad exploration and analysis. (a) One was that the study of terrorism was a "taboo" subject, generally left untouched by most social scientists and academic programs. (b) Given the controversial nature of the phenomenon, its treatment was pregnant with misconceptions and emotive language that more often than not reproduced ethical confusion, simple labeling, and intellectual hollowness. (c) The bulk of the literature gave a piecemeal, anecdotal, and highly simplistic treatment of terrorism. (d) Though the underlying themes of violence, power and politics were always present, little was done in assessing terrorism from a systemic and analytical perspective. Instead, a preferred line of thinking emphasized its criminal or purely pathological nature, and proceeded to list a number of prescriptions to deal with its "evil". (e) In the same vein, most writers were more prone to describe and condemn symptoms, rather than addressing root causes, or looking at the context of terrorism. (f) An inordinately large proportion of the authors presented an extreme right-wing view, attempting to equate terrorism with "communism" of leftist politics, while largely ignoring state and right-wing manifestations. (g) Most importantly, an even larger proportion did not connect terrorist behavior with systemic violence, nor did they address the basic issue of its pedagogy.

As the date of the conference neared, I realized that the central themes underpinning the meeting were almost by default rooted in perceptions quite similar to those prevailing in the literature. For one thing, the leitmotifs of the event were the theses of the World at Bay[16] and the "terror network,"[17] both reflecting the Centre for the Study of Conflict in the United Kingdom and the writings of Claire Sterling and Robert Moss.[18] The principal audience of the closed symposium were chiefs of intelligence and police, as well as other experts, civil servants, and officials from a number of Western countries and lower-level jurisdictions.

The nature of the audience, implied a professional and "technical" slant, presented as a compelling response to an assumed global predicament. Rather than looking at the problem, this deontological stand promoted a solution. In this sense, the answer clearly preceded the question. Antiterrorist know-how appeared to substitute a one-size-fits-all prescription for an analysis of the causes, circumstances, and effects of terrorism. "Expert" knowledge in this context meant a "hard" national security response: expanding the power of security forces, integrating their efforts across boundaries, sharing intelligence, and rolling back legal impediments to carry on their vital institutional missions. In a Cold War context, the forementioned position also involved the implicit and very ideological stance of looking at dissent and leftist politics as a breeding ground of terrorism. From a pedagogical point of view, the structure and presuppositions of the meeting presented the prospects of learning reenforcement through positive feedbacks.

Against this background, and using an array of disparate materials, I sought to create a conceptual framework for a critical analysis of terrorism from an integrated, comparative, and systemic perspective. The initial task was to place the terrorist phenomenon in the larger context of violence and politics. Most importantly, I attempted to present a more nuanced and multisided view of the subject, by stressing that terrorism is not an ideology, but a method (or means), to exercise power through extreme fear in the pursuit of political goals. The corollary of this instrumental view—terrorism as an immoral but calculated and rational strategy—was that terrorists pursued diverse ideological objectives: Right, Left, or center. Therefore, terrorism had to be explained and understood in specific historical and structural circumstances, focussing on functions and effects (terrorist acts), rather than in the a-priori labeling, or disqualifying of "enemies" as "terrorists." An important, and disturbing, consequence of this conceptualization was that terrorism and counterterrorism often end up as dialectically interrelated strategies. Worse, counterterrorism can become a semantic construction to separate "good" from "bad" violence, even in the absence of a real threat. Although I was not dealing directly with moral and normative issues, the analytical framework was aimed at setting the basis for questioning self-serving hypocrisy and double standards. Above all, my intention was to deal with a comprehensive and nuanced picture, separating myth from reality.

It was a welcome surprise to listen to Professor Lebow's presentation. Rather than the litany of self-serving condemnations and prescriptions I came to expect, his empirical study of the politics of terror in Northern Ireland was an inspiring and sophisticated account, with methodological and analytical rigor. Without common intent, our respective works complemented each other. This may have shocked part of the audience—those expecting academic reenforcement to their convictions—but apparently inspired all the other participants. The outcome of my research was a paper subsequently published by the Atlantic Council of Canada, as part of an edited collection.[19] As an outcome of the conference I was invited to give an interview to Robert Collison for *Saturday Night* magazine.[20] Also Peter Sypnowitch, then editor of *Weekend Magazine* asked me to write the feature story for a special issue coinciding with the anniversary of the assassination of former Italian prime minister, Aldo Moro, by the Red Brigades.[21] It was followed by several other pieces.[22]

Terrorism as a Window to Critical Learning

On the basis of this work, in 1980 I was asked by my department Chair to offer, on an experimental basis a general interest undergraduate course on the topic. As conventional Political Science dryness was ever less appealing to students, it appeared logical that such a jazzy subject could help to reduce a declining enrolment trend. The idea was to splice a terrorism course at the junior level in the general area of International Relations/World Politics, but without mandatory prerequisites, so it could attract a large contingent across campus.

Though I had reservations with this idea, it appeared to me that the analysis of the terrorist phenomenon could have added significant intellectual value if well grounded on theories of violence, conflict, international politics, and social psychology. While sensationalism, anecdote, and emotive and ideological stands pointed to the possibility of a counterproductive learning outcome—the reenforcement of prevailing stereotypes—it also presented some advantages. One was the provision of a visible "problematic" focus (in a Popperean sense) to approach politics in general. The other was in offering a challenging point of entry for undergraduate students willing to engage in critical analysis.

I prepared a syllabus, utilizing and updating the bibliography I had collected for the ACC conference. To this I added my own writings, ongoing research, and a select amount of germane Social Science literature. Audiovisual materials were an integral part of the course. The main objective was not to make just an attractive and "interesting" package. Focusing on morally abhorrent political behavior was but a window—a sort of Brechtian alienation—to gain understanding of power processes and their premises, often taken for granted in less controversial settings. To compensate for the absence of prerequisites, strong emphasis was put on academic rigor, and procedures were set in place to make sure that the rather heavy bibliography was read and understood. Also, seminars for the critical analysis and discussions of the themes contained in the bibliography and audiovisual materials were established, all complemented by demanding evaluative criteria.

The course attracted a large contingent of students, especially for a third-year elective, but the increases were by no means dramatic: some 20 percent above the comparative cohort. The bulk of the participants were Political Science (Comparative Politics, International Relations, and International Politics) students as well as from the International Development program I chaired. Between 1980 and 1982, "The Politics of Terror" was offered three times. Lectures, seminars, and audiovisuals were complemented by a large 2-day role-playing exercise "The Road to Armageddon." The effort integrated two World Politics/International Relations classes with my own. Over 200 students, six TAs, and the three instructors participated. The scenario was aimed to give an experiential, albeit contrived, view of a multilayered, multi-actor interaction in a complex and conflictive global game where terrorist incidents could act as triggers in superpower confrontation over the Middle East. It was in essence an application of a 1914 Sarajevo-like incident in a complex, layered bipolar world with numerous transnational and subnational actors. The structure of the game was based upon three levels of actors, as in a Greek tragedy. The "gods" (instructors and Teaching Assistants) set and interpreted the rules, kept records and tallies of interactions, acted as umpires, and sometimes introduced exogenous events and multiple obstacles to the game. The "heroes" were the major players proper (the global power configuration, with superpowers, alliances, international regimes, and client states), representing national and institutional interests, whose decisions were critical. The "chorus" were the subnational actors and groups that acted either as dependents of, or with relative autonomy from, the "heroes." Irrespective of the dysfunctions introduced by the "gods" in the various runs within each game, nuclear confrontation was always avoided. However, in the periphery of the superpowers, uncontrollable subnational conflicts by proxy became prevalent.[23]

This teaching effort coincided with the emergence of important reflective writings on the subject.[24] The dominant "world at bay" thesis, attempting to link terrorism with the "evil empire" and domestic dissent, soon fell into disrepute, as the excesses of counterterrorism and national security doctrines became exposed. The counterinsurgent view of terrorism had been severely challenged by critical research. The controversy between the conventional and the critical camps appeared closed: the critical stand seemed to have won the day. However, the "terroristologists" in universities, think tanks, and private consultancies that provided intellectual inputs to the security practitioners would not vanish.

The Soviet invasion of Afghanistan (following the Iranian revolution), as well as the unfolding of the Central American civil wars indicated a willingness of the West to support, train, and finance "freedom fighters." These included groups like the Afghani *mujahadeen*, or the Nicaraguan *contras*, or pro-government paramilitaries (like the Latin American death squads and regular security forces) whose tactics were hard to separate from terrorism. In this context, the pretended moral high ground held by the hard-liners could be overturned in the face of growing evidence, including declassified documents. The focus on terrorism had the potential for backfiring, and therefore lost its ideological usefulness. Furthermore, the collapse of the Soviet Union, the legacy of the proxy wars, the reduction of tensions in Southern Africa, Latin America, Northern Ireland, and the Middle East, and the growing resort to use conventional force, further pushed terrorism out of the headlines.

Despite its popularity and its relative success, the experimental course had some negative consequences. Some colleagues increasingly attacked it as "justifying terrorism," or "teaching an evil doctrine," or "undermining Western values." Others, including a Dean, complained about the security problem posed by simulations, which fed into the rumor mill about terrorism's training grounds. At any rate, I was beginning to get frustrated too, as a yet quite small, but persistent percentage of the participants remained stuck in conventional, and even extremist mind-sets. These were glamorizing violence and looking at the course as a feeder of "soldier-of-fortune" type fantasies. In 1982, upon considerate reflection I decided to discontinue the course and devote my interests to new pursuits, though I continued research on the subject.

Broadening the Analytical Window

In the mid- to late 1980, my research had centered on three subjects. One was the so-called democratic transition in Latin America, away from the National Security regimes (and state terrorism) and into restricted democracies.[25] Another was the impact as technology on development.[26] The third topic was food security.[27] While the later presented ostensibly some solution of continuity with terrorism—especially from the perspective of the "food weapon"—the other two appeared to be quite unrelated. However, at a deeper epistemological level, I was already beginning to structure a framework of convergence. For one thing, development had remained a central preoccupation of mine since early on. So were peace and my concern with the dysfunctions of "national security." My very interest in repressive politics and state terrorism had been an attempt to come to grips with the inner workings of development models and their mechanism for conflict management.[28] Furthermore, in my experience with the South Commission,[29] I had witnessed first hand a changing configuration of the world order, from bipolarity and the Three Worlds of development to a form of muted unipolarism. This reordering had meant also a redefinition of the "traditional" relationship between development and security. Also, my association with the Pan American Health Organization had maintained my interest in the relationship between environment, nutrition, health, science and technology, administration, and development. Food security was also a bridging preoccupation in the spheres of security and development.

There were two institutional associations that played a major role in terms of contributing to the forementioned paradigmatic convergence, and to a redefinition of terrorism. One was my working as a consultant for the International Development Research Centre's (IDRC) South–North Project. (1987–1989). The other was my sabbatical at the UN Economic Commission for Latin America and the Caribbean in 1990. My IDRC work put me in the middle of an institutional effort to rethink the pattern of global relations and international cooperation in the context of the end of the Cold War. The series of internal panel discussions around the South–North project had broadened the scope of the original intent of reexamining development, by raising the thesis of "mutual vulnerability." This idea dawned on me in 1988 as I was trying to characterize the mutual-assured destruction (MAD) concept of nuclear deterrence and its functional equivalent in a post–Cold War world. As mentioned, it meant that the integrity of a system, and that of its apparently "stronger" sectors, was conditioned by its most vulnerable components. Although I had presented these concepts in an internal memo,[30] and referred to mutual vulnerability in a subsequent article on refugee flows,[31] the first published item mentioning human security and mutual vulnerability was a chapter on democratic transitions in Latin America.[32] Other pieces were to follow,[33] culminating in the first edition of *Human Security and Mutual Vulnerability*[34] that appeared late in 1995.

The theme of terrorism reemerged in my writings, this time in a broader context of mutually reciprocating systemic dysfunctions—environmental, economic, social, political, and cultural crises—whose net effect was a heightened level of mutual risk, vulnerability, and insecurity. From this viewpoint, terrorism is one among several political manifestation of violence closely related to a failure of governance (conflict management), occurring at the intersection between domestic and global politics. In this line of reasoning, terrorism is closely related to a set of interconnected manifestations of an imbedded and global political crisis.

(a) One is the growing number of failed states resulting from fiscal and economic breakdown, loss of sovereignty, legitimacy crises, and expanding internal conflicts. These conflicts are, in turn, fueled by acute resource plundering and accelerated by a vigorous arms trade.

(b) Another is the surge of irredentist forms of ethnic and religious nationalism. These emerge as a reaction to modernization and political breakdown and as a search for collective identity.

(c) A third is the resurgence of neo-fascist, xenophobic, and extreme right-wing tendencies in developed countries, emanating from severe socioeconomic disruptions and alienation.

(d) A fourth involves expanding criminality enhanced by authoritarian, ineffectual, unaccountable, and/or corrupt law enforcement. A manifestation of this trend is the configuration of police states where civil society is criminalized by "countercrime."

(e) Finally, is the growing irrelevance of democratic politics resulting from neoliberal policies and the subsequent loss of legitimacy and sovereignty of the nation-state. With traditional safety nets and social capital eroded by modernity and state welfare minimized by restructuring, civil society oscillates between apathy and frustration.

A promising line of inquiry on the problem is to approach it from the three-layered framework (or "images") for the analysis of conflict proposed by Kenneth Waltz.[35] At the broader level of the international system, terrorism is as a form of surrogate war whose incidence increases as existing power balances—as well as nation-states—disintegrate, and as subnational forces challenge a crumbling global order. The end of bipolarity has implied that superpower constraints upon client-states, especially in the Middle East have loosened. Also, given the fact that the remaining superpower has actively discarded multilateral international instruments, the arenas for institutionalized interaction have been greatly reduced.

At the national level, the fracturing of states, combined with persistent economic decline and the concomitant inability of elites to compromise in power-sharing formulas has led to protracted conflict. This situation has been complicated by two factors. One is the aforementioned resurgence of militant religious and ethnic nationalism. The other is the dramatic transformation of the world order itself, from muted bipolarity to aggressive unipolarity under U.S. control. Whether the more diffuse asymmetry of the post-1989 system, or in the neo-imperial manifestations of the present, the net effect of unipolarity is a weakening of the protective economic, legal and military "hard shell" for most nation-states. Without these constrictive centripetal attributes, and in the absence of surrogate regional and supranational structures, nation-states have lost structural integrity. These mega-trends, in the midst of a purposeful shrinking of multilateralism and a weakening of international law, have enhanced the volatility of a system where might makes right. A new Hobbesian "state of nature" has emerged simultaneously in both the international and domestic spheres.

In the ensuing lawlessness and power vacuum, terrorism and its dialectical opposite—counterterrorism—become viable options. Violence is the political currency where neither acceptable rules of the game, nor legitimate and effective "authoritative" arbitration are possible. Though eminently symbolic, terrorist deeds imply utmost destructive force, not necessarily in its amount, but in intensity and intent. The outrages perpetrated, however, are not purely gratuitous, "voluntaristic," psychotic, criminal, or symptomatic rage. Rather, and irrespective of its aims, terrorism is first and foremost rational: a cold-blooded, immoral and calculated strategy. It targets an adversary's "soft belly" of unsuspected victims to effect political aims through the management of fear. As a tool of struggle, the so-called war of the flea[36] is fundamentally geared to elicit an adversary's overreaction that ultimately is designed to work to the perpetrator's advantage.

Terrorism is therefore a system, with a specific context, a culture, structures, processes, and effects. It emerges from a milieu and history in which one or many actors are prone to commit violent acts. It is mediated by a culture or subcultures where violence is justified and learned. It expresses itself in organized forms, either by permeating, transforming and polarizing existing structures and practices, or by creating its own "terrorist/antiterrorist" configuration. As a process, terrorism reproduces itself through multiple spirals of actions and retaliations. These dynamics have the effect of radically altering the terms of reference of political life and reproducing the all-encompassing nature of fear.

Two important points in the characterization mentioned earlier need to be highlighted. One is that terrorism and counterterrorism are often dialectically intertwined as two explicit or implicit sides of the same coin. The other is that the culture of violence is induced by learning through a pedagogy of violence. This term, which I have derived from Freire's conceptualization of the "pedagogy of oppression,"[37] suggests that individuals, groups and entire societies can be taught extreme brutality. As Milgram's experiment[38] suggests, socially induced extreme behavior can and does affect perfectly functional individuals, who are provided with a justifying and supporting framework for cruelty.

In fact, many organizations that put human life in harms ways exclude psychopaths, preferring instead perfectly functional individuals. The latter, through dehumanizing and systematic training, and behavioral conditioning, are made dysfunctional. They become co-dependent upon asylum-like collectives,[39] or "families," made of those already initiated, outside whose boundaries they have difficulties in living a full-time normal life. This pattern presents strikingly similarities with the socialization of gangs, hooligans, child soldiers, terrorists, and security forces.

The moral double standard here is that, while society outwardly condemns life-threatening behavior for individual gain, personal identity, or social change, it glorifies it as it relates to high moral purpose (e.g. for God and country, or "national security"). This is reinforced by the deep machismo in the collective imaginary of pop culture: movies, television programming, comics, sports, and video games. This pro-violence attitude has long crossed the cultural, ethnic, and gender divides. Identity and violence, as noted in Fanon's account,[40] go hand-in-hand: "we fight, therefore we are." All around us violence is glorified in the name of history, destiny, or patriotism. It also sells and it is newsworthy. Not only dying for the fatherland is sweet and honorable as the Roman motto states, more so it is killing for it.

The Pedagogy of Violence

Most important, this cultural software is not innate, but taught. The professionalization of violence makes trespassing ethical thresholds a mere technical matter. Most important, however is the generalized acceptance of violence—and war—as a morally viable alternative among those who are not specifically trained for killer roles. There are two basic manifestations of the pedagogy and culture of violence. One is the explicit induction of individuals and groups by means of professional or paraprofessional training in "best practices." The other is a more implicit, subtle, and systemic pedagogy, seemingly outside intentional settings. In the second case, the culture of violence is imbedded by multiple influences, from peer groups, to daily activities, to the media, games, artistic and leisure undertakings, and above all by the allegedly neutral educational system. I am not talking here only about "patriotic" and xenophobic rituals, like pledges of allegiance among grade and high school youngsters. I am referring mostly to the largely a-critical way subjects like History or Political Science are taught, especially in universities. More specifically, one needs to pay close attention at the way the subject of terrorism is constructed and presented, as well as its ideological uses. The terrorist label is far too easily applied to anybody who, in the eyes of the existing political authorities is defined as the current "enemy." Witness the widespread and now growing racial or security profiling, hidden under the "us" versus "them" idiom, or under the clash of civilization[41] scenarios. Scholarship is often complacent not only by not challenging these stereotypes, but also for giving authoritative support to political prejudice.

CONCLUDING REFLECTIONS

This brings me to the second date, as well as to the end, of this narrative: September 11, 2001. The collapse of the Twin Towers and the direct hit on the Pentagon with all their gore and loss of innocent life, also ushered in a new politics and a newspeak. Terrorism became the central preoccupation in North America, and by extension in the entire globe. President Bush's "crusade" on terror became an all-encompassing global undertaking, semantically dwarfing everything else. By inducing a suspension of judgement and most forms of critical thinking, the word "terrorism" is now part of the mass hysteria of the terror system itself.

A hard-line response, along the standard prescriptions already dreamed by the terroristologists of the 1970s resulted in a severe political closure, authorized arbitrariness, extreme concentration of power, significant erosion of civil liberties and due process, unprecedented in past wartime situations. It also projected itself into a strong military reaction abroad. The action against the Taliban regime in Afghanistan, soon after the terrorist attacks, enjoyed a significant support from the international community. The American tragedy had become humanity's tragedy and hunting and punishing the perpetrators an act of self-defense. Subsequently, President Bush's war shifted into a unilateral, seemingly unconnected, and internationally resisted, expansion of the conflict into a Saddam Hussein's Iraq. For all the bad deeds of the former ally, once armed by both superpowers to undermine revolutionary Iran, there seemed to be little convincing evidence of an Al-Qaeda connection, or a threat to U.S. security posed by weapons of mass destruction.

Nevertheless, in many respects the American overreaction is understandable. For the first time since the 1860s, the population had become directly exposed to the horrors of war in its own territory. For a country that for

140 years has had the privilege of not experiencing the down side of war, vulnerability, mutual or not, is an uncomfortable feeling. Yet, it was not the first terrorist incident on American soil. The Oklahoma City bombing of 1995 by domestic white supremacists killed nearly 200 innocent civilians. But it paled in intensity and symbolism compared to the attacks on the Pentagon and the Twin Towers. Nor was 9/11 the first episode of international terrorism in the United States. The 1993 bombing of the very same Trade Center by Islamic fundamentalists, though smaller in scale, produced scores of civilian casualties and widespread panic.

However, and this refers back to the beginning of my narrative, the first international terrorist activity resulting in the killing of an American civilian happened in Washington DC in 1976. It was carried out by General Pinochet's intelligence services DINA, assisted by a right-wing anti-Castro cell (with connections to the Watergate affair) and managed by Michael Townley, an American with shady linkages to the intelligence community. The operation involved complex planning and coordination among many agencies and individuals. The explosion of a bomb planted in the car of former Chilean ambassador, Orlando Letelier, killed him and his American assistant, Rony Moffit. It also injured the latter's husband.

What made this event peculiar is not only that it happened in the nation's capital, in Embassy Row, near Dupont Circle. It also occurred at a time when the director of the forementioned DINA, General Manuel Contreras, was in the payroll of the CIA.[42] The Agency (headed in 1976 by George Bush Sr.), under the leadership of John McCone, had been actively involved in the 1973 coup that overthrew and killed President Allende. The investigation of this possible "friendly fire" incident in Washington dragged on for years in U.S. and Chilean courts. Though finally the prosecution managed to establish immediate penal (but not political) culpability, it left far too numerous loose ends and crucial questions unanswered. Certainly the White House did not retaliate against the regime that planned, financed, and perpetrated the bombing. This tolerance went on even when it was known that these ostensibly criminal activities were part of a wide international operation coordinating five military dictatorships (codenamed "Condor") and aimed at the elimination and terrorizing of opposition figures and their families.

The story behind the assassination on Embassy Row is quite revealing in the sense that it encompassed a wide network of operatives—government officials, military personnel, ideologically like-minded groups, and hired guns. Most important, the bulk of these operatives had been trained to perform Cold War–related duties in and by the United States itself, allegedly to defend the interests of the "Free World." It was in the discharge of their official mission, or as trained "freelancers" that they performed the 1976 bombing and other deeds throughout the Americas and Europe.

The Condor experience shares a great deal with the training of Islamic fighters in Afghanistan and Saudi Arabia to combat the Soviets throughout the 1980s. Osama bin Laden was a main financier, mentor, and ally of these groups, and once he enjoyed strong U.S. backing. An organizational outcome of this undertaking was the loosely structured "franchise" under his command known as Al-Qaeda, Arabic for the base. The ultra religious and business leader was also a conduit for the secret war that ultimately bled the USSR. In the 1976 episode, the terrorists killed what they saw as enemies of the Free World in U.S. territory. If Americans were on their way they likely saw them as either "bad" people or simply dismissed as "collateral damage." The more vicious Al-Qaeda strain of religious fundamentalists of 2001 stroke massively at the symbolic heart of the remaining superpower (and once ally), whose culture and arrogance they had learned to hate as much as they did the Soviets'. In either case, the chickens had come home to roost; except than in the Chilean case, toppling a government and neutralizing exiles was, by comparison to the anti-Soviet campaign, just small fry.

The assassins of the recent September 11 had undoubtedly a better and more efficient organization than their Condor predecessors. The Base was truly transnational, in the mold of a corporation, and effectively equipped to function in a global society. They had ostensibly planned their operations on their own for many years, starting with their test-run at the World Trade Center in 1993, advancing through the devastating attacks on the U.S. embassies in Kenya and Tanzania in 1998, and the USS Cole off Bahrain in 2000. Intelligence and operation analysis, as well as strategic planning, appeared to have been careful, including the manipulation of symbols, the possible reverberations in the economy, and even anticipating U.S. reactions. They seemed to know how and where to strike, down to the uses of commercial planes as missiles, and the determined fanaticism and discipline of offensive suicide. They likely had a competent knowledge of American myths, distopias, and psychology (both elite and mass), including the staging of Hollywood style catastrophes and dark fantasies dwelling in the collective imagery. Most important, they operated—as did their 1976 counterparts—from the perverse logic of the pedagogy of violence. They saw themselves as soldiers with a technology of death accomplishing a mission; and in reality they so evolved from amateur retailers of violence to professional wholesalers by unleashing hell.

The impact of the 2001 terrorist attacks, unlike all previous incidents, is not so much a function of the large scale, salience, and brutality of the acts themselves, but of the responses it has elicited. The international community is today in greater disarray, as they grope with a new global reality. International law and organization, in the long run the only effective mechanisms to control and prevent terrorism, appear currently unable to present a coherent response. This further undermines international conventions, collective security, and multilateralism. At the level of the nation-states, especially in the remaining superpower, the terror scare, multiplied by unrelated events, such as the Anthrax episode or the sniper incident, has resulted in a curtailment of civil freedoms, and open debate, leading to a peculiar and hegemonic form of authorized totalitarianism. Terrorism has also provided a justification for steamrolling an ultraconservative political agenda that threatens democracy not only in the United States but beyond its borders too.

A similar closure obtains at the level of foreign policy and international interactions. The articulation of a "friend–foe" doctrine, reflective of the domestic closure of the "open society" has impacted everybody. It has weakened alliances and various forms of regionalism and has configured new forms of global enmity. At the domestic level, interpersonal suspicion, xenophobia, and collective paranoia become pervasive. The once independent press has become homogeneous and essentially a mouthpiece for government policy and ideology: a thinly veiled propaganda tool in a holistic, generalized, and never-ending war. Terror alerts remind citizens of the need to internalize fear in the name of security and not to question authority. It seems that the pedagogy of violence has mutated into the more invasive and acute pedagogy of fear.

It is ironic that despite all the intelligence before the events, and even more so after, Osama bin Laden is still at large. The perpetrators of the Anthrax scare have not been caught. Despite persistent blows to its organization in Afghanistan and the Pakistani border, Al-Qaeda is still lurking in the dark; Afghanistan appears a long way from becoming stable and rebuilding civil society. All this is happening while the Palestinian–Israeli conflict— a fundamental source of terrorist activity—continues its barbarous escalation. In the mantra of terrorism and the possible war on Iraq, this human tragedy in the Eastern Mediterranean has become somewhat shelved and lost. What about contemporary Colombia? Are the Revolutionary Armed Forces of Colombia (FARC) another component of David Frumm's most unfortunate "axis of evil" cliché? Is the United States ready to invade Colombia and Venezuela to stop terrorism? The only response to the multiple crises seems to be more of the same prescription and intellectual and moral myopia that brought about the crises in the first place. It seems that learning is caught in a dysfunctional loop of self-reenforcing feedbacks.

We hear nowadays many answers and solutions. Most of these are virtually the same as those proclaimed by those experts espousing the "world at bay" and "terror network" theses a quarter century ago. At any rate, these formulas are ineffectual anyway. Most of them are dangerous. To work, prescriptions need to be connected to critical problems. But, in the absence of reflective thinking, these problems are not posed, or probing questions are not raised. One thing is clear, magic bullet like, technical solutions to a complex problem such as terrorism are not working. Have those in power ever questioned our learning about the subject and about the pedagogy and culture of violence that supports this learning? Have we tried to see ourselves as part of the problem? Finally, have we seriously considered looking at the horror, and the mirror, of terrorism from the prism of what UNESCO calls a "culture of Peace"?[43]

Notes

1. See Dorothy Smith, *The Everyday Life as Problematic: A Feminist Sociology* (Toronto: University of Toronto Press, 1987), p. 1.

2. J. Nef, *Human Security and Mutual Vulnerability. The Political Economy of Development and Underdevelopment* (Ottawa: IDRC Books 1999), pp. 2–21.

3. Cf. Gabriel Garcia Marquez, "The Death of Salvador Allende," *Harper's* No. 248 (March 1974), pp. 46–53.

4. See Armando Uribe, *The Black Book of the American Intervention in Chile* (Boston: Beacon Press, 1975), passim; also Victor Marchetti and John Marks, *The CIA and the Cult of intelligence* (New York: Knopf, 1975).

5. See the *Rettig Report*, Raul Rettig, "Informe de la Comision Nacional de Verdad y Reconciliacion," official unabridged text, Nos. 1, 2, and 3, special edition of *La Nacion* (March 1991).

6. "Neoliberalism and the Chilean Model: A Forerunner of the New World Order," in Gordana Yovanovich, ed., *The New World Order: Corporate Agenda and Parallel Reality* (Kingston: McGill-Queens' Press, 2003), pp. 89–105.

7. Edward Feit, *The Armed Bureaucrats. Military-Administrative Regimes and Political Development* (Boston: Houghton-Mifflin, 1973).

8. This concept is derived from Paulo Freire's "pedagogy of oppression." See Paulo Freire, *The Pedagogy of the Oppressed* (New York: Continuum, 1983).

9. See Gabriel Almond and Sydney Verba, *The Civic Culture. Political Attitudes and Democracy in Five Nations* (Boston: Little, Brown and Co., 1965), p. 13.

10. J. Nef, "The Politics of Repression: The Social Pathology of the Chilean Military," *Latin American Perspectives*, Vol. 1 No. 2 (Summer/Fall, 1974), pp. 58–77.

11. Marcio Moreira Alves, "Urban Guerrillas and the Terrorist State," in Jon Rosenbaum and William Tyler, eds., *Contemporary Brazil: Issues of Economic and Political Development* (New York: Praeger, 1972), p. 51.

12. Cf. Ned Lebow, "Sectarian Assassination in Northern Ireland," in John Carson, ed., *Terrorism in Theory and Practice* (Toronto: The Atlantic Council of Canada, 1978), pp. 22–37.

13. See Karl Popper, *Conjectures and Refutations; the Growth of Scientific Knowledge* (New York: Basic Books, 1962), pp. vii–viii, 27–29, 33–65.

14. See e.g. James Davies, *Human Nature in Politics. The Dynamics of Political Behavior* (New York: John Wiley and Sons, 1963), pp. 64–103; also Ted Gurr, *Why Men Rebel* (Princeton, N.J.: Princeton University Press, 1970).

15. See e.g. Jürgen Habermas, "What does a Crisis Mean Today? Legitimation Problems in Late Capitalism," *Social Research*, Vol. 40, No. 4 (1973), pp. 643–47.

16. See the 1978 WHYY-TV documentary, produced by Edward Karayn, "Terrorism/The World at Bay."

17. See Arye Neier, "Review of *The Terror Network: The Secret War of International Terrorism*, by Claire Sterling," *The Nation* (May 9, 1981), pp. 373–75.

18. See Fred Landis, "Robert Moss, Arnaud de Borchgrave and Rightwing Disinformation," *Covert Action*, No. 10 (August–September 1980), pp. 37–44.

19. "Reflections on Terrorism: Domestic and International Perspectives," in Carson, ed., *Terrorism in Theory and Practice*, pp. 4–21.

20. Robert Collison, "The New Barbarism," *Saturday Night* (January–February 1980), p. 15.

21. "Reign of Terror," *Weekend Magazine* (cover story), May 5, 1979, pp. 4–12.

22. See "Importing State Terrorism," *The Nation*, Vol. 231, No. 2 (July 12, 1980), pp. 54–56; "Terrorismo: Política del Miedo," *Relaciones Internacionales*, No. 7 (October 1984), pp. 77–86; "Peru's 'Shining Path,'" (with J. Atlin),

International Perspectives (July–August 1985), pp. 25–28, 5–34, "Symbolic Politics," *New Internationalist*, No. 160 (June 1986), pp. 8–9; "Terrorismo y política: algunas consideraciones básicas," in Augusto Varas (comp.), *Paz, Desarme y Desarrollo en América Latina* (Buenos Aires: Grupo Editor Latinoamericano, 1987), pp. 131–49; "The Spiral of Violence: Insurgency and Counter-Insurgency in Peru" (with J. Vanderkop), *North/South. Canadian Journal of Latin American and Caribbean Studies*, Vol. 13, No. 26 (Fall 1989), pp. 53–77; "El fenómeno terrorista: una perspectiva global y algunas consideraciones empíricas y teóricas" (con E. A. Cebotarev) in Augusto Varas, ibid., pp. 69–89.

23. The evaluations from those retained (about 60% of the intake) were extremely good and very encouraging. Students' interest, knowledge, and depth of understanding of politics, society, history, and ethics, beyond the subject matter of the course, had grown substantially. The simulation game was highly praised by its participants and showed increased degrees of awareness, and intellectual sophistication, as compared with the more conventional teaching.

24. Edward Herman, *The Real Terror Network. Terrorism in Fact and Propaganda* (Cambridge, Mass.: South End Press, 1982).

25. On "restricted democracy," see Gullermo O'Donnell and Philippe Schmitter "Tentative Conclusions About Uncertain Democracies" in Volume IV of Guillermo O'Donnell, Philippe Schmiter, and Laurence Whitehead, eds., *Transitions for Authoritarian Rule. Prospects for Democracy* (Baltimore: The Johns Hopkins University Press, 1986), pp. 6–72.

26. See "Science, Technology and Underdevelopment: A Conceptual Approach," with O. P. Dwivedi and J. Vanderkop, *Canadian Journal of Development Studies*, Vol. XI, No. 2 (December 1990), pp. 223–40; also *Ethics and Technology*, with J. Vanderkop and H. Wiseman, joint editors (Toronto: Wall & Thompson 1989).

27. J. Nef and J. Vanderkop, *Food Systems and Food Security in Latin America and the Caribbean: Politics, Ideology and Technology*, with J. Vanderkop (Guelph: Centre for Food Security Research, 1989); also "Food Systems and Food Security in Latin America: A Systemic Approach to Politics, Ideology and Technology," with J. Vanderkop, in J. I. Bakker, ed., *The World Food Crisis: Food Security in Comparative Perspective* (Toronto: Canadian Scholars' Press, 1990), pp. 97–136.

28. "Stalemate and Repression in Southern Cone: An Interpretative Synopsis," *New Scholar*, No. 8 (1983), pp. 371–85.

29. The South Commission, *The Challenge to the South: The Report of the South Commission* (Oxford: Oxford University Press, ca.1990).

30. "South-North: A Framework for Analysis," background document for the Presidential study group on South–North relations (Ottawa: IDRC, 1989).

31. "The Politics of Refugee Generation in Latin America," Glendon College, Centre for Refugee Studies, York University, 1989. It appeared in Howard Adelman, ed., *Refugee Policy. Canada and the United States* (Toronto: York Lanes Press, 1991), pp. 52–80.

32. See "Democratization, Stability and other Illusions: Militarism, Nationalism and Populism in the Political Evolution of Latin America with Special Reference to the Chilean Case," in Mark Dickerson and Stephen Randall, eds., *Canada and Latin America: Issues to the Year 2000 and Beyond* (Calgary: The International Centre, University of Calgary, 1991), pp. 73–122.

33. I prepared a number of papers on the subject as companion texts to invited lectures at the DND's former National Defence College at Kingston, and the Staff College in Toronto. Using this conceptual framework, I wrote "The Politics of Insecurity in Latin America," in Jan Black, ed., *Latin America. Its Problems and its Promise*, third edition (Boulder: Westview, 1997), pp. 203–31.

34. See our, *Human Security and Mutual Vulnerability. An Exploration into the Global Political Economy of Development and Underdevelopment* (Ottawa: IDRC Books 1995).

35. Kenneth Waltz, *Man, the State, and War* (New York: Columbia University Press, 1959).

36. Robert Taber, *The War of the Flea; A Study of Guerrilla Warfare Theory and Practise* (New York: L. Stuart, 1965).

37. Freire, *The Pedagogy of the Oppressed*.

38. Stanley Milgram, "Obedience [motion picture]" (New York: New York University Film Library, 1965).

39. Erving Goffman, *Asylums; Essays on the Social Situation of Mental Patients and Other Inmates* (Chicago: Aldine Pub. Co. [1962, c1961]).

40. Frantz Fanon, *Les damnes de la Terre* (Paris: F. Maspero, 1968).

41. Samuel Huntington, "The Clash of Civilizations?" *Foreign Affairs*, Vol. 72, No. 3 (2003), pp. 1–25.

42. See "Chile Security Chief was CIA Informer," *BBC News*, Internet service, September 19, 2000, 23:24 GMT, 00:24 U.K.

43. For an overview of UNESCO's Culture of Peace project, see http://www.unesco.org/cpp/uk/.

II

AMERICA AND THE WORLD

5

Doomed To Suspicion: A Qualitative Inquiry of Selected Middle Eastern Students' Experiences on American Campuses after September 11, 2001

Casandra Culcer

On September 11, 2001, not just three buildings were struck by hijacked planes, but the very feeling of people's security has been struck hard at, and also their feelings of trust toward anyone who looks, speaks, or behaves differently. During the weeks following the terrible tragedy, the media reported numerous incidents where peaceful individuals became victims of violent and misdirected retaliation only because they were identified with the ethnic and religious groups to which terrorists are supposed to belong. The Middle Eastern look has suddenly become dangerous in America.

The president George W. Bush, himself, expressed his concern that innocent people might uselessly be hurt by angry citizens seeking revenge against the terrorists. On September 17, 2001, at the Islamic Center in Washington, D.C., the president said, "Americans who mistreat Muslims should be ashamed." The president emphasized the fact that, "in our anger and emotion, our fellow Americans must treat each other with respect."[1] In a briefing held at the FBI Headquarters during the same day, Robert Mueller, the Director of FBI, was reporting the fact that the Bureau was already investigating 40 cases of hate crimes against Arab American citizens and institutions.[2]

On the other hand, in their endeavor to identify and prevent potential threats against public safety, the law enforcement authorities took various types of actions, some of which being much likely to affect negatively a great number of peaceful individuals. For instance, the police made plans to interrogate about 5,000 young men from Middle Eastern countries who are in the United States on temporary visas, in order to obtain any information that might lead to terrorist organizations and activities.[3] In the opinion of Imad Hamad, of the Arab American Anti-Discrimination Committee, quoted in an article written by Andrew Gumbel, this is "the clearest message to both the Arab-American community and to society at large—the government believes that young Arab men are, by definition, suspicious and possibly dangerous."[4] In October 2002, leaders of Arab American and African American communities in Detroit denounced "the racial profiling against Middle Eastern men by the U.S. government."[5]

A report posted on the webpage of the Human Rights Watch, entitled "Presumption of Guilt: Human Rights Abuses of Post-September 11 Detainees"[6] states that,

> the lives of many who came to the United States with high hopes for a better life have been harmed by the practices documented in this report. Their lives were turned upside down when their nationality and religion drew the government's attention although they were never charged with terrorism.[7]

The report shows that after September 11, 2001, the law enforcement authorities started questioning thousands of individuals whom they considered could give any information about possible terrorist activity. However the report determined that,

> the decision of whom to question often appeared to be haphazard, at times prompted by law enforcement agents' random encounters with foreign male Muslims or neighbors' suspicions. The questioning led to the arrest and incarceration of as many as 1,200 non-citizens, although the exact number remains uncertain.[8]

The majority of people who have been detained consist of Muslim men who are not U.S. citizens. This is not surprising since the 19 alleged hijackers were all men, citizens of Middle Eastern nations, and Muslim. However the Human Rights Watch points out,

> suspicion that other terrorists in the United States might have a similar profile to the alleged hijackers is no justification for abrogating the rights of the Muslim immigrant community. National origin, religion, and gender do not constitute evidence of unlawful conduct.[9]

Very true.

On American campuses the population of international students includes an important number of students from Middle Eastern countries. After the terrorist attacks it seemed somehow expectable that the Middle Eastern students might have to face incidents of ethnoviolence. According to The Baltimore-based National Institute Against Prejudice and Violence (Prejudice Institute), approximately 25 percent of minority students are the victims of at least one ethnoviolent incident during a school year.[10]

Eva Wong and Susan Tracz, from CSU (California State University) Fresno, in their study on International Students' Perceptions of Ethnoviolence, point out the fact that there is a reach bibliography dealing with racism directed at American minorities in higher education, but very few studies focus on international students.[11]

The category defined as international students consists of those students who are not permanent residents of the United States. The most salient characteristic of this group is its diversity. These people have in common the fact that they come from different countries very diverse in terms of cultural traditions, socioeconomic characteristics, forms of political government, and systems of education. They also have in common the fact that, with few exceptions, English is not their native language. They all have the willingness to study in American universities, which they consider to be the world's best universities. And they all need to adapt to a new cultural environment.

For each international student one of the most important goals is to become integrated in the campus community and to function efficiently in this environment. In order to achieve this goal, each individual goes through a very challenging experience. This experience is also unique, being determined by a variety of factor, from demographic characteristics—such as the type of personality, personal values, life priorities of each individual—to local and circumstantial factors, like the campus culture, the type of housing, roommates, classmates, and the like.

The Middle Eastern students are themselves a group with a high level of diversity. That is why I considered that research instruments measuring central tendency and standard deviation could lead to erroneous conclusions and I chose to conduct a qualitative study rather than a quantitative one. Besides, the qualitative methods should enable the researcher to distinguish nuances that could not possibly be checked on a Likert scale.

I tried to find out what it is like to be a man with Middle Eastern looks on an American campus after the terrorist attacks of September 11. Does this mean that an individual student has to face hostile attitudes from other members of the campus community? Does it mean that he can no longer feel secure in that learning environment and, therefore, he can no longer be focused on his learning?

In order to answer these questions, I initially conducted open-ended interviews with five students from two mid-western American public universities and from one Canadian public university. Then I continued with follow-up inquiry, after one year from the terrorist attack, interviewing two more students from Middle Eastern countries and also keeping in touch with all the initial participants.

My participants came to study in the United States from different Middle Eastern countries, and at different moments in their academic career. All of them considered that they can get the best possible education only in the United States, which should lead them to the highest professional achievements.

Question: Why did you come here?

Jamal, who came from Jordan in August 2001, answered

> Jamal: I'm here to do my Ph.D. in Mathematics. And this is *the only reason* why I'm here.

Now, if I were to answer the same question, I would of course say that I came for a Ph.D. program, but I would probably also say that I am here to learn more about this country, its people, its cultural and democratic values. Of course, I wouldn't add all these when answering to a policeman or to an INS official, but when speaking to a person who is also a student, I think I would. Jamal's need to emphasize that "this is the only reason" for him to be here actually shows a defensive attitude. It shows his awareness of the fact that his mere presence in this country might raise suspicions.

Tareq came from Egypt, in 1998, when he was only 17 years old, to study Pharmacy. For him the transition from adolescence to adulthood took place here, in the environment of an American campus. The important stages of intellectual and moral development associated with this transition occurred to him under the general paradigms governing the American learning communities. But he still looks different and that is why Tareq had sometimes to face occasional intolerant attitudes. He, however, emphasized that this would happen even before September 11, and also that it would not happen on campus.

> Tareq: I used to walk in the streets and one guy asks me, "where are you from?" And I say, "I'm from Egypt." He is like, "well, go back home!" I'm like, "what do you mean, 'go back home?' why are you telling me that? The reason I'm here is to study, and I'm paying money to be in school. So there is no reason for me to go home. I'm not here working or anything, I'm here just to get my education and then go home."

I tried to find out how satisfied my participants were with their overall campus experience. All of them declared that, so far, generally speaking, they had good experiences. I also wanted to know whether they would socialize more with American students, with compatriots, with international students, or just with students from their department, no matter what national origin they had.

> Jamal: My colleagues in the Math Dept, most of them are Chinese, so I don't have the chance to socialize with American students, but I'm teaching two undergraduate courses at the university and in these courses, yes, my students are all Americans and I treat them with respect and they do the same to me.

Rasool, is a doctoral student in educational technology who came from Iran in 1999. He started with a masters program completed in some other American university.

> Rasool: There, it was a small campus, and most ...all of my friends were international students.... As far as the department is concerned, since I was a GA, most

of the time I would work in the department, so basically I didn't have that much time to socialize, or go out.

Tareq, on the other hand, I would say, is quite a popular guy. But he is still an undergraduate, and has had plenty of time to become popular.

Tareq: I have so many friends, from all kind of countries, and specially from the U.S. . . . I have friends.

Zaher is Lebanese and he came to the United States in 1997. He is also in a Ph.D. program in technology.

Zaher: I didn't have much in terms of involvement in the American society.

Question: You didn't because you were very busy with your studies?

Zaher: I think the objective was to come to study, and I think that I was very fortunate in my second year to get a fellowship, and so I said, "I got this fellowship, let me focus and get my studies," because finance would have been a problem. My social interaction was basically campus-related, so to say.

As I have already stated, in conducting this study, I was mainly interested in determining whether or not anything had changed in the way other people on campus behaved toward these Middle Eastern students after the events of September 11, 2001.

Jamal: No . . . as far as I'm concerned. Everything is normal with me, the professors explain to me the same way as before, because they know that it wasn't my fault. We are all sorry for what happened, but it didn't affect me, actually. They treat me in the same way they used to before that event.

I must admit that I was a little bit surprised by his answer, because only minutes before, I thought I heard him tell a different story. But that was in a private conversation, and off the record. It seemed to me that he was speaking about a rather cold atmosphere, and about faculty being more demanding and less understanding toward his first year problems of adjustment. But I also know that he grew up in a culture where a man is not supposed to whine about difficulties, but he has simply to face them with dignity trying to deal with them at the best of his capabilities.

However, a little bit later he did mention something he had noticed while teaching his undergraduate courses.

Jamal: Well, you can see *some looks* in some students who, maybe, have lost some dear people in the tragedy. So you just can't take it away because *they feel that it's your fault*. . . . But *you just can feel the look* in their faces, but they are not doing anything else, you know.

Tareq: Actually, I have been treated the same. Nothing has affected the relationship between me and my friends . . .

I have also many Arab friends who came here, they are living here, and you don't really feel like they have experienced anything yet. We might have *a couple*

of looks here, a couple of looks there, but everybody gets looks like that, even before
September 11.

Rasool: No, faculty, not at all. They didn't have any kind of negative reaction, the
faculty or the staff. But students, I don't say that they had any negative reaction,
but I could say that the way they look at me...I could feel that it is slightly
different. The *way they look*...or, even, some times...it just seemed to me, that
they would ignore my smile.

Question: Do you mean people whom you know?

Rasool: Usually, people would smile while you pass by. Still they do, but I could
say that it changed a little bit after September 11. Sometimes there is no smile, as
if *they try to ignore*...In few cases I saw that. I could feel that, yeah...Which, *it
did bother me*.... I understand it, I can understand it, you know...yes, I could
say that it changed a little bit.

Question: Does this make you feel uncomfortable?

Rasool: No. Not really, because I can understand it. I realize why they are angry
or why they are sad...or, they may generalize it, consider all the Middle Eastern
people as potential agents involved in this kind of activities. It didn't bother me
that much. *I feel kind of sad*, but it doesn't bother me. *I don't complain*...

Of course, his self-esteem would not allow him to complain. He knew
from the very beginning that achieving his professional goal was not going
to be easy at all. But since he made the commitment, he works hard and tries
to stay focused on his study, no matter what changes of climate would occur
on campus. However, he did feel a change of attitude toward him, and this
has clearly affected him. Whether or not it did affect his schoolwork, it could
hardly be determined. He would never claim that, for instance, he lost a
number of points in a midterm exam because the general atmosphere on
campus became suddenly less friendly.

The existing research shows that a hostile and prejudiced environment
is a constant source of stress, which reinforces a sense of alienation in students, hindering their personal and academic development. International
students on U.S. campuses have a high level of satisfaction if the campus
climate does not encourage any form of discrimination against them, and
does not reveal a negative attitude toward their home countries.[12]

Question: Do you feel that now you may no longer be safe here?

Rasool: No, no. I don't...No, I wouldn't think like that. Sometimes I would be
concerned, sometimes if I walk on campus...with some of my Arab friends who
are Muslims...Sometimes I would talk to them and I would tell them, "OK,
guys, it's better to be a little concerned, for instance, *don't talk in Arabic in public.*" Not just because people are mean, just because...you know, they might
think negatively towards you. Sometimes I am concerned about Arab people.
Sometimes I might think about myself, because I kind of look like those people.
But I didn't have any major fear or any major scare, of that.

Question: Didn't it occur to you that you might be...

Rasool: *A target?*

I must admit that, in the context of our conversation, I would have never used the word "target." It came out of his mind, from which he was making efforts to eliminate any "major fear or scare." On the other hand, even some high-level politicians publicly declared that, in their opinion, it would be "reckless to ignore the fact that a person might be speaking Arabic or reading the Koran."[13]

My Canadian participant, Ahmad, came to the United States from Syria, 11 years ago, to continue his education as a medical doctor.

> Ahmad: I did not feel hostility based on September 11, by itself. *The only hostility I experienced concerned my profession.* I have a medical degree from my home country, and I was mistreated in a medical hospital in a residency program. I faced discrimination in the medical field, being a foreign medical graduate, . . . obviously for economical and competition reasons.
>
> Question: After September 11, did you feel any change in the attitude of people on campus towards you or other people from Middle Eastern countries?
>
> Ahmad: Honestly, I haven't heard. You know, my university is small, and . . . I did not hear of any *major discrimination* issue on campus, . . . or major racial harassment . . .
>
> But I have found some negative reactions . . . for instance some Muslim friends, who, after I expressed my anger against the Muslim extremists, they felt harassed and they stopped talking to me and they repeated that they were Muslims. And other friends, . . . they were right wing, protestant Christians, who did not mistreat me, but they, you know, they think that this is done simply and purely by *evil*, nothing else, and I don't believe that evil is the cause of it. It's caused by *hatred*, but there is a reason why those people hate Americans and we should look for that reason. These people are always justifying this cause on biblical . . . or whatever we call it, and I don't agree with it. I agree on scientific explanations.

Ahmad is a person who likes to communicate, to share his ideas and judgments with other people, whether they might agree with him or not. From the Myers-Briggs[14] perspective, he is definitely an E (extrovert) type, and so is Tareq, while Jamal and Rasool, both of them are rather I (introvert) types, who would participate in a dialogue, but would probably not be the ones to initiate it. For extroverts, like Ahmad and Tareq, the effect of any unfriendly look is probably more superficial than it is for introverts. But they are more likely to ask in a straightforward manner what the problem is and in a violent type of environment, they would be more exposed to violent reactions.

The conclusion might be that, since no one got anything worse than "looks," it means that, at least in this geographic area of mid-western United States and Ontario, Canada, the campus climates are relatively civil, and the probability of serious incidents is much lower than out, in the larger community. But, I knew that there were issues about which my participants would not speak if asked directly. Therefore I tried to provoke them to discuss these issues in a somehow larger context.

I asked Zaher:

Question: Did you ever feel marginalized, somehow treated differently by American students or faculty because you are a foreigner?

Zaher: I feel, that's interesting, because having an accent...because you have an accent, then you tend to get the feeling that there's a turn off. When you begin to talk, automatically...you have an accent, so the communication tends to break down immediately.

International students are more likely to communicate with other international students, not necessarily from their own country.

Zaher: I socialize primarily with international students. I think it is a little easier, for different reasons...in terms of...I guess we have more in common, it is more easier

My comment: But when you speak of international students, this is a very comprehensive term, that includes people from eastern Europe, like myself, from China, from Africa, from the Caribbean...

Zaher: Yes, we are different, but, in this case, we have something in common. You have commonness in terms of the same program, the same courses, you don't have to step out too far to get there.

I am an international student myself, I speak with an accent, I had problems myself, and sometimes I could feel the "look" that tells you that you are an outsider, and "you don't belong here."

The social comparison theory developed by Leon Festinger[15] states that "people have a need to evaluate their opinions and their abilities" comparing them with those of peers. The social influence can be informational and normative. People try to evaluate their own beliefs based on information received from their peers. Within groups judgments tend to follow a group norm, which is internalized by the group members. This may happen either from the individual's desire to be correct in one's judgments or from the desire to have a good standing among the members of the group. When people adopt the group's opinions and behavior because they are concerned about their image within the group and about the way they may be treated by the other members of the group we are speaking about normative social influence. Even after being removed from a certain group an individual would usually hold on to the norm of the group.

International students are people who voluntarily left the groups to which they belonged and chose to live in a totally new type of social environment. At the beginning they try to understand this new environment in order to identify the norms and the values they need to adopt in order to be accepted by the other members of the learning community in which they want to be integrated.

The language barriers cannot be overcome with a dictionary. The meaning of the words composing a language is embedded in social paradigms, which are grounded in a commonality of tradition, of understanding specific metaphors or allusions to certain myths or heroes. Social paradigms also include some "self-evident" truths, which may be completely different for various cultures. When you, an international student, are told that your situation is a kind of "Catch 22," the dictionary won't be of much help.

There is an extremely large number of norms that an international student needs to identify, learn, and eventually adopt. They may refer to the tone and volume of speech, face expressions, body language, manner of addressing various persons in various positions, behavior related to specific circumstances, dressing codes for different occasions, and the like. If a student has recently come from a very different culture he or she may notice how different they look compared to his or her local peers.

It is not clear when normative social influence produces real change in behavior and/or opinions and when people are speaking and/or acting in a certain way only to maintain a favorable image about themselves within the group. In order to understand when the normative influence produces real change and when it does not, Herbert Kelman[16] identified three distinct situations: compliance, identification, and internalization.

Compliance is just an apparent attitude, which does not involve real change of ideas. It lasts only as long as the individual is aware that he or she is under surveillance. On the contrary, internalization represents a real change of ideas under the influence of a credible source. Identification also involves the emotional side of one's personality. It is a real change that occurs as a result of the positive feelings the individual has toward the source, with whom he or she would like to identify. The change usually lasts as long as the admiration for the source lasts. This is the case of mentors and various types of role models.

Group membership has a very important role in defining personal identity including perceptions of self-concept and self-esteem that result from social comparisons. The greatest dilemma for an international student is whether or not adopting certain norms of their new social environment represents an implicit rejection of their old norms, the ones that contributed to the shaping of their personality, to making them who they are. There may be moments when an international student would wonder if he or she is still the same person, or if there is someone else taking possession of their body and mind. In such moments the student's self-concept and self-esteem may be seriously challenged.

According to the social comparison theory, people tend to compare themselves with similar others, which leads to "strong pressures toward uniformity in groups." The members of a group compare their opinions and/or their performance.

Opinions are subject to discussion or "talk." The talk tends to reach consensus, and those who expose deviant opinions are rejected from the group with hostility. The uniformity of opinion defines the group boundaries. Usually those with extreme opinions compromise and the group finds an equilibrium somewhere in the middle. However when the opinion involves important values the groups tend to adopt extreme positions. The consensus in this case is polarized. People try to prove that they support the relevant value of the group as much as, or even more than other members of the group.

A problem for international students is the fact that usually people consider them a priori ignorant or indifferent to the locally shared values. In many cases this is not true. The most important values are universal, human values. They represent the ethical foundation for most of the largely spread religions of the world.

Sociological research shows that the existence of different groups with different values leads to intergroup hostility. This is the default rule unless two or more groups have a "superordinate goal" that will enhance joint or coordinate efforts to achieve it, while reducing the intergroup hostility and even defining a single larger group. That is what campuses all over the nation try to achieve when they articulate their mission and educational goals.

Although it is clear that efforts are made to promote diversity and intercultural communication on campuses, those individuals who are different from the larger majority and are not willing to reshape their personality up to that point where it would match the majority pattern, would rather be tolerated than integrated in the community.

International students face various types of problems about which they are willing to talk with other fellow students. They want to know what these ones think, how they would deal with one issue or another. And the fact that their fellow was born on the opposite hemisphere doesn't really matter.

On the other hand, at least in the mid-west, some kind of communication gap seems to exist, maybe because some people tend to exaggerate their concern for other persons' privacy. For an international student it doesn't take long to understand that "how u doin" actually means "hi," and that you are supposed to answer "good," or "fine," even when you feel like you are dying. The only available listeners for an international student's problems, worries, or concerns are other international students, who might have had similar experiences, or sometimes different experiences about which one should better know and be prepared for them. The existence of a communication gap between international students and the majority within a campus community hinders the intercultural mutual understanding, and it can also generate the feeling of alienation in some international students.

The "Model Questionnaire for Assessing Campus Climate" published by the Prejudice Institute in 1995 and revised with the national Victimization Study,[17] includes a list of 18 effects of perceptions of ethnoviolence. I am mentioning a few of them here, which in my opinion, should raise higher levels of concern. These are:

Felt more nervous than usual
Became withdrawn
Felt as if you didn't want to live

Had trouble concentrating, working
Felt very angry
Afraid of having more trouble in your life
More prayer or Bible study/meditation

An individual who has come to the point of experiencing these types of effects, who becomes withdrawn, and seeks refuge in prayer or meditation, can eventually be misguided and manipulated by some ill-intentioned spiritual mentor. I don't want to be misunderstood. I have a deep respect for any person, who practices any religion, but when religious meditation becomes a refuge from real life, we might have a problem. No matter what type of problems, a supportive and caring community can offer the help or the advice a person might need, and also, in some cases, it can prevent someone from engaging oneself in possible antisocial behavior.

opinion

After one year, from the terrorist attacks I interviewed Ibrahim and Salim, two undergraduate students from Kuwait. Both of them came to the United States in August 2001. They told me that they can remember the events of September 11 "as if it happened yesterday." When I asked if those events have in any way affected them, they started to tell me how they were emotionally affected.

> Ibrahim: First of all, when we saw what happened we were terribly sad about what happened, and had the same feeling as if our family were in those two towers.

I insisted that they tell me about their experiences as Middle Eastern men after those events.

> Ibrahim: We experienced some harassment from people, because you know, Bin Laden as an Arabic person, coming from the Middle East, some people, like . . . when they get so, so . . . sad about what happened they just think that Bin Laden reflects who all the Middle Easterners are. But, no! What they are doing is *exactly opposite to what our religious principles and what our religion just say.* And we stand totally against what happened.

However, they told me that not all the people identified any Middle Eastern person with terrorists and their leader. They both emphasized the fact that any incident of hostility on campus they experienced happened off campus.

> Salim: I can remember a direct incident. It was like 3 o'clock in the morning and we were having dinner, and this man, who was drunk, was just moving back and forth around our table and just saying, in a low voice, that he's gonna get us, he's just waiting for us to finish. We waited then he left.
>
> Question: So he was threatening you?
>
> Salim: Yes he was threatening us.
>
> Question: Did you feel insecure?
>
> Salim: Oh, no! No, no, no! Because legally he doesn't have the right, and on top of that, he is a drunk man.

The young Middle Eastern man could not allow himself to admit that he might have felt any fear at all. His dignity and his self-esteem required him to prove that he was in control of the situation. And in order to find the strength to stay in control the couple of young Muslim men observing the tradition of Ramadhan,[18] were trustfully relying on the protection of the American law. However, they knew that if a violent conflict would have happened the law enforcement authorities could not determine immediately whose fault it was, but they were thinking that since the threatening man was drunk, this could indicate that he was the one looking for trouble.

> Salim: We just stayed there waiting for him to go. We didn't even look at him as if he wasn't there. But it just gave us a bad feeling that some Americans think that we agree with what happened. But in fact we are totally against what happened

Again, my participants pointed out that this type of incidents never happened on campus.

> Ibrahim: When the American Government said that the suspect was from the Middle East, our Embassy talked to the university...to all the universities in America, that Kuwaiti students should have the excuse to...not to attend for one week. We attended, and everything was totally normal. They...they treated us so well! I was surprised about that. Students and faculty...In fact faculty, they treated us even better than before.

I asked my participants how they perceived the people's attitude toward Middle Eastern persons after one year of continuous campaign against terrorism in general, and Middle Eastern terrorism in particular.

> Salim: This had a negative effect and a positive effect to our culture. Some people, like...got an idea about Middle Easterners as terrorists. Other people have the opposite idea.

In fact, especially in learning communities there was a growing interest in studying about Islam and about Middle Eastern cultures. People have learned to make the distinction between fundamentalist factions and the authentic Islamic doctrine. One example is a course project on Cultural Perspectives of Islamic Society and Schools, which was a mid-term assignment for undergraduate students at the University of Toledo (UT). The students presented this project on October 16, 2002 and some of their findings have been posted in the hallway of the Department of Theory and Social Foundations of Education, at UT.

But in spite of the civility and understanding they generally find on campuses, the situation of students from Middle Eastern countries is still very unsure. Here's what Ibrahim told me about his personal experience at the airports.

> Ibrahim: When I have some flights between states, it was so much security. It was on every airport. But when I came to boarding, it happened to me three times,

actually. They told me that it was a random... we randomly chose you to look in your bag. And it happened three times in a row. I don't think it was random...

Salim told me about problems other students had with the immigration authorities.

Salim: My fellow mates who study in the United States of America, when they came back to renew their visas to come back and continue their studies, although they were enrolled to classes, when they came to the Embassy to renew their visas they didn't extend it—just cancelled their visas. And... my other friend, he used to study here at this university, he has a visa which expires in 2005, but he asked them at the Embassy if it was possible to go to another university—he was going to the university of Tampa—to enroll over there with his student visa, they told him that "we're gonna check about that," and if this is not possible he should continue his studies here. What they did was they cancelled his visa and they didn't give him a visa for Tampa.

Ibrahim: Some students with scholarships from the government, they had GPAs more than 3.8 and were accepted in the university... like top ten universities, but they didn't get their visas. This all started in the summer.

The conclusion was that for them it was a risk even to go home to visit their families, because they could easily expect that they would not be allowed to return to school.

Salim: We're going to go back anyway. And if we have our visas cancelled, we're going to stay there.

In other words, "we do value the education we came to get here, but if we really are unwelcome we'd better stay away." There is dignity and there is also a certain degree of bitterness in this attitude. Hopefully they will be able to finish their studies and return to their countries after they graduate to promote the ideas of democracy, respect, and tolerance that confer the strength of American society. It is significant to mention that in the United States there are approximately 500,000 international students from all over the world who contribute annually some $9 billion to the national economy.[19]

A very important factor in attracting and retaining new students by an institution of higher education is the students' perception of the campus climate.[20] Educational administrators and faculty should be sensitive to perceptions, needs, and concerns of international students. The presence of international students on American campuses contributes to the enrichment of the learning environment, sets the lines for future economic and diplomatic links.

Concluding this study, I should at least try to answer the question, what it is like to be a Middle Eastern male student on an American campus. Does this mean that the person is doomed to suspicion? Is this type of student facing any real danger on an American campus? The answer revealed by the inquiry, actually depends on the definition we might want to associate with the concept of "danger."

If we simply mean physical danger, the answer is clearly, "no." The campus environment seems to be a safe place for Middle Eastern students, although they may face serious threats anywhere outside the campus.

If we consider only strong, well-balanced personalities, goal-oriented, and confident in their capacity to overcome difficulties, the answer could be, "not really." Again, we should only have in mind the campus environment, although this time we will also include in our definition the threat of psychological harm.

For everyone else, the answer is "yes." However it is only to some extent more "dangerous," than to be just "different" from the majority. To what extent? We should reflect upon this, and, eventually, conduct further studies in order to find out more.

Notes

1. W. S. Ross, "Bush at Islamic Center Urges Tolerance Towards Arab-Americans," U.S. Department of State—International Information Program (September 27, 2001), <http://usinfo.state.gov/topical/pol/terror/01091721.htm> (October 1, 2001).
2. Mueller and Ashcroft Briefing, "F.B.I. Director Denounces Attacks Against Arab-Americans," U.S. Department of State—International Information Program (September 17, 2001), <http://usinfo.state.gov/topical/pol/terror/0109170.htm> (October 1, 2001).
3. A. Gumbel, "Fears of Witch-Hunt as Police Question Arab Men" *Independent News* (November 28, 2001), <http://news.independent.co.uk/world/americas/story.jsp?story=107156> (February 8, 2002).
4. See note 3.
5. N. Warikoo, "Black, Arab-American Leaders Assail Racial Profiling," *The Detroit Free Press* (January 11, 2002), <http://www.freep.com/news/locway/deport11_20020111.htm> (February 8, 2002).
6. Human Rights Watch, "Presumption of Guilt: Human Rights Abuses of Post-September 11 Detainees," <http://hrw.org/reports/2002/us911/Index.htm#TopOfPage> (January 28, 2003).
7. See note 6.
8. See note 6, <http://hrw.org/reports/2002/us911/USA0802.htm#P139_18291> (January 28, 2003).
9. See notes 6–8.
10. H. J. Ehrlich, 1999, "Campus Ethnoviolence," in F. L. Pincus and H. J. Ehrlich, eds., *Race and Ethnic Conflict: Contending Views on Prejudice, Discrimination and Ethnoviolence*, 2nd ed., (Boulder, CO: Westview Press), pp. 277–90.
11. E. Y. W. Wong, and S. M. Tracz, 2001, "A survey of international students' perceptions of ethnoviolence," paper presented at the annual meeting of Mid-Western Educational Research Association, Chicago (October 2001).
12. R. Petrucci, and H. Hu, "Satisfaction with Social and Educational Experiences Among International Graduate Students," *Research in Higher Education*, 36(4) (1995), pp. 491–508.
13. G. Appelson, "Oklahoma Governor Favors Profiling in Terror War," Reuters—Politics (February 2, 2002), <http://dailynews.yahoo.com/h/nm/20020202/pl/lawyers_profiling_dc_1.html> (February 8, 2002).

14. I. B. Myers, 1987, *Introduction to Type: A Description of the Theory and Applications of the Myers-Briggs Type Indicator*, 4th ed. (Palo Alto, CA: Consulting Psychologists Press).

15. L. Festinger, "A Theory of Social Comparison Process," *Human Relations*, 7 (1954), pp. 117–40.

16. H. Kelman, "Processes of Opinion Change," *Public Opinion Quarterly*, 25 (1961), pp. 57–78.

17. H. J. Ehrlich, "Prejudice and ethnoviolence on Campus," *Higher Education Extension Service Review*, 6(2) (1995), pp. 1–15. Ehrlich, "Campus Ethnoviolence," pp. 277–90.

18. "For over one billion Muslims throughout the world, Ramadhan is a special month of the year. During the month of Ramadhan, Muslims fast from dawn to sunset everyday. Ramadhan was the month in which the first verses of the holy Qur'an were revealed to Prophet Mohammad. It is a time for inner reflection, devotion to God and self-control. The sighting of the new moon at the end of Ramadhan heralds the celebration of Eid ul-Fitr," retrieved from <http://www. ummah.org.uk/ramadhan/> (January 31, 2003).

19. William J. Clinton, "Memorandum for the Heads of Executive Departments and Agencies on International Education Policy," April 19, 2000, <http:// exchanges.state.gov/education/remarks/whstatement.htm> (February 8, 2002).

20. C. M. Cress and L. J. Sax, "Campus Climate Issues to Consider for the Next Decade," *New Directions for Institutional Research*, 25(2) (1998), pp. 65–80.

6

9/11 AND CIVIC ILLITERACY

John Marciano

There is no better way to love one's country, no better way to fulfill its greatness, than to entertain critical ideas and engage in the pursuit of social justice at home and abroad.

Michael Parenti

PART I

In an article on what students should learn about the terrorist attacks of September 11, 2001, *New York Times* foreign affairs correspondent Thomas Friedman writes, "[t]his is a moment for moral clarity."[1] He would first require of students an essay from the humorist and writer Larry Miller, who asserts "that our country has, with all our mistakes and blunders, always been and always will be the greatest beacon of freedom, charity, opportunity, and affection in history."[2]

Friedman would also require students to read *An Autumn of War: What American Learned from September 11 and the War on Terrorism* by the military historian Victor Davis Hanson, who argues that our war against terrorists preserves Western civilization with "its uniquely tolerant and human traditions of freedom, consensual government, disinterested inquiry and religious and political tolerance." Hanson states that his civic literacy education about America was formed in multiracial rural California schools during the 1960s, where he and his classmates "developed a sense of American exceptionalism—a deep appreciation for just how distinctive the culture of the United States had proved to be over two centuries and more, and how it belonged to and benefited all of us."[3]

At that time, Americans "knew that their country was not merely different from others, but that it was clearly superior in its rare democratic government, tolerance for religious differences, spirit of liberty, and allowance for dissent.... The confidence that sprang from such knowledge...also gave citizens the ability...at home to create a real sense of national harmony."[4] The Mexican Americans in Hanson's school and community, however, were not part of the "national harmony" and "rare democratic government"; they were second-class citizens in a racist country. But this racism and national chauvinism did not made a dent in Hanson's euphoria about the "good old days" in California, nor in his present work that sings the praises of America—evidently blind to the pervasive inequalities that have marked U.S. history, especially its civic life. There is a voluminous historical record put forth by outstanding scholars and writers that documents these inequalities.[5]

In the war on terrorism, Hanson wonders how "a nation [can] struggle against enemies who do not tolerate dissent, do not allow freedom, when many of its own citizenry, especially in our schools, are not quite sure why or how we as a people are different and therefore can or should succeed?" These critical "values and ideals... should be second nature to every American. But sadly they often are not—and cannot be when so many of our youth have neither facts about nor confidence in their own American heritage."[6]

In his book, Hanson claims that we are in "our own bloody war against tyranny, intolerance, and theocracy, an age-old fight against medieval foes who despise modernism, liberalism, and freedom, and all the hope that they bring for the human condition."[7] He further asserts, "America is not only the inheritor of the European military tradition, but in many ways its most powerful incarnation. Our multiracial and radically egalitarian society has taken the concepts of freedom and market capitalism to their theoretical limits...."[8] This egalitarianism is so "radical" that the richest 5 percent of Americans with incomes of at least $250,000 make 25 times more than the poorest 20 percent at $10,000.[9] The disregard for the empirical evidence that contradicts Hanson's assertion of a "radical egalitarian" society[10] is less a commentary on this historian than on those in the mass media and education who are awed by his claims.

Supporting Hanson's and Friedman's views on terrorism is William Bennett, a leading conservative and former secretary of education. Currently codirector of Empower America, a policy organization, Bennett passionately defends the lofty principles and traditions that have shaped this country; he applies them to his discussion of 9/11 and "the war on terrorism." These principles and traditions include "justice, liberty, government with the consent of the governed, and equality under the law." These are the basic truths that must be taught to our youth so that they understand that they live in a "free, self-governing society [that defends] those ideas which together make for freedom and self-government."[11]

Alongside the fundamental principles and truths that youth should know, however, Bennett sees a "dark side": such principles have not guided all governments in the world, and applying "universal" standards will show that some nations "are simply awful."[12] His latter assertion is certainly true; however, only official U.S. enemies seem to be "awful," never its friends, and it is not included among the "awful." Bennett believes that we must teach youth "the whole truth" about other nations, but this high standard is not applied, for example, to U.S. policies against American Indians, nor to its support of undemocratic and murderous regimes in the world.[13]

September 11, argues Bennett, "had a riveting effect on the entire world, and not least on our own children.... For the youngest, the terms were most simple—'bad men did something very wrong that hurt a lot of people'—but also the most truthful." He claims that we should have responded to September 11 with the children's "kind of moral clarity...that calls evil by its true name: Terms like 'evil,' 'wrong' and 'bad' were rightly put back into the lexicon. [It] also requires that we point to what is good and right and true [about our country].We are living in a teachable moment, but some would squander this moment, or repudiate it altogether as though we have nothing to learn, nothing to teach."[14] The children's "truth," however, is rarely used as a foundational principle by which to judge the actions of the United States or its allies, as Bennett and other supporters of the U.S. war on terrorism have a double standard regarding the use of state-sanctioned violence in the world (see note 13).

Bennett also asserts that those in colleges and universities who have criticized the war on terrorism have sent out "a muddled and dishonest response to the [9/11] attacks."[15] He names just one academic, however: Eric Foner of Columbia University, a distinquished historian and former president of the American Historical Association. Who are the others and what are the institutions? U.S. intellectuals who have signed public statements against U.S. terrorism or a war in Iraq represent a very small percentage of those in the academy; and as of this writing (March 2003) only one college or university president has taken such a public stand. How many intellectuals have publicly sided with the anti-imperialist and antiwar analysis of Noam Chomsky, Michael Parenti, or Howard Zinn? Bennett's assertions about the raging Left criticism in the academy are bogus, but he gets much media time to present them—unlike those he attacks.[16]

Bennett is also deeply distressed by a survey about the war on terrorism that showed college students' "ignorance of our national leaders, an ignorance of world events, and an ignorance of what it means to be an American..." The first lesson of 9/11, he argues, should be "about America. Love of this country must be learned; we cannot assume it will grow without cultivation." American patriotism is best served and the strongest "when it is rooted in knowledge about this nation's heritage in the context of world history." In this way, youth can understand "that this is, indeed, a great land. To do so, children must be taught that there are moral absolutes; that right and wrong do exist. For too long, those in elite circles have told us that right and wrong are merely opinions or matters of personal taste. No serious thinker can see September 11 as anything but evil and wrong—terms that the academy has mocked and now fails to recognize in their starkest terms."[17]

Who are these unnamed elitists in the academy, essentially a code term used to attack those such as Chomsky who criticize U.S. policies? The dissenters to U.S. policy cited in this chapter do not take a relativist position on the issue of terrorism; they are attacked precisely because of their strong opposition to it—especially when committed by the United States.

In summary: for Bennett, one of the great lessons of 9/11 is we must teach "morality and patriotism, two ideas that have lost favor." Young people must be taught about the things that make the country great. "They should learn the [founding] bedrock principles [and] ideas like equality, freedom and justice under the law.... Nowhere else has freedom flourished as it has in America; never before in the history of the globe have so many benefitted because there is a land of the free and the home of the brave. Even with its faults, America remains the best nation on earth.... A fair reading of our history will reveal, once again, that we truly are 'the Last, best hope of Earth.' "[18]

Bennett and Hanson merely rehash the arguments presented in Allan Bloom's *The Closing of the American Mind* in the 1980s. Bennett's American celebration echoes Bloom, who believed, "the United States in one of the highest and most extreme achievements of the rational quest for the good life according to nature." Despite its violent origin, slavery and subsequent history, Bloom asserts that the Founders created a system of government in America that was based on "freedom and equality, hence the consent of the governed."[19] He wrote this in the 1980s, when the U.S. armed and funded the contra terrorists in Nicaragua, engaged in economic and military attacks on Cuba, and supported South African apartheid within that nation and in its wars in Angola and Mozambique—among other international actions. In Bloom's mind, however, this era was the "defining moment in world history, the one for which we shall forever be judged," because "the fate of freedom in the world" was the responsibility of "our regime."[20]

PART II

How do we counter the dominant views about imperialism and terrorism? Perhaps we should begin with basic definitions, different questions and assertions, and then placing the actual historical record alongside the assertions put forth by Bennett, Bloom, and Hanson. In the analysis that follows, I rely on the definition of imperialism provided by Michael Parenti: "Imperialism...is the process whereby the rulers of one country use economic and military power to expropriate the land, labor, markets, and natural resources of another country in order to attain even greater capital accumulation on behalf of wealthy interests at home and abroad."[21] Official U.S. documents define terrorism as "the calculated use of violence or the threat of violence to attain goals that are political, religious, or ideological in nature. This is done through intimidation, coercion, or instilling fear."[22]

Given the definitions mentioned here, provocative questions arise in reponse to the assertions put forth by Miller, Hanson, and Bennett: Were the U.S. government's wars against Native Americans a "blunder" and "mistake"? Was the enslavement of African people a "mistake" committed by powerful officials who simply overlooked this crime against humanity? Was U.S. terrorism in the late twentieth century against Chile, Cuba,

El Salvador, Grenada, Guatemala, Nicaragua, and Panama a "blunder" committed against our Latin American neighbors? Can we reconcile the "values and traditions and freedoms embraced by Western civilization" that Bennett, Bloom, and Hanson laud, with the deaths of millions of indigenous people at the hands of colonial Spain, England, Holland, Belgium, and France? Were these too simply "blunders" and "mistakes"?

As I have argued elsewhere, there is a different view of our history, patriotism, terrorism, and war that rarely makes it into our schools and mass media. This radical "other side" must be made known if we are to think about the distortions, omissions, and lies that shape history lessons about the country, terrorism, and its wars. This side must be presented if youth are to move toward the essence of "civic literacy"—the ability to think critically and objectively about the nation's fundamental premises and policies. For the most part, influential educators—who include important journalists and intellectuals such as Friedman, Bennett, Bloom, and Hanson—faithfully support a dominant-elite view of patriotism, militarism, and terrorism; this perspective, however, undermines thoughtful and active citizenship in a democracy. Educators and mass media pundits offer the youth a view of U.S. policies that promotes civic illiteracy and turns civic responsibility into patriotic conformity. Despite the many claims that civic literacy is vital to education and democracy, patriotic and militaristic propaganda has dominated history lessons in the mass media, schools, and colleges. Such miseducation leaves citizens and students unable to make reasoned judgments about the terrorist acts of 9/11, in particular, and international terrorism in general, preparing them to give unthinking support to U.S. policies.[23]

The dominant elite of transnational capitalists, influential educators, and public officials that governs the nation and shapes it civic debate, fears what Harvard scholar and former Pentagon official Samuel Huntington called "the democratic distemper" in the people, especially the youth. If they question and then challenge policies, this elite will face an "excess of democracy" of the kind that emerged in the 1960s when social movements confronted authorities and established policies. Huntington's essay, written for the powerful and influential Trilateral Commission, is an important document for those who wish to understand the dominant elite's response to the progressive movements of the 1960s and 1970s.[24]

The history lessons passed on in the mass media and schools about 9/11 in particular, and patriotism, war, and terrorism in general, are educational tools in the struggle to vaccinate the hearts and minds of youth against this "democratic distemper." The elite fears that civicly literate and activist youth will become informed and involved citizens; civic instruction in our schools and mass media, therefore, is organized to prevent such a danger. Civic illiteracy is perfectly reasonable once we understand the nature and purpose of "citizenship training" in the schools: to undermine the critical and liberating potential of education.[25]

A critical and open debate in our schools and media that accurately presents the radical "other side" of 9/11 and terrorism would raise fundamental questions about the nature of imperialism and terrorism in the transnational capitalist system. This radical view was expressed by the late journalist Andrew Kopkind. Writing shortly after the conclusion of the Persian Gulf War in 1991, Kopkind argued, "America has been in a state of war—cold, hot and lukewarm—for as long as most citizens now living can remember"; this state of war has "been used effectively to manufacture support for the nation's rulers and to eliminate or contain dissent among the ruled." This "warrior state is so ingrained in American institutions…in short, so *totalitarian*—that the government is practically unthinkable without it." But this war mentality is a good cure for "democratic distemper," because it "implies command rather than participation, obedience over agreement, hierarchy instead of equality, repression not liberty, uniformity not diversity, secrecy not candor, propaganda not information."[26] This warrior system influences every institution in our society; it stands in stark contrast to rhetoric on American democracy, patriotism, and Western values put forth by Bennett, Friedman, and Hanson.

My *Civic Illiteracy and Education* asserts that we must have a vision of civic literacy that challenges the dominant view of U.S. history and terrorism. This new vision and approach are needed to counter patriotic and militaristic indoctrination. Our social and educational institutions, media pundits, public officials, and influential educators continue to pledge allegiance to compassion and peace, while the nation's leaders and policies remain militaristic and violent. We need to understand how educators support these destructive policies, and how a genuine civic literacy can help to transform them.[27]

This civic literacy must begin with the actual public record of what the Unites States has actually done throughout the world, especially since World War II—one of empire and terrorism that has resulted in the deaths of millions throughout Central and South America, Africa, and Asia. The facts of and behind U.S. actions in this period are clearly documented, yet mass media commentators and leading intellectuals continue to project the image of a benign and peace-loving nation. William Blum has compiled an extensive list of U.S. terrorism since World War II; it includes the planning or actual assassinations of the following foreign officials since 1950: Zhou Enlai, prime minister of China; Kim Il Sung, premier of North Korea; Jawaharlal Nehru, prime minister of India; Gamal Abdul Nasser, president of Egypt; Brig. Gen. Abdul Karim Kassam, leader of Iraq; Jose Figueres, president of Costa Rica; Patrice Lumumba, prime minister of the Congo; Ngo Dinh Diem, president of South Vietnam; Charles DeGaulle, president of France; Fidel Castro, president of Cuba; Che Guevara, Cuban leader; Salvador Allende, president of Chile; Michael Manley, prime minister of Jamaica; Ayatollah Khomeini, leader of Iran; Miguel d'Escoto, foreign minister of Nicaragua; Saddam Hussein, leader of Iraq; and Slobodan Milosevic, president of Yugoslavia.[28] To this list can be added U.S. interventions in other countries since 1945: China, France, Italy, Greece, Philippines, Korea, Germany, Iran, Guatemala, Indonesia, Iraq, Soviet Union, Vietnam,

Cambodia, Laos, The Congo/Zaire, Brazil, Dominican Republic, Cuba, Chile, South Africa, East Timor, Angola, Nicaragua, Grenada, Panama, Afghanistan, El Salvador, Haiti, Somalia, Mexico, Columbia, and Yugoslavia.[29]

These assassinations, covert actions, and interventions clearly fall under the definition of terrorism, but one would be hard-pressed to find these actions condemned as such by mass media pundits or influential educators. Therefore, we must challenge the common and selective political use of "terrorism" in order to understand its ideological use here in the United States. We can begin with the writings of Noam Chomsky, "arguably the most important intellectual alive" in the words of a *New York Times* reviewer. It is a testament to the effectiveness of U.S. propaganda that someone of Chomsky's stature, known and respected worldwide, still remains marginalized and relatively unknown in this country. I taught more than 6,500 students in 32 years at SUNY Cortland: few had heard of him or the other writers cited in this essay, and it was extremely rare to find a student who had read any of his works. Chomsky personifies the grand tradition of speaking/writing against dominant-elite power—as did W. E. B. DuBois—by courageous and admirable movements and individuals.[30]

The official U.S. definition of terrorism cited here is concrete enough to condemn Israeli terror against Palestinians. But as Chomsky argues, Israel is a U.S. ally and by definition incapable of engaging in terrorism, just as the United States could not have engaged in terrorism against Nicaragua in the 1980s by arming and funding the contras who murdered thousands of people in that Central American nation. However, the United Nations condemned the U.S.-sponsored contra war and the World Court ruled in favor of Nicaragua; the Reagan administration ignored this verdict and Congress rewarded the contras with increased aid. As a result of its contra war against Nicaragua, "the U.S. is the only country that was condemned for international terrorism by the World Court and . . . rejected a Security Council resolution calling on states to observe international law."[31]

The late social theorist Eqbal Ahmad argued that most citizens lack historical context when it comes to terrorism and terrorists. They do not understand that "terrorists change. The terrorist of yesterday is now the hero of today, and the hero of yesterday becomes the terrorist of today [e.g., Saddam Hussein, supported by the United States in his war against Iran and his repression of the Kurds]. In a constantly changing world of images, we have to keep our heads straight to know what terrorism is and what it is not. Even more importantly, we need to know what causes terrorism and how to stop it."[32] Ahmad also addressed a fundamental characteristic of terrorism: the principle of selectivity. We "denounce the terror of those groups of which are officially disapproved [but] applaud the terror of those groups of whom officials do approve. Hence, President Reagan's statement, 'I am a contra.' We know that the contras of Nicaragua were by any definition terrorists, but the media heed the official view . . . ." We also need to confront the fact that "the dominant approach also excludes from consideration the terrorism of friendly governments, as was pointed out above [viz. Israel against the Palestinians]. Thus, the United States excused, among others, the terrorism of Pinochet.... And it excused the terror of Zia ul-Haq, the military dictator of Pakistan...."[33]

Ahmad's prescription concerning terrorism is clear and simple: we must avoid "double standards.... Don't condone Israeli terror, Pakistani terror, Nicaraguan terror, El Salvadoran terror, and then complain about Afghan... or Palestinian terror.... Do not condone the terror of your allies. Condemn them."[34] The official condemnation of terror by the United States, however, excludes the illegal violence of its allies and itself: "torture, burning of villages, destruction of entire peoples [and] genocide [are] outside the definition of terror, which is to say the bias of terror is against people and in favor of governments. The reality is that the ratio of human losses between [official acts by armies and other terrorists] has been one to a thousand. For every life lost by unofficial terrorism, a thousand have been lost by the official variety."[35] The "retail terrorism" of unofficial individuals and groups that oppose the United States receives a great deal of attention in the mass media, which ignore the vastly greater "wholesale terrorism" of the United States and its client-states.

Political analyst Michael Parenti addresses the matter of retail vs. wholesale terror, and the hypocrisy on international terrorism. Despite overwhelming evidence, the mass media and influential educators refuse to acknowledge that "US leaders have been the greatest purveyors of terrorism throughout the world. In past decades they or their surrogate mercenary forces have unleashed terror bombing campaigns against unarmed civilian populations...causing death and destruction to millions of innocents.... Of course hardly a word of this is uttered in the corporate media [or mainstream educational circles], leaving Bush and company free to parade themselves as champions of peace and freedom."[36] Those in "official circles or corporate media [never] acknowledge how, for more than a half century, US military forces (or their US-supported surrogates) have repeatedly delivered mass destruction upon unarmed civilian populations in Latin America, Asia, Africa, the Middle East, and—with the 1999 bombings of Yugoslavia—even Europe, pernicious acts of terrorism that go unexamined" in our mass media and educational system.[37]

The fears and myths regarding terrorist attacks against the United States continue despite the actual power of the armed forces here. Parenti points out that the United States "expends more military funds than all the other major powers combined. The US military establishment consists of about a half-million troops stationed at over 395 major bases and hundreds of minor installations in 35 foreign countries; more than 8,000 strategic nuclear weapons and 22,000 tactical ones; [and] a naval strike force greater in total tonnage and firepower than all the other navies of the world combined...."[38]

When these truths are suppressed by the mass media and ignored or marginlized by the likes of Friedman and Bennett, it creates " a void...in our national discourse" and "a democracy devoid of the democratic debate that might challenge the ideology of practices of its leadership. The media attempt to fill this void with endless puffery, limited secondary issues, public personality profiles, and various scandal stories."[39] Given the dominant elite's fear about "democratic distemper" among youth, the lack of substantive debate about the American Empire and terrorism is quite functional: passivity is preferred over the rebellions of the 1960s and 1970s.

U.S. military dominance and support of brutal governments that do not address "the well-being of their peoples but... transnational corporations and the US national security state"[40] form the foundation of national security state terrorism. This is articulated in a blunt and honest manner by the *New York Times* Thomas Friedman, who offered up the intimate relationship between the capitalist market and militarism: "The hidden hand of the market will never work without a hidden fist. McDonald's cannot flourish without McDonnell Douglas, the designer of the F-15. And the hidden fist that keeps the world safe for Silicon Valley's technologies is called the US Army, Air Force, Navy and Marine Corps."[41]

The terrorism double standard that Parenti critiques is revealed when we look at the countries that are attacked or aided: "US leaders have consistently supported rightist regimes and organizations and opposed leftist ones...."[42] Rightist regimes are thought to be "'friendly to the West,' a coded term for 'pro-capitalist.' Conversely, leftist ones are labeled as 'anti-democratic,' 'anti-American' and 'anti-West,' when actually what they are against is global capitalism...." In pursuit of this selective policy, "US leaders have supported some of the most notorious rightwing autocracies in history, governments that tortured, killed [and] mistreated large numbers of their citizens.... Washington also assists counterrevolutionary groups that have perpetrated some of the brutal bloodletting against civilian populations in leftist countries...." These actions, thoroughly documented by journalists Robert Fisk, Amy Goodman, and John Pilger, and by the *Monthly Review, The Nation,* and the *Progressive,* "are seldom if ever treated in the US [mass] media."[43] Too few citizens and students have knowledge of this total public record; thus, they are unable to reflect critically on such issues and then act as democratically empowered citizens.

The United States has also attacked, covertly or directly, "reformist or revolutionary governments" in Cuba, Angola, Nicaragua, Cambodia, Iran, and Jamaica. "These... wars of attrition extracted a grisly toll on human life and frequently forced" governments to abandon their progressive efforts and "submit to IMF dictates, after which the US-propelled terrorist attacks ceased." And finally, since World War II, U.S. invasions and aerial attacks—against Vietnam, Laos, Cambodia, Lebanon, Grenada, Panama, Iraq, Somalia, Yugoslavia, and Afghanistan, among others, have produced "a record of direct military aggressions unmatched by any communist government in history."[44]

Historian Howard Zinn has challenged a basic assertion of Bennett et al., and President Bush, that the United States is "a peaceful nation." "Bush hasn't read any history and does not remember any history," Zinn states, as the United States has been engaged "in wars and military actions for a long time. You can't tell the Native Americans we were a peaceful nation as we moved across the continent and engaged in hundreds of wars against the Indians. The United States engaged in at least twenty military interventions in the Caribbean in the first twenty years of the last century. And then from World War II through today, we've had an endless succession of wars and military interventions."[45] Those who call the United States a "peaceful nation" forget "an enormous amount of history.... even a small amount part of it would be enough to suggest that we have not been a peaceful nation. In fact, it is safe to say that since World War II, there has not been a more warlike nation in the world than than the United States."[46] The war on terrorism that Bush offers as the "way to combat terrorism is just what other presidents...have offered before: the pursuit of domination over whole areas of the world. The horror of the terrorist attacks we experienced on September 11 is something that people in other parts of the world—Southeast Asia, Iraq, Yugoslavia—have experienced as a result of our bombings, of terrorism carried out by people we have backed and armed."[47]

There is a chasm dividing the analysis that Zinn, Blum, Chomsky, and Parenti have of U.S. history, from Bennett's and Hanson's reading of the same. When the lessons of 9/11 are examined, past experience tells us that Zinn's controversial assertions will not receive a fair hearing in our classrooms and mass media; they will be marginalized or ignored. I have read the *New York Times* almost every day for the past 40 years, as well as the *Los Angeles Times* each day since moving to California in 2000. I cannot recall a single news article or editorial in these sources or any television commentary that supports the assertions on war and terrorism made by Zinn et al. in this chapter. Discussions with more than 1,500 teachers in my graduate courses over 32 years reveals a similar pattern: not a single one could recall using the term "terrorism" in their classes to refer to any U.S. action in recent decades. The invisibility of U.S. terror is also what Bill Griffen and I found in our secondary history textbook study on the U.S.–Vietnam War, and what I found in my updated analysis of such textbooks in *Civic Illiteracy and Education* (see note 22). In 48 texts surveyed, for example, the word "terror" does not appear with regard to U.S. actions in that war. To have a rigorous and civically literate debate on terrorism and related political issues in the media and education, therefore, the dissenting arguments presented by Zinn et al. must at least be granted a fair hearing.

John Pilger, the English-based journalist, calls the war on terrorism "fraudulent: that its prosecutors are themselves terrorists from a greater league and that their actions will, at the very least, produce more carnage and martyrs." The United States is diseminating "an insidious propaganda that says a crime is not a crime if 'we' commit it."[48] The "medieval blockade" against Iraq has caused immense suffering and "the facts are not in dispute, though rarely published....•The United Nations Children's Fund, Unicef, says that every month up to 6,000 children die mostly as a result of the blockade. This is twice the number of deaths in the Twin Towers and another vivid reminder of the different value of different lives."[49]

As I have argued elsewhere, becoming civicly literate about these issues of patrotism, war, and terrorism is not merely a minor debating point in another educational report or academic publication. What we learn about U.S. policies can literally mean devastation or peace, especially for the poor in the Third World. As Zinn states, "we can reasonably conclude that how we *think* is not just mildly interesting, not just a subject for intellectual debate, but a matter of life and death."[50]

When all is said and done, the present Bush II national security state policies remain grounded in principles that were articulated in 1988 by his father George Herbert Walker Bush, former president and head of the CIA: "I see America as the leader, a unique nation with its special role in the world. This has been called the American century, because in it we were the dominant force for good in the world . . . . now we are on the verge of a new century, and what country's name will it bear? I say it will be another American century."[51] This "American century" ideology of empire is supported by Bennett, Friedman, Hanson, and other mainstream intellectuals and journalists who promote and defend a "Manifest Destiny" that has brought terror to every corner of the world. But their claims of noble visions, national documents, commencement addresses, and history lessons cannot hide imperial assumptions and policies that were bitterly condemned some more than 150 years ago by Henry David Thoreau. Reflecting on the nature of the U.S. government during the era of slavery and aggression against Mexico, Thoreau declared that he could not "without disgrace be associated with it."[52] Despite his critique and those of dissidents cited in this essay, the principles articulated by former President Bush have helped to indoctrinate generations of students and citizens; the lessons of 9/11 have simply followed this path of civic illiteracy.

NOTES

The foundation of this chapter was presented in a much shorter version at the Annual Meeting of the American Educational Studies Association, October 31, 2002, Pittsburgh, Pennsylvania.

1. Thomas L. Friedman, "9/11 Lesson Plan," *The New York Times*, September 4, 2002, A21.
2. Larry Miller, "You Say You Want a Resolution," *The Weekly Standard*, January 14, 2002, quoted in Friedman.
3. Victor Davis Hanson, "The Civic Education America Needs," *The City Journal*, Vol. 12, No. 3 (Summer 2002), p. 1.
4. Ibid., p. 4.
5. See, e.g., the insights on class, gender and racial conflict found in the works of Angela Davis, *Women, Culture and Politics* (New York: Random House, 1989); Frederick Douglass, *Narrative of the Life of Frederick Douglass, An American Slave* (New York: Modern Library, 2000); W. E. B. DuBois, *The Souls of Black Folk* (New York: Dover Publications, 1994); Linda Gordon, *Woman's Body: Woman's Right: Birth Control in America* (New York: Penguin Books, 1990); Emma Goldman, *Anarchism and Other Essays* (New York: Dover Publications,

1969); June Jordan, *Technical Difficulties: Selected Political Essays* (London: Virago Press Limited, 1992); Gerda Lerner, ed., *Black Women in White America: A Documentary History* (New York: Vintage Books, 1992); Manning Marable, *The Great Wells of Democracy* (New York: BasicCivitas Books, 2002); Judith Stepan-Norris and Maurice Zeitlin, *Left Out: Reds and America's Industrial Unions* (New York: Cambridge University Press, 2003); Ronald Takaki, *A Different Mirror: A Multicultural History of America* (Boston: Little, Brown and Co., 1993); Howard Winant, *The World is a Ghetto: Race and Democracy Since World War II* (New York: Basic Books, 2001); Howard Zinn, *A People's History of the United States, 20th Anniversary Edition* (New York: Harper-Collins, 1999); and Michael Zweig, *The Working Class Majority: America's Best Kept Secret* (Ithaca, New York: Cornell University Press, 2000).

6. Hanson, "The Civic Education," p. 6.
7. Victor Davis Hanson, *An Autumn of War: What America Learned From September 11 and the War on Terrorism* (New York: Anchor Books, 2002), p. 5.
8. Ibid., p. 7.
9. Doug Henwood, "Not Such a Good Year, 2001," *Left Business Observer*, #103, No. 4, p. 4; www.leftbusinessobserver.com.
10. See Chuck Collins and Felice Yeskel, *Economic Apartheid in America: A Primer on Economic Inequality and Security* (New York: New Press, 2000); Kevin Phillips, *Wealth and Democracy: A Political History of the Rich* (New York: Broadway Books, 2002); and Henwood's *Left Business Observer*.
11. William Bennett, *Our Children and Our Country: Improving America's Schools and Affirming the Common Culture* (New York: Simon and Schuster, 1988), p. 203.
12. Ibid., pp. 203–04.
13. The evidence for this assertion is overwhelming, and includes the works of Gilbert Achcar, *The Clash of Barbarisms: Sept 11 and the Making of the New World Disorder* (New York: Monthly Review Press, 2002); Eqbal Ahmad, *Confronting Empire: Interviews with David Barsamian* (Boston: South End Press, 2000); William Blum, *Killing Hope: US Military and CIA Interventions Since World War II* (Monroe, Maine: Common Courage Press, 1995); Richard Drinnon, *Facing West: The Metaphysics of Indian-Hating and Empire-Building* (Norman, Oklahoma: University of Oklahoma Press, 1997); Roxanne Dunbar-Ortiz, *Indians of the Americas: Human Rights and Self-Determination* (New York: Praeger, 1984); Jane Franklin, *Cuba and the United States: A Chronological History* (New York: Ocean Press, 1997); Donald A. Grinde and Bruce E. Johansen, *Ecocide of Native America: Environmental Destruction of Indian Lands and Peoples* (Sante Fe, New Mexico: Clearlight, 1995); Edward S. Herman, *The Real Terrorism Network* (Boston: South End Press, 1982); Michael Parenti, *The Sword and the Dollar: Imperialism, Revolution, and the Arms Race* (New York: St. Martin's Press, 1989); *Against Empire* (San Francisco: City Lights, 1995); and *America Besieged* (San Francisco: City Lights, 1998); Stephen Rosskamm Shalom, *Imperial Alibis: Rationalizing US Intervention After the Cold War* (Boston: South End, 1993); Holly Sklar, *Washington's War on Nicaragua* (Boston: South End, 1988); and Henry David Thoreau, *Anti-Slavery and Reform Papers* (Montreal: Harvest House, 1963).
14. William Bennett, "Teaching September 11," *The Wall Street Journal*, September 10, 2002, A12.
15. Ibid.
16. Norman Solomon's critical analyses consistently reveal a mass media that promote the official government line and spokesmen such as Bennett, while

ignoring or marginalizing dissenters such as Noam Chomsky and Howard Zinn. See, e.g., Solomon's "The Conventional Media Wisdom of Obedience," www.znet.org, March 13, 2003; and numerous reports found in FAIR: Fairness & Accuracy in Reporting: www.fair.org.

17. Bennett, A12.

18. Ibid.

19. Allan Bloom, *The Closing of the American Mind: How Higher Education has Failed Democracy and Impoverished the Souls of Today's Students* (New York: Simon and Schuster, 1987), p. 39.

20. Ibid., p. 158.

21. Michael Parenti, *The Terrorism Trap: September 11 and Beyond* (San Francisco: City Lights Books, 2002), p. 108.

22. Noam Chomsky, *9/11* (New York: Seven Stories Press, 2001), p. 90.

23. John Marciano, *Civic Illiteracy and Education: The Battle for the Hearts and Minds of American Youth* (New York: Peter Lang Publishers, 1997), pp. 1–2, and arguments presented throughout the book. This work builds on an analysis of secondary history textbooks and U.S. foreign policy found in William L. Griffen and John Marciano, *Teaching the Vietnam War: A Critical Examination of School Texts and An Interpretive Comparative History Utilizing The Pentagon Papers and Other Documents* (Montclair, New Jersey: Allanheld and Osmun, 1979); reissued as *Lessons of the Vietnam War*, 1984. An excellent source that supports our critical historical and educational analysis is James W. Loewen's *Lies My Teacher Told Me: Everything Your American History Textbook Got Wrong* (New York: The New Press, 1995).

24. Samuel Huntington, "The United States," in Michael Crozier, Samuel Huntington, and Joji Watanuki, *The Crisis of Democracy: Report on the Governability of Democracies to the Trilateral Commission* (New York: New York University Press, 1975), p. 102.

25. Marciano, *Civic Illiteracy*, p. 2.

26. Andrew Kopkind, "The Warrior State: Imposing the New Order at Home," *The Nation*, April 8, 1991, p. 433.

27. Marciano, *Civic Illiteracy*, p. 6.

28. William Blum, *Rogue State: A Guide to the World's Only Superpower* (Monroe, Maine: Common Courage Press, 2000), pp. 38–40.

29. Ibid., pp. 126–67.

30. Chomsky's works include *American Power and the New Mandarins* (New York: Pantheon, 1969); *For Reasons of State* (New York: Pantheon, 1973); *The Faithful Triangle: The United States, Israel, and the Palestinians* (Boston: South End Press, 1983); *The Culture of Terrorism* (Boston: South End, 1988); *Manufacturing Consent* (New York: Pantheon, 1988), with Edward S. Herman; *Necessary Illusions: Thought Control in Democratic Societies* (Boston: South End, 1989); *Deterring Democracy* (New York: Hill and Wang, 1992); *World Orders, Old and New* (New York: Columbia University Press, 1994); *Understanding Power: The Indispensable Chomsky* (New York: The New Press, 2002); *9/11* (New York: Seven Stories Press, 2002); and *Power and Terror: Post-9/11 Talks and Interviews* (New York: Seven Stories Press, 2003).

31. Chomsky, *9/11*, p. 44.

32. Eqbal Ahmad, *Terrorism: Theirs and Ours* (New York: Seven Stories Press, 2001), pp. 12–13.

33. Ibid., pp. 15–16.

34. Ibid., p. 24.

35. Ibid., p. 53.
36. Parenti, *The Terrorism Trap*, p. 7.
37. Ibid., p. 18.
38. Ibid., p. 19.
39. Ibid., p. 20.
40. Ibid., p. 43.
41. Thomas Friedman, *The Olive Tree and the Lexus* (New York: Farrar, Strauss & Giroux, 1999), p. 373.
42. Parenti, *The Terrorism Trap*, p. 75.
43. Ibid., pp. 76–77.
44. Ibid., p. 81.
45. Howard Zinn, *Terrorism and War* (New York: Seven Stories Press, 2002), p. 50.
46. Ibid., p. 52.
47. Ibid., p. 10.
48. John Pilger, *New Rulers of the World* (London: Verso Press, 2002), p. 8.
49. Ibid., p. 8.
50. Howard Zinn, *Declarations of Independence: Cross-Examining American Ideology* (New York: HarperCollins, 1990), pp. 1–2.
51. Quoted in Robert Bellah et al., *The Good Society* (New York: Random House, 1992), p. 245.
52. Thoreau, *Anti-Slavery*, p. 127.

7

Cultural War through Sound Bytes: The Assault by the American Council of Trustees and Alumni on Critiques of U.S. Foreign and Military Policy Following September 11

Stuart McAninch

Following the events of September 11, 2001, an organization named the American Council of Trustees and Alumni (ACTA, whose website is www.goacta.org) released a report entitled *Defending Civilization: How Our Universities Are Failing America and What Can Be Done About It*. One of the report's authors is Jerry L. Martin, president of ACTA and a former official at the National Endowment for the Humanities as well as a former chair of the philosophy department at the University of Colorado at Boulder. The other author is Anne D. Neal, vice president and general counsel for ACTA and a former official at the National Endowment for the Humanities (NEH). In that report, the authors contrasted the condemnation of the terrorist attacks by political leaders, who "called evil by its rightful name," with the responses of college and university faculty, who failed to call evil by its rightful name.[1] Resolute statements from George W. Bush, Tom Daschle, Trent Lott, and Rudolph Giuliani were contrasted with 115 campus responses, which the authors depicted as being illustrations of either moral equivocation or outright condemnation of America. The public statements by the political leaders depicted a clear-cut struggle between good (represented by the U.S. government) and evil (represented by the terrorists and those who sponsored them). The major problem, from the standpoint of the authors, is that the faculty members whom they castigate in their report refuse to recognize what should be the obvious moral nature of the struggle—and, furthermore, these faculty members are in a position to directly influence through their teaching, writing, and social activism how college and university students as well as social groups outside higher education understand that struggle.

Some critics of the report have maintained that it is McCarthyist in nature. In the original version of the report, names were attached to the 115 campus responses.[2] The ACTA announced that the list of responses and the attached names would be sent to 3,000 college and university trustees.[3] While the authors removed the names from subsequent versions of the report, a number of the names could still be found on the organization's website in an issue of its publication, *Inside Academe*.[4]

Moreover, the responses, drawn from media sources, are brief and taken out of context. They range in length from a single sentence to two paragraphs. Most are direct quotations. Some, however, are the authors' own allegations of irresponsible statements and behavior or of intimidation of faculty and students who support government policy. While the statements are taken out of the contexts in which they were made, Martin and Neal told readers what we need to understand:

> Rarely did professors publicly mention heroism, rarely did they discuss the difference between good and evil, the nature of Western political order or the virtue of a free society. Indeed, the message of many in academe was clear: BLAME AMERICA FIRST.[5]

Hence, it was not only that names were attached by the authors of the report to statements taken out of context. The statements were then identified as being disloyal to "America." Such practices lend credence to the charges of McCarthyist tactics made by critics of the report.

The inclusion of the 115 campus responses also illustrates the problematic nature of the authors' methodology and reasoning. The authors made vague reference to "our intellectual elites" (apparently a critical mass of leftist, left-leaning, and/or left-intimidated tenured faculty and university administrators) who enforce a "dominant campus ideology":

> Students have reported more and more that they are intimidated by professors and fellow students if they question "politically correct" ideas or fail to conform to a particular ideology.

And:

> Students and often professors, especially if they are untenured, are reluctant to question publicly the dominant campus ideology. In several cases where they did so, college administrators were quick to clamp down on their activities, until faced with a public uproar.

The evidence for such sweeping claims regarding American university cultures and the politics of knowledge on university campuses is anecdotal: namely, the 115 campus responses. If one looks at those responses that are quotations, they are an eclectic lot. While many of the quotations included in the responses are attributed to members of university and college faculties and administrations, others are from students. Still others are from speakers not affiliated with the universities and colleges named, or—in some cases—whose relationships to those universities and colleges are not identified. Some quotations are from signs and posters, and, in other cases, they are evidently drawn from titles of events. These responses are not only out of context and eclectic; they are also highly selective in terms of the institutions from which they are drawn. Of 115 responses, 37 were drawn from three campuses: the University of North Carolina-Chapel Hill (14 responses), Brown University (12 responses), and the University of California-Berkeley (11 responses). Harvard University, the City University of New York, and the Massachusetts Institute of Technology collectively account for 17 more.[6]

Moreover, the authors' representation of the ideologies of those academics, students, and others who oppose U.S. military and foreign policy is contradictory. Hence, the "dominant campus ideology" enforced by "our intellectual elites" is evidently characterized by both moral relativism and a tendency "to suggest that Western civilization is the primary source of the world's ills—even though it gave us the ideals of democracy, human rights, individual liberty, and mutual tolerance."[7] The authors' argument at this point is not coherent.

Incoherent rhetoric about "intellectual elites" and "dominant campus ideology" and anecdotal evidence serve to identify this report as propaganda rather than reasoned academic discourse. It is reasonable to conclude that the cursory and logically flawed critique of the ideologies of campus dissenters, which decontextualizes and caricatures those ideologies, was not the result of bad writing or lack of intelligence on the part of the authors. Rather, the purpose of the document is suggested by the dramatic language ("BLAME AMERICA FIRST"), and the numerous emotionally stirring, but unsubstantiated assertions (e.g., "[m]oral relativism has become a staple of academic life in this country") extracted from the text and highlighted in bold print in the margins. Illogic and incomplete analytic development of a critique are not germane to the authors' purpose for the document; dramatic language and pithy statements that can be picked up by media are. However, if this is propaganda, it is politically potent propaganda—and deconstruction of it can provide insight into a key ideological struggle characterizing American universities during the last three-and-a-half decades. The report also affords another challenge worthy of reasoned academic discourse: if what the authors provide is two-dimensional caricatures of fundamental dissent by academics against U.S. foreign, national security, and military policy, how can those of us who engage in such dissent present dissenting thought within an adequate intellectual and social context?

* * * * * * * * * * * *

The ACTA report needs to be placed within the context of the overall agenda of the organization. Lynne Cheney played the most instrumental role in founding the ACTA in 1994. Both Martin and Neal served in the

NEH during her years as chair. The ACTA provides a vehicle for furthering the kind of conservative cultural and political agenda that has characterized her work and that of her predecessor as chair of the NEH, William Bennett (who serves as a member of the ACTA National Council). The organization has published reports calling for the strengthening of English and history requirements in universities and colleges in order to ground students in the foundations of Western civilization. Such calls are coupled with critiques of "political correctness" on campuses, which ACTA publications identify as the influence of radical multiculturalist, feminist, and leftist theories and the suppression of viewpoints in academic discourse not consistent with those theories.

The organization has sought to influence higher education policy through such measures as annual roundtables for educational leaders and trustee workshops in Colorado and Florida. The ACTA maintains the Institute for Effective Governance, the Center for Higher Education Policy, Trustees for Better Teachers, and the Governors Project as means to increase its influence among political and educational leaders and to promote its projects and programs. It has sought to influence philanthropic gifts through publication of a donor's guide and maintenance of a donor's working group. It has forged networks with other academic groups with similar agendas like the National Association of Scholars and the Education Leaders Council. It also places considerable value on the publicity afforded by media appearances, press releases, and the influence of ACTA publications on media commentary. Hence, this document must be understood within the context of a multifaceted ACTA strategy to maximize its influence within higher education in order to advance its conservative agenda.

As Henry Giroux has noted, the ACTA report also needs to be placed within the context of a developing critique of the fundamental dissent among academics against both corporate capitalism and U.S. foreign and military policy—dissent that became widespread by the 1960s.[8] For those who have read earlier documents in this genre of critique, the charges leveled in "Defending Civilization" are likely to be familiar. One can, for instance, see those charges articulated at more length in Paul Gagnon's *Democracy's Untold Story: What World History Textbooks Neglect*, published in 1987, and *Democracy's Half-Told Story: What American Textbooks Should Add*, published in 1989. While ostensibly critiques of commonly used high school history textbooks, Gagnon's works provide a wide-ranging denunciation of what he depicted as an "industry of blame," characterized by excessive and unbalanced criticisms of American institutions and ideals and spawned by those who during the crises of the 1960s and early 1970s became "indifferent to, or even alienated from, American democracy, out of disillusion over its failings in practice."[9] He especially located the roots of these excessive and unbalanced criticisms by academics in the critiques of American military and foreign policy during the Vietnam era. Gagnon never explicitly identified who engages in the industry of blame, except when he made references in both books to revisionist historians who place more blame for the origin of the Cold War on the United States than on the Soviet Union. Gagnon apparently approved of excluding such "revisionist" viewpoints from the classroom: "None [of the world history textbooks which he reviewed] pretends to take up the revisionist debate; each is content to state the obvious."[10]

As in Martin's and Neal's later report, Gagnon criticized academics who challenged the moral legitimacy of capitalism and the U.S. government as betraying their vital mission as academics to pass on to the next generation those political traditions that he associated with democracy. Also like Martin and Neal, Gagnon emphasized that preparing students to play their necessary role of safeguarding American democracy entails "our transmitting to each new generation the political vision of liberty and equality that unites us as Americans—and a deep loyalty to the political institutions our founders put together to fulfill that vision."[11] Unfortunately, realization of this primary civic goal in American schools has been seriously threatened by "a certain lack of confidence in our own liberal, democratic values" and "an unwillingness to draw normative distinctions between them and the ideas of nondemocratic regimes" among some educators.[12] Like Martin and Neal, Gagnon depicted historical ignorance among American youth as being a primary symptom of this failure by academics to fulfill this mission.

While Gagnon permitted some criticism of American institutions, he set clear ideological limits on what could be legitimately criticized. It is legitimate to speak of the American government's excesses, mistakes in judgment, or occasional failure to implement democratic principles in the conduct of foreign and military policies, but according to Gagnon's own formula for addressing such flaws, one must treat them ultimately, to borrow a phrase from John Lewis Gaddis, as "examples of tolerating evils in the pursuit of good."[13] Certainly, American foreign and military policies at times were enacted in ways that were harmful to other peoples and deceitful to the American public, but such activity was conducted by leaders who were genuinely trying to confront severe threats to American security, who often lacked adequate information on which to base decisions, who often had to make decisions based on partisan political considerations rather than purely objective and disinterested analysis or moral reasoning, and who often faced complex dilemmas for which there were no clear-cut and neat moral solutions.

To speak of the U.S. government as motivated in large part by an imperial agenda clearly fell outside of the pale of legitimate academic critique and debate for Gagnon. Educators can discuss evils pursued by men with good intentions; educators can debate with each other and their students whether certain compromises with principles should have been made, and what factors caused American leaders to believe them necessary at the time. To question, however, whether the intentions of American political leaders were in fact good places one in the camp of revisionist historians who cannot—or will not—see the obvious. To deny good intentions—as Alan Tonelson, associate editor of *Foreign Policy* magazine, argued in a 1986 review of Noam Chomsky's *Turning the Tide*—"reflects a failure to think of United

States national interests in a Hobbesian world in which tragic choices are sometimes unavoidable."[14]

As in the case of Martin's and Neal's report, it is especially important to place Gagnon's books within the context of the institutional support for them. In the case of the work of Gagnon, the power of the ideas is far more political than it is intellectual. In the case of the work of Martin and Neal, the power is entirely political since the rhetoric never progresses beyond crude propaganda. At least in Gagnon's books, there was considerable coherence as well as some development of argument.

Gagnon's books were published by the American Federation of Teachers, as part of the Education for Democracy Project. The Education for Democracy Project was, in turn, a joint project of the AFT, the Educational Excellence Network, and Freedom House. The Educational Excellence Network was founded by Chester Finn and Diane Ravitch in 1981 and later incorporated into the Thomas B. Fordham Foundation, in which Chester Finn serves as president. Freedom House was represented in Gagnon's books as "a national organization that monitors political rights and civil liberties around the world and that has spent 40 years educating the public about the nature and needs of democracy and the threats to it." The ideological framework structuring that monitoring during the late 1980s was, not surprisingly, consistent with both Gagnon's argument and American foreign policy at the end of the Cold War. [15]

Funding for Gagnon's books came from a range of public and private sources: the U.S. Department of Education, the National Endowment for the Humanities (during the period in which Lynne Cheney served as chair), the California Department of Public Instruction, the Pew Charitable Trusts, and a number of private foundations. Gagnon himself served during this period "as consultant to the National Center for History in the Schools based at the University of California, Los Angeles and funded by the National Endowment for the Humanities."[16]

While Gagnon's books may not evoke widespread recognition today, it should not be surprising that the ideas have reemerged in Martin's and Neal's ACTA report. Gagnon's books refined an ideological formula for attacking the legitimate place of fundamental critique of the capitalist economy and State which, in effect, appears to have become incorporated into the ideological store of ideas preserved through an interlocking set of public and private institutions: the NEH, the U.S. Department of Education, the Thomas B. Fordham Foundation, the ACTA, and the like. One also sees the same names emerge in positions of leadership in this interlocking set of institutions: Lynne Cheney as chair of the NEH, founder of ACTA, and wife of the vice president of the United States; Chester Finn as assistant secretary of the U.S. Department of Education, cofounder of the Education Excellence Network, founding partner and senior scholar with the Edison Project, president of the Thomas B. Fordham Foundation, fellow at the Hudson Institute and Manhattan Institute, and member of the National Council for ACTA; Diane Ravitch as assistant secretary of the

U.S. Department of Education, cofounder of the Education Excellence Network, chair of the textbook advisory committee for the Education for Democracy Project, distinguished visiting fellow at the Hoover Institute, senior fellow at the Brookings Institute, and trustee for the Thomas B. Fordham Foundation.

It is important to note that Gagnon's books themselves were hardly original in terms of the kind of critique of fundamental dissent he constructed. Many of the ideas in those books could be found in Diane Ravitch's *The Revisionist Revised: A Critique of the Radical Attack on the Schools*, a review of the literature on the history of American education invited by the National Academy of Education and funded by a Ford Foundation grant.[17] In that book, published in 1978, Ravitch argued that American society and education had, due to the influence of "the democratic-liberal tradition" on reform efforts, become over the course of the nation's history incrementally more democratic and humane. Given the strength of that tradition, American society is "a society that would ultimately be compelled by its own democratic creed to confront its prejudices and discriminatory practices and seek to abolish them." The "consensual political process" in the United States that has been shaped by the democratic-liberal tradition is "a manifestation of democratic, pluralist politics, in which many groups and individuals press for their own interests and arrive at a resolution which satisfies most of the participants and crushes none."[18]

Much like Gagnon, Ravitch dismissed the "radical attack" (in this case, on the schools) as hopelessly flawed due to its rigid economic determinism, and due to its subsequent failure to acknowledge the extent of pluralism and opportunity or the potency of either the democratic-liberal tradition or of reform efforts in American history. Hence, the work of those she identified as radical historical revisionists—historians like Michael Katz, Clarence Karier, Joel Spring, Samuel Bowles, Herbert Gintis, and James Anderson—suffers from more than just flaws in research methodology or occasional erroneous factual claims (although Ravitch sought to provide examples of both). Rather, their work was presented as irremediably distorted and slipshod. Consequently, their claims of persistent institutionalized oppression and hegemony were dismissed by Ravitch as not even being worthy of serious academic attention—just as Gagnon would dismiss in 1987 arguments that maintenance of empire has been the most important motivation of American foreign and military policy as not even being worthy of serious academic attention.

Michael Katz provided a rebuttal to *The Revisionists Revised* in which he maintained that Ravitch's dismissal of critical historical scholarship depended on her refusal to acknowledge differences in interpretation among those she labeled as radical historical revisionists and on distortions of their positions.[19] Katz also noted that copies of the books were sent by the National Academy of Education to publishers of the historians she criticized, to deans of education, and to some historians (although not to Katz himself or to others whom she attacked).

In the cases of the works by Martin and Neal, Gagnon, and Ravitch cited here, their goal is not sustained criticism of the methodologies and interpretations of those academics whose work denies the democratic nature and moral legitimacy of U.S. foreign, military, and national security policy and of capitalism. It is not an effort to identify flaws, on the one hand, but also, on the other hand, to identify aspects of interpretation and research that possess intellectual merit and deserve careful consideration. Katz was correct to refer to the kind of criticism they engage in as an "attack" rather than as reasoned, methodical academic criticism.[20] This "attack" was (and is) aimed at excluding fundamental critique of U.S. governmental policy and capitalism from academic discourse. Moreover, the careful construction and refinement of an interlocking set of institutions that have sustained and amplified this attack during the last three decades indicates a well-developed understanding on the part of its architects (Diane Ravitch, Chester Finn, Lynne Cheney, etc.) of the politics of ideas. Those architects are masters at the very politicization of academic discourse that they decry.

★★★★★★★★★★★★

How, in the face of this sustained attack, can one represent the intellectual and social vitality of the kind of scholarship and dialogues being dismissed as the products of academics who are isolated from the mainstream beliefs and values of the American public and who "BLAME AMERICA FIRST"? One means for doing so lies in consideration of two of the most dynamic areas of historical research during the last four decades: social history and labor history. Rather than positing a monolithic "America," works in these areas have by their very nature required careful analytic differentiation between American businesses and the State, on the one hand, and American communities and social groups, on the other.[21] Those histories provide considerable support for the conclusion that the struggle for democracy in American history has been primarily sustained by grassroots movements strongly grounded in community and labor organizations and values. Powerful traditions of fundamental dissent against the State and capitalism have been sustained by those organizations and values: from the inception of a civil rights movement grounded in developing African American culture and the tactics of resistance to slavery within black communities during the colonial period to the GI and veterans' antiwar movement of the 1960s and 1970s grounded to a significant extent in the working-class community and family values shared by most of the "New Winter Soldiers."[22] To the extent that the State has been pluralistic rather than simply the hegemonic guardian of the interests of the most economically powerful institutions and individuals, that pluralism has been forced by the pressure of nonelite movements. Often, those movements have generated critiques of the closely interrelated State and capitalist economy as being anti-democratic.

When Martin Luther King, Jr. stated in 1967 that "I knew that I could never again raise my voice against the violence of the oppressed in the ghettos without having first spoken clearly to the greatest purveyor of violence in the world today—my own country," he was not engaging in politically correct blaming of America first.[23] He was engaging in a critique of State violence and imperialism—a critique rooted in three centuries of civil rights activism against State-sanctioned violence and oppression. Likewise, as a soldiers' and veterans' movement against U.S. military policy developed during the 1960s and 1970s (and continued into the subsequent decades), it was informed by a sense that the State (and for at least many, a sense that capitalism as well) had betrayed what those soldiers and veterans had learned in home and community was best about America.[24]

These two illustrations indicate that analytically one of the problems with the condemnation of fundamental dissent by Ravitch, Gagnon, Martin, and Neal is the conflation of blaming the State and capitalism with blaming America. For Martin Luther King, Jr. and for antiwar soldiers and veterans, there was (and, in the case of the latter, still is) a clear-cut distinction between these two forms of blame. Moreover, Martin's and Neal's representation of fundamental political–economic critiques following September 11, 2001 as the socially and culturally isolated view of radical professors living insular lives within their universities and colleges fails to take into account (as did the earlier work of Gagnon and Ravitch) the roots of those critiques within long-standing social movements in this country.

One of the 115 pieces of anecdotal evidence in Martin's and Neal's document is a statement attributed to a professor of English at Rutgers University: "[W]e should be aware that, whatever its proximate cause, its ultimate cause is the fascism of U.S. foreign policy over the past many decades."[25] In fact, many of the statements appear to suggest a distinction between a proximate cause rooted in the actions of the hijackers and the terrorist network that supported them and an ultimate cause rooted in the interrelated impacts of capitalism and U.S. military and foreign policy on Muslim nations.

Martin's and Neal's argument obviously depends on the condemnation of the contention that U.S. military and foreign policy is fascist. It is important to understand, however, that their argument also depends on the condemnation of the analytic distinction between proximate cause and ultimate cause of the events of September 11. To maintain this distinction is to maintain the possibility of a complex moral and political–economic understanding of those events: on the one hand, those events were caused by the planning and action of a terrorist network; on the other, analysis of the political–economic context demonstrates the depiction of the United States as either innocent victim or righteous avenger to be hopelessly inadequate intellectually and morally.

Martin and Neal are consequently in the position of having to condemn academic inquiry itself as well as radical political–economic interpretations in order to prevent that possible understanding. This is further illustrated by their inclusion of the following statement attributed to a speaker at the University of North Carolina-Chapel Hill among their anecdotal evidence:

> The question we should explore is not who we should bomb or where we should bomb, but why we were targeted. When we have the answer to why, then we will have the ability to prevent terrorist attacks tomorrow.[26]

It is clearly not wrong to argue that scholarly interpretations that depict U.S. foreign, military, and national security policies as fascistic should be subject within universities and colleges to testing and debate and to a weighing against scholarly counterinterpretations. Within the field of history, for instance, such testing, debate, and weighing are necessary for any meaningful study of historiography. However, the propagandistic nature of their work indicates that promoting the critical weighing of conflicting interpretations is not the real agenda of Martin and Neal. Rather, the real agenda is to suppress those interpretations and lines of inquiry that might foster fundamental dissent against foreign, military, and national security policies and against capitalism. Analysis of their work in light of the earlier work by Paul Gagnon and Diane Ravitch—and in light of the historical development of a network of institutions to support such work—indicates that Martin's and Neal's ideas are not new. It also indicates that despite calls by the ACTA to free the pursuit of knowledge in universities and colleges from political ideology, their own work is a prime illustration of the politics of ideas. *Defending Civilization* is not written in such a way as to stimulate rational argument; rather it is written in such a way as to stimulate sound bytes for public condemnation of misrepresented arguments.

NOTES

1. Jerry L. Martin and Anne D. Neal, *Defending Civilization: How Our Universities Are Failing America and What Can Be Done About It*, revised and expanded (Washington, D.C.: American Council of Trustees and Alumni, 2002), p. 1.
2. Ibid., p. 9. For contentions regarding the McCarthyist nature of the report, see ibid., pp. 32, 35–37; Julianne Malveaux, "The New McCarthyism," *Black Issues in Higher Education* 18, No. 22 (December 20, 2001): 43; Matthew Rothschild, "The New McCarthyism," from http://www.progressive.org/0901/roth0102.html.
3. Eric Scigliano, "Naming—and Un-naming—Names," *The Nation*, December 31, 2001, 16.
4. *Inside Academe* 6, No. 4 (Fall 2001): 2, 5.
5. Martin and Neal, *Defending Civilization*, p. 3. The emphasis is in the original.
6. Ibid., pp. 5–6, 13–29.
7. Ibid., pp. 5–6.
8. Henry A. Giroux, "Democracy, Freedom, and Justice after September 11th: Rethinking the Role of Educators and the Politics of Schooling," *Teachers College Record* 104, No. 6 (Summer 2002): 1138–62.

9. Paul Gagnon, *Democracy's Untold Story: What World History Textbooks Neglect* (Washington, D.C.: American Federation of Teachers, 1987), p. 17; Paul Gagnon, *Democracy's Half-Told Story: What American History Textbooks Should Add* (Washington, D.C.: American Federation of Teachers, 1989), p. 165; Stuart McAninch, "Cold War Paradigms and the Post-Cold War High School History Curriculum," *Theory and Research in Social Education* 23 (1995): 34–52.

10. Gagnon, *Democracy's Untold Story*, p. 132; Gagnon, *Democracy's Half-Told Story*, p. 133.

11. Gagnon, *Democracy's Half-Told Story*, p. 161.

12. Gagnon, *Democracy's Untold Story*, p. 15; Gagnon, *Democracy's Half-Told Story*, pp. 162–63.

13. John Lewis Gaddis, *The United States and the End of the Cold War: Implications, Reconsiderations, Provocations* (New York: Oxford University Press, 1992), p. 53.

14. Alan Tonelson, "Institutional Structure Blues," *NY Times Book Review*, April 13, 1986, p. 28; Noam Chomsky, *Turning the Tide: U.S. Intervention in Central America and the Struggle for Peace* (Boston: South End Press, 1985).

15. Gagnon, *Democracy's Untold Story*, p. 3; Gagnon, *Democracy's Half-Told Story*, p. 3; Beth Sims, *Workers of the World Undermined: American Labor's Role in U.S. Foreign Policy* (Boston: South End Press, 1992).

16. Gagnon, *Democracy's Untold Story*, p. 3; Gagnon, *Democracy's Half-Told Story*, pp. 3–4.

17. Diane Ravitch, *The Revisionists Revised: A Critique of the Radical Attack on the Schools* (New York: Basic Books, 1978); Michael Katz, *Reconstructing American Education* (Cambridge, M.A.: Harvard University Press, 1987), p. 145.

18. Ravitch, *The Revisionists Revised*, pp. 4–5, 14–15, 17.

19. Katz, *Reconstructing American Education*, pp. 144–52.

20. Ibid., p. 144.

21. See, e.g., Herbert Gutman, *Work, Culture & Society in Industrializing America* (New York: Vintage, 1977); Howard Zinn, *A People's History of the United States* (New York: Harper and Row, 1980); Sean Wilentz, *Chants Democratic: New York City & the Rise of the American Working Class, 1788–1850* (New York: Oxford University Press, 1984); David Montgomery, *The Fall of the House of Labor: The Workplace, the State, and American Labor Activism* (Cambridge, U.K.: Cambridge University Press, 1987); James Anderson, *The Education of Blacks in the South, 1860–1935* (Chapel Hill: The University of North Carolina Press, 1988); American Social History Project, *Who Built America? Working People & the Nation's Economy, Politics, Culture & Society*, 2 vol. (New York: Pantheon, 1989); Marjorie Murphy, *Blackboard Unions: The AFT & the NEA, 1900–1980* (Ithaca, N.Y.: Cornell University Press, 1990); Ruben Donato, *The Other Struggle for Equal Schools: Mexican Americans During the Civil Rights Era* (Albany: State University of New York Press, 1997); Denise Gelberg, *The "Business" of Reforming American Schools* (Albany: State University of New York Press, 1997); Philo Hutcheson, *A Professional Professoriate: Unionization, Bureaucratization, and the AAUP* (Nashville: Vanderbilt University Press, 2000); Patricia Carter, *"Everybody's Paid but the Teacher": The Teaching Profession and the Women's Movement* (New York: Teachers College Press, 2002).

22. Ira Berlin, *Many Thousands Gone: The First Two Centuries of Slavery in North America* (Cambridge, M.A.: Belknap Press, 1998); Richard Moser, *The New*

   Winter Soldiers: GI and Veteran Dissent During the Vietnam Era (New Brunswick, N.J.: Rutgers University Press, 2002).

23. Martin Luther King, Jr., "A Time to Break Silence," in *Unwinding the Vietnam War* (Seattle, W.A.: Comet, 1987), pp. 427–40.

24. Moser, *The New Winter Soldiers*.

25. Martin and Neal, *Defending Civilization*, p. 14.

26. Ibid., p. 23.

III

Selected National Case Studies (Indonesia, Iraqi-Kurdistan, Northern Ireland, and Sierra Leone)

8

COMMUNICATION AND *DAKWAH*: RELIGIOUS LEARNING GROUPS AND THEIR ROLE IN THE PROTECTION OF ISLAMIC HUMAN SECURITY AND RIGHTS FOR INDONESIAN CIVIL SOCIETY[1]

Andi Faisal Bakti

[handwritten: Takes an opportunity to explore a muslim Religious learning and tone point to similar + di better other muslims Religious learning groups + western civilization]

INTRODUCTION

Islamic religious study or learning groups are not only unique in the teaching and learning processes they adopt, but also in their ability to mobilize, on a regular basis, a large part of the population in support of causes to which they hold dear. In this respect, these groups have a widespread and penetrating impact on life in Indonesia.

Unlike the formal secular and religious education,[2] which follow curriculum set by the State,[3] Islamic religious learning groups operate on an informal basis, and are therefore flexible in the kind of themes they address. These themes, which may relate to sociopolitical, economic, or cultural issues are subject to change based on perceived needs.

This chapter[4] provides a background to Islamic learning groups, in particular, Dewan Dakwah Islamiyah Indonesia (Indonesian Islamic Missionary Council, hereafter Dewan Dakwah), and its notion of what it means to promote civil society.

For being so narrow in its interpretation of human rights, it seems that Dewan Dakwah is at odds with the Western concept of human rights that appears accommodating even to those who espouse different "truths."

Many Muslim leaders take their cue of what constitutes civil society, which characterizes it as an ideal peaceful society (*baldatun thayyibatun wa rabbun ghafuur*). This ideal state is what Muhammad is believed to have attained at Medina and is the model that Dewan Dakwah strives to attain.

In the ideal civil society of Dewan Dakwah's aspiration, citizens will be able to exercise the Islamic notion of democracy, expressed through *musyawarah* (negotiation) and *mufakat* (consensus). Such a state also allows citizens to observe the law revealed by God for which violators need to be given a reminder, warned, and, as the case may be, tried by the authorities (the state). A state that does not punish such violations needs to be criticized. For a Dewan Dakwah leader, this "watchdog" role belongs to religious learning groups whose criticisms can extend to individuals, institutions, companies, or government apparatuses, including bureaucrats, the military, the police, and judges. This role seems in line with Janoski's definition of civil society, which underlines the importance of discourses between the four spheres of civil society: the state, public, the market, and the private spheres.[5]

The discerning reader, however, would perceive that Dewan Dakwah's ideal, corresponds to a certain view of Islamic purity, for which all elements of society must fall in line.

In any case, Dewan Dakwah considers it a fundamental right not to be threatened by any of the other spheres, so that a state of comprehensive human security encompassing the social, political, and economic, can be attained. This supports Dupont's definition of human security as "any significant threat from external sources or from within a state, will be deemed a threat to security."[6]

This chapter uses the (ethnographic ethnomethodological) approach to highlight some of the perspectives on human rights and security found within Dewan Dakwah, an organization that has gained a reputation for being fundamentalist, so labeled, because of being critical, modernist, textualist, literalist, and for objecting to internal and external values and traditions/cultures (qualified as non-Islamic).

In analyzing this organization from the perspectives of fundamentalism, human security and rights, as well as civil society the following questions emerge. What led to the founding of Dewan Dakwah? Why is Dewan Dakwah reactive to perceived threats? What role does Dewan Dakwah play in protecting human and security rights? Which specific human rights does it address? To what extent must an equitable social organization guarantee individual freedom of will and act to safeguard the dignity of individuals and their quality with respect to rights and obligations? How does Dewan Dakwah work to achieve its mission, vision, and goals? And how does this group link these elements with civil society, both as means and ends?

FUNDAMENTALISM, CIVIL SOCIETY, HUMAN AND SECURITY RIGHTS, AS UNDERSTOOD IN (MUSLIM) RELIGIOUS LEARNING GROUPS

Historical Basis of Religious Learning Groups

Religious learning groups make up the oldest Islamic system of education. Introduced by Muhammad (A.D. 570–632), religious education is commonly believed by Muslims worldwide to have begun with Muhammad's first revelation (the collection of Muhammad's revelation became later known as the Qur'an) and his ensuing prophetic task in A.D. 610.

Rejected by Meccans[8] and wary of the public scene, Muhammad established an informal and clandestine religious group, Darul Arqam, to convey the divine messages to its members, which extended to entrepreneurs, bureaucrats, aristocrats, generals, opinion and group leaders, as well as members of suppressed groups, such as slaves and women.

Driven to leave for Yathrib (now Medina),[9] Mohammad negotiated with the various clans of Jewish, Meccan immigrants, and Medinans, and eventually declared the Constitution of Medina, to be observed by all.[10] A political establishment was born, and with the construction of a mosque, a center of Islamic activity, religious learning gained momentum. Muhammad hitherto became the political leader of the Medina city-state, independent from other authorities, preaching monotheism, negotiation, respect for human beings, the environment, and observance of laws, identified as ways of worshiping God.

Today, religious learning groups emerge wherever there are Muslims. Peripatetic religious leaders travel widely, as freelancers or voluntary preachers; as in the past, many are merchants[11] who apply one of Muhammad's Hadith: "Convey the words of God even if one verse only." However, the Qur'an specifies, "No compulsion [should be exercised] in religious propagation and the messages should be delivered using wise persuasion, equal negotiation and rational argumentations." However, some Muslim leaders have ignored these guidelines, and exhibit extremism.

Islamic learning groups have been key actors in uniting the diverse communities of the Malay world. Indeed, in Indonesia alone, with over 300 ethnic groups, an "imagined community" in Anderson's terms,[12] came first and foremost to be united religiously, as Sunni Muslims, with educational and financial ties to Middle Eastern Islamic teachers and philanthropists.

Dewan Dakwah: An Active Islamic Learning Group in Indonesia

Dewan Dakwah was founded on February 26, 1967 in Jakarta by Muhammad Natsir (1908–1993), the first prime minister of Indonesia (1949–1950), (in order to propagate Islam internally (to remove syncretism, superstitions, and un-Islamic innovations), and externally (to peacefully introduce Islam to individuals such as animists who do not belong to religions officially recognized in Indonesia.[13])

Initially perceived as liberal,[14] Natsir's political struggle for an Islamic state failed and his party (Masyumi) was dismantled by Soekarno. Imprisoned and released years later under Soeharto, this internationally respected charismatic leader shifted his strategy to the development of informal education. This shift in strategy did nothing to change the original goal of Natsir: to establish an Islamic state (political Islam) and related law, based on Islamic democratic system as opposed to merely protecting (i.e. offering security) Muslims from perceived threats.

Fundamentalism

[handwritten: Here we say fund... is more Christian than Muslim.]

Fundamentalism, from Latin, *fundamentum*, means foundation, basis, or root. Primarily, "fundamentalist" refers to someone who believes in a religious textual foundation, be it the Bible or other scriptures. As a term that was initially associated with Christians, the use of the term *fundamentalist* as an exclusive characterization of Islam is inappropriate.

According to the *Encyclopedia of Americana*,[15] fundamentalism is a militant, conservative, Protestant movement, which emerged in the United States of America in the 1920s. This movement holds the Bible as the only truth, and rejects inventions and the use of science and technology. Similarly, so-called Muslim fundamentalists believe in the truth of the Qur'an, a text kept in its original Arabic form, but subject to continuous (re) interpretation and explanation or *tafsir* (exegesis). As with the *shari'a*, numerous and distinct *tafsir* are found in the Islamic world. The label "fundamentalist" is used by Western media and a few Muslim scholars, including Bassam Tibi,[16] Abdul Mulkhan,[17] even if Islamic purification and pro-science movements in Islam encourage the education and development of science within society.

Human Rights

[handwritten: Here we say Human Rights was in Muslim first]

Muslim scholars have extensively worked on defining human rights in Islam and compared them with the Western understanding of the words. Arguing that the Western concept of human rights emerged long after it was introduced in Islam, Abu A'la Mawdudi, a Muslim scholar who is strongly respected in Dewan Dakwah, writes: "The practical proof and demonstration of these concepts can only be found at the end of the eighteenth century in the proclamations and constitutions of America and France."[18] Unlike Mawdudi, whose stance appears rooted in a narrow translation of a few Qur'anic verses,[19] Bassam Tibi insists that the "*shari'a* is at odds with individual human rights. Islamic fundamentalists believe that there are specifically Islamic human rights...Human rights are not restricted to one religious community."[20] "Apologetic Islamic writers argue, (in a very unspecific way) that human rights have always existed in Islam. References to the [Qur'an] and to the sayings of the Prophet serve as the ground for the needed evidence. Old symbols are filled with new meaning. This choice between the scriptural understanding of Islam on the one hand, and the social science analysis on the other, may also be applied to the legal discussion of Islamic Law and to its compatibility with human rights."[21]

However, in the deeply religious and traditional context of the Dewan Dakwah, a religious scriptural definition of human rights is crucial and Islamic human rights need to emerge to fit the Islamic context. Considering that human rights elements are brushed over in the Qur'an it seems that the broader, all-encompassing human rights that go beyond an individual's religion should be attributed to the West. This is pivotal, if the Islamic world and the West wish to communicate. In Western countries such as the

[handwritten vertical left margin: Devise a te: determine how one learns.]

Netherlands, the United Kingdom, and the United States, the concept of human rights and freedom of worship has allowed Muslims to build viable communities where they can worship freely. The question thus arises as to how to avoid coercion and seduction in religious conversion, and how predominantly Islamic countries such as Indonesia are willing to grant similar rights to non-Muslims to build similarly viable communities in a predominantly Islamic environment.

Civil Society

The concept of civil society is translated in Indonesia as *masyarakat madani*, or *masyarakat sipil*.[22] For those who prefer the former translation, referring to an ideal Muhammad's city-state of Medina, the city, which Muhammad turned into an ideal Islamic city-state, civil society is not new to Islam. Those who adopt the latter translation, however, believe civil society is a modern expression, born in the Western tradition (Europe), in modern times. It is therefore impossible, according to them, to apply these terms retroactively to a Muslim society. However, despite the similarity in pronunciation, the concept of "civil" cannot be translated into *sipil*. Indeed, while "civil" is an adjective in English, *sipil*, a noun in Indonesian, is the antonym of *militer* (military), which is not at all what a civil society is meant to be. Olaf Schumann also defines civil society as *masyarakat madani*.[23]

Unlike authors who first introduced the terms civil society, such as Marx, Hegel, Gramsci, Habermas, Cohen, and Arato, Indonesian Muslims understand civil society in terms of the public sphere per se, versus the state sphere. The role of the market and private spheres is not mentioned. How then can one establish a civil society without a balance of power between spheres? For example, civil society cannot exist without State intervention to regulate society. Thus, civil society has to be understood both as a means and an end of discourse, according to its four spheres, suggested by Janoski,[24] in order for us to be able to apply the concept as a development approach and analysis of human security and rights.

DEWAN DAKWAH: ITS OBJECTIVES, VISION, AND MISSION

Dewan Dakwah oversees a network of Islamic learning groups, and trains religious trainers in an informal educational setting. Its headquarters occupy the former office of Masyumi. This is a missionary organization engaged in the *dakwah bilisanil hal* (Islamic propagation through words and actions), educating, and strengthening the intellectual capacity of the Islamic community toward the full application of Islamic law. The mission of Dewan Dakwah calls for *amar ma'ruf nahi munkar* (commanding good and forbidding bad conduct, as a core of Islamic teachings). The organization sends out its trainers to preach in mosques across the country: in urban, isolated rural areas, and other islands. Dewan Dakwah organizes intellectual activities, sets up printing/publishing houses, journals, a human welfare program, worshipping and social facilities as well as educational institutions through various bureaus, committees, social work organizations, and autonomous bodies within their own organizational structures.[25]

DEWAN DAKWAH AND ITS UNDERSTANDING OF HUMAN RIGHTS PROTECTION

The strongest concern of Dewan Dakwah is protecting the human rights of Muslims by securing the Islamic teaching, and purifying it from both internal and external contamination. Internal contamination includes superstitions, syncretism, tribalism, and un-Islamic religious innovations; external contamination includes secularism, materialism, hedonism, communism, capitalism, and Christianization.

Secularism

Dewan Dakwah's anti-secularist stance is made abundantly clear through speeches and interviews granted by the organization's leadership as well as through its printed media with numerous articles advising Muslims that "secularism can make Muslims forget their religious activities and tasks. For Dewan Dakwah, being religious in all aspects of life, including the way the State operates, guarantees safety in the Hereafter." Despite its broader activities, Dewan Dakwah appears to take a reductionist approach to good deeds (*amil salihat* and *hasanat*), as defined in Islam, focusing rather on the five pillars of Islam: confession, prayers, fasting, almsgiving, and pilgrimage. While many Qur'anic verses extend this definition to development, members of Dewan Dakwah tend to have a strongly spiritualized, ritualized, formalized, and "pillared" understanding of them. Indeed, Dewan Dakwah offers a spectrum of human development activities, but its criticisms against perceived threats overshadow its own social commitment to humanity.

Among others, the State Institute of Islamic Studies (IAIN), a network of 14 centers of higher education and 35 colleges across the country, has a strong footing in the Indonesian society. For sending hundreds of graduate students abroad (Canada, United States, Europe, and Australia) to study Islam, the IAIN is sharply criticized by Dewan Dakwah: "Why does the government send Muslims to study Islam in Western secular universities [as opposed to the Middle East]? These graduates will no doubt become secularized!" said a chief of secretariat, supported by the treasurer of Dewan Dakwah.

Capitalism/Materialism/Nihilism

Capitalism is seen as a possible road to materialism, leading Muslims to abandon spirituality (become nihilistic), and to accumulate wealth without limits. For Dewan Dakwah, rich people, following the Islamic teaching, should share their wealth with the needy. Moreover, there is a fear that capitalism would simply accelerate the exploitation of the natural resources of the Muslim world. Dewan Dakwah preaches caution to Muslims in that respect. Capitalism, in addition to materialism and nihilism, is seen as "basically tyrannical and corrupted, and functions at the expense of people in the developing world, in particular in the Muslim world. Thus, a Muslim has the right to reject them."

Socialism/Communism and Atheism

These Western-based philosophies, according to a Dewan Dakwah organizer of a training-the-trainer workshop, "are dangerous for Muslims, who have the right to reject such notions. These beliefs can lead Muslims into disregarding God, and eventually become *kafir* (infidel), which will lead them to Hell fire." The history of Communism and its brutalities throughout Indonesian history is repeatedly mentioned by Dewan Dakwah speakers, as a reminder of the worst. In fact, when Abdurrahman Wahid (Indonesian president in 1999–2001, and former Nahdlatul Ulama leader) wanted to lift the decree that forbids Communism in Indonesia, Dewan Dakwah, among others, vehemently opposed this possibility. When questioned about this contradiction to the right to freedom expressed in the Qur'an, a speaker and secretary of Dewan Dakwah retorted that Communism is born out of violence. In one of his speeches, this individual said: "while Habibie produced more than a hundred decrees to establish democracy for the sake of the people, all Abdurrahman Wahid thought about was to lift the decree banning Communism. How ridiculous Wahid is!"

Christianization/Hedonism

Among the most challenging threats perceived by Dewan Dakwah is the Christianization of Indonesia, supported by the Christian West (financial aid, military, development policy under the so-called diaconal programs) supported by the Jewish community. This aggressive Christianization "happens right in the private homes of Muslims," says a Dewan Dakwah leader. Dewan Dakwah believes that Muslims who convert become apostates. They have been coerced and seduced by gifts from Evangelists (Jehovah Witnesses), Catholic missionaries, and Protestant *zendings*. For Dewan Dakwah, this is clearly an attack on *human rights*! "It is not an issue of religious freedom," adds a preacher. "Of course, in Islam, anyone can decide his or her religion. However, the issue here is the use of coercion and seduction. We strongly object!"

When apprised of the Qur'an's acceptance of Christians and Jews as People of the Book,[26] one respondent says: "Christians, in particular, in the West are hedonists who ignore their own belief." Dewan Dakwah indeed fears that Indonesian Christian converts will turn to hedonism, a terrifying thought. "In addition, Christians are different today than in Jesus' time." In this respect however, Dewan Dakwah limits itself to a strong and persistent verbal (*lisan*) criticism.[27]

Comparing Muslims to Christians. Why Muslims are violent?

Regarding the portrayal of Muslims as violent by the Western media, a
Dewan Dakwah speaker explained: "Violence in a Muslim basically comes as
a reaction to and protection against external invasion/intrusions. While the
Qur'an teaches love and respect of human rights, the Bible clearly teaches
violence, killing, burning." It is indeed ironical that both Christians and
Muslims seem to focus on the violence preached in each other's sacred book.

Syncretism/Superstitions/Innovations *3 notes*

These are considered to be contaminants of the Islamic tenets. "These local
beliefs have to be purified," said a treasurer of Dewan Dakwah. "These are
not congruent with *tawhid* (monotheism). Every Muslim who wishes to
preserve his or her truly Islamic belief should try his or her best to clean him
or herself from TBC" (*Tachayul, Bid'ah and Churafat*;[28] superstitions, innovations, and syncretism). T and C are related to local beliefs, while B is
attributed, for example, to new elements in worship, and new prophets such
as Mirza Ghulam Ahmad (1839–1908), the Ahmadiyah founder. Asked why
people cannot freely choose what to believe, the same respondent argues:
"Since these are Muslim, it is our right to remind them these beliefs are not
Islamic." While it looks at purifying Islam from its meshed-in local beliefs
and traditions, Dewan Dakwah ignores Islam's acceptance of local values
(*'urf*), beyond those practiced during Muhammad's life. Purity is a relative
and elusive concept calling for some flexibility on the part of Dewan Dakwah
where no direct contradiction of Islam is evident.

Tribalism */ level*

Dewan Dakwah is also very wary of tribalism, or *'asabiyah* (local-ethno group
sentiments). "This is non-Islamic, as it could lead to separatism and exclusivism, resembling the pre-Islamic pride for one's own ethnic group and clan
and a tendency to be excessively protective against potential interference,"
explained a secretary of Dewan Dakwah. There is some incongruity in this
testimony and Dewan Dakwah seems to send mixed messages. While it perceives tribalism as un-Islamic, it struggles for an Islamic nationalism in
Indonesia, another form of exclusivism. Thus, the same protectionism it fears
from tribalism, Dewan Dakwah practices against perceived internal threats.

Fundamental Rights need Protection

Feeling threatened by external and internal attacks, and following the five
fundamental human rights (necessities) in Islam,[29] Dewan Dakwah struggles
to protect the following Islamic rights. *IRs*

The Right of Belief

The protection of religious and spiritual rights (Islam for Dewan Dakwah).
Dewan Dakwah respects other religions, as long as their members do not

coerce or seduce Muslims into conversion, a practice that violates the human rights of religious freedom. While conversion is accepted in Islam as a personal choice, one respondent suggests, "government should regulate conversions and forbid religious seducers and coercers from converting those who already have a religion (as opposed to animists)." On the one hand, Dewan Dakwah seeks to "purify" Islam against local beliefs, such as animism, or even Javanism (pre-Islamic religion), through an active Islamization process; and yet it is against active Christianization. "After the 350-year colonization of Indonesian Muslims by the Christian West [Dutch]," says a speaker in a Dewan Dakwah mosque, "cultural and economic imperialism remains. Muslims should have the right to protect once again their religion from this hegemony and tyranny."

The Right to One's Soul and Body

Dewan Dakwah also relates protection of one's soul with the right to life. According to a librarian of Dewan Dakwah, "a soul is sacred, and thus Islamic. Whoever tries to kill Muslims, to separate their soul from their body, is violating the right to life. Citing a Qur'anic verse (5:32; 17:35), "Killing one person in Islam is killing all human beings; and saving one's soul is saving all human beings," for him, "Muslims are strongly forbidden to kill others, except in the application of justice (Islamic law). Similarly, others are not supposed to kill Muslims. A Muslim has the right to protect him or herself. In fact, the right to one's soul also includes right of free movement and residence, and the right to obtain medications, to have a livelihood and all which is necessary in a person's life to defend him or herself from banishment." Regarding the justification for cutting off the hand of a thief or stoning an adulterer, a Dewan Dakwah mosque organizer notes: "These punishments aim at setting an example for others." Without a comprehensive comparison, this respondent is convinced, "This deterrent fosters a greater stability than imprisonment, as we observe in those Muslim countries which apply the *shari'a*."[30] Perhaps, a fresher interpretation of the Qur'an in this respect is pivotal. For example, a hand can be interpreted as a means/power to work, to make money. Imprisonment can be seen as cutting the "hand" of the perpetrator, who cannot make a living anymore. This metaphor hand/livelihood or hand/power is commonly found in the Qur'an and can be understood as such in the context of crime.

The Right to One's Mind

This includes mental, psychological, intellectual rights, as well as the protection of body rights. The mind is very central in Islam. According to a sermon, "We are not supposed to corrupt someone's mind. A right to a healthy mind is protected in Islam, and explains why alcohol and drugs are rejected. Whoever provides these to Muslims violates the right to live and think normally. Among others, bars and other establishments should be banished by law." On a different occasion, another speaker declared that smoking is also unlawful in Islam, since tobacco causes 25 diseases. It not only violates the body of the smoker, but also affects non-smokers, children, and asthmatic people. This speaker is convinced tobacco should be forbidden in Indonesia, as it is, according to him, in Egypt, but this remains to be confirmed.

The Right for Protection of Family and Community ✓

This protection is an Islamic obligation (highest among the list of duties for Muslims). A trainer explained, "members of an Islamic community and family should struggle to protect their rights against possible violations. Whoever helps a Muslim under attack, is a hero, and whoever dies doing so is a martyr, the highest position in paradise. Thus, family and community rights are part of the human rights to be protected. These rights also include the right to a family, to marriage, the right for various ethnic groups and races to exist." Regarding the concept of polygamy in the context of family protection, one trainer noted, "While men enjoy sex all the time, women are limited by their menstruations, the fact that they give birth, and their menopause. Since Islam forbids sex outside of marriage and during menstruation, allowing a man to marry more than one woman is humane." Here, the context of the Qur'anic text needs to be taken into account, as it emphasizes that men, since they cannot be fair (financially, emotionally, and physically) to more than one wife, should only marry one. In addition, the essence of the verse was emphasis on fairness to women and to orphans.

The same narrow interpretation is found on the question of the veil (*hijab*) with one speaker claiming that "the veil basically protects women from sexual harassment, rape, and abuse." Actually, the Qur'anic verse (24:31), asks women to cover their *juyub* (lower neck, chest, and breasts) and *furuj* (genitals), without reference to other parts of their body. Finally, both males and females are asked to control themselves in their dealings with the other sex, and to avoid staring in order to avoid the commission of any "crime."

The Right to Wealth or Property
or the Protection of Material Rights ✓

The protection of one's property is highly respected in Islam, and includes the right to acquire property and to protect it, as well as the opportunity to work and be involved in economic activities. As one regular mosque member notes, "Whoever attempts to go against this right, can be tried, and the legal system in Muslim countries allows cutting his or her hand(s) as an effective way to limit such violations. Also included in the list of violations are corruption, manipulation, and excessive interest charges (usury)." The apparent double standard in the interpretation of inheritance law in Islam (males would receive double the share of females) needs to be reexamined as the present context no longer justifies the differential treatment of sexes. When the Qur'anic verse (4:11) in question is interpreted by Dewan Dakwah as, "two [inheritance shares] for males, one for females," that is, a ratio of 2 : 1, it can be argued that what is meant in the text is an equivalence (not a ratio): if a male receives two inheritance shares, they must be equivalent to the female's share $(2 = 1)$, an interpretation that is more in keeping with the essence of the Qur'anic message (4:7), saying, "there is a share for males and a share for females from what is left by parents...."

In the case of witness accounts (two female witnesses for one male), as commonly interpreted from verse 2:282, we could rather stress the meaning of *al-waw*, which could mean *or* rather than *and*, thus stating that males and females are equal. In addition, Qur'anic punctuation was introduced at a later date, and could account for this narrow interpretation (i.e. the possibility of a comma missing before "two women witnesses"). Also, the strong emphasis and narrow interpretation by Dewan Dakwah reflects the way the group defines a normal (civil) societal life.

DEWAN DAKWAH'S INVOLVEMENT IN CIVIL SOCIETY

Let us analyze this involvement in relation with four spheres:

The State Sphere

The founder of Dewan Dakwah eventually gave up politics to turn to the task of propagating Islam. However, politics remain crucial for this group. Dewan Dakwah is very critical of government, in particular on the implementation of a secular state. It struggles for the reinforcement of a law against, syncretism, authoritarianism, corruption, and aggressive Christianization. Dewan Dakwah demands the adoption of an Islamic state. In particular, a treasurer of Dewan Dakwah regrets that a recent general assembly of parliament failed to return the seven missing words (making it an "obligation for Muslims to practice Islamic law") within the ideology of the state, the Pancasila initially formulated in the Jakarta Charter in June 1945.[31]

The Public Sphere

The major socioreligious organizations in Indonesia, such as the Muhammadiyah and the Nahdlatul Ulama (NU),[32] are not keen to establish an Islamic State and Dewan Dakwah speakers tend to be very critical of this stand. However, when it comes to purifying Islamic teachings from syncretism, innovations, and superstitions, Dewan Dakwah seems to be in line with the Muhammadiyah and, for this reason, both groups are seen as modernist organizations. They return to the Qur'an and reject syncretism, encourage rational reasoning, using modern organization/school systems, modern technology/science. On the contrary the NU, while perceived as a traditionalist movement, is more accommodating in this respect.

Dewan Dakwah also criticizes Paramadina, another leading religious learning group led by Nurcholish Madjid, who holds a Ph.D. from the University of Chicago, as being dangerous to Islamic teachings. Despite misrepresentation, this scholar is seen as promoting secularism and as having been influenced by Judeo-Christianity and Zionism during his studies in the United States.

Dewan Dakwah is against his promotion of pluralism and his belief that Islam, Christianity, and Judaism are equal according to the Qur'an (5:69).

The Market Sphere

Dewan Dakwah indirectly receives funds from Aquamas, a mineral water producer, and Astra Motors, a Japanese vehicle company, which encourages its employees to channel donations to Dewan Dakwah. Without direct link in cash-flow, the Muamalat Bank also rents an office in Dewan Dakwah headquarters. Natsir was also very influential in attracting donors to sustain Dewan Dakwah activities. However, the economic security of the Dewan Dakwah is ensured by *zakat* (almsgiving), *sadaqah* (charity), *infaq* (donation), or *waqaf/hibah* (house or land donation) as well as organizing regular pilgrimages to Mecca.

The Private Sphere

Dewan Dakwah approaches religious individuals deeply concerned with developing the Islamic mission at all levels. In urban areas, Dewan Dakwah has a close relationship with former Masyumi party members. Being limited in their scope of activities, former members of this party feel they are fighting a common enemy, that is, state leaders, solidarity ties and trust that their party will emerge once again.

In rural areas, speakers trained within Dewan Dakwah are trusted to deliver the Islamic messages to Muslims and non-Muslims in isolated areas. On their approach to non-Muslims, a former teacher in Irian Jaya explained: "We pray in front of them; we cook in front of them. They ask questions, they prefer our cooked food to their raw one. They are eventually interested to join us. When they see us pray, they ask more questions: we answer that we are praying to God, and they want to learn about praying, about God and Islamic teachings, and eventually adopt Islam, without forcing and seducing them." To what extent seduction is absent from the education/Islamization process remains to be researched.

Thus, the private sphere as understood and invested by Dewan Dakwah activists involves personal links for financial support and humanitarian support (both in intellectual and practical terms).

Summary and Recommendations

Dewan Dakwah is neither fundamentalist in the Christian understanding of the term, nor overreactionist. Rather, it follows a rather distinct path to protecting human security and rights of Muslims in order to lead to civil society. However, the approach of this group is rigid, politicized, and less communicative with internal or external threats. Furthermore, the group focuses on Islamic rights, based on outdated Islamic laws, themselves unfair to localities, religious minorities, women, and to those who are perceived as breaking the law: thieves and adulterers. While the Qur'an is often and repeatedly translated by Muslim scholars, and is open to new and fresh interpretations, reformist Muslims, such as members of Dewan Dakwah, limit themselves to an outdated textual interpretation of the scriptures, without giving much consideration for contextual meaning. The group is also not at ease with foreigners (the West) and with local values. Despite its goal of protecting the human rights of Muslims, and of negotiating a comprehensive security in order to promote the emergence of a civil society, Dewan Dakwah members demonstrate low self-esteem and exclusivism, which comes across in their lack of trust for other religions. However, Dewan Dakwah's strengths at this point lie with its nonviolence and its persistence in criticizing corruption, manipulation, authoritarianism, and dictatorship. Unlike FPI (Front Pembela Islam, Islamic Defense Front) and Laskar Jihad, other religious discussion groups, for example, Dewan Dakwah does not teach violence but is very vocal in its criticism.

The Dewan Dakwah membership seems to have dwindled and lost some of its strength and popularity since the death of its founder. It might be time for the group to shift toward a more positive and tolerant approach to its Islamic mission, as it also claims to be preaching.[33] There is perhaps no better way to demonstrate its commitment to tolerance than for Dewan Dakwah to work with other spheres of civil society and go beyond religious and cultural boundaries. In fact, a Dewan Dakwah activist, now minister of Human Rights and Justice, Yusril Ihza Mahendra, seems to adopt this approach. Expressing his opinion on the issue of initiating an economic relationship with Israel, and, although criticized by colleagues on his stand, he commented that, in Islam: "Pure theological spiritual activities (the worship of God) of course cannot be tolerated, but we are allowed to associate with other religious believers in secular life. There is nothing wrong with working with Jewish people and others..."[34]

The practice of the pillars of Islam, which tend to be highly spiritualized and formalized with the Dewan Dakwah, has to be balanced with another pillar, the pillar of good deeds to human beings and the environment.

In the aftermath of 9/11, two conflicting discourses emerge between the West and the Islamic world. While the West (Capitalist) distrusts and fears Muslims as an emerging challenge following the downfall of communism, Muslims also perceive the Christian West, supported by Jews, as a strong external threat of being imperialist to their security and rights to live cooperatively with all components of the human family. Intercultural communication and reconciliation of both perceptions is highly needed. Educational support would have a far greater impact than military support in Muslim countries as demonstrated by the support the West is giving to the consolidation of higher Islamic education in Indonesia.

NOTES

1. This research was conducted during my appointment as a research fellow of IIAS/ KNAW/CNWS/ISIM program on "The Dissemination of Religious Authority in

20th Century Indonesia," IIAS, Leiden, The Netherlands. My deepest gratitude goes to those individuals involved in granting me this research funding.
2. Andi Faisal Bakti, "Indonesia—Education System," in *Encyclopedia of Modern Asia*, ed. David Levinson and Karen Christensen (New York: Charles Scribner's Son), summer 2002, pp. 59–61.
3. *Formal public education* in Indonesia is provided by two main national networks of institutions: a secular one from kindergarten to university, and a parallel religious network. Although Islamic in essence due to its mostly Muslim population, the secular network offers only two hours a week of religious education (Islam when more than ten students are Muslim, other religions under the same conditions). Subjects include social and natural sciences. In the religious network, students study religion (philosophy, law, etc.) as well as extra subjects, some including English, social and even natural sciences. As a result, students of the religious network acquire a broader knowledge, although somewhat more superficial than in secular schools. Religious formal education is sought after by parents who wish their children to be good Muslims and sound citizens. The religious network (20% of the student population of all ages), including religious schools *(madrasah)*, promote tolerance and pluralism. According to the population census of 1990, 84.1% of the population [179.3 million] older than ten years of age are literate. At the basic education level, including Madrasah Ibtidaiyah [State religious schools], 92.16% of children age 7–12 years attended school in 1992; at junior secondary level, 53%; at secondary school level, 35%; and at higher learning institutes 7.5%. See *Education in Indonesia* (Jakarta: Ministry of Education and Culture, 1993), pp. 4–6. Although not free, a compulsory nine-year basic program of education was initiated in 1994 for students between the age Six and 15.

Private education in Indonesia, offered by a variety of networks, secular and religious, is in full expansion today. Private schools remain expensive, but are crucial in accommodating those who are not accepted in public schools. Christian private schools are known to offer better schooling, facilities, and outcome for their graduates, and they are more expensive than others. There are two categories of Islamic private schools: traditional *(pesantren)* and modern *(madrasah)*. Traditional *pesantren* are usually free, sponsored by organizations or wealthy individuals. They teach Islamic subjects (philosophy, law, reading of the Qur'an, and other religious texts), and traditionally use classical and medieval books written in Arabic. The purpose is to transmit to "students" Islamic teaching, including tolerance and respect of others. Thus, violence is not at all part of the teaching, except within very few groups, such as FPI and Laskar Jihad, which emerged two years ago. In fact, since the late 1970s, in order for their graduates to have access to civil service jobs, *pesantren* have had to strengthen their curriculum with the study of social sciences. Some *pesantren* have gone one step further by calling themselves "modern" in order to attract students and their parents: they promote a joint religious-modern science education, and emphasize the study of both Arabic and English (the term "modern" refers here to the fact that students sit in chairs—not on the floor—, classes follow set schedules as opposed to prayer times, and new texts are introduced—in Indonesian and English. Considered expensive, students in modern *pesantrens* hire various teachers, as opposed to one charismatic religious teacher in traditional ones. However, although students tend to be more critical and have a wider knowledge in modern *pesantren*, many parents find that the quality of their children's religious knowledge has decreased.

Informal education: parents of children in the public secular and religious systems, and in private Islamic institutions as well, tend to look for a balance in their children's education, between excellence in secular subjects and in-depth knowledge and practice of Islam. As school and work in Indonesia resumes early afternoon, it has become common to send children to informal afternoon religious classes, and for teenagers and adults to join religious discussion groups during the same period as well as on weekends. Indeed, it is an obligation for Muslims to at least have read the Qur'an once in their lifetime, then to understand it, to practice its teachings, and to analyze it in view of their everyday life and that of human beings in general. There are 162,944 discussion groups in Indonesia, each with a core of 20–100 regular participants. See H. A. M. Romly, *Fungsi Majlis Taklim dalam Era Globalisasi* (The Role of Religious Learning Groups in the Era of Globalization) (Jakarta: Ditjen Bimas Islam dan Urusan Haji Proyek Penerangan, Bimbingan dan Dakwah/Khutbah Agama Islam Pusat, 1993), p. 10. Dewan Dakwah organizes all levels of informal education from age six to late eighties. Their schools are free of charge, funded through donations, almsgiving, charity, gifts of wealthy people.

4. Previous works on Dewan Dakwah include: William Liddle, "*Media Dakwah* Scripturalism: One of Islamic Political Thought and Action in New Order Indonesia," in *Toward a New Paradigm: Recent Developments in Indonesian Islamic Thought*, ed. Mark R. Woodward (Tempe: Arizona State University Program for Southeast Asian Studies, 1996); and Asna Husin, "Philosophical and Sociological Aspects of Da'wah: A Study of Dewan Dakwah Islamiyah Indonesia," Unpublished Ph.D. Thesis, Columbia University, 1999. While Liddle's work is basically a sharp analysis of Dewan Dakwah's magazine as a scripturalist work, Husin's takes a descriptive approach, which falls short of analyzing Dewan Dakwah philosophy and activities.

5. Thomas Janoski, *Citizenship and Civil Society: A Framework of Rights and Obligations in Liberal Traditional, and Social Democratic Regimes* (Cambridge: Cambridge University Press, 1998).

6. Alain Dupont, "Comprehensive Security and the Issue of Migration and Ethnic Conflict," in *Conceptualising Asia-Pacific Security*, ed. Mohammad Hasan (Kuala Lumpur: ISIS Malaysia, 1996), pp. 67–80.

7. Fieldwork was conducted from July through December 2002. Interviews with Dewan Dakwah's leaders, teachers, speakers, staff, librarians, journalists, regular members, were conducted by myself in the organization's mosque (Al-Furqan), office, conference room, in corridors, library, bookstore, stairs, and other occasions and places where we agreed to meet. I thank the CEO of Dewan Dakwah who allowed me to conduct interviews. Although my research encompasses several places and religious institutions and learning groups, in particular in Jakarta, for this particular Chapter, I only quote those who were directly involved in the Dewan Dakwah central headquarters and Jakarta provincial office. I met 35/50 staff members; 50/70 regular speakers in pre-sermon briefing sessions; attended 20 Friday sermons in 15 mosques followed by interviews. During the 29 days of Ramadhan daily discussions were attended by well over 1,000 participants each day. I attended youth camps for Southeast Asia where speakers are trained by Dewan Dakwah as speakers. For the purpose of confidentiality, names were not mentioned, only the position occupied by respondents in taped interviews.

8. Mecca, Saudi Arabia, is the focus of the annual pilgrimage of the world's Muslims.

9. A city in Saudi Arabia, the second holy city after Mecca.

10. Ibrahim Abdullah al-Marzouqi, *Human Rights in Islamic Law* (Abu Dhabi: no publisher mentioned, 2000).

11. Andi Faisal Bakti, *Islam and Nation Formation in Indonesia: From Communitarian to Organizational Communications* (Jakarta: Logos, 2000).

12. Benedict Anderson, *Imagined Communities: Reflections on Origin and Spread of Nationalism* (London: Verso, 2nd ed., 1992).

13. Islam, Christianity, Hinduism, and Buddhism.

14. See Charles Kurzman, ed., *Liberal Islam: A Source Book* (New York: Oxford University Press, 1998).

15. R. Scott Appleby, "Fundamentalism," in *The Encyclopedia of Americana* (Danbury, Connecticut: Grolier, 2002), pp. 164–67.

16. Bassam Tibi, "From Clash of Civilizations to International Morality: Islam, Tolerance, and the Secular Concept of Human Rights," in *The Interplay of Islam, Cosmopolitanism and Human Rights: The Views of Intellectuals from the Transmediterranian*, ed. Herman de Leeuw. Proceedings of the First "Diagnosis" Meeting (Rotterdam: October 1994).

17. Abdul Munir Mulkhan, *Neo-Sufisme dan Pudarnya Fundamentalisme di Pedesaan* (Neo-Sufism and the Fading of Fundamentalism in Rural Areas) (Yogyakarta: UII Press, 2000).

18. Abu A'la Mawdudi, *Human Rights in Islam* (Leicester: The Islamic Foundation, 1976), p. 13.

19. See Katarina Dalacoura, *Islam, Liberalism, and Human Rights: Implication for International Relations* (London: I. B. Tauris, 1988), pp. 49–53.

20. Tibi, "From Clash of Civilizations," p. 25.

21. Ibid., p. 26.

22. For further discussions on the uses of both terms, see Hendro Prasetyo and Ali Munhanif et al., eds., *Islam & Civil Society: Pandangan Muslim Indonesia* (Insights on Indonesian Muslims) (Jakarta: Gramedia Pustaka Utama, 2002); Various authors in *Jurnal Pemikiran Islam Paramadina* 1, No. 2 (1999): 7–87.

23. Olaf Schurmann, "Dilema Islam Kontemporer: Antara Masyarakat Madani dan Negara Islam" (Contemporary Islamic Dilemma: Between Civil Society and Islamic State). Ibid., pp. 48–75.

24. See note 5.

25. See Thohir Luth, *M. Natsir: Dakwah dan Pemikirannya* (M. Natsir: His Mission and Thought) (Jakarta: Gema Insani, 1999), pp. 53–62

26. Like Christians, Jews are recognized in Islam as People of the Book (Truth revealed by God). Their religion is recognized as a true religion acceptable by God like Islam (Qur'an: 5:69). This verse, however, is not very commonly quoted in Dewan Dakwah.

27. Unlike Dewan Dakwah, other Islamic groups (FPI, Laskar Jihad) used violence against those whom according to them, practice hedonism (e.g. attacks on bars etc.), which was condemned by many Muslim leaders in Indonesia.

28. Terms introduced by a large socioreligious organization in Indonesia, the Muhammadiyah, in the early twentieth century.

29. See al-Marzouqi, *Human Rights*, pp. 143–45.

30. Some translations of the Qur'an (5:38), regarding males and females convicted of stealing, literally understand the cutting of their hand, as understood and practiced by conservative *shari'a* interpreters.

31. Natsir, along with other leaders, had signed a petition against Soeharto, for using his military might in ruling the country.

32. Each claims to have around 30 million members and followers. They each own and operate hundreds of schools, clinics, orphanages, and are known to have been tolerant and working closely with the government's program for Indonesia's economic and social development. The Muhammadiyah was established in 1912, the NU, in 1926.

33. Luth, *M. Natsir*, pp. 122–23.

34. *Media Dakwah* (January and February, 2000): 3.

9

Human Security and Education in a Conflict Society: Lessons from Northern Ireland

Matt Cannon

Introduction

The lessons learned from attempts to resolve and contain the conflict in Northern Ireland provide a valuable empirical example of the role played by human security issues in addressing terrorism in conflict societies. Northern Ireland demonstrates the paradox of education in regard to conflict. Identity plays a significant role in maintaining division between the Unionist and Nationalist communities, and for the most part remains segregated, reenforcing identities and perpetuating conflict. A system of segregated education between the two communities contributes to the sense of competing identities and the notion of an "other." However, the experience in Northern Ireland also demonstrates the potential of education to curb conflict through projects focused on peace building.

In its 1994 *Human Development Report* the UNDP highlighted the significance of human security. In doing so the UNDP identified the risk to security posed by issues that threaten the individual, which in turn could impact international order.[1] In essence the provision of basic human needs has the potential to impact international security. The working notion of human security discussed in this chapter is based on the contribution of human security outlined by Nelles, which stresses conflict prevention and nonmilitary solutions to conflict or human rights abuses while responding to injustices that create unmet basic needs. "Educational empowerment" in Northern Ireland was restricted to a segregated school system that reenforced misunderstanding and prejudice between traditions.

Two opposing understandings of the nature of education are evident in this case study. The first perceives education as a way of preserving differences based on socioeconomic, religious, language, nationality or other forms of identity. For some groups, separate and distinctive schools are a desirable way of preserving identity, and they feel it necessary if their particular form of difference is to survive and prosper. Occasionally such schools seek to proselytize, but more often they are exclusive—exclusive because the group has deeply felt religious convictions, or wishes to preserve a particular cultural identity, is a minority within the society, or has a particular power-base that it is reluctant to share.

This chapter concentrates on the transition from the former view of segregation and identity preservation to the latter view of education as a tool for promoting reconciliation and understanding between communities in a state with multinational or conflicting identities. The lessons from Northern Ireland can best be understood as a transition from a singular system of segregated education toward a fragmented system coping with attempts at integration and reconciliation between two communities in a post-conflict scenario.

CONFLICT IN NORTHERN IRELAND

The history of conflict in Northern Ireland occupies a great deal of space in conflict resolution literature.[2] For the purposes of the discussion in this chapter it is useful to give a brief background to the conflict in Northern Ireland. The conflict is characterized by two distinct identities. The Nationalist/Republican identity is associated with the movement to end the partition of the island of Ireland that took place in the 1920s as a result of the Irish War of Independence and the resulting Treaty. The partition of Ireland after the War of Independence left a two-thirds majority in Northern Ireland, in which Roman Catholics comprising the minority of the population were in favor of Irish reunification, while the Protestant majority wished to remain under British rule. Encouraged by the Civil Rights Movement in the United States, the clash between the Protestant/Unionists and the Catholic/Nationalists came to a head in what is now referred to as "the Troubles." As a result of the ensuing violence the British government suspended the Northern Ireland parliament in 1971 and assumed direct rule.

As the Civil Rights Movement in the United States unfolded during the 1960s, a civil rights campaign emerged in Northern Ireland that focused largely on grievances concerning social injustices against Catholics in housing, employment and electoral issues. A series of protests and reaction by the state incited civil unrest in the late 1960s. This was followed by the deployment of the British Army in support of the local police, the Royal Ulster Constabulary (RUC). Although the initial role of the army was one of peacekeeping, the relationships between the security forces and the Catholic community quickly deteriorated. It was within this climate that paramilitary activity becomes increasingly evident, starting with the Irish Republican Army (IRA) organizing an armed campaign. The campaign of the IRA was based on its stated aim to bring about the end of the Northern Ireland state as a separate entity and have a single Irish state that included the six counties in the North. The campaign of the IRA, and smaller nationalist paramilitary groups such as the Irish National Liberation Army (INLA), has lasted for over 30 years. Republican/Nationalist insurrection has been accompanied by violence from Unionist/Loyalist paramilitary groups such as the Ulster Volunteer Force (UVF), the Ulster Freedom Fighters (UFF) and the Red Hand Commandos, the Loyalist Volunteer Force (LVF) and the Ulster Defence Association (UDA). Since 1969 more than 3,600 people have been killed as part of the Troubles in Northern Ireland.

The present population of Northern Ireland is approximately 1.5 million, the majority of whom are of Protestant denominations, but estimates based on the 1991 Census suggest that the Catholic population has risen to over 40 percent. Voting at elections in Northern Ireland corresponds closely to a pattern whereby most Catholics vote for Nationalist parties (which aspire to a single, united Ireland) and most Protestants vote for Unionist parties (which wish Northern Ireland to remain part of the United Kingdom).

The period after the outbreak of the Troubles was characterized by an ongoing struggle between the Loyalist and Republican paramilitaries and involving the British and Irish governments. After a lengthy period of conflict and negotiation between the various parties and governments, a significant step toward a sustainable peace was made with the declaration of a cease-fire and the signing of the Belfast/Good Friday Agreement in 1998, leading to the establishment of the Northern Ireland Assembly and a power-sharing Executive.[3] The new institutions remain fragile and sectarian violence continues, though at reduced levels.

As a result of political agreement, Northern Ireland provides an example of a conflict society that has achieved a relative degree of success in achieving a level of reconciliation through the containment of violent conflict embodied in the Good Friday/Belfast Agreement. John Darby's control model examined the reasons why Northern Ireland remained a low-intensity affair and concluded:

> that long familiarity with inter-community conflict within the North of Ireland has led to the evolution of effective control mechanisms to control it; that these mechanisms arise from the mundane and essentially local accommodations reached in their own localities...and that the efficiency and variety of these mechanisms hold the key to explaining why a conflict of such duration has not produced more serious levels of violence. They have amounted, so far, to a major and effective control against the conflict expanding into a genocidal war.[4]

A noteworthy feature of the Northern Ireland conflict is the existence of a narrow middle ground, that is, community efforts to breach the divide promulgated by paramilitaries. Cross-community contact contributes to maintaining this middle ground by promoting contact and communication between Catholics and Protestants. This is particularly important during episodes of heightened community tension. Cross-community contact can make it more difficult to "dehumanize" the other community. In this respect the cross-community activities may not have a direct impact that could claim to resolve the conflict, but it is tenable that, along with many other controls on the conflict, they have contributed to maintaining this narrow but vital middle ground in Northern Ireland. It is in this context that the contribution that education can make to the improvement of relationships between Catholics and Protestants in Northern Ireland has also become a focus for action.[5]

The history of Northern Ireland profoundly impacted on the development of the education system. Segregation existed prior to the Troubles and further resistance to integration was reinforced by the outbreak of violence in 1969. A range of approaches emerged from within the communities and from government agencies, and the interaction of these raises interesting questions about the relative merits of interventions in the structure and process of education.[6] The current education system in Northern Ireland is relatively small. Statutory education involves approximately 970 primary, 166 secondary and 70 grammar schools. The system is administered by a central Department of Education and five local authorities (known as Education and Library Boards). There also exists a statutory Council for Catholic Maintained Schools and the government provides funds for the Northern Ireland Council for Integrated Education (NICIE) to coordinate the development of a small but growing number of integrated schools (27 primary and 17 secondary in 1999). There are five basic categories for schools in Northern Ireland that include: *Controlled Schools, Catholic Maintained Schools, Other Maintained Schools, Voluntary Grammar* and *Grant Maintained Integrated Schools.* The majority of Protestant children in Northern Ireland attend state *Controlled Schools,* whilst the majority of Catholic children attend *Catholic Maintained Schools.* These are essentially Protestant and Catholic schools and provide for the bulk of the population. The other categories comprise a smaller percentage of the population, including *Other Maintained Schools* that are essentially Protestant schools managed by a Board of Governors and the *Voluntary Grammar Schools* that are owned by a Board of Trustees and also managed by a Board of Governors. The *Grant Maintained Integrated Schools* are essentially mixed schools, for Catholic and Protestant children. The education system also includes eight Irish language schools, some of which receive grant-aid from the government, and ten independent Christian schools associated with the Free Presbyterian Church that do not receive government funds.

As it stands segregated education continues to dominate the system in Northern Ireland with a majority of pupils attending mainly Protestant "controlled" or mainly Catholic "maintained" schools, most of which are also segregated by ability and some by gender. The system is segregated by religion; by ability (and some would argue social background) in that a selection system operates at age 11 to decide which children attend grammar schools (more than one-third of children in second-level education attend grammar schools); and often by gender (particularly in second-level education where a quarter of the secondary schools and almost half of all grammar schools are single sex). Only a small minority of pupils attend integrated schools where equal numbers of Protestant and Catholic pupils are educated together. Integrated schools are attended by approximately equal numbers of Catholic and Protestant children and, in terms of pupil enrolments, represent less than 3 percent of the school population.[7]

Education and Segregation

Education presents a paradox for those examining it with a view toward understanding conflict. In the first instance education can be perceived as a causal factor in conflict. Education can be used to preserve and in some ways promulgate an identity, concentrating on differences in socioeconomic status, language or nationality. Segregated schooling has an immediate impact on the contact between pupils from different traditions, hindering the possibility of reducing prejudices that lead to conflict. Furthermore, as Catholic and Protestant schools developed separately, school curriculum was affected by and contributed to the division in Northern Irish society. Catholic and Protestant schools conveyed historical and political issues to their students with a subjective approach to events.[8] Although the early work on the subject suggested that a definitive answer to the question was not possible, later research supported the belief that segregated schooling plays a contributory part in so far as significantly different activities were encouraged within the two sets of schools, ultimately encouraging a cultural apartheid. This cultural apartheid—the very separation of Catholic and Protestant children into different schools encouraged suspicion and developed group differences and tribal loyalties. Furthermore this social apartheid is enhanced by the culture of apartheid in each school, a phenomena referred to as a "hidden" curriculum. The hidden curriculum concerns itself with school values, rituals, group loyalties, peer influences and friendship patterns, which established a basis upon which society later builds a superstructure of political, demographic, recreational and social segregation.[9] Polarization between communities is further intensified at schools where the curriculum and contact between students represent the subject viewpoint of a particular community. Differences in curriculum content may contribute to the development of a sense of distinct, separate and adversarial identities.[10] Differences are compounded in the school by symbols that include rituals, flags and statues that may be taken for granted by one identity, but could make the other group feel ill at ease, because these symbols represented an alien culture.[11]

Equity issues form the foundation for understanding how the transition can occur in which education moves from being a dividing aspect of conflict to a positive influence on peace building. The first studies examining equity concentrated on the relative advantage and disadvantage between Catholics and Protestants.[12] Segregated schooling and structural issues over equality led to further polarization between communities as Catholic students were marginalized by a poorly resourced education system.[13] Attempts were made to explain the difference in education between the communities, including differences in school size and provision of specialist teaching space that contributed to consistently lower levels of recurrent funding for Catholic schools.[14] It was also implied that Catholic schools were less disposed to approach government for funding for historical and perceptual reasons.[15] Furthermore equity issues arose over the capital funding of Catholic schools. Traditionally the Catholic schools were run on a voluntary basis, making the trustees of the school responsible for the building and capital development of the schools. This changed prior to the outbreak of the Troubles, reaching a stage where Catholic voluntary schools received grants covering 85 percent of certain capital costs. Negotiations followed during the 1970s between the government and Catholic schools over further funding. Eventually agreements over higher funding from state sources were agreed to if the Catholic schools agreed to a reduction in representation on school management boards.

By the late 1980s several arguments contributed to further change in the level of capital funding for Catholic schools. The introduction of a statutory curriculum created a requirement for all schools by law to provide the same educational opportunities to their pupils. It was accepted that the differential in unemployment levels between Catholics and Protestants was partly linked to school provision, resulting in a political effort to address the problem of differential capital funding between schools. Catholic schools in Scotland were used as an example, citing that the arrangements there allowed 100 percent capital funding for integrated schools highlighting the possibility of a school with a particular identity being able to operate without its governing body being dominated by a single interest group. The outcome of these arguments was that the government, in consultation with the Catholic bishops, introduced a mechanism by which Catholic schools could opt for 100 percent capital funding and legislation to make this possible was enacted in 1993.[16]

In an effort to remove the disparity in education between communities the Education Reform (NI) Order 1989 included a provision for the local management of schools (LMS) whereby each school was allocated a recurrent budget. The budget was determined by a formula dependent on pupil numbers. It was hoped that this would help relieve some of the differences between the communities in regard to the funding of education. The act also took other steps to change the education situation in Northern Ireland, moving it from a divisive promoter of conflict in Northern Ireland to a contributor in seeking reconciliation between communities. The Education Reform (NI) Order 1989 included a number of provisions for the encouragement of the development of integrated schools, created a mechanism for funding and placed a statutory responsibility on government to support integrated education.

Education and Reconciliation

Since the Troubles, schools have been increasingly drawn into the spotlight in terms of how their activities take account of the conflict that is taking place within the wider society. This culminated in the introduction of new and significant initiatives, including legislation and government policies, which ascribe a more prominent role for schools in the improvement of relations between the two main communities in Northern Ireland. In broad terms, these policies support interventions in both the process of education (through curriculum reforms and associated intergroup contact) and the structure of education (through consideration of equity issues between existing schools and support for the creation of new, integrated schools).[17]

In practice three strategies were advanced to promote reconciliation through education.[18] The first involved curricular initiatives such as the Schools Curriculum Project, developed in the Queen's University of Belfast in 1973, and the Schools Cultural Studies Project, developed in the New University of Ulster in 1974.[19] These efforts laid the groundwork for a more comprehensive effort on the part of the Northern Ireland Council for Educational Development that produced guidelines for Education for Mutual Understanding (EMU) that included, among other things, community relations issues. The second strategy involved the development of integrated schools. Gallagher points out that all but two of the planned integrated schools are new schools, rather than old schools changing their status. In a period of falling school enrolments, with primary and secondary schools closing down it was much more difficult to open new schools without causing resentment.[20] The third strategy was to be incorporated in preexisting schools system, promoting interschool links with a view to promoting reconciliatory attitudes. Previous attempts were often ad hoc, relying on the involvement of a small number of motivated teachers for their success. A study based in the Centre for the Study of Conflict developed a model for interschool links that aimed to give the links a greater degree of permanence by institutionalizing them.[21]

Curriculum Changes

Although teachers and academics were active from the early seventies, the government in Northern Ireland was more hesitant and cautious about suggestions that schools should be involved with community relations issues. By the 1980s the Department of Education began to address community relations issues. The first public commitment on the part of government to community relations came from the 1982 production of a circular, *The Improvement of Community Relations: the Contribution of Schools.*[22] The publication signaled the beginning of formal government support for addressing community relations through education. Established in 1983, the Northern Ireland Council for Educational Development (NICED), a quasi-government curriculum development body, became involved in the issues of education and community relations. It began by establishing a committee with a brief to develop ideas about education that would be inclusive to both traditions in Northern Ireland. This approach would later earn the name, Education for Mutual Understanding (EMU).[23] The need for an educational program that would contribute toward improving community relations but could be delivered irrespective of what type of school an individual attended was the impetus for the creation of the EMU. The NICED committee appointed two field officers. It also produced a guide to the EMU for teachers that attempted to introduce schools to EMU activities both within and between schools.[24] This was followed and eventually superseded by the Education Reform (NI) Order, 1989. The Education Reform Order based its work on the EMU principles set out by the NICED, calling for two "cross-curricular themes" related to the issue of community relations, Education for Mutual Understanding and Cultural Heritage.[25] The statutory requirement to include these themes in the curriculum of all schools took effect from 1992 and the aims and objectives state that as an integral part of their education the themes should enable pupils "to learn to respect and value themselves and others; to appreciate the interdependence of people within society; to know about and understand what is shared as well as what is different about their cultural traditions; and to appreciate how conflict may be handled in non-violent ways."[26] The Education Reform (NI) Order, 1989 also placed a statutory responsibility on school governors to report annually to parents on steps taken to promote the EMU.

The aims and objectives of the EMU and Cultural Heritage gradually seeped into the overall schooling thereby forming an integral part of programs of study in all subjects, although there has been some criticism as to the extent to which some schools have adopted a "minimalist" approach to the EMU.[27] In addition it has become clear that many schools also see the aims being communicated less formally by the nature of relationships within the schools, and between the school and the wider community. In this sense many schools claim that the aims of the EMU are already implicit in their whole-school ethos. Whilst the themes are a mandatory feature of the curriculum, cross-community contact with pupils in other schools remains an optional strategy that teachers are encouraged to use. Although curriculum change has provided an opportunity for contact, changing the curriculum on its own cannot guarantee a wholesale change in attitudes or perceptions.

Integrated Education

The debate over integrated education became increasingly vociferous after the Troubles. In addition comparisons between the civil rights movement in the United States and Northern Ireland brought comparisons with the movement toward integrated education. Although this was an unlikely prospect in Northern Ireland immediately after the Troubles it did drive many to consider rethinking how segregated schooling had contributed to building opposing identities.

The first substantial research into integrated education developed out of the School Links project, a Ford Foundation Research Initiative that was published in 1977 as *Education and Community in Northern Ireland, Schools Apart?*[28] It attempted to understand the ways in which the two systems were different. The findings suggested that the development of integrated education was unlikely in the foreseeable future, but almost without exception, all those who were interviewed expressed some anxiety about the effects, or even just the possible effects, of complete segregation.[29] The second study, *Schools Together?* measured the amount of contact that existed between Catholic and Protestant Schools.[30] The results stated that little contact actually existed even though claims were made about contact and cooperation between the sectors.

The campaigning parent group All Children Together (ACT) established the first integrated school, Lagan College, in Belfast in 1981. In 1985 three more integrated schools opened in Belfast offering parents in the city an alternative choice to the existing segregated schools. Prior to this some schools were religiously mixed but where this happened it had more to do with local circumstances, and the religious mixing did not extend to governors or teaching staff. Individuals or independent groups carried out most of the studies and attempts at integration, which grew out of earlier notions about contact and segregated education. Meanwhile the British government was slow to enter the difficult subject of integrated education and its hesitancy was demonstrated by the late date in which government action was eventually taken in the 1980s with the formation of the NICIE.

Early attempts at bridging cross-community divides grew out of the aftermath of the Troubles. The beginnings of these developments came from committed individuals with a personal conviction that education and the indoctrination of identity contributed to misunderstandings related to the Troubles. In addition, although these early projects were conducted with a view of approaching primary- and second-level schools they were often conducted with the support of third-level institutions. The first and most notable of these developments was pursued by a Belfast school principal who persuaded the Northern Ireland Ministry of Education to fund a project on education and community relations.[31] The project was focused mainly on curriculum development and became based in Queen's University.

Following on from the initial success of the project run in Queen's University, two parallel projects were conducted with the guidance of the University of Ulster. The first of these explored a Social Science Curriculum that would be inclusive of all the identities in Northern Ireland, bridging the previous divide of segregated perspectives on the development of social and political history in Britain and Ireland. The second project focused on religious education based on respect and tolerance for diversity in religion with particular emphasis on the divide between the two major religious communities in Northern Ireland. Although neither project developed beyond its original small remit, both projects were pioneers in the area of religious and social education for understanding, establishing a context for future projects. These projects did not cover a large area and had little in the way of immediate impact upon the manner in which education was pursued in Northern Ireland. The significance of these early projects was that they formed the foundation for the work of the NICIE.

The NICIE, established in 1987 was to coordinate efforts to develop integrated education and to assist parent groups in opening new integrated schools. As a result of growing interest in integrated education outside of Belfast a total of ten integrated schools were established across Northern Ireland by 1989. The fact that the integrated movement both generated and funded its own central organizing Council, in addition to demonstrating significant numbers of enrolments at existing schools, contributed to a changed atmosphere in the political environment in the form of gradual government support.

The Education Reform (NI) Order, 1989 offered provision for Northern Ireland's existing schools to "transform" to integrated status, providing funding in the form of retrospective capital to integrated schools lifting much of the financial burden from parents and school officials. This allowed the officials to focus on developing schools that concentrated on promoting understanding and respect for pupils from different religious traditions. The NICIE began a consultation process with the existing integrated schools, resulting in an agreed Statement of Principles that continues to underpin the ethos and practice of integrated education ever since. The Statement of Principles provided for religious balance in pupil enrolments, teaching staff and governors. New schools would have to agree to these principles as a prerequisite of NICIE support and assistance.[32]

Although some progress has been made over the issue of integrated education, it continues to face many difficulties. Several factors inhibit the establishment of new integrated schools including strategic issues concerning a selective secondary education system, government financial constraints on capital development and the introduction of an "open enrolment" policy that may create difficulties for schools trying to manage equal representation of both communities. In lieu of these events there has been a significant shift away from establishing new integrated schools toward the "transformation" of existing schools to becoming more integrated. This has mainly involved existing "Protestant" schools trying to make the school more open and inclusive. Transforming the culture and ethos of these schools in this way is only beginning. The outcome of this transformation may be a sense of loss within the Protestant community of its schools whilst the Catholic sector remains largely intact due to Catholic commitments to provide a Catholic education. In the long term these commitments may have a negative impact on relations between the two communities.

ALTERNATIVE EDUCATION: INVOLVING THE COMMUNITY AND VOLUNTARY SECTOR

Although curriculum change and integration have led to some degree of understanding, there still remains a great deal of work in regard to the contribution of education to conflict resolution in Northern Ireland. The priority of the schools to deliver education, their ties to funding and ties to their respective communities act as a barrier to concentrated involvement in the role as peace builders. Instead Northern Ireland has witnessed the growth of an active voluntary and community sector that has taken up the role of facilitator between schools, thereby providing programs of interschool contact, mutual understanding and respect that some schools are restrained from pursuing due to constraints on funding and reservations on the part of school management. In this sense education becomes one part of a larger effort to manage conflict by promoting human security through nongovernmental, voluntary and community efforts.

The content of community relations programs involves the development of cross-community contact and cooperation between existing community groups, voluntary bodies and schools for the encouragement of mutual respect and understanding between the communities. Aspects of School Links programs have advanced to become a part of more focused reconciliation and conflict resolution work. There are three main forms of statutory support in Northern Ireland. These include: a special Central Community Relations Unit, established by government in 1987 to coordinate the programs, find community relations work and ensure government departments look at the community relations impact of all their policies; the Community Relations Council, a statutory body providing support and facilities for organizations operating at the local level to promote contact between the communities. Parallel to this work is a cultural traditions program to promote respect for local cultural diversity. The Council tries to ensure that issues of sectarianism and community relations are on the agenda of as many organizations or groups as possible. A further initiative has been the use of local district councils to improve community relations through funding for community relations officers. Despite some initial suspicion from Unionist councilors, all of the 26 councils now have community relations officers and programs. The objectives of this program are to develop cross-community contact, promote greater mutual understanding and increase respect for different cultural traditions.[33]

For the time being the status quo will largely remain with regard to integrated education. Education should be recognized as one part of a larger movement toward peace building in a post-conflict society. While the attempts to achieve equity, agreement on curriculum and explore the possibilities of integration, the voluntary and community sector continue to offer alternatives to education that could complement the current situation. It appears that the most valuable initiative may be to use a consultative process with school, youth and community groups asking them what they and others envisage "peace" to be and how they see a culture of reconciliation and tolerance being developed. This incorporates cooperation between the schools, government and nongovernmental actors promoting a broader sense of the impact of education on community relations.

CONCLUSION

There is a problem in evaluating any of the above strategies: it is by no means clear what are the best methods of promoting community relations in the short or longer terms.[34] In addition, the educational system does not

Peace building [handwritten marginal note]

exist in isolation from the rest of society in Northern Ireland. While the adult community continues to be characterized by political polarization and division, it may be unfair to foist the solving of the problem onto the shoulders of the children.[35] Peace building is the effort to promote human security in societies marked by conflict. The overarching goal of peace building is to strengthen the capacity of societies to manage conflict without violence, as a means to achieve sustainable human security.

The steps taken in Northern Ireland to achieve the foundation of an agreement between conflicting parties owes part of its success to a gradual bottom-up process that involves several actors. Education is a key actor in this development. The experience in Northern Ireland demonstrates that educational alternatives including peace building/bottom-up and ensuring equity in education must complement changes in curriculum and approaches to integration. At a local and regional level these are key factors in bringing about the resolution of conflict in Northern Ireland. Despite recent progress in Northern Ireland some problems remain and persist as sticking points to a definitive peace. Notwithstanding the emergence of a multitude of grassroots and community groups and the development of government-sponsored initiatives designed to encourage cross-community contact and involvement from the late 1980s onward, residential segregation is greater than ever. One of the more controversial moments for the newly devolved government in Stormont was the appointment of Martin McGuinness's, a central figure in the Republican Sinn Fein party, to the position as Secretary for Education. His choice of the position belies the importance that it plays in the conflict between Nationalists and Unionists. Additionally schools, particularly separate schools continue to be flashpoint between the conflicting communities, as was illustrated by recent tension surrounding the Holy Cross School in North Belfast. Although progress has been made education will have difficulty nurturing tolerance in a society that continues to suffer divisions. It is clear that in order to succeed, education must be one part of a larger organized effort to promote peace building in conflict and post-conflict societies.

NOTES

1. United Nations Development Programme, *Human Development Report* (New York/Oxford: United Nations Development Programme/Oxford University Press, 1994), pp. 22–24.
2. For more in-depth description of the background see John Darby, "Conflict in Northern Ireland: A Background Essay," in *Facets of the Conflict in Northern Ireland*, ed. Seamus Dunn (Gill and Macmillan, 1995).
3. Sean Hopkins, "'The Good Friday Agreement in Northern Ireland," *Politics Review*, 8, 3 (1999): 2–6.
4. John Darby, *Intimidation and the Control of the Conflict in Northern Ireland* (Dublin: Gill and Macmillan 1986).
5. Alan Smith, "Education in Northern Ireland," in *Facets of the Conflict in Northern Ireland*.

6. Alan Smith, "Education and the Peace Process in Northern Ireland," presented to the Annual Conference of the American Education Research Association (Montreal, April 1999).

7. http://cain.ulst.ac.uk/ni/educ.htm.

8. Sean Farren, "Education and National Identity in Northern Ireland," *Aspects of Education: Journal of the Institute of Education, University of Hull*, 54 (1997): 82.

9. John Darby et al., eds., *Education and Community in Northern Ireland: Schools Apart?* [and] *Schools Together?* (Coleraine: University of Ulster, 1989).

10. A good example of this is the difference in teaching languages: in Catholic grammar schools Irish is taught as part of the curriculum, however it is not a part of Protestant schools, which see it as the language of their adversary.

11. Murray holds that, regardless of similarities in what is taught in the schools, segregated schooling initiates children into the conflict by emphasizing and validating group differences and hostilities, and encouraging mutual ignorance and, perhaps more importantly mutual suspicion, see Dominic Murray "Identity: A Covert Pedagogy in Northern Irish Schools," *Irish Educational Studies*, 5, 2 (1985): 182–97.

12. In an effort to understand whether aspects of the segregated system of schooling had contributed to higher levels of unemployment amongst Catholics, the Standing Advisory Commission on Human Rights commissioned a number of research studies that investigated various explanations leading to research that identified underlying differentials in funding between Catholic and Protestant schools, see Standing Advisory Commission on Human Rights, *Annual Reports* (London: HMSO, 1989, 1990, 1991, 1992).

13. An unanticipated finding concerning recurrent funding revealed consistently higher levels of per capita funding in favor of Protestant pupils within primary, secondary and grammar schools, see Osborne, Robert D., Cormack R. J. and A. M. Gallagher, "The Funding of Northern Ireland's Segregated Education System," *Administration: Journal of the Institute of Public Administration of Ireland*, 40:4, (1992/1993): 316–32.

14. Robert Osborne, Robert Cormack, and Anthony Gallagher, eds., *After the Reforms: Education and Policy in Northern Ireland* (Newcastle upon Tyne: Ashgate Publishing Ltd, 1993).

15. Dominic Murray, "Identity," pp. 182–97.

16. Robert Osborne, Robert Cormack, and Anthony Gallagher, eds., *After the Reforms: Education and Policy in Northern Ireland* (Newcastle upon Tyne: Ashgate Publishing Ltd, 1993).

17. Alan Smith, "Education in Northern Ireland."

18. Seamus Dunn first highlighted these strategies in Seamus Dunn, *Education and the Conflict in Northern Ireland: A Guide to the Literature* (Coleraine: University of Ulster, Centre for the Study of Conflict, 1986).

19. See J. Malone, "Schools and Community Relations," *The Northern Teacher*, 11, 1 (1973): 19–30.

20. A. M. Gallagher, *Education in a Divided Society: A Review of Research and Policy* (Dublin: Gill and Macmillan, 1995).

21. This project, involving primary and post-primary schools in a small market-town in the west of the province, was supported by the Western Education and Library Board see Seamus Dunn and Alan Smith, *Inter School Links* (Coleraine: Centre for the Study of Conflict, University of Ulster, 1989).

22. "Every teacher, every school manager, Board member and trustee, and every educational administrator within the system has a responsibility for helping children learn to understand and respect each other." Northern Ireland, Department of Education, *The Improvement of Community Relations: the Contribution of Schools* (DENI: Circular 1982/21).

23. The EMU "Education for Mutual Understanding is about self-respect and respect for others, and the improvement of relationships between people of differing cultural traditions."

24. Northern Ireland Council for Educational Development, *Education for Mutual Understanding—A Guide* (Belfast: NICED, 1988).

25. Common History (1990) and Religious Education (1993) curricula were introduced as compulsory elements of the Northern Ireland Curriculum, as were the cross-curricular themes Education for Mutual Understanding and Cultural Heritage (1992).

26. Northern Ireland Curriculum Council, *Cross-curricular Themes—Guidance Materials* (Belfast: NICC, 1990).

27. Alan Smith, "Education and the Peace Process in Northern Ireland."

28. John Darby et al., *Education and Community in Northern Ireland, Schools Apart?* (Coleraine: University of Ulster, 1977).

29. Alan Smith, "Education in Northern Ireland."

30. Seamus Dunn et al., *Schools Together?* (Coleraine: Centre for the Study of Conflict, University of Ulster, 1984).

31. J. Malone, "Schools and Community Relations," p. 1.

32. Alan Smith and Seamus Dunn, *Extending Inter School Links: An Evaluation of Contact Between Protestant and Catholic Pupils in Northern Ireland* (Coleraine: Centre for the Study of Conflict, University of Ulster, 1990).

33. Derek Birrell, "Social Policy Responses to Urban Violence in Northern Ireland," in Seamus Dunn, ed., *Managing Divided Cities* (Keele: Keele University Press, 1994).

34. A. M. Gallagher, *Education in a Divided Society.*

35. Ed Cairns, *Caught in Crossfire: Children and the Northern Ireland Conflict* (Belfast: Appletree, 1987).

10

Education and Human Security in Sierra Leone: Discourses of Failure and Reconstruction[1]

Robert Krech and Richard Maclure

Introduction

Sierra Leone's recent decade-long civil war was remarkable not only for the horrific and often seemingly random violence perpetrated on civilian populations, but as well for the large-scale involvement of children and youth as armed participants in the conflict. In considering the underlying and proximate factors that led to the complete collapse of human security and the engagement of children as combatants and victims in this conflict, it is clear that the role of education was both significant and complex. Indeed, as a system inextricably linked to a failed state, public education is widely regarded as having contributed to the deterioration of human security in Sierra Leone and to the extraordinary participation of children in conflict. Yet after 11 years of conflict, and with the country struggling to come to terms with its nationwide civic trauma and with the enormous challenge of social and institutional reconstruction, education is now ironically regarded as playing an important role in fostering peace building and national reconciliation. Hopes for education today in many respects mirror similar aspirations and expectations that underscored educational expansion during the years following Sierra Leone's independence.

These contradictory perspectives—of education as a failure and a causal factor of children's involvement in war, and now as a key instrument for national reconstruction—are problematic, largely because they hinge on deterministic notions of education as an autonomous force for change. In this chapter we argue that education in the context of Sierra Leone has been, and continues to be, highly constrained by political, economic, and ideological forces that are national and international in scope. As such, the nature and effects of education are complex and must be examined not as discrete phenomena that are inherent to a particular system or institution, but rather consist of an accumulation of characteristics and events that derive directly from these overriding forces. From this perspective we examine the relationship between education and the breakdown of human security in Sierra Leone, and the more recent international efforts to support education as a basis for the reinstatement of human security in the current post-conflict circumstances. Before discussing the particular case of Sierra Leone, however, we briefly review changing discourses of education in developing countries and how these discourses relate to both the breakdown and the reconstruction of human security.

THE EVOLVING RELATION BETWEEN EDUCATION AND HUMAN SECURITY IN DEVELOPING COUNTRIES

From the early 1960s to approximately the mid-1980s, a set of clearly articulated assumptions helped foster a remarkable consensus about the importance of publicly funded and managed national education systems. Education was widely accepted as a critical investment in human capital formation and subsequent economic growth and in the formation of national citizenries having common allegiance to the nation-state. During this period, therefore, governments generally invested heavily in systems of public schooling. Such investments were also undertaken in response to popular demand, for families and communities increasingly came to regard formal schooling as a significant channel for enhancing their children's long-term economic and social security. Up until the mid-1980s, a commonly accepted principle was that the enrolment of children in state-sponsored schools offered families the prospects of significant financial and social rewards in a world that was clearly changing. Among children and parents alike, it was generally assumed that the further youngsters advanced through the school system, the greater were their opportunities for attaining employment in the public sector or in the modern industrialized private sector.[2]

Yet by the mid-1980s the public and private aspirations attached to national education systems had begun to appear hollow in much of the developing world, particularly in Africa. Far from being a cohesive institutional mechanism for inducing planned social change, it had become apparent that education was profoundly affected—and constrained—by prevailing forms of societal governance. The notion of education as an investment in human capital development was being undermined by widespread evidence of poor quality, irrelevance, and waste, and by the failure of national, political economies to ensure full and effective _utilization_ of human capital. With the phenomena of educated unemployment and underemployment, popular convictions about long-term occupational rewards and personal fulfillment that were supposed to follow from education were dissipating and were being replaced by widespread school leaver disillusion and frustration. Likewise, as the fiscal solvency of many governments declined in the wake of global economic recession and the imposition of structural adjustment programs in the 1980s, it became clear that education systems could no longer be sustained through public expenditures. Invariably this led to the incipient privatization of education as families had to absorb greater costs of erstwhile?

schooling. Inevitably, too, the ideal of education as a means of fostering social equity and enhancing socioeconomic mobility was negated by the increasingly transparent role of education in reinforcing and reproducing entrenched social and economic divisions. In many countries, education was functioning much more as a selective mechanism of human screening than it was as a form of human resources development. By the late 1980s, throughout much of the developing world, the erstwhile function of education as a form of state legitimation was overshadowed by its status as the embodiment of flawed and fragile states. Indeed, the weaknesses of national education systems underscored the flaws of state-centered development strategies and the declining legitimacy of many central states.[4]

Coinciding with concerns about the incapacity of national education systems to engender national economic growth and a common adherence to the nation-state, the global community began to pay increasing heed to the insecurities of intra-national tensions and outbreaks of armed conflict within national boundaries. Since the end of World War II, in fact, the majority of major conflicts have been *within* rather than *between* nation-states. Yet such intra-national civil wars became even more pronounced following the end of the Cold War in 1989. Many of these conflicts could no longer be contained by erstwhile Cold War support for numerous debt-ridden, delegitimized states.[5] Particularly disturbing has been the severe harm that most such civil conflicts have inflicted on unarmed women and children.[6] According to some observers, among whom Kaplan is probably the best known, the eruption of civil strife in many parts of the developing world is an indication of the resurrection of premodern tribalism and ethnic rivalry that has generated a corresponding descent into social chaos.[7] Yet a growing body of scholarly literature has rejected this type of reductionist claim. Instead of explanations that point to generealizable or "traditional" causes of contemporary civil wars, it is becoming increasingly apparent that the breakdown of human security in developing countries is often the result of severe impoverishment and socio-economic disparity that have been exacerbated by globally induced factors such as market deregulation, structural adjustment programs, state corruption, and the politics of foreign aid. In such contexts, the struggle for power and legitimacy tends to shift away from institutions of the state and tend to be diffused among other non-state actors. Most prominent among these are traditional ethnic and religious leaders, erstwhile soldiers transformed into warlords, and private entrepreneurs.

In order to finance and sustain the struggle for power, competing national actors invariably have sought assistance from a host of international sources. These usually include foreign governments, private corporations, criminal networks, and donor agencies, all with diverse and frequently competing agendas that impinge on the processes and outcomes of civil strife. Invariably, too, in contexts where the authority of central states has dissipated, and where the struggle for power and legitimacy has become increasingly fluid and involves a multitude of alliances among diverse national and international interests, the propensity for violence and the breakdown of human security has increased.[8] In such circumstances, weapons tend to be dispersed among civilian populations and the new brokers of power work to fan and exploit sources of disenchantment and frustration among local groups. As has become evident in the last decade, children and youth are particularly vulnerable to this type of violent exploitation, not only as victims of violence, but also as perpetrators of violence. The phenomenon of child soldiery has thus become a disturbing feature of many civil conflicts.

That so many children and young adolescents have been drawn into violent conflicts has raised concerns about the nature of education in societies that have been prone to lapse into fratricidal conflict, and about the apparent causal connection between frustrated educational aspirations of many youth, and subsequent manifestations of youth anger and organized youth violence. In addition, however, despite the evident failure of national education systems to live up to hoary ideals as instruments of social engineering and national development, there is growing attention to the ideal of education as a basis for alleviating the effects of violent civil conflict. From this perspective civil wars are now commonly regarded as complex humanitarian emergencies, in large part because of the effects that such conflicts have on unprotected and highly vulnerable civilian populations.[9] Depicted as multidimensional crises that almost always result in "some combination of mass population movement, severe food insecurity, macro-economic collapse, and acute civil and military conflict including genocide,"[10] complex humanitarian emergencies are invariably intertwined with a complete breakdown of human security.

In response to such crises, the diverse international community of UN organizations, bilateral foreign aid agencies, NGOs, and human rights groups are now generally quick to collaborate in mobilizing resources for humanitarian relief. Until recently, such relief was widely assumed to be oriented toward the alleviation of physical needs. Responses to emergencies, therefore, typically involved obvious life-saving measures such as water supply and sanitation, food aid, shelter, and primary health care.[11] Increasingly, however, in accordance with the UN Convention on the Rights of the Child that was formally adopted in 1989, education is now widely accepted as a fundamental right as well as a basic need for the balanced psychosocial development of all children, including all those who have been displaced and otherwise victimized by war. This was recently reinforced at the 2000 World Education Forum in Dakar.[12]

Within the last decade, therefore, alongside the long-standing discourse of education for development which, as we have noted, has been the target of substantial criticism, has emerged the interrelated concepts of education as humanitarian relief and education as a force for peaceful reconciliation and social reconstruction. As relatively short-term humanitarian relief, educational interventions are regarded as being essential to bolster human security and the overall well-being of children in the immediate aftermath of traumatic conflict. In operational terms, rapid emergency education programs, which have most often been targeted toward children in camps set up temporarily for refugees and internally displaced people, are managed by international donor agencies that provide packages of pedagogical and recreational materials, and often short-term training of rapid education teachers as well. The main purpose of emergency education programs is to help traumatized children to settle immediately into a structured learning environment. This is regarded as crucial for normaliz*and* ing stressful situations following the disruption of family and social life, and for helping children to develop coping strategies that will facilitate confidence building and emotional security. Likewise, education as humanitarian relief is seen as a way to protect children from various forms of exploitation to which they are easily exposed as a result of their vulnerability.[13] In these circumstances, rapid humanitarian education usually consists of basic literacy and numeracy, as well as subjects related to the awareness of environmental and health hazards, and the rudiments of peaceful conflict resolution.[14]

For longer-term rehabilitation, the notion of education for reconstruction is now also regarded as essential for societies that have been severely disrupted by civil conflict. This of course is a much longer-term process that involves the rebuilding and refurbishing of schools, the retraining of teachers, the development of new curricula with heavy emphasis on peace education, and the production and distribution of new teaching and learning materials. As it is widely conceptualized, education as a force for social reconstruction is an alternative form of investment, one that focuses on the psychological rehabilitation and eventual reintegration of former child combatants and other war affected children and youth into new productive and socially accepted roles.[15] In effect it is an investment in the development of long-lasting human security.

What we have outlined here are two quite distinctive discourses of education in developing countries. From one perspective, education is viewed as having not only failed to live up to early promises of facilitating economic growth and equitable national development, but as having given rise to widespread youth disillusion and anger with the existing structural status quo. From another perspective, however, education continues to be regarded as a *yet,* benign force that is essential for the peaceful reconstruction of societies that *the* have been torn apart by severe civil strife. In our view, however, both these *author's* contradictory perspectives are simplistic, emphasizing the capacity of educational systems to function as independent catalysts of dramatic change, but failing to capture the essence of national education systems as dependent on the dynamics of the political economies in which they are situated. The case of Sierra Leone, to which we now turn, offers an illustration of the misplaced hopes that have been—and continue to be—heavily invested in education as a force for the guarantee of human security in a fragile sociopolitical and economic context. *perspective #1*

The Collapse of Human Security in Sierra Leone: Education and Unemployment

Siaka Stevens and Joseph Momoh

Sierra Leone was established as a British colony in 1808, and for the next century and a half it served primarily as an exporter of raw materials to the metropolitan power. In 1961, in line with Britain's commitment to disengage from the vestiges of empire, Sierra Leone attained its formal independence. From the outset, however, burdened with the legacy of indirect rule that had privileged a small number of indigenous elites and an undiversified economy based on monopoly-owned commercial and mining enterprises, Sierra Leone was a profoundly weak state.[16] In 1967 Siaka Stevens gained the reins of power, and over the next 25 years the state was transformed into a kleptocratic regime that functioned essentially to reinforce Stevens's control over the country's economic resources. As head of what has been characterized as a "shadow state," Stevens's economic and political perfidy was extensive.[17] In conjunction with a handful of associates, he "privatized" the most lucrative sectors of the national economy and gained tight control over the production and sale of diamonds, oil, and rice. Competition and the development of new industries beyond Stevens's control were stifled and political authority was maintained through an elaborate patronage network. Although an estimated 80 percent of Sierra Leone's population lived in rural areas, rural development under Stevens's administration was ignored. Cash crops were underpriced by the government and little was done to extend electricity, potable water, or road networks to rural regions.[18] Given the personalization of central power, state institutions were enfeebled and Sierra Leone's economy remained as undiversified as it had been during the colonial era.

By the early 1980s, despite its abundant natural resources and a large pool of human capital, Sierra Leone had entered a period of acute economic crisis. It was clearly unprepared to withstand the impacts of the oil shocks during the mid-1970s and the subsequent global recession of the early 1980s. As the costs of fuel and imported manufactured products rose and prices for raw commodities declined, the value of Sierra Leone's currency dropped. Inevitably these shocks exacerbated the impoverishment of the vast majority of Sierra Leone's population. In order to relieve pressure on the prevailing system of clientelist government, Stevens increasingly relied on foreign aid to help pay his clients and maintain the bare minimum of state structures that legitimized government by patronage. This necessarily reduced the available revenue for developing the state institutions, resulting in a decline in state spending on health and education by 60 percent, and all the while generated a growing national debt.[19]

In 1985 Stevens resigned from the presidency. Unfortunately, his successor as dictator-president, Joseph Momoh, made little attempt to alter practices of clientelism and primitive accumulation that had been entrenched during Stevens's regime. Yet with Sierra Leone's impoverishment and growing international indebtedness, Momoh did not have the unbridled discretionary authority of his predecessor. Instead, under pressure from the International Monetary Fund (IMF) and the World Bank, he was forced to begin an ostensible process of fiscal and bureaucratic reform as a conditionality of much needed international loans. This entailed a dramatic downsizing of the state that had become the largest employer in the country. By 1994, 15,000 government employees (40 percent of the public service) had been laid off and the mood of Sierra Leone's population had become deeply embittered.[20]

The Education System: Exemplifying State Failure

In this context of crumbling political and economic vitality, Sierra Leone's education system is clearly perceived as integral to the wider failings of human security. Beginning under British colonial rule, Sierra Leone's education system consisted of schools largely established by Christian missionaries to spread the gospel and to create a local comprador class that would be inured to British manners and taste and would assume jobs as teachers, clergy, and low-level administrators. Inevitably, as cadres of school graduates became implicated in the administration of British indirect rule, schools in Freetown and in the interior became instruments of indigenous elite formation. At the time of Sierra Leone's independence, the school system was a prototype colonial academy, skilled at producing cohorts of elite urban functionaries attuned to interests and *mores* that had emanated from the colonial power rather than from the societies of the indigenous population. Yet as such, for a new and untested national government, the school system was ill-suited to be transformed into a system of mass education capable of adjusting to the cultural and linguistic differentiation of diverse local people. Nor, because of its colonial heritage, was it aligned with the complex and multitudinous developmental needs of the country.[21]

Nevertheless, over the next three decades the school system expanded steadily, in large part because of the universally accepted rationale that education was a long-term investment in the modernization of the country and a means by which families—particularly those members who completed their schooling—could achieve a degree of socioeconomic mobility. This perspective of the public and private gains from education was reinforced by numerous international aid agencies that were keen to assist in Sierra Leone's human resource development.[22] Unfortunately, however, the structure and content of the system remained essentially unchanged. For three decades after formal independence until the descent into civil war, Sierra Leone's formal educational system retained its elitist, precolonial character, emphasizing a system of rote teaching and learning that terminated with a series of final examinations designed to select a relatively small proportion of individuals for further schooling and hence for the promise of economic advancement and improved social status.

Securing our schools.

he events that took place at this time + in concluding that.

School curricula bore little relation to the sociocultural backgrounds of most pupils, nor to the immediate socioeconomic realities that confronted children who left schooling either prematurely or with school certificates. Yet confidence in the system remained remarkably steadfast until at least the late 1970s, mainly because of the widespread assumption that Sierra Leone's formal economy would grow to accommodate school graduates, and that agriculture would remain sufficiently large and productive to absorb young people with minimal or no education.[23] Consequently, although sporadic efforts were made to reform the system through the introduction and expansion of more technical and vocational options that might match burgeoning sectors of production and employment possibilities, there was neither popular demand nor political will to sustain fundamental educational reform.

By the early 1980s, however, it had become apparent that the school system itself was unable to live up to expectations of being both an engine of growth and a vehicle for social mobility.[24] While the education system had steadily expanded and had received public resources that were second in volume only to military spending, vast numbers of children were still unable to gain access to school. Indeed, by the late 1980s, only 59 percent of eligible children were enrolled in schools and the illiteracy rate stood at 80 percent.[25] For many children the promise of future advancement via schooling was therefore denied to them. Qualitatively the system was also replete with deficiencies. Not only was the hoary academic, examination-oriented curriculum unable to provide skills and knowledge for even middle-level labor needs, but growing numbers of students were dropping prematurely out of school as well, often because of their poor academic achievement or their inability to adjust to a frequently harsh authoritarian school environment.

With the government unable to sustain the increasing financial burden of the system, and with the imposition of structural adjustment measures designed to scale back public expenditures, the costs of sending children to school began to devolve onto families. Payment of school fees, uniforms, and books and other sundry school materials became normative household expenditures. This increase in the private costs of schooling penalized poor, mostly rural households, and thus had the effect of exacerbating the role of schooling as an agent of socioeconomic stratification that favored an affluent few.[26]

In a social climate that had engendered among children and youth the perception that farming was a demeaning occupation and that with even some education they were entitled to the rewards of public sector jobs and corresponding heightened social status, the dysfunction between schooling and subsequent employment opportunities became a source of deepening disillusionment.[27] Added to this sense of injustice was an increasing perception among secondary and university students that in light of what was widely recognized as gross misappropriation of resources by those in power, the most senior government officials were working against their interests.[28] In effect, therefore, for growing numbers of youth who had never had access to school, or who had been forced to drop out of school, or who graduated from school but found themselves without the corresponding status and rewards they had come to expect, it was not education per se that was the source of their disillusion and anger, but rather the failed *promises* of education. Fully aware of the interests of a rapacious governing elite, many children and adolescents were thus only too willing to demonstrate resistance and outrage.

Start here

HUMAN SECURITY, EDUCATION, AND CHILD SOLDIERY IN SIERRA LEONE: A CAUSE-EFFECT RELATION?

With the gross appropriation of Sierra Leone's political opportunities and theft of economic resources in combination with an exclusive and irrelevant education system, it is not surprising that so many youth were drawn into the conflict that broke out between the RUF and the government of Sierra Leone. Paul Collier dismisses pure grievance as a cause of war, citing economic opportunity instead as the more potent driver of conflict,[29] but Sierra Leone's case challenges this finding in favor of a more sophisticated explanation for why children participated in the conflict. Although numerous children were abducted and otherwise forcibly conscripted into participating in the conflict through brutal physical and psychological means, there were nonetheless many children and youth who fought and participated voluntarily in brutal attacks on defenseless victims.[30] Reasons for such participation have been recognized as varied and complex. As Bangara states:

> [T]he combatants themselves [were] pulled by a complex of contradictory forces: the pursuit of the long-standing goals of political liberation; the opportunities which war provided to loot the resources of the forest and the property of villagers for personal and collective gain; a "lumpen" type of unaccountable, free-wheeling behaviour, which drugs and other anti-social behaviour-inducing mechanisms have generated or sustained.[31]

Most significantly, a lack of educational opportunity and being denied a voice in local level decision-making is also identified as a cause of youth involvement in violence. David Keen quotes a Catholic Relief Services staff who states,

> The educational system has increased rebel and soldier numbers. A lot drop out of school early, and these do not have fair job opportunities. And having gone to school, they do not want to go back to their villages and till the land. They feel their friends will laugh at them, and say you are still farming even though you went off to school. They saw that being a rebel you can loot at will, then you have a sway over your former master, who used to lord it over you, or the others who might have laughed. You might as well go to the bush and become a rebel. There is no master there.[32]

Keen continues by saying that "abuse by youth in SLA and RUF forces can be explained as reflecting the deep resentment of young men denied a substantial role or status within their communities. Teenage fighters repeatedly humiliated chiefs and local 'big men'. Violence such as this may have aimed to heal what Nigerian writer Femi Osofisan has called the 'wound of invisibility.' "[33] Either excluded from education altogether, or denied opportunities to obtain jobs and to participate in local and national power arrangements that they had come to expect as the fruits of their schooling, the grievance of youth was easily exploited by unscrupulous greedy leaders such as Foday Sankoh. It seems that on some level, the RUF and other fighting forces attracted youth because war offered the potential of a better life with more respect than what national and local leaders could offer.[34] As Abdullah and Muana have indicated, by tapping into widespread youth alienation, the RUF was able to offer a "simplistic political analysis" to many such youth who were seemingly convinced.

> The RUF's consistent "political" message to recruits was simply that the country was immensely rich in mineral wealth, controlled by a few Lebanese and business men with political connections, that the time for reasoned debate had passed, and that lasting solutions to the country's chronic economic and political problems could be found only through an explosion of destructive violence.[35]

What is clear, then, is that vast numbers of children and youth were overcome by dislocated social identities and by deep-seated outrage. Underdeveloped and in need of imaginative reforms as far back as the early 1960s, Sierra Leone's fragile educational system was entirely undermined—as was the political economy of the country as a whole—by a rapacious kleptocratic "government." Ultimately the educational system—established as a state institution—failed because a strong representative state was never established in Sierra Leone. Instead, a predatory "shadow state" functioned on the basis of primitive accumulation and clientelist patronage. A viable educational system, especially one that was inherently weak to begin with, could not possibly function effectively in such a context.

EDUCATION IN POST-CONFLICT SIERRA LEONE: AGENT OF HUMAN SECURITY OR RELAPSE OF MISPLACED ASSUMPTIONS?

Reintegration of both former adult and child combatants, in part through education, has been recognized as essential to sustainable peace building by the United Nations since the beginning of the 1990s.[36] Reintegrating child soldiers has a practical history in aid agency programs operating as part of peace-building efforts in Mozambique, Uganda, El Salvador, and Liberia, and largely focuses on family reunification, education support, and support for finding employment, along with meeting psychosocial needs.[37] While the Convention on the Rights of the Child (CRC) guides reintegration "theory" for children, the literature for children shares a concern with the wider literature on adult reintegration, that children receive education so as to become "constructive members of civil society" and gain employment.[38] Education, employment, and economic security of the children's family is said to be linked to successful social reintegration and preventing re-recruitment,[39] and is also said to be integral to normalizing children and providing them with a new context and a new identity apart from that of a combatant.[40]

This thinking on reintegration for peace building has permeated the international response for children in Sierra Leone. This response has been coordinated by the UNICEF, who as the lead agency in reintegrating child combatants, has championed education as integral to their reintegration resulting in a fairly uniform programatic approach to child reintegration among the NGOs.[41] In its relationship with the Ministry of Youth, Education, and Sports (MYES) and often through the NGOs, UNICEF's Education Sector has supported the rehabilitation of schools (i.e. rebuilding schools, and restocking them with furniture, teaching and learning materials, and staff), and three main emergency education programs: the Rapid Response Education Programme (RREP) provides children with six months of intensive schooling to "catch them up" and assist with their reinsertion into the regular system; the Complimentary Remedial Education for Primary Schooling (CREPS) provides six years of primary schooling compressed into three, aimed at children older than primary school age to allow them to gain what they missed; and the Community Education Investment Programme (CEIP) is a program that provides teaching, learning, or recreation materials to schools that admit former child combatants to classes waiving their school fees.

With UNICEF support, the MYES reforms to schooling have resulted in a clear policy on the curriculum and structure of education in Sierra Leone that emerged from intensive consultations with international education experts. Reforms are intended to counter the colonial roots of Sierra Leone's education system by creating a curriculum with a distinct vocational stream of equal status to the academic stream to produce "middle level skills" such as mechanics, electricians, masons, contractors, and the like in addition to supporting the Education For All (EFA) goals of free and compulsory quality basic education. Primary schooling was also shortened by one year to help more students graduate quicker, and so reduce the drop-out and failure-to-access rates, increase literacy, and increase skilled labor. As told in interviews, many people in the MYES believe strongly the education system failed Sierra Leone's children and youth, and apportion blame on themselves for the anger and marginalization of youth.[42]

Education and the Discourse of Reconstruction

Amidst this array of international and national educational responses, three lines of thought under girding the discourse of reconstruction emerged regarding why education is critical to reintegrating former child combatants and so build peace. The first line of thought, most notably from the UNICEF and international NGOs, is a rights-based discourse that children have a right to education and education is in the best interests of the child (for their healthy development, and to create stability and normalcy for the child and community after the conflict).[43] The second line of thought, one less discussed, is more pragmatic wherein children are viewed as a security risk both prior to becoming soldiers and after demobilization. Even during the tenuous months of post-conflict settlement, children were still considered at risk of recruitment into an armed force if they were idle on the streets or in their villages. Children who were unable to afford schooling, who were school leavers (drop-outs or fail-outs), or graduates with no employment became idle and involved in what some agencies called "antisocial behavior" such as crime, drug use, prostitution, exploitive labor, and street violence. Involvement in such behavior is said to increase their vulnerability and risk of recruitment and abduction. In a similar fashion, child combatants though regarded on the one hand as victims, are also regarded as having enormous potential for violence. School is then said to occupy children so they do not become a security risk.[44]

The almost inviolable claim of the child's right to education can be seen to coalesce with the thinking on children as a security risk to support the idea that education or schooling would prepare children for their future, giving them new identities as productive citizens by replacing the gun with a pencil (or hammer, or other trade tool). Recognizing the right to education and the need to occupy children, international aid agencies and the Government of Sierra Leone (with the help of such agencies) operationalized these mutually supportive lines of thought within Sierra Leone through emergency education programs, and also in the MYES' reforms of the formal education system along the lines of EFA goals and new vocational curricula. These discursive practices institutionalized the idea that education would help children prepare for their futures, making emergency education necessary for reintegration. They likewise made education reforms to address the illiteracy, exclusion, and irrelevant schooling plaguing Sierra Leone's education system necessary for renewed long-term development that would hopefully prevent future violent conflict. The clear desire from Sierra Leone's children and youth for education has only served to justify this broad conviction.[45]

The coalescence of these two lines of thought produced a third line of thinking, that education interventions in Sierra Leone reflect what was realistically programable and fundable given the constraints of donor funding frameworks in Sierra Leone's emergency and transition.[46] As reported at an interagency meeting on reintegration held in Freetown, Sierra Leone in April 2002, the NGOs complained that there was little available economic baseline data to correlate Sierra Leone's emerging post-conflict labor/employment needs with education and training programs. Arguably this suggests that emergency education and reconstruction programs are guided less by rigoros evidence associated with peace building or future development, but instead represents a systemic logic inherent certainly in emergency programing but also in development aid. The dominance of the "input–output" measurable results model of programing poses the threat of further reinforcing the necessity of emergency education and education for reconstruction in their current programatic forms and latent discursive logic.[47])

At least two implications for these lines of thought comprising the discourse of education for reconstruction in Sierra Leone's post-conflict period are evident. Foremost, emergency education and education for reconstruction in Sierra Leone appears to be an iterative process where education is both an agent of social reconstruction and an object of reconstruction itself, largely by means of outside financial and technical resources. This is evident in the lines of thinking that education is necessary for peace building because it is a child's right, is a solution to security threats, but especially that education helps prepare children for their futures. As a response to the trauma and victimization so many children experienced in Sierra Leone, children benefited from emergency education. But simultaneously, international agencies are investing financial and technical resources in reconstructing the education system, which will ideally in turn assist with reconstructing Sierra Leone's war-torn society.

This first implication suggests a second one, which itself stems from the line of thinking that education interventions reflect the exigencies of what is programable and fundable in a post-conflict emergency and transition. Superficially, there is a risk of implementing emergency education and education for reconstruction in a kind of narrow "recipe" format that may not live up to the ideal of "empowering" youth, with the reconstructed education system falling back into the old pre-conflict model of a hierarchical formal school system geared mainly to academic learning and exam success despite the current reform efforts. On a deeper level, given that external aid agencies have become major players in Sierra Leone's reconstruction process, their relationship with each other, the reemergent state, and local communities must be carefully articulated. This is a pertinent issue in light of Sierra Leone's conflict as the contemporary role of aid agencies in fostering education as a form of peace building must be reconciled with the historic role these same agencies have had in supporting systems of education underlying competitive, market-oriented capitalism. The suggestion then with regards to these implications is that while efforts to establish education more firmly as a valid and legitimate part of emergency response are necessary, practitioners in the field of emergency education and education for reconstruction should be critical practitioners. This means probing the poorly understood issue of how education actually builds peace without getting lost in the logic of the aforementioned discourses or the urgency of the technical questions of implementation.

CONCLUSION

The relation between the pre-conflict school system and the breakdown of human security that led to the civil war was evident but ambiguous. For although education was a factor strongly underlying youth disenchantment, it is erroneous to regard education per se as a direct causal factor of open conflict. Instead, for some children education was irrelevant, for others it did not live up to what they had assumed was the promise of what it could deliver, and still for others it represented a service that was denied to them. While clearly a source of youth frustration and disillusion, the school system in Sierra Leone was itself undermined from the very start by larger forces upon which it depended for its structure, scope, and orientation. In Sierra Leone, the patrimonial "shadow" state created by Stevens and reproduced by his successor Momoh was so corrupt that at best it failed to facilitate development and at worst spoke the unfulfilled promise of education that generated frustration and wrath that—in a climate of structural violence—left children and youth vulnerable to the breakdown of human security.

Eleven years later, the discourse of education as an agent of post-conflict rehabilitation and reconstruction has become prominent in Sierra Leone. Education is now seen as the basis for reestablishing human security in the aftermath of a hideous civil war. So far, however, little is known about how such an education "system" is developed and sustained, especially when trauma has severely disrupted an entire society, and when the government itself is having to be "reconstructed." What we fear in examining the case of Sierra Leone's civil conflict is that the discourses that drove emergency education and education for reconstruction in Sierra Leone embody the same assumptions that continue to pervade development education. The assumptions that education would modernize the postcolonial African state has produced fragmented and questionable results. Despite the obvious innovations in education interventions in emergencies and reconstruction, these interventions seem to function as stop-gap measures until development education can resume. Sierra Leone has never experienced state-led education for development, and it is uncertain if it ever will unless Sierra Leone's leaders accompany education reforms with responsible governance that can capitalize on that country's abundant natural and human resources.

In sum, just as the discourse of pre-1990 education for development can be regarded as limited in its effect on what eventually befell Sierra Leone, so in the post-2000 era, while it is hoped that education can help to transform structures of violence, those foundations are essentially rooted in political, economic, and ideological forces that are not themselves easily or rapidly transformed. The connection between education and human security in a context of a fragile state remains fraught with uncertainty and complexity.

Notes

1. This chapter is based on field research and interviews conducted by the authors with UNICEF, the Sierra Leonean Ministry of Youth, Education, and Sports (MYES), the Sierra Leonean Ministry of Social Welfare, Gender, and Children's Affaires (MSWGCA), and NGO staff in Sierra Leone in 2002.
2. J. W. Meyer, "The Social Construction of Motives for Educational Expansion," in B. Fuller and R. Rubinson, eds., *The Political Construction of Education* (New York: Praeger, 1992); K. M. Lewin, "Education in Emerging Asia: Patterns,

Policies, and Futures in the 21st Century," *International Journal of Educational Development* 18 (2) (1998), pp. 81–118.

3. T. J. LaBelle and C. R. Ward, "Education Reform When Nations Undergo Radical Political and Social Transformation," *Comparative Education* 26 (1) (1990), pp. 95–106; L. Ratinoff, " Social Policy Issues at the End of the 20th Century," in D. Morales-Gomez, ed., *Transnational Social Policies: The New Development Challenges of Globalization* (Ottawa: International Development Research Centre, 1999).

4. Paul-Albert Emoungu, "Education and Primitive Accumulation in Sub-Saharan Africa," *Comparative Education* 28 (2) (1993), pp. 201–13.

5. David Keen, "Incentives and Disincentives for Violence," in *Greed and Grievance: Economic Agendas in Civil Wars*, Mats Berdal and David M. Malone, eds. (Boulder, Co.: Lynne Rienner Publishers, 2000), pp. 19–21.

6. Gantzel has estimated that unarmed women and children account for 90% of the casualties in civil conflicts over the last half century (Klaus Jürgen Gantzel, "War in the Post–World War II World: Some Empirical Trends and a Theoretical Approach," in *War and Ethnicity: Global Connections and Local Violence*, David Turton, ed. (Rochester, NY: University of Rochester Press, 1997), p. 126; UNDP, *Human Development Report 1994* (Oxford and New York: Oxford University Press, 1994, p. 47.

7. Robert Kaplan, "The Coming Anarchy." *The Atlantic Monthly.* 273 (2) (February 1994), pp. 44–76.

8. Mark Duffield, *Global Governance and the New Wars: The Merging of Development and Security* (London: Zed Books, 2001), pp. 13–15; *The New Humanitarianisms: A Review of Trends in Global Humanitarian Action*, Joanne Macrae, ed., Humanitarian Policy Group Report 11, April, 2002; Mary Kaldor, *New and Old Wars: Organized Violence in a Global Era* (Cambridge: Polity Press, 1999).

9. Cf. Mark Duffield, "The Political Economy of Internal War: Asset Transfer, Complex Emergencies and International Aid," in *War and Hunger: Rethinking International Responses to Complex Emergencies*, J. Macrae and A. Zwi, eds. (London: Zed Books, 1994), pp. 50–69.

10. Michael Bryans, Bruce D. Jones, and Janice Gross Stein, "Mean Times: Humanitarian Action in Complex Political Emergencies—Stark Choices, Cruel Dilemmas," report of the NGOs in Complex Emergencies Project, *Coming to Terms* 1 (3) (January 1999), p. 1, n. 1. Cf. also Jeni Klugman, *Social and Economic Policies to Prevent Complex Humanitarian Emergencies: Lessons Learned from Experience* (Helsinki: UN University, 1999), pp. 1–6.

11. *The Sphere Project: Humanitarian Charter and Minimum Standards in Disaster Response* (Geneva: The Sphere Project, 2000).

12. *Dakar Framework for Action, paragraph 8*, April 2000. Quoted in UNESCO. *Guidelines for Education in Situations of Emergency and Crisis. EFA Strategic Planning*, Kacem Bensalah, ed. (Paris: UNESCO, 2002), p. 8.

13. UNICEF, *Education in Emergencies and for Reconstruction. Document No. UNICEF/PD/ED/99-1* (New York: UNICEF, 1999); Margaret Sinclair, *Planning Education in and after Emergencies* (Paris: UNESCO/IIEP, 2002), p. 27; K. Bush and D. Saltarelli, *The Two Faces of Education in Ethnic Conflict: Towards a Peacebuilding Education for Children* (Florence: Innocenti Research Centre, UNICEF, 2000), pp. 14–16; Margaret Sinclair, "Education in Emergencies," in J. Crisp, C. Talbot, and D. B. Cipollone, eds., *Learning for a Future: Refugee Education in Developing Countries* (Geneva: UNHCR, 2001), pp. 7–9.

14. P. Aguilar and G. Retamal, *Rapid Educational Response in Complex Emergencies: A Discussion Document* (Geneva: IBE, 1998).

15. J. Boyden and P. Ryder, *Implementing the Right to Education in Areas of Armed Conflict* (Oxford: 1996), pp. 43–45, available on-line at http://ineesite.org/core/default.asp.

16. Richard Jackson, "The State and Internal Conflict," *Australian Journal of International Affairs* 55 (1) (2001), p. 67. The problem of weak statehood is discussed at length in Robert H. Jackson, *Quasi-States: Sovereignty, International Relations and the Third World* (Cambridge: Cambridge University Press, 1990). Useful sources on Sierra Leone's political and economic formation are: Ian Smillie, Lansana Gberie, and Ralph Hazleton, *The Heart of the Matter: Sierra Leone, Diamonds, and Human Security* (Ottawa: Partnership Africa Canada, 2000), pp. 38–41; Earl Conteh-Morgan and Mac Dixon-Fyle, *Sierra Leone at the End of the Twentieth Century. History, Politics, and Society* (New York: Peter Lang Publishing Inc., 1999), pp. 41–43; John Bobor Laggah, Joe A. D. Allie, and Roland S. V. Wright, "Sierra Leone," in *Comprehending and Mastering African Conflicts*, Adebayo Adedji, ed. (New York: Zed Books, 1999), pp. 176–77.

17. William Reno, *Corruption and State Politics in Sierra Leone* (Cambridge: Cambridge University Press, 1995), p. 14. Stevens built a "shadow states" in the sense that he destroyed and manipulated formal state institutions to benefit himself and his clients.

18. Victor A. B. Davies, "Sierra Leone: Ironic Tragedy," *Journal of African Economies* 9 (3) (2000), p. 354.

19. Ishmail Rashid, "Subaltern Reactions: Lumpens, Students, and the Left," *Africa Development* 22 (3–4) (1997), pp. 24–25; William Reno, *Warlord Politics and African States* (Boulder, Co.: Lynne Rienner Publishers, 1998), p. 116; Department of Education, *New Education Policy for Sierra Leone* (Freetown, Sierra Leone. July, 1995), p. vii.

20. Reno, *Warlord Politics*, p. 118; William Reno, "Ironies of Post-Cold War Structural Adjustment in Sierra Leone," *Review of African Political Economy* 67 (1996), p. 11.

21. Kingsley Banya, "Illiteracy, Colonial Legacy and Education: The Case of Modern Sierra Leone," *Comparative Education* 29 (2) (1993), pp. 164–66.

22. Between 1960 and 1970 primary enrolment increased from 81,881 to 166,107, and then to 263,724 by 1981 (Karl-Heinrich Hildebrand, *"Bookish" Knowledge or Empowering Capacities? Education and Social Development in Sub-Saharan Africa with a Case Study of Sierra Leone* (Frankfurt/Main: Verlag für InterKulturelle Kommunikation, 1991), p. 59).

23. Ibid., pp. 62–64.

24. Ibid., p. 64.

25. UNICEF, *A Humanitarian Appeal for Women and Children. January–December, 2002. Sierra Leone*, Document provided in Freetown, Sierra Leone, May 2002; Department of Education, *New Education Policy for Sierra Leone*, Freetown, Sierra Leone, July, 1995, p. v; Interview #065, Freetown, Sierra Leone, May 2002.

26. Banya, "Illiteracy," p. 159; Kingsley Banya and Juliet Elu, "Implementing Basic Education: An African Experience," *International Review of Education* 43 (5–6) (1997), pp. 485–86.

27. ILO, *Paper Qualification Syndrome* (PQS) *and Unemployment of School Leavers. A Comparative Sub-Regional Study*, Geneva: ILO, 1982, pp. i–iii; Wright, "Sierra Leone," p. 22; Interview #712, Freetown, Sierra Leone, May 2002.

28. Yusuf Bangura, "Understanding the Political and Cultural Dynamics of the Sierra Leone War: A Critique of Paul Richards's *Fighting for the Rainforest,*" *Africa Development* 22 (3–4) (1997), pp.133–34. Bangura states that state functionaries and company officials were "dominant figures in the process of destroying the formal institutions for resource extraction, the management of public sector enterprises, and the regulatory regime that had ensured the transfer of revenues from such ventures to the state." (133). Bangura also notes this excluded youth from benefiting from this scheme (134).

29. Paul Collier, "Doing Well Out of War: An Economic Perspective," in *Greed and Grievance: Economic Agendas in Civil War,* Mats Berdal and David M. Malone, eds. (Boulder, Co.: Lynne Rienner Publishers, 2000), pp. 91–111.

30. Angela McIntyre, Emmanuel Kwesi Aning, and Prosper Nii Nortey Addo, "Politics, War, and Youth Culture in Sierra Leone: An Alternative Interpretation," *African Security Review* 11(3) (2002); Interviews #123, 210, and 263, March 2002, Bo, Sierra Leone.

31. Bangura, "Understanding the Political," p. 130.

32. Quoted in David Keen, *The Economic Function of Violence in Civil Wars. Adelphi Paper 320* (Oxford: Oxford University Press for the International Institute for Strategic Studies, 1998), p. 48.

33. Ibid., p. 48. What Keen expresses in the two quotes from his work were told to the authors by many in Sierra Leone within official and unofficial conversations.

34. David Lord, "Introduction: The Struggle for Power and Peace in Sierra Leone," *Accord* 9 (2000), available on-line at http://www.c-r.org/accord/accord9/intro.htm.

35. Ibrahim Abdullah and Patrick Muana, "The Revolutionary United Front of Sierra Leone: A Revolt of the Lumpenproletariat," *African Insurgencies,* Christopher Clapham, ed. (Oxford: James Curry, 1998), p. 179.

36. Kofi Annan, *The Causes of Conflict and the Promotion of Peace and Sustainable Development in Africa,* Report of the UN Secretary-General, A/52/871. S/1998/3/318 (New York: United Nations, 1998); Kofi Annan, *Disarmament, Demobilization, and Reintegration in a Peacekeeping Environment. Vol. 1 and 2.* (New York: Lessons Learned Unit of the UN Department of Peacekeeping Operations, 1999); Kees Kingma, "Demobilization of Combatants After Civil Wars in Africa and their Reintegration into Civilian Life," *Policy Sciences* 30 (3) (1997), p. 153; Nat J. Colletta, Markus Kostner, and Ingo Wiederhofer, *Case-Studies in War-to-Peace Transitions. The Demobilization and Reintegration of Ex-Combatants in Ethiopia, Namibia, and Uganda,* World Bank Discussion Paper No. 331 (Washington, D.C.: The World Bank, 1996); Nat Colletta et al., *The Transition from War to Peace in Sub-Saharan Africa* (Washington, D.C.: World Bank, 1996).

37. Guy Goodwin-Gill and Ilene Cohn, *Child Soldiers: The Role of Children in Armed Conflicts* (Oxford: Clarendon Press, 1994), pp. 138–40; United Nations, *The Impact of Armed Conflict on Children,* Report of the Expert of the Secretary-General, Ms. Graça Machel, submitted pursuant to General Assembly Resolution 48/157, A/51/306, August 26, 1996, paragraph 49–57.

38. Rachel Brett, "Child Soldiers," in *the Firing Line: War and Children's Rights* (London: Amnesty International, 1999), p. 68; e.g. Nicole Ball with Tammy Halevy, *Making Peace Work: The Role of the International Development Community. Policy Essay No. 18* (Washington, D.C.: Overseas Development

Council, 1996), pp. 42–43. The authors refer to child soldiers' needs in reintegration, but the focus remains on adults.

39. Margaret McCallin, "Community Involvement in the Social Reintegration of Child Soldiers," *Rethinking the Trauma of War*, P. J. Bracken and C. Petty, eds. (New York: Free Association Books, 1998), p. 72; Verhey, 18–19.

40. United Nations, *Impact of Armed Conflict on Children*, paragraph 54. See also *The Machel Review 1996–2000. A Critical Analysis of Progress Made and Obstacles Encountered in Increasing Protection for War-Affected Children*, UNICEF/UNIFEM/Norway/Canada, 2000, p. 7.

41. UNICEF, *Children Affected by Armed Conflict: UNICEF Actions* (UNICEF: New York, 2002), pp. 40–41; UNICEF, *A Humanitarian Appeal for Women and Children. January–December 2002. Sierra Leone*, Received at UNICEF Freetown Office.

42. Interview #034, Freetown, Sierra Leone May, 2002; Interview #649, Freetown, Sierra Leone May, 2002. Sierra Leone's literacy rate for ages 15+ is 30% (40% for males and 20% for females), with a net enrolment rate for children aged 5–12 of 42% (44% for boys and 40% for girls). Additionally, 85% of all children who enter grade 1 reach grade 5 (Government of Sierra Leone, *Survey Report on the Status of Women and Children in Sierra Leone at the End of the Decade*, November 2000). An internal document given by a UNICEF staff member in Sierra Leone of February 2002 gives the same numbers.

43. Interview #321 and #558, Freetown and Bo, Sierra Leone, May 2002.

44. Interview #002, 003, 005, Bo, Pujahun, and Freetown, Sierra Leone, March–April 2002.

45. According to interviews with UNICEF staff, when children were asked what they wanted most now that the war was over, they most often said education. Interview #692 and #065, Freetown, Sierra Leone, April and May 2002.

46. Interview #754 and #649, Freetown and Bo, Sierra Leone, April and May 2002.

47. Terje Tvedt, *Angels of Mercy or Development Diplomats? NGOs and Foreign Aid* (Oxford: James Curry, 1998), pp. 75–93.

11

Education of a Non-State Nation: Reconstructing a University in the War Zone of Iraqi Kurdistan[1]

Shahrzad Mojab and Budd Hall

Introduction

Education has been an indispensable institution of nation building and state building, and is often seen in terms of its emancipatory, enlightening, and progressive potential. However, it has been a site of struggle between conflicting interests that are at times irreconcilable. This chapter examines the conflict over higher education in the context of competing nation-building projects that involved genocide, linguicide, ethnocide, and unceasing war. The nation-states of Turkey, Iran, and Syria have used their educational systems in order to assimilate the Kurds into their Turkish, Persian, and Arab ethnic polities. In these nation-building projects, education was one of the means for perpetrating violent forms of linguicide, ethnocide, and genocide against the Kurds,[2] and as such this chapter fits into this book's exploration of education's role in violence and peace-making, as well as reflections on the role of Western universities in assisting the construction of civil society.

The focus of the chapter is the struggle for a Kurdish university in Northern Iraq in the context of the nationalist movement of the Kurds who were seeking autonomy within the borders of the Iraqi state. This conflict has created one of the world's most enduring war zones since 1961. The chapter is a study of the (re-)construction of a university in the course of unceasing destruction. When we visited the University of Sulaimani, our plan was to participate in a process of nation building through education and the expansion of civil society in that region of the world; this support marked one of the first academic efforts in North America to promote higher education as a peace effort in a major war zone. Moreover, this initiative challenged the more conventional, state-centered, postwar reconstruction efforts by approaching "reconstruction" as a sustainable, bottom-up, and self-managed process. Denying the Kurds the right to have a university of their own (located in Kurdistan and teaching in Kurdish) was, for Iraq and other states, an important component of the policy of denying them the status of a nation or even a national minority. After the 1991 Gulf War and the formation of the Regional Government of Kurdistan in 1992 (in the "safe haven" region), the (re-)construction of a higher education system was a component of the Kurdish nation-building project, which included, among other institutions, a parliament, a civil and military administrative structure, a court system, an airport, and state-run radio and television networks. All these steps toward nation and state building were constrained by the United States and the United Nations, which did not allow the secession of the Kurds from the Iraqi state. Internal conflicts between the two ruling political parties, the Patriotic Union of Kurdistan and the Kurdistan Democratic Party, also constrained the role of the universities, which resisted their "fratricidal war" of the mid-1990s.

The People, the Land, and the National Struggle: An Overview

The Kurds, totaling between 25 and 30 million people, are frequently mentioned as a typical "proto-nation," an ethnic group possessing all of the characteristics of a nation except their own state. The majority of the Kurds live in Iraq (23 percent), Turkey (19 percent), Iran (10 percent), and Syria (8 percent).[3]

Britain occupied three provinces of the Ottoman Empire during the last year of World War I, and called it Iraq. With the formation of the League of Nations in 1920, Britain became the Mandatory Power ruling over the new country until it became an independent Arab monarchy in 1932. In spite of disputes over borders and territory, there were no armed conflicts between Iraq and its neighbors from 1925 until 1980. However, the Kurds and the Assyrians were, from the very beginning, struggling for national rights, especially self-rule in the form of independence or autonomy. At the same time, social movements of women, students, workers, and peasants, and political groups such as communists and various Arab nationalists, continued to challenge the status quo.

However, the formation of the Iraqi nation-state was associated, like many other cases, with the use of violence. The army was frequently used against the Kurds in the 1920s and the 1940s. The pro-British monarchy was overthrown in 1958 in a coup d'etat led by nationalist Arab officers. The Kurds enjoyed more freedom under the new republican regime, which they supported. However, they revolted in 1961 when the government began to crack down on the opposition that included the Kurds who were demanding autonomy, including educational rights. The use of military power to arrest Kurdish leaders led to armed resistance, which continued until the Gulf War of 1991. Western powers and Israel and Iran, among others, intervened in various ways during its long history. After nine years of intermittent war, the Kurds reached a settlement with the government in 1970, which, if implemented, would have created an autonomous Kurdish region by 1974. However, the United States, Israel, and Iran encouraged the Kurdish leadership to reject the settlement. The United States was concerned about

Baghdad's close relations with the Soviet Union, and its border disputes with its client-state—Iran.

Iraq declared war on the Kurds at the end of the four-year truce (the impact of this development on the future of the university will be discussed later). The United States, Israel, and Iran provided the Kurds arms and logistics. However, they abruptly abandoned the Kurds after a year of destructive war when Iran and Iraq resolved their differences in March 1975. The Kurdish side was defeated. This war inflicted extensive damage on life and property. It created waves of refugees, estimated at more than 100,000, who fled to Iran, Turkey, and Western countries.

After the defeat of the Kurds, the Iraqi government created a buffer zone on its borders with Iran. This was done through the destruction of mountain villages along the border. All village buildings and springs of water, the lifeblood of the community, were destroyed; millions of land mines[4] were planted in the villages and on their farms so that no one, peasants or guerrillas, could resettle there. However, Kurdish armed resistance resumed in 1976. The government pursued a policy of revenge rather than amnesty and reconstruction. In the aftermath of the 1979 Revolution of Iran, Iraq attacked the Islamic state, and unleashed the longest war of the region (1980–1988), which led to enormous destruction in the two countries. The United States intervened by helping Iraq.

The two major Kurdish political parties, the Patriotic Union of Kurdistan (PUK) and the Kurdish Democratic Party (KDP), lead the armed struggle against Baghdad, although one of them (the PUK) tried in vain to negotiate a deal in 1984. During the last phases of its destructive war with Iran, Iraq conducted a genocide of the Kurds in 1988. Known as *Anfal* ("spoils of war"), the genocidal campaign eliminated an estimated 180,000 people. Between 1975 and 1991, several thousand villages were destroyed in the predominantly rural society of Kurdistan. Iraq also used chemical bombs against the Iranian army and its own citizens in the Kurdish town of Halabja, which led to the killing of more than 5,000 people.

During the Gulf War of 1991, led by the United States, President George Bush encouraged the Kurds of Iraq to revolt against Baghdad. When they revolted, the United States abandoned them. Saddam's army attacked them and some three million escaped into the snow-covered mountains in late March and April. The United States refused to take any responsibility, arguing that this was an ancient tribal war. When forced into action because of the pressure of world public opinion, the United States and the United Kingdom created a so-called safe haven for them, with a no-fly zone that is being guarded, until today, by American and British air forces.

Millions of people continue to suffer from the impact of the 1991 war. The Kurds suffer from the economic embargo on Iraq, and the double embargo of Iraq on the Kurds, and the third layer of embargo imposed by neighboring states on the land-locked Kurdish "safe haven." This "safe haven" has, however, been unsafe for the people living there. It has been regularly occupied by the Turkish army, the Iraqi army (once), and the

Iranian army (several incursions); it also experienced intermittent war between the two ruling Kurdish parties from 1994 to 1996. Moreover, the Islamic fundamentalist armed groups funded and organized by Iran, the Taliban regime, and Saudi Arabia, among others, have occupied some territory on the Iran–Iraq border and have waged war against the Kurdish government. However, the people of the region have not failed to reconstruct their war-torn country in spite of insurmountable challenges. One of their more visible achievements is reconstructing a university in the midst of unceasing destruction.

FROM MOUNTAINS TO CLASSROOMS: REBUILDING A UNIVERSITY IN A WAR ZONE

Perhaps the most remarkable phoenix arising from the ashes of more than 150 years of suffering and displacement has been the rebirth of the University of Sulaimani.[5] Following the creation of the "safe haven," one of the first things done was to reopen the University of Sulaimani at the sight of the former Iraqi military training facilities. This was done largely by the people of Sulaimani who made extraordinary donations to help with the restoration of the university. In the latest address at the opening page of *The University of Sulaimany: Prospectus, 2000–2001*, the president of the University states:

> An enormous task faces the University at present: the task of taking an active part in the process of restructuring the country, democratizing the society and its educational system and raising a new generation of educated men and women who are well-qualified to build a society, in which every member accepts and respects the authority of law.[6]
> This has not been an easy undertaking.

The first university in Iraqi Kurdistan was established in 1968 in the city of Sulaimani; it was the fifth university in Iraq. In keeping with its geopolitical location within Northern Iraq, the university has maintained a PUK orientation throughout its history. The university began with three colleges of agriculture, science, and engineering. In 1970, the government issued a peace accord known as "The 11 March 1970 Peace Accord," which according to McDowall "was not only the best deal the Kurds of Iraq had been offered, but it has remained the Kurds' favored foundation stone for future relations with the rest of Iraq."[7] Several articles directly addressed the educational and cultural rights of the Kurds:

> Article 1. The Kurdish language shall be, alongside the Arabic language, the official language in areas with a Kurdish majority; and will be the language of instruction in those areas and taught throughout Iraq as a second language.
> Article 3. Kurdish education and culture will be reinforced.
> Article 5. Kurds shall be free to establish students, youth, women's and teachers' organizations of their own.[8]

It was based on the promises of this peace accord that the university began to expand in the early 1970s. During this time the university was reasonably funded and the following colleges were added: Arts (1971–1972), medicine (1974–1975), economics and administration (1975–1976), and education (1976–1977).[9] The life of this newly established institution was disrupted in 1974 when the truce between the Kurds and the central government of Baghdad collapsed. A report by "Support Committee for the University of Salahaddin" describes the scene on campus:

> many members of staff and students fled to the mountains and the studies in the university were suspended for 5 months.... Many academics and students were harassed, transferred by decrees, driven out, arrested or even executed. Funds started to dry up. The secret services and the Ba'th party started to interfere in the day-to-day running of the university.... On campus interrogation and even torture of dissidents, Kurds as well as others, became part of the daily university life.[10]

Finally, in 1981, the university was moved from Sulaimani to Hewler (Erbil) and its name was changed to the University of Salahadeen: "The change of the name was significant, as it clearly indicated that the government of Baghdad had other plans for the university. It intended to remove it from the Kurdish-populated area of Iraq to the Arab-populated Tikrit, the center of Salahaddeen Province of Iraq and the birth-place of Saddam Hussein."[11] This was a significant political decision by the Iraqi Government, which left the Kurds without an institution of higher learning for another decade. In the 1980s, "the atmosphere of terror continued and intensified. University funds were at the mercy of the security agents.... In 1982 to 1984, the university was the focus of a peaceful protest campaign which was confronted with the utmost brutality and some protesting students were shot and killed inside the university campus."[12]

Following the Kurdish uprising in March 1991, the discussion to reestablish the university in Sulaimani began. The newly appointed Kurdistan National Assembly adopted a resolution in October 1992 to reopen the university and by November 15, teaching resumed. Since then, the university has faced many academic and administrative problems, the most significant of which is its isolation regionally and internationally. The double embargo imposed on the Kurdish region has created a massive shortage of resources, including teaching staff and materials. The economic shortage is further aggravated by the special relationship between Kurdish authorities and the Iraqi regime: "On the one hand, the area is cut off from and independent of Baghdad; on the other hand, the Kurds have been granted no legislative power and still have to defer to the Iraqi legislation and administration."[13]

Despite all obstacles, the university succeeded in receiving membership in the International Association of Universities (IAU) in 1998 and attracted the academic support of other internationally renowned institutions such as the

University of Toronto (Canada) and Stockholm University (Sweden).[14] It also has pursued its goal of expanding. Since 1991, when the Iraqi government withdrew its forces from Kurdistan, "no student from the region...has been admitted to the Iraqi universities."[15] Another significant initiative has been resuming the publication of the journal *Zankoy Sulaimany*, the official university publication (October 30, 1995).[16]

By early 2003, the university consisted of 13 colleges: Administration and Economics, Agriculture, Commerce, Dentistry, Engineering, Fine Arts, Languages, Law, Medicine, Physical Education, Science, Social Science, and Veterinary Medicine. These colleges are grouped under two clusters: Pure and Applied Sciences, and Humanities and Social Sciences. It had a total of 231 faculty members, 5,801 undergraduate students, and 184 graduate students.[17] The institution is administered by the University Council, which consists of the president, assistants to the president, deans of the colleges, and representatives of faculty members. Until 2000–2001, all 16 members of the council were men.

Building Links Across Borders

As was mentioned earlier, one of the goals of the University of Sulaimani was to receive international recognition. The administrators have strived hard to prove the scientific capacity of the university and establish a sound reputation in the region. The institution, furthermore, symbolizes the deep-seated ambition of the Kurdish nation for advancing their culture, language, and education autonomously. Thus, under the section of "Academic Organization and Educational Objectives" (*The University of Sulaimany: Prospectus, 2000–2001*) it is stated:

> For a country that is struggling to build a new democratic society, the necessity to develop a new democratic tradition in education is of the utmost importance. It is, therefore, vital to break from the party-dominated educational system of the past and to put an end to its brainwashing methods whereby the students were taught what to think and not how to think...The aim should be the raising of a new generation of educated men and women who are able to respond to the challenges of tomorrow's problems.

The Memorandum of Understanding (MOU) between the Ontario Institute for the Studies in Education of the University of Toronto (OISE/UT) marks one of the first academic efforts in North America to promote this aspiration of the Kurds. Let us first review the history and mechanism of this memorandum. The Department of Adult Education and Counselling Psychology (AECP) at OISE/UT has been supporting research activities involving Kurds since 1997. It has been the home of the International Kurdish Women's Studies Network and the Kurdish Women Research Resources.[18] On the basis of the activities of these research projects, the need for expanding beyond diaspora and collaborating with the academic institutions in the region was felt. The University of Sulaimani in Iraqi Kurdistan was among the first universities to reach out to us.

In February 2000, the first visit from the University of Toronto by Budd Hall was undertaken. It was the result of a formal invitation by the president of the University of Sulaimani, Dr. Kamal Khoshnaw. The purpose of the visit was to open up opportunities for mutual collaboration between the two institutions. It was also an opportunity for Canadian academics to learn something about a region that is very little understood. Upon return from Iraqi Kurdistan, Professor Hall briefed the then minister of Foreign Affairs and International Trade, Lloyd Axworthy, the minister of International Development, the Canadian International Development Agency, and members of the academic community.

What strikes most visitors to the University of Sulaimani is the democratic "feel" of the institution. Students bustle from class to class laughing and teasing each other. The classrooms are filled with challenging debates about the various competing scholarly discourses as well as passionate views about the international scene. Most importantly, there is sense of an entire new generation of leadership with a deep pride in their Kurdish language and culture and a sophisticated approach to regional politics. The university administration supports a modernist democratic vision and is eager to establish academic connections between their university and the international community of academic and cultural interchange.

The challenges however have been enormous. The government of Iraq has been sitting on the UN committee that controls the spending of the Oil-for-Food funds (this issue will be discussed later). There are no Kurds represented on that committee. Baghdad has consistently forbidden the purchase of most contemporary scientific and cultural books for the University of Suleimaniah or for other postsecondary institutions in the region. The library of the university remains mostly empty shelves with books donated by professors who have studied abroad and who brought books home with them. The recent establishment of an Internet research and communications center at the university has meant that much communications and research can now be done through this medium. Funding for studies abroad is very limited as these purposes are not supported under the Iraqi-monitored UN program.

During his visit to Iraqi Kurdistan, Professor Hall and colleagues from the University of Sulaimani drafted a tentative MOU that included a list of areas of potential collaboration between the two institutions. Following this successful event, a meeting of "Founding of University of Toronto-University of Sulaimani Cooperation" was called in May 2000. The committee members consisted of students, faculty members from across various departments of the University of Toronto, the International Development Business Initiative, and members of the Kurdish community. Another meeting of this committee was also organized in July 2000. The results of these meetings were communicated with colleagues at the University of Sulaimani. In both meetings the following issues remained as priorities: Finalizing the MOU between the two institutions; arranging for the collection and the shipment of library resources; facilitating the participation of faculty members and students in the first academic conference held in September 2000 at the University of Sulaimani; seeking funding for establishing a Community Education Center at the University of Sulaimani; and arranging for a faculty member from Kurdistan to attend OISE/UT in order to pursue a graduate program. A proposal for the creation of a Community Education Center was chosen as an important next step for international cooperation. The purposes for the center was the creation of training and skills enhancement opportunities for adult men and women in disadvantaged situations in the region so that they have educational opportunities that have been denied them because of the years of war and violence. The exchange agreement has already resulted in the admittance of the head of the English Department of the University of Sulaimani into the graduate studies at OISE-University of Toronto.

Shahrzad Mojab's trip coincided with the opening of the "First Scientific Conference of Sulaimani University, September 27–28, 2000." One of the doctoral students at the Department of Political Science of the University of Toronto also attended the conference and presented a paper.[19] A significant achievement of this visit was the signing of the MOU. The event was covered in all the local media and was broadcast via the satellite TV station KurdSat. Various meetings were arranged for Professor Mojab on campus, among them one inclusive meeting with women faculty members. She also gave a lecture on the topic of academic freedom based on her comparative research in the Middle East.[20] Shahrzad recounts her experience with the University of Sulaimani as follows:

The University of Sulaimani was a familiar but distant campus for me. It was familiar because it reminded me of the college where I conducted my undergraduate studies in Tehran in the mid-1970s. The physical layout, the furniture, the interaction of young men and women in the courtyard of the campus, all belonged to a familiar era of my campus life in Iran. There was something else that was familiar though now distant—the hierarchical relations among faculty members and administration and between them and students. That too reminded me of the long struggle of students and faculty members on Iranian campuses for democratization of university relations, for access to and participation in decision-making processes, and for university autonomy, that is, the separation of university and state powers. Considering the circumstances under which the University of Sulaimani was operating, I was wondering where and how even to open up a space for dialogue on these topics. I am not suggesting that our colleagues and students at the University of Sulaimani were not preoccupied with these ideas, rather my concern continues to be the conditions under which the university manages itself. The condition of semi-military occupation, war, total dependency on international funds, and multiplicity of states, that is, the sovereign state of Iraq, the defacto state of Regional Government, and the supranational state of the United Nations, all of which intersect in order to deny the Kurds statehood. These material conditions, undoubtedly, complicate further the planning, direction, and aspiration of the university. The driving force was the dream of building a self-reliant and sovereign Kurdish nation through their struggle on the educational battlefield.

A daunting task was accessing the funds that came from the United Nations Security Resolution (UNSR) 986, the Oil-for-Food program. The UNSR 986 allocated 13 percent of the total income to the reconstruction of the Northern Iraq.[21] There is much evidence about the misuse and abuse of this fund.[22] For most of its spending, the university had to submit a request to the Ministry of Higher Education, which would then present the request to the special UN–Iraq Committee; after the approval by this committee, the proposal would go to the UN headquarter in New York for final authorization.[23] University administrators all complained about this unnecessarily lengthy and bureaucratic process that was described to me as a symptom of a non-state status.

EDUCATION OF A NON-STATE NATION

Kurdish nationalism, like other nationalist movements, has seen education as a major site of nation building. In the case of the Kurds, the violent repression of their language by the state in Turkey, Iran, and Syria has made native-tongue education a matter of life and death for the nation.[24] The states that rule over the Kurds have used the official state language (Turkish in Turkey, Persian in Iran, and Arabic in Syria and Iraq) as a means of assimilating the Kurds. Thus, demands for language rights are, in the Kurdish case, inseparable from demands for education rights.

In the Republic of Turkey, formed in 1923, the use of the Kurdish language, in writing and speaking, was criminalized, and various governments used a diversity of measures in order to eliminate the Kurdish language. Turkey tried to prevent the use of the Kurdish language even in the Kurdish diasporas of Europe.[25] However, Turkey currently aspires to become a full member of the European Union (EU). Under the pressure from the Union, a bill was introduced into the parliament in 1991 to allow the use of spoken Kurdish, though only in private spaces. Broadcasting in the language or speaking it in government offices or for election campaigns continued to be illegal. Pressed by the EU, Turkey in 2002 allowed the use of the language in education, although on a very limited scale, for example, on weekends, only to a certain age group, and with state-controlled content (only Turkish government propaganda).[26]

Iran adopted a similar policy of linguicide (the deliberate killing of a language) under Reza Shah Pahlavi (1925–1941) and, with less harshness, under the last king of the dynasty (1941–1979). Native-tongue education was illegal, although speaking the language in private was tolerated. Although article 15 of the constitution of the Islamic Republic of Iran (since 1979) allows "the teaching of ethnic literature in the school together with Persian language instruction," various governments have refused to implement the article by including in the curriculum the teaching of

Kurdish or other non-Persian literatures. In recent years, however, private teaching of Kurdish is allowed, while there has been no ban on publishing and broadcasting in the language.

In Iraq, Kurds demanded native-tongue education on all levels (primary, secondary, and tertiary) from the beginning of the formation of the Iraqi state under British occupation. The League of Nations, which supervised the British Mandate over Iraq, recognized the right of the Kurds to native-tongue education. However, Britain was wary of the spread of Kurdish nationalism as it was a potential threat to the Arab state that it was building, as well as to the neighboring states where the Kurds were being suppressed. Under these conditions, in spite of the increasing pressure of the Kurds for more schools, the emerging Iraqi state and the British mandatory power did not allow the teaching of Kurdish in more than two dozen primary schools. The mandatory power rejected the demand of the Kurds for Kurdish language secondary and higher education. To give one example, Britain complained to the League of Nations in 1929 that the "opening of three new elementary schools has not appeased the discontent of the Kurds with the general educational policy of the [Iraqi] Government. This discontent takes the form of complaining:—(a) that there are not enough Kurdish elementary schools, (b) that there is no Kurdish training college...."[27] The Mandatory government tried to provide "A fair answer to these complaints...(a), if true of Kurdistan, is equally true of the Arab speaking areas; (b) that a separate training college is neither practicable nor in the interests of the Kurds themselves...."[28]

After the fall of the monarchy in 1985, the Kurds again demanded native-tongue education on the secondary and tertiary levels. This demand was again rejected. During the autonomist movement of 1961–1975, a period of intermittent armed conflict between the two sides, the demand was repeated during various negotiations, leading ultimately to the establishment of the University of Sulaimani. However, the medium of instruction was not Kurdish except in the department of Kurdish language and literature.

War, State Violence, and Education

While this chapter is being written and prepared for publication (March 2003), the political map of the region is in the process of being redrawn, probably with much bloodshed and massive destruction of the institutions that temporarily brought the Kurds closer to the sense of a nationhood with a limited regime of self-rule. The fate of the University of Sulaimani is unknown. However, a decade of Kurdish experiment with autonomous state building seems to be over. The future, postwar order, will be, at best, a semblance of a federated province, whose autonomy depends on the whim of a centralist regime in Baghdad.

In fact, the United States and Britain have never been interested in settling the status of the Kurds in Northern Iraq. The Kurdish authorities remained legally bound to the sovereign rule of the Iraqi state. A 2002

UN-Habitat report states: "The Local Authorities in the Governorates operate within the general legal framework of Iraqi law, with various revisions. There is no constitution or legal framework independent of Iraqi law, and the Iraqi constitution."[29] Carver, after reviewing the definitions of state, also concludes, "Iraq/Kurdistan is not a *state* nor has it been recognized as such by any national or international governing body."[30] She also provides us with this thought:

> Looking specifically at Iraq/Kurdistan, perhaps the two worst case scenarios would be either war between an Iranian-backed PUK and an Iraqi-backed KDP, or an internationally-tolerated suppression of a movement for an independent Kurdistan, by Turkish, Iraqi, Iranian and/or Syrian troops. Whatever the US action, and whatever the proximate results, it must be concluded that the already unstable "statelets" will further destabilise.[31]

In this context we argue that the expansion of academic, cultural, and nongovernmental relations represents a promising avenue for the pursuit of peace and the strengthening of democratic institutions in the region. Canadian academic interest in the region continues to grow. The Faculty of Education and the Center for Global Studies at the University of Victoria are the latest Canadian institutions to express a specific interest in the region. In February 2003, a joint letter from the director of the Center for Global Studies and Budd Hall (the current Dean of the Faculty of Education)[32] at the University of Victoria proposed to the Canadian minister of Foreign Affairs that Canada make the strengthening of universities in Kurdish Northern Iraq its priority for international development in the area. It offered to take a leadership role along with the University of Toronto and other international academic and development specialists in supporting university–community capacities and faculty development given the opportunity to do so.

To conclude, the founding of a Kurdish university in Iraq spanned a period of five decades of struggle (from the 1920s to the late 1960s), and involved a persistent conflict between the Kurds, Britain (the founders of the Iraqi state), and various Iraqi regimes, both monarchical and republican. Reflecting on the troubled life of the University of Sulaimani, we argue that the strong resistance to the Kurdish demand for an institution of higher education was rooted in the empire-building interests of Britain and nation-building projects of various Iraqi regimes. The colonial regime and the nation-state it established in Iraq were determined to contain Kurdish nationalism, which was relentless in its demand for self-rule leading eventually to statehood. When the university was finally established in 1968 under the pressure of years of armed struggle, it was forcefully controlled by Baghdad to ensure that it would remain loyal to the state.

When the university was reconstructed under the auspices of the United Nations in the "safe haven," state sovereignty continued to shape the life of the university. The Iraqi state was potently present, under the UN flag, in the "safe haven." Here the unequal division of power was most prominent.

While we were not able to ship (under the auspices of the United Nations) books from Toronto to the book-hungry library of the University of Sulaimani, the Turkish state was able to violate international law and the very principles of the UN by readily moving its army into the "safe haven."

The university played a positive role in promoting peace and peaceful coexistence in Iraqi Kurdistan under conditions of internal conflict between the two Kurdish political parties that shared power between 1991 and 1994, and later divided into two separate administrations. It also contributed to the formation of a civil society and public spheres that enhanced democratization. However, this experience offers critical insight on current thinking about reconstruction of war-torn societies,

The literature on reconstruction is oblivious to two crucial factors. First, the idea of reconstruction is not examined in the context of enduring destruction. The destruction of life, social relations, or institutions of civil society takes many shapes. In the Middle East, for example, a combination of national, regional, and international forces combine to regularly perpetrate genocide, gendercide, linguicide, ethnocide, and ecocide in the Kurdish regions. Based on the Kurdish case, we can demonstrate that the postcolonial nation-state has engaged in more mass killing of citizens than its colonial predecessors. In this context, reconstruction does not and cannot catch up with the forces of destruction. Second, education has been reduced to its most rudimentary form, that is, formal education at elementary and secondary levels or some limited skill-training module. In the region, in particular, the idea of emancipation, consciousness raising, or education for liberation is not accepted by the state or by most NGOs, as a vital component of reconstruction efforts. If some historians convince us that people make their own history, we see in the Kurdish case people who are not allowed to be agents of historical change.

A major question remains to be the conditions that (re-)produce destruction. And what is the role of education in constraining the machinery of war and destruction? The worldwide peace protests of early 2003 should be interpreted not as an appeasement of despots like Saddam Hussein, but rather as a genuine revolt against the destructive powers of high-tech, globalization, and imperialism.[33]

NOTES

1. We would like to thank Omar Sheikhmous, Amir Hassanpour, and Stephan Dobson for their assistance in the writing of this chapter, and especially Lydia Shaswar who provided additional information for us.
2. On the relationship between genocide and education, see Tove Skutnabb-Kangas, *Linguistic Genocide in Education—Or Worldwide Diversity and Human Rights?* (London: Lawrence Erlbaum, 2000); on the educational and linguistic genocide of the Kurds see ibid, pp. 364–65; Amir Hassanpour, "The Politics of A-Political Linguistics: Linguists and Linguicide," in Robert Phillipson, ed., *Rights to Language: Equity, Power, and Education* (London: Lawrence Erlbaum), pp. 33–39; and Desmond Fernandes, "The Kurdish Genocide in Turkey, 1924–1998," *Armenian Forum*, 1, No. 4 (1999): 57–107.

3. Kurdistan Region of Iraq, *The University of Sulaimany, Prospectus, 2000–2001,* The University of Sulaimany Press. An electronic copy of this document was provided for us by Lydia Shaswar who prepared that document for the University.

4. On the issue of land in Carver writes, "There are more than 10 million land in and a large quantity of unexploded ordnance in Iraq/Kurdistan. According to the UN, which has been working to clear the land, it could take between 35–75 years. Land in have killed up to 3,000 people since 1991 in Iraq/Kurdistan and casualties remain high;" Natasha Carver, "Is Iraq/Kurdistan a State such that it can be said to Operate State Systems and Thereby Offer Protection to Its 'Citizens?'" *International Journal of Refugee Law,* 14, No. 1 (2002): 57–84.

5. The spelling of the word "Sulaimani," a major city in Iraqi Kurdistan where the university is located, varies in different documents. We have adopted the preceding spelling, however, in quoting documents we have adhered to original spelling and names.

6. All the statistical data and other information on the University of Sulaimany is based on: Kurdistan Region of Iraq.

7. David McDowall, *A Modern History of the Kurds* (London: I. B. Tauris, 2000), p. 327.

8. All the 15 articles are quoted in ibid., pp. 327–28.

9. Kurdistan Region of Iraq, p. 11.

10. Support Committee for the University of Salahaddin (formerly Sulaymaniyah University) in Kurdistan-Iraq, n.d.

11. Kurdistan Region of Iraq, pp. 11–12.

12. Carver, "Is Iraq/Kurdistan a State,"

13. Rasmussen, Lene Kofoed (1999) *The System of Education in Iraq,* Danish Refugee Council. Copenhagen, Denmark, pp. 30, 40.

14. An important initiative by the Kurdish diaspora in Britain was the establishment of "Support Committee for Higher Education in Iraqi Kurdistan," which provided information on the three universities in the region: Salahaddin University, Dahuk University, and Sulaimani University. The group also assisted these institutions through fund raising and linking them with academic community in Europe.

15. See note 3.

16. Ibid.

17. Ibid.

18. The International Kurdish Women's Studies Network was established in 1997; Shahrzad Mojab was one of the founding members of this network. Check the following website for more information: http://www.oise.utoronto.ca/projects/kwnet. The website for the Kurdish Women Research Resources was also created in 2002 with funding from two SSHRC grants: (1) New Approaches to Lifelong Learning, coordinated by Professor David Livingstone at OISE/UT; and (2) War, Diaspora, and Learning: Kurdish Women in Canada, Britain, and Sweden, conducted by Shahrzad Mojab: see http://www.fcis.oise.utoronto.ca/~mojabweb.

19. For a fuller account of Shahrzad's experience in Kurdistan, see Mojab (forthcoming), "The Bleeding Borders: Gender, Nation, and State Boundaries."

20. Shahrzad Mojab, "Civilizing the State: the University in the Middle East," in S. Inayatullah and J. Gidley, eds., *The University in Transformation: Global Perspectives on the Futures of the University* (Greenwood, Westport: 2000), pp. 137–48, and Shahrzad Mojab, "The State, University, and the Construction of Civil Society in the Middle East," *Futures,* special issue on "The Future of the University," 7 (September 30, 1998), pp. 657–67.

21. According to the UN Office of the Iraq Programme, "Oil-for-Food—The Basic Facts, 1996 to 2000," since December 2000 the revenue has been divided in the following way: 53 percent for humanitarian supplies in the center and south of Iraq, 13 percent for supplies in the three northern governorates, 30 percent for the UN Compensation Fund administered from Geneva, 2.2 percent for the UN's cost administering the humanitarian program, 0.8 percent for the administration of the commission responsible for disarmament and 1 percent to the escrow account.

22. See, e.g., R. M. Ahmad, "Use and Abuse of Iraqi Kurdistan Share from UN Oil-for-Food Program," June 18, 2001, www.KurdishMedia.com; Rizgar Khoshnaw, "Please Stop Bilking the Oil-for-Food Proceeds," December 10, 2001, www. KurdishMedia.com.

23. The UN document mentioned earlier (see note 20) explains this process as "All contracts signed by the Government come to the Office of the Iraq Programme in New York for processing and, in most cases, circulation to the 661 Sanctions Committee for its consideration. Some contracts can now be approved by the Secretariat of the United Nations on the basis of lists approved by the committee in the 'fast track procedure.'" See also *Human Rights Watch World Report 2002*, section on "Iraq and Iraqi Kurdistan."

24. See note 2.

25. Tove Skuttnabb-Kangas, *Linguistic Genocide*.

26. For more on Turkey language policy see Tove Skutnabb-Kangas, "Linguistic Human Rights in Education and Turkey—Some Inter Comparisons," invited plenary paper at the International Conference on Kurds, the European Union and Turkey, Copenhagen, Denmark, October 14, 2002 (available at http:// babel.ruc.dk/~tovesku/); and Burton Bollag, "Silenced Minority," *The Chronicle of Higher Education* (July 19, 2002), A34–36 (also available at http://chronicle. com/world).

27. *Report by His Majesty's Government in the United Kingdom of Great Britain and Northern Ireland to the Council of the League of Nations on the Administration of 'Iraq for the Year 1929,'* (London: His Majesty's Stationary Office, 1930 (Colonial No. 55)), pp. 139–40.

28. Ibid. The conflict over the expansion of schools and the demand for a Kurdish college is recorded in other British reports to the League of Nations. For instance, the *Report by His Majesty's Government in the United Kingdom of Great Britain and Northern Ireland to the Council of the League of Nations on the Administration of 'Iraq for the Year 1928* (London: His Majesty's Stationary Office, 1929 (Colonial No. 44), p. 132) wrote:

> The opening of 5 new primary or elementary schools in the course of the year [1928] in Kurdish areas has satisfied everyone except the Kurds themselves. It is not easy to hold a just balance between the claims of Kurdish and Arab areas for new schools, or persuade the responsible authorities that the number of pupils is not the only justification for the opening of a new school. If it were so, the Arab areas would get a larger share of new schools than they actually do get. Another difficulty is that whereas the Government holds that the present 30 Kurdish primary and secondary schools represents the maximum to which the Kurds are entitled, most Kurds regard, or profess to regard, this as a minimum. Yet apart from questions of right or wrong, it is clear that the country cannot at present afford a separate training college and separate higher schools for Kurdistan, even if such were proved to be in the interests of the Kurds themselves.

29. UN-Habitat, Disaster Management Programme and Settlements Rehabilitation Programme, "Gender Situation Report—Northern Iraq" (November 2002), p. 7.
30. Carver, "Is Iraq/Kurdistan a State," p. 60; italics in original.
31. Ibid., p. 82.
32. Professor Hall moved from OISE/UT to Victoria University in 2001.
33. For more on this see Naom Chomsky, "Confronting the Empire" (February 1, 2003), available on ZNet.

IV

COMPARATIVE AND REGIONAL PERSPECTIVES (CENTRAL ASIA, EAST AFRICA, EGYPT, TAIWAN, AND USA)

12

The Changing Role of Education in a Post-September 11, 2001 World: Perspectives from East Africa, Taiwan, and the United States

Sheng Yao Cheng and W. James Jacob

Introduction

The aftermath of the terrorist attacks on New York City and Washington D.C. on September 11, 2001, impacted not only the United States but also the entire world. International economies suffered as the world was forced into a semi-critical economic recession. The foundation stones of democracy were challenged as terrorists targeted not only the United States, but also the symbols of the current capitalist ideology.[1] Differences between people, nations, religious beliefs, ethics, and values are at the very heart of this new era in world politics. What role should education play in this international crisis? In this study, we examine the potential role education will play in the aftermath of the September 11, 2001 terrorist attacks, by offering several perspectives from East Africa, Taiwan, and the United States. After providing these three international cases, we juxtapose the information presented and provide our recommendations and conclusions.

Ubuntu: Perspectives from Kenya, Tanzania, and Uganda

Education plays a key role in how societies in East Africa formulate and deal with issues of terrorism, security, and ultimately peace. East Africans are not strangers to terrorism, war, and the impacts of foreign powers on their national interests. In this section, we provide country perspectives from Kenya, Tanzania, and Uganda on how each country has addressed the issues of education and terrorism, and how the idea of *ubuntu* is an essential African philosophy of both.

The Concept of Ubuntu and Its Relationship
to Education and Terrorism

We begin with the concept of ubuntu, which views the individual as a component of a greater (inclusive) collective whole, and stresses social consciousness and unity.[2] Ubuntu places the interests of others first, especially as they associate individual relationships with their respective families, communities, and ultimately nations. The term has been "viewed as a basis for a morality of co-operation, compassion, communalism, and concern for the interests of the collective respect for the dignity of personhood, all the time emphasising the virtues of that dignity in social relationships and practices."[3] Bishop Desmond Tutu described a person with ubuntu as open and available to others, affirming of others, not feeling threatened that others are able and good, for he or she has a proper self-assurance that comes from knowing that he or she belongs in a greater whole and is diminished when others are humiliated or diminished, when others are tortured or oppressed, or treated as though they were less than who they are.

Tutu also feels that ubuntu connotes community, with the understanding that it's impossible to isolate persons from community, that there's an organic relationship between all people such that when we see another, we should recognize ourselves and the God in whose image all people are made. Interdependence and reciprocity, not independence and self-sufficiency, are the keys here. As Tutu magnificently says, "A self-sufficient human being is subhuman. I have gifts that you do not have, so consequently, I am unique—you have gifts that I do not have, so you are unique. God has made us so that we will need each other. We are made for a delicate network of interdependence."[4]

The concept of ubuntu takes on new meaning as terrorism continues to pervade throughout East Africa. Education also plays a fundamental role in the concept of ubuntu, by providing a means of expanding individual experience to a broader context. Ubuntu's relationship to terrorism and education is that both are realities of East African and global societies, therefore, both education and terrorism can be conceptualized within the nexus of each individual's life in Kenya, Tanzania, and Uganda. The realization of a terror-free society begins with the individual.

Ubuntu is also a concept that requires a reciprocal relationship in order to realize its potential impact on society. Africans have mixed feelings regarding the way the United States and other Western nations have responded to global problems in addition to terrorism. Many African leaders felt that the U.S. government showed little support at the World Summit on Sustainable Development 2002, held in Johannesburg, South Africa.[5] Yet others felt the opposite in January 2003, when the Bush administration offered a substantial commitment toward prevention and treatment of the HIV/AIDS pandemic in sub-Saharan Africa.[6] The war in Iraq has also brought mixed feelings amongst East Africans.[7] East Africans long for the realization of an ubuntu-based society, where peace is the standard in the hearts of the people. It is difficult to see this reality without a total commitment from the global community. Western nations should seize the opportunity to embrace the concepts of ubuntu.

Terrorism on East African Soil

On August 7, 1998, the U.S. embassies in Nairobi, Kenya, and Dar es Salaam, Tanzania were simultaneously bombed killing 224 people. An additional 4,500 people were injured in these events. Although thwarted, an attempt was made on the same day to bomb the U.S. embassy in Kampala, Uganda. Thus, even though the U.S. embassies and its citizens were targeted in these coordinated attacks, many innocent Kenyans and Tanzanians lost their lives and several thousands were impaired or severely injured for life.[8] As a result of these attacks, the East African community established a Joint Committee to coordinate their actions against terrorism.

As East Africans watched the horrific events of September 11, 2001 in New York and Washington D.C., they felt sympathetic and in many regards could relate with the victims as very few others on the earth could. In an address to the United Nations on October 4, 2001, Bob F. Jalang'o said, "All nations, irrespective of their size, might or influence; and all people, irrespective of their colour, sex, race or religion, are directly or indirectly affected by terrorism."[9] It was clear that this was not just an event that impacted citizens of the United States alone. Largely through the media, this became a world event, one that East Africans could watch from their own homes.[10] Yet, the overwhelming response of support by the U.S. citizens for the families of the victims of September 11, brought feelings of animosity to many Kenyans and Tanzanians who never received such support from the U.S. government or its citizens when the embassies were attacked in 1998.

The successful bombings of U.S. embassies in Nairobi and Dar es Salaam, along with the failed attempt in Kampala, convinced U.S. government officials that their downtown embassy locations in East African urban centers were too dangerous to defend against would-be terrorists. Thus, they have constructed new embassy buildings in suburban locations in Kenya, Tanzania, and Uganda that are built to withstand car bombs, unlike previous office-building embassies in downtown urban centers.

Although Al-Qaeda has been weakened since the U.S.-led coalition invasion and overthrow of the Taliban in Afghanistan, continued terrorist attacks during 2002 in Tunisia, Bali, Kuwait, and Kenya demonstrate that it has not been destroyed. Al-Qaeda continues to act on its own in small factions throughout the earth. On November 28, 2002, this was witnessed when Al-Qaeda operatives detonated a car bomb killing three tourists and 12 Kenyans at the Paradise hotel in the resort coastal city of Mombasa, Kenya. In concert with the hotel attack, Al-Qaeda loyalists attempted to kill 261 people aboard an Israeli passenger plane when they fired two surface-to-air missiles that narrowly missed their target. Once again Kenyans suffered from terrorist tactics aimed at foreign targets. From the recent terrorist events in East Africa, the Kenya, Tanzania, and Uganda governments have increased security at key transportation hubs and tourist locations.[11]

Since Yoweri K. Museveni overthrew Milton Obote's regime in 1986, the people of Uganda have faced terrorism by two primary factions: the Lords Resistance Army (LRA), in the Northern Region of Uganda, and the Allied Democratic Forces (ADF) in South-Western Uganda. LRA rebels are known for attacking innocent bystanders for political purposes. In July 2002, LRA rebels attacked a secondary school in Northern Uganda and took many female students hostage. Unfortunately, this has been a recurring theme in Uganda, despite relative stability in the central-Kampala region. The LRA method of terror is the maiming and cutting off of body parts of innocent children and women and kidnapping the survivors, taking them to their bases outside Uganda. The ADF's method has been characterized by the use of terrorist bombs placed in public vehicles or crowded shopping areas in Kampala, and other urban centers in Uganda.

Education: An Avenue for Addressing Terrorism

Education is viewed by the governments of Kenya, Tanzania, and Uganda as a primary avenue for addressing terrorism and peace. Yet, it is difficult to implement rapidly on a national level as education systems in East Africa have rarely changed since independence.[12] Changes are particularly difficult when the national curricula are based on a colonial system of education, which is in many cases contradictory to what is contextually relevant for students, teachers, and communities in Kenya, Tanzania, and Uganda. Radical changes are required in education systems in East Africa, as education is often viewed as a catalyst for change. Education provides an avenue to address the issues of terrorism and other modern problems facing Africa today, such as HIV/AIDS and poverty. Perhaps one of the reasons HIV/AIDS has had such rampant devastation in sub-Saharan Africa over the past two decades is because of the lack of a national and multi-sectoral response to battle this tremendous disease. East Africa, the traditional seedbed of HIV and AIDS, has seen many different approaches for dealing with the epidemic. Uganda is heralded throughout the world as being only one of two countries worldwide to reverse the adult infection rate curve of its citizens.[13] This success is attributed to a multi-sectoral approach in a climate of total government support. Perhaps chief among the various sectors is the role education has played in disseminating prevention and control of the disease on a national level. Kenya and Tanzania have not been as successful in dealing with the HIV/AIDS epidemic, primarily because the heads of state have not placed the epidemic as a priority in their respective national contexts. Just as education plays an integral role in dealing with the HIV/AIDS epidemic, so must it in addressing the relatively new dynamic of global terrorism. Without top-level government support and a nationwide response through formal and nonformal education avenues, it will be difficult to confront complex terrorist network in East Africa.

Possible solutions for the future include adapting local knowledge, values, and philosophies (such as the concept that are of ubuntu) into the national education curricula in East Africa.[14] In this way, Africans can build on cultural concepts that are already part of their way of life. The education of each child is traditionally a community-based effort in African societies.[15] Changes in the predominantly Western model of education in East Africa must occur so that students are able to integrate the school curriculum with the realities of everyday life. As alluded to earlier, terrorism is one of these realities for many East Africans. Whatever changes that are implemented by governments and school administrators, must also coincide with global trends so that students are able to move within the world that we live.[16] This global dynamic—balancing the global and the local—creates a difficult dilemma for educators in East Africa in dealing with current issues of terrorism, HIV/ AIDS, and poverty alleviation.

TAIWAN: LIFE EDUCATION IN TAIWAN AFTER SEPTEMBER 11, 2001

Many equate the terrorist attacks on the World Trade Center and the Pentagon as an overt attack on global capitalism and American military power.[17] This section looks at a Taiwanese perspective on September 11. One of the most obvious effects of September 11 is the economic impact it has had on the world. As *The China Post* explains, "the September 11 attacks have caused a steep decline in private consumption, particularly in the United States where Taiwan relies heavily for its exports of semiconductors and electronics products."[18]

Other areas affected by the events of September 11 include politics, culture, and education. For the purpose of our discussion here, we focus on education. In order to better understand what impact September 11 will have on education in Taiwan, we must first discuss the historical background of the relationship between Taiwan and Mainland China. Following this historical framing, we discuss the changes and reforms of Taiwan education in the aftermath of September 11.

Historical, Social, and Political Background of Taiwan

After overthrowing the Ching dynasty, the Republic of China (ROC) was established in 1911. This was a defining moment for the Chinese because it meant that 5,000 years of imperial rule had officially ended and a brand new united states of China had been established. Unlike the autocracy of the Ching dynasty, the new republic was set up as a democratic and liberal country.

But this major change proved to be short-lived. In 1949, due to opposing sociopolitical ideologies, Taiwan and Mainland China separated into two parts. The Kuo Min Tang (KMT) occupied the island of Taiwan and the Chinese Communist Party (CCT) captured the Mainland of China (Chow, 2000). With the outbreak of the Korean War in 1950, U.S. President Harry S. Truman ordered the 7th Fleet into the Taiwan Strait to prevent a possible Chinese attack on the island. This event marked the first time the United States had intervened in the conflict between the island and mainland. The United States considered Taiwan a buffer against communist expansion in East Asia and provided the island money and military supplies.

Later, Lee Deng-Hui, former president of the ROC, tried to strengthen diplomatic relations with countries around the world, including the United States. In 1995, he traveled to the United States and met with President Bill Clinton. As presidential elections neared in 1996, tensions between the Mainland and Taiwan reached new heights when China conducted several missile tests in the Taiwan Strait throughout the month of March. Many in Taiwan thought that the Mainland was trying to influence voting in the election by the show of military force.[19]

The United States responded by sending warships to the Straits in what would become the largest show of naval force since the Vietnam War. President Clinton ordered two aircraft carrier battle groups to patrol the area. The elections went forward as planned and Lee decisively won a second term.[20]

In 1997, as Britain prepared to return control of Hong Kong to China, Taiwan conducted live military exercises in the Straits. Experts believe this maneuver sought to demonstrate to the Mainland and the World that Taiwan would not follow the Hong Kong example. The United States began shipping fighter jets to Taiwan that year and the pro-independence Democratic Progressive Party won municipal elections on the island itself.[21]

In 1999, President Lee announced that Taiwan enjoyed a "special state-to-state relationship" with China. This statement of implied state sovereignty angered Beijing. Taipei backed away from the position, but talks between the two leaderships were cut off.[22] After the rapid economic development of the past several decades, Taiwan has arrived at a pivotal juncture of economic transformation and must find new ways to maintain competitiveness in a globalized world.[23]

Curriculum and Educational Reform
Concerning Terrorism in Taiwan

Due to several confrontations and the continuous threat with its giant neighbor, Mainland China, Taiwan continuously maintains security alertness in the Taiwan Strait. Due to the political violence periodically experienced in the Mainland, peace and life education have become very important issues of school curricula. And after September 11, 2001, Taiwanese educators realize that life and peace education are essentials in today's world, perhaps even more than ever before. Furthermore, teachers remind their students not to view the media as a means of disseminating information, much of which is often misinterpreted and one-sided.

Life Education

Life education has always been one of the key issues in school curricula, but since September 11 it has increased meaning. There are three Chinese concepts of life education that focus on the following relationships: an individual with her/himself, an individual with others, and an individual with nature.[24]

In the "individual with her/himself" concept, students are taught how to face all aspects of one's life, from birth to death, on an individual level. After September 11, teachers should pay more attention to how society can face the realities of death. Especially in the teenage years, it is difficult for most students to conceptualize death in their own lives. September 11 changed this perspective. Feelings of terror and helplessness permeated society when the students saw the news of the World Trade Center (WTC) and Pentagon terrorist attacks on television and the Internet.

The "individual with others" perspective positions the tensions between Mainland China and Taiwan in a similar vein with the recent conflicts between the United States and the Islamic terrorists. Issues raised in this perspective include addressing how one side can rejoice in the September 11 terrorist events while the other is left to suffer. Teachers should use this concept to help students discuss possible solutions to these dynamic and often negative relationships between two groups of peoples.

The final concept looks at the relationship between an "individual and nature." In this concept, humanity has the responsibility to protect the environment, and maintain it for future generations who will depend on the earth for sustenance.

Peace Education

There were two world wars during the twentieth century, which caused millions to die and suffer because of family and personal losses. After 1949, Taiwan and Mainland China have been in a situation of turmoil and recurring conflicts. Peace education has thus played an integral role on both sides of Taiwan Strait.

After September 11, students in Taiwan felt terrible about the events during the WTC collapse. September 11 provides teachers and parents with a unique opportunity to lead students to rethink a potentially peaceful future between Taiwan and Mainland China.[25]

Teaching Portfolios from a Taiwan Elementary School Teacher

This section follows the ideas of a Taiwan elementary school teacher who tried to use September 11 as a guide to help students reflect on the various roles the media plays in disseminating information.[26]

Instructive Goals:

1. To analyze the reporting methods, which mass media, used during the September 11 event.

2. To understand the difference between covering a news item and translating a news item.
3. To think about and recognize blind spots in the messages when Taiwan mass media quoted CNN directly without verification.
4. To keep an eye on the historical factors of terrorists' anti-United States actions.
5. To improve the proper attitude toward messages and information from the media and sources used by news reporters and agencies.

Teachers should Help Students to Think about the Following Questions

1. The international news broadcasts in Taiwan always included network icons from CNN, ABC, or NBC, so what can we learn from this?
2. The international news in Taiwan always quotes from foreign news reports directly, relying almost entirely on second-hand information and not primary sources.
3. In the final part of every international news broadcast, Taiwan reporters conclude by saying "some reporter translated and edited from CNN or ABC." But in almost all local news broadcasts, reporters said "some reporter covering a news item." What is the difference between these two statements?
4. All translated and edited news information is easy to be controlled by the original reporters and news agencies; the political intonations often mislead the direction of the various readers and audiences.
5. After the discussion of these issues, how will you "view" the news and the messages they portray?
6. We need to be open to receive various kinds of information but learn to develop media literacy skills to enable us to criticize and filter media messages.

Considering the political situation between Taiwan and Mainland China, September 11 teaches the people of both countries about the need to develop peaceful solutions to our differences. The teachers should use the curriculum of life education to interpret the meaning of cooperation and harmony with other peoples, countries, religions, and cultures. And students should be taught about how to make the world a better place with the ultimate goal of peace. Furthermore, teachers could use this incident as an opportunity to ana-lyze the possible misleading influence of the media, mass communication, and help students to develop skills to become media literate.

UNITED STATES: WHAT EDUCATIONAL LESSONS CAN THE UNITED STATES LEARN FROM SEPTEMBER 11, 2001?

Referring to the historic situation presented by September 11, 2001, we now examine the role education should play in the aftermath of terrorist attacks in the United States. Starting with the twin foundations of moral and peace education, we also examine cultural imperialism, media literacy, religious tolerance, and education on a national level.

The Need for Moral Education

Moral education is an essential element for educators in the United States today. Moral education also recognizes the connection between spirituality and the critical reasoning that is crucial to democracy. The moral education context involves initiation into, and renewal of, communities devoted to nondogmatic ideals located beyond both the self and the collective.[27]

According to Hanan A. Alexander,[28] the United States and all Western societies are plagued with a moral inarticulateness and thus rendered unable to decipher between what is good and what is evil. Thus for some, American culture is saturated with immoral influences, as "they all wreak their own brands of spiritual devastation, all in the name of freedom and peace."[29] In the process of meeting the needs of every minority, what is popular with the masses, and focusing what is politically correct, the United States has in some degree lost its moral compass. We must reverse the trend toward moral degeneration. Alexander further claims, "It is crucial that we send a message to the world that we will not be divided by terror." According to Alexander, the task of moral education is to target the root of the moral decay, and that means addressing the three democratic values of freedom, critical thinking, and fallibility.[30] A great moral reformation will occur only as moral education takes place in the hearts, minds, and lives of each of us. We argue that following the terrible events on September 11, moral education must be reinvestigated as a priority in the schools of America.

Peace Education as a National Goal

In an increasingly globalized world, where the United States is a key player in both international economics and cultural dissemination, peace education should have a crucial place on a national level. Peace education employs a nonviolent theory and shows that "language and culture—our ways of creating and perpetuating our reality—can impose minimal aggression while maximizing the potential for peacemaking."[31] Joan Bondurant believes that education is an essential element for obtaining peace, stating that nonviolent "propaganda must be made an integral part of the movement. Education of the opponent, the public, and participants must continue."[32] Though the end goal of all education is peace, moral education claims that there are times when we must stand up for right and decency, for freedom and civilization, to defend the cause of liberty.[33]

Potential Instigator of International Cultural Imperialism

Whether intentional or not, the United States is often considered a leading catalyst in the process of neocolonialism throughout the world. Hollywood, news networks, MTV, sports figures, national interests, and corporations are no longer just U.S. entities but reach out to the masses of the world through the postmodern dynamics of globalization. The cultural, economic, or political domination of one country over another fits the definition of what Peter McLaren terms *cultural imperialism*.[34] With the escalating impact of modern communication, technology brings the previously isolated world closer in virtually every part of life. This hegemonic paradigm,[35] where nations are forced to interact on a global rather than a national or regional level, is the natural product of international free markets, postcolonialism, and globalization.[36] Educators must realize that the perception of the United States as a neocolonial state is legitimate and must be taken into account if notions of moral and peace education are to succeed.

The Influence of the Media

The issue of media literacy is closely related to cultural imperialism. With the development of the Internet and other advances in technology, the media has become an ever more pervasive influence on children and citizens alike. The influence of media in its various forms is significant in the United States and in many countries of the world. Children and adults around the world are able to view footage of terrorists such as Osama bin Laden speaking in his own words about his joy over the widespread impact of the September 11 attacks. The debate on whether or not the United States and a coalition of other nations should go to war against Iraq, and then the actual war with Iraq, are additional international spectacles. Citizens in most countries are able to witness acts of terror and war, through newspapers, magazines, and television screens, sometimes as they are unfolding live. The sniper shootings in the Washington D.C. area are vivid examples of this. The boundaries of government and journalism are blurred as news correspondents are allowed to travel with United States and foreign military to observe military action firsthand. We would argue that given the pervasiveness of the media and recent world events, the effects of the media on children must be considered and addressed in the educational realm.

U.S. citizens live in a democratic society in which the media are not generally required to filter the news and information they present and are allowed to report on all aspects or developments. Of course, the military does not release strategic information, but most other aspects are transparent. Media outlets in a democracy are free to produce news as they see fit. Therefore, we would not support a limitation of the media's right to free speech. Instead, we would support the education of children and other citizens in the area of media literacy. Children must learn to be skeptical of everything they see and read and to consider those who may have had an influence on the portrayal of certain situations and news items. Individuals must develop media literacy skills in order to decode and interpret the various modes of the media.[37]

Religion and International Awareness

Education about religion, or education with religious aspects has been a heated subject for many years in the United States. The separation of church and state has been a mainstay of public education since battles over the issue were waged in the 1960s. The fate of this issue was sealed with the *Engel v. Vitale* Supreme Court case of 1962, which involved turmoil over a prayer by the New York State Board of Regents that was read aloud in public schools at the time. On June 25, 1962, the Court ruled that the Regents' prayer was unconstitutional. This issue continues to be contested, however. On one side of the debate, religious groups and political leaders argue that America's children should be allowed religious instruction in public schools. On the other side of the issue, separationists argue that the church should remain outside the realm of public education. In the current multicultural, multi-ethnic setting of the United States, allowing one religion to prevail in public schools might serve the dominant interest, and may further marginalize those already on the periphery. We would argue that teaching about various religions should be part of any public school curriculum in the United States.

Curriculum and Global Education

Until September 11, President George W. Bush had made it clear that reforming education was his primary domestic goal. Reforming education was the chief pillar of Bush's presidential campaign and this commitment has carried over into the recent *No Child Left Behind Act of 2001*, which was signed into law on January 8, 2002. However, we argue in this section that the Bush administration has struggled to link the domestic priority—education—with the country's new international agenda against terrorism. We feel that in order for peace and moral education to be successful and viable in the United States, the government must emphasize this link and its importance must be substantiated on state and national levels.

Though the federal system in the United States allows for the governance of education primarily at the local level, national curricula and debates play an important role in the shaping of state and local curricula. The Bush administration's *No Child Left Behind* (2001) educational plan "is the most sweeping reform of the Elementary and Secondary Education Act (SESA) since it was enacted in 1965."[38] In the plan, the federal government assumes shared fault for some of the problems inherent in the educational system, and suggests that it must take action to recognize and reward successes and sanction failure in the system.

The president's educational reform plan was written before the tragedy of September 11, in a time when the domestic agenda may have possibly outweighed the international one in the United States. However, the Bush administration acknowledged the importance of education for the multicultural population of the United States in the document. In the foreword to the plan, President Bush states: "...[T]oo many children in America are segregated by low expectations, illiteracy, and self doubt. In a constantly changing world that is demanding increasingly complex skills from its work-force, children are literally being left behind." Though the Bush administra-tion did not address globalization directly, this statement makes it clear that they are working toward education that fits into the world scene of globalization and international interaction.

Earl H. Fry, Stan A. Taylor, and Robert S. Wood argue that due to the interdependencies of today's globalized world, America has become vincible or vulnerable. The only alternative would be isolationism, which would go against the grain of the underpinnings of democracy in America.[39] In a time in which the world has become more interdependent and the United States cannot act on its own, the Bush administration has chosen to take a firm stance against nations that support or harbor terrorists.[40] In his January 2002 State of the Union address, President Bush continually spoke of the war on terrorism as the response to the events of September 11. He took the unusual approach of acknowledging a democratic senator, Ted Kennedy, who was vital to the passing of the *No Child Left Behind Act*, indicating that bipartisan decisions and actions are possible and necessary at this time. Although he did not connect it directly, some would argue that by men-tioning this successful accomplishment of the education act, President Bush implied that this unified, bipartisan milestone could be built upon to relate more closely in a post–September 11 world. Later, Bush continued his diplomatic zeal when he addressed the United Nations in an attempt to build an international coalition of nations to battle against terrorism in Iraq. Yet, failure to enlist a large coalition of nations left the United States and its allies to address the Iraqi crisis independent of the UN endorsement. We would argue that this historic period is precisely the time in which at least some of the principles of moral education and peace education should be incorporated on a national level.

We would also argue that education has an essential role to play in the post–September 11 United States. The educational system in the United States should begin to revitalize at least some of the principles of moral edu-cation and peace education. Educators should take into account ideas around cultural imperialism, media literacy, and religious tolerance, as dis-cussed earlier. Furthermore, at a time when the federal government is tak-ing a more active role in education, the moment to integrate some of these ideas has arrived. Unfortunately, it has taken a severe incident such as the September 11 attacks on the United States to remind us that we need to think in terms of international peace and understanding again. Instead of taking a reactionary stance, we must do all we can to foster the peace and international understanding that was engendered after World War II, when so many of the world's international exchange and peace organizations were founded. Education is a prime outlet for fostering international peace and understanding.

ANALYSIS AND CONCLUSION

What are the lessons that we should learn after September 11, 2001? Should we focus on the worldwide economic decline? Or should we stress the possible conflicts and antagonisms that inevitably exist in a global market economy? Facing this international scene of terrorism—the recent bombing in Bali; the snipers terrorizing the Washington D.C. area; the hostage crisis in Russia; and the war with Saddam Hussein and Iraq—what role can education play to improve the overall situation? Under the rubric of these questions, we analyze educational perspectives from East Africa, Taiwan, and the United States. Table 12.1 shows a comparison of each country in matrix format with the educational issues discussed throughout this chapter: peace education, moral education, national curriculum and global education, terrorism, religion, media literacy, and cultural imperialism.

Let us summarize our main conclusions and recommendations. First, we advocate that peace education could be the crucial concept for all of our cases after September 11, 2001. In East Africa, the concept of ubuntu consists of peace and love at both the individual and communal levels. Both Kenya and Tanzania articulated peace and love as objectives in schools after U.S. embassy buildings were attacked in 1998. In Taiwan, educators should try to lead students to rethink the possible peace between Taiwan and Mainland China. The United States is a key player in both international economics and cultural dissemination; peace education should therefore have an eminent place on a national level.

Second, we stress that moral education should be the important target after the disaster. Schools play a crucial role for disseminating values and morals in the lives of students in East Africa. The curriculum of Life Education leads students in Taiwan to think about the relationships between an individual and herself/himself, an individual and others, and an individual and nature. In the United States, moral education also recognizes the connection between spirituality and the critical reasoning that is crucial to democracy, and its context involves initiation into, and renewal of, communities devoted to nondogmatic ideals located beyond both the self and the collective.

Third, we emphasize the importance of the relationship between national curriculum and globalization. Where current East African education systems are based on a colonial model of education, the national curricula must find avenues for incorporating current dilemmas facing Kenya, Tanzania, and Uganda such as HIV/AIDS, terrorism, and poverty. This emphasizes the need for national curricula to be based on relevant needs rather than simply stepping stones toward higher education, which is only accessible to a small percentage of the respective populations. In Taiwan, the curriculum of Life Education keeps an eye on global village, and stresses the impact of an individual and others' perspective: a nation relating with other nations, a culture interacting with and other cultures, especially in a globalized world. The Bush administration's *No Child Left Behind* acknowledged the importance of

Table 12.1 Issues of educational comparison from East Africa, Taiwan, and the United States

Issues for comparison	East Africa (Kenya, Tanzania, and Uganda)	Taiwan	United States
Peace education	The indigenous concept of ubuntu consists of peace and love, beginning with the individual and extending throughout society. Kenya, Tanzania, and Uganda have incorporated peace and love as objectives for dealing with acts of terrorism in their respective countries.	After September 11, students in Taiwan felt bad about the terrible events during the terrorist attacks. Teachers should try to lead students to rethink the potential for peace between Taiwan and Mainland China. To face the tension between both sides of the Taiwan Strait, education in Taiwan should play a role to keep peace in the world.	In an increasingly globalized world, where the United States is a key player in both international economics and cultural dissemination, peace education should have a crucial place in the national curriculum. Peace education employs a nonviolent theory and shows that language and culture can impose minimal aggression while maximizing the potential for peacemaking.
Moral education	Schools serve a crucial role in disseminating moral values in the lives of students. Ubuntu is viewed as a basis for morality of cooperation, compassion, communalism, and concern for the interests of the collective respect of each individual, while simultaneously emphasizing the importance of relationships and community.	Similar to moral education, curriculum reform in Taiwan pay more attention to Life Education. It leads students to think about the relationships between an individual and herself-himself, an individual and other, and an individual and nature.	Moral education is an essential element for educators in the United States today. Moral education also recognizes the connection between spirituality and the critical reasoning that is crucial to democracy. The moral education context involves initiation into, and renewal of, communities devoted to nondogmatic ideals located beyond both the self and the collective

Curriculum and global education	Sometimes it is difficult for colonial style of education to deal with current problems facing Africa today. These needs to be a delicate balance between the local and the global, as East African governments must help make national curricula relevant to their people, but also provide students with skills necessary to operate in market-driven economy.	The curriculum of Life Education keeps an eye on the global village, and stresses the impact of an individual and other perspectives: a nation relating with other nations, a culture interacting with and other cultures, especially in a globalized world.	The Bush administration, in *No Child Left Behind* (January, 2001), acknowledged the importance of education for the multicultural population of the United States, making it clear that the United States is working toward education that fits into the world scene of globalization and international interaction.
Perspectives on terrorism	Terrorism is an East African as well as a global problem. Making ubuntu part of each individual's life provides a positive example of how to deal with terrorism and other associated problems from an indigenous perspective.	Due to the 50-year confrontation between Taiwan and Mainland China, people in Taiwan have developed a strong antagonism to terrorism, especially after the 1996 missile test in the Taiwan Strait from Mainland China.	Terrorist groups are based on evil and destructive values and morals. These groups will do everything in their power, by whatever means available, to bring down the three fundamentals of moral education. Their leaders strive to woo the masses with sophistry, and to take control of the society.
Perspectives on religion	Political and social tensions have traditionally existed along religious and ethnic lines. The study of religion in schools is an integral part of understanding these differences.	The key concept of Life Education is to help students respect and coexist with different religions and cultures.	Education about religion or education with religious aspects has been a contentious subject for many years in the United States. The need to practice religious tolerance has rarely been more severe than in the post–September 11 world.

Table 12.1 (*Continued*)

Issues for comparison	East Africa (Kenya, Tanzania, and Uganda)	Taiwan	United States
Media literacy	Globalization has made various modes of mass media available to East Africans (TV, Internet, and more sophisticated communication mediums). These tools can affect individuals in both positive and negative ways. Thus, it is mandatory for individuals to develop media literacy skills to decipher between good and bad	Mass media should not mislead the judgment of audiences and students. Education should train students with critical media literacy skills to decode possible wrong messages.	The issue of media literacy is closely related to cultural imperialism. With the development of the Internet and other advances in technology, the media has become an ever more pervasive influence on children and citizens alike. The influence of media in its various forms is significant in the United States and in many countries of the world.
Cultural imperialism	Kenya, Tanzania, and Uganda have only experienced approximately 40 years of independence from European colonization. The concept of ubuntu eliminates hierarchical differences between individuals, communities, and nations. If put on a national level, ubuntu recognizes the reciprocal necessity for nations to work together for the betterment of the world.	After the colonial domination by Holland, Spain, and Japan, Taiwanese learn how to face political and economic imperialism, but now are faced with cultural imperialism in a globalized world. Teachers should teach their students to see the real world, and avoid personal biases when casting judgment.	Whether intentional or not, the United States is often considered a leading catalyst in the process of neocolonialism throughout the world. Hollywood, news networks, sports figures, national interests, and corporations are no longer just U.S. entities but reach out to the masses of the world through the postmodern dynamics of globalization.

education for the multicultural population of the United States, and provides a malleable framework that fits into the world scene of globalization and international interaction.

The various perspectives and definitions presented bring us to our fourth issue—terrorism. In East Africa, the general view is that terrorism is not just an international problem, but is something that every East African must deal with. Making ubuntu a part of each individual's life provides a positive example of how to deal with terrorism from an indigenous perspective. Stemming from the 50-year confrontation between Taiwan and Mainland China, people in Taiwan have developed a strong antagonism to terrorism, especially after the 1996 missile test in the Taiwan Strait from Mainland China. Americans view terrorism as an evil and antagonist to democracy and freedom. The terrorist attacks on September 11 provided a latent validity to the U.S. government's stance to fight against international terrorists.

Fifth, after September 11, the religion issue has seized the attention of the education field. Political and social tensions in East Africa have often developed along ethnic and religious lines. In Uganda, the Lord's Resistance Army that has opposed the government for over 15 years is based on an extremist religious belief. Al Qaeda operatives targeting a hotel and passenger plane in Mombassa, Kenya, were obvious religious statements against Israel. In Taiwan, the key concept of Life Education is to help students respect and coexist with different religions and cultures. In the United States, education about religion, or education with religious aspects has been a contentious subject for many years in the United States. The need to practice religious tolerance has rarely been more severe than in the post–September 11 world.

Sixth, we examined the role of the media and propose the need for and development of media literacy skills. Globalization has witnessed increasing access to the media in East Africa. The mass media mode of education can work both ways as either an instigator for or against terrorism. Individuals must develop media literacy skills to decipher between these differences. In Taiwan, mass media should not mislead the judgment of audiences and students. Education has the obligation to train students with critical media literacy skills to decode possible wrong messages. For the United States and much of the rest of the world, the issue of media literacy is closely related to cultural imperialism. With the development of the Internet and other advances in technology, the media has become an ever more pervasive influence on children and citizens alike.

Finally, cultural imperialism and postcolonialism are essential ingredients when rethinking the role education should play in the aftermath of September 11, 2001. Kenya, Tanzania, and Uganda have only experienced some 40 years of independence from colonial rule. Recognizing that the colonial education systems are not sufficient to deal with the multiple problems that exist in Africa, the concept of ubuntu is viewed by many as a means for overcoming these ailments. After the colonial domination by Holland,

Spain, and Japan, Taiwanese have learned how to face political and economic imperialism, but now are faced with cultural imperialism in a globalized world. Teachers should teach their students to see the real world, and avoid personal biases when casting judgment. Whether intentional or not, the United States is often considered a leading catalyst in the process of neocolonialism throughout the world. Media networks, blockbuster movies, sports figures, national interests, and corporations thrive in a global market economy; these entities influence not only those in the United States, but also the masses of the world.

NOTES

1. Bruce Nussbaum, "9.11: What Has Change?" *BusinessWeek*, September 16, 2002; "A Night Fell on a Different World," *The Economist*, September 7–13, 2002.

2. We have chosen to use the Zulu word *ubuntu*, even though this same philosophical concept exists in East African languages as well. In Swahili, the indigenous lingua franca of East Africa, the word *harambee* has a similar meaning with *ubuntu*. *Harambee* means that people unite and come together for a common purpose or goal and for the good of all the people in a community. In Kenya, e.g., *harambee* schools have been organized by communities and other social efforts like health clinics. In Lugandan—the indigenous language spoken by the Buganda, the largest ethnic group in Uganda—the word *ekikuungo* has a very similar meaning to *ubuntu*, and is defined as people getting together to pursue common endeavors for the well-being of all members of society. *Ekikuungo* builds on the spirit of love, respect, solidarity, and cooperation as the driving motivations for a group. *Ekikuungo* involves efforts toward improving humanity and human service—i.e., building bridges, wells, and building schools together. The concept of ubuntu relates very well in an East African context as it does in the southern, Zulu-speaking region of the African continent.

3. J. Mokgoro, *Ubuntu and the Law in South Africa* (Johannesburg: Konrad-Adenauer-Stiftung, 1998). See also Moboge B. Ramose's definition of ubuntu in *African Philosophy through Ubuntu* (Harare: Mond Books, 1999).

4. Michael Jesse Battle and Desmond Mpilo Tutu, *Reconciliation: The Ubuntu Theology of Desmond Tutu* (Cleveland, OH: Pilgrim Press, 1997), p. 35.

5. One of the most controversial issues at the World Summit was the U.S. stance against the Kyoto accord it signed along with 54 other countries in 1997 in Japan. Many African nations felt that the United States should have taken a lead role to halt global warming; the U.S. position claimed that it will not back a treaty that will harm the U.S. economy. Furthermore, the U.S. government did not want to be constrained to industrial emissions standards when other world powers, such as India and China, were not required to sign the same declaration. For more information see Robert Lempert, "Missed Opportunities in Johannesburg," *United Press International* (October 22, 2002); Associated Press, "Protests Mark End of World Summit," *The East African Standard* (September 5, 2002); "Summit Negotiators Reach Deal on Kyoto Text," *South African Press Association* (September 1, 2002); Nate Heard, "The World Summit on Sustainable Development," *The Reporter* (Fall 2002): 23.

6. Mike Allen and Paul Blustein, "Unlikely Allies Influenced Bush to Shift Course on Aids Relief," *Washington Post* (January 30, 2003), p. A1; Kevin J. Kelly, "AIDS: 'Gunslinger' Bush to Africa's Rescue," *The East African* (February 3, 2003).

7. See, e.g., Mugumo Munene, "Kenya Opposed to War on Iraq without Un Mandate," *The Nation* (March 21, 2003); "Why Government Backed U.S.-Led War Against Saddam," *The New Vision* (March 24, 2003); "MPs Shocked on Govt's Backing of War on Iraq," *The New Vision* (March 25, 2003); Absalom Kibanda, "Even with a $1.4bn Account, War Makes Tanzania Restless," *The Monitor* (March 19, 2003); "If Bush Intends to Be Headman of Global Village, Villagers Need a Say," *BusinessDay* (March 26, 2003).

8. See John Kamau, "Kenya: Yes, So What?" *NewAfrican*, No. 408 (2002): 13; Daudi N. Mwakawago, "Tanzania: Measures to Eliminate International Terrorism," Statement to the 56th Session of the United Nations General Assembly (New York: United Nations, October 4, 2001). Mwakawago is the ambassador of the United Republic of Tanzania to the United Nations.

9. Bob F. Jalang'o, "Kenya: Measures to Eliminate International Terrorism," Statement to the 56th Session of the United Nations General Assembly (New York: United Nations, October 4, 2001). Jalang'o is the ambassador of Kenya to the United Nations.

10. Rajeev Bhargava, "Ordinary Feelings, Extraordinary Events: Moral Complexity in 9/11," in *Understanding September 11*, edited by Craig Calhoun, Paul Price, and Ashley Timmer (New York: New Press, 2002), p. 322.

11. Terrorist attacks have significantly impacted the economies of the East African region. Tourism, trade, and travel all suffer from the aftershocks of such events. See Lucy Ndichu and Dorah Nesoba, "Minister, U.S. Envoy Differ on Terrorist Danger to Kenya," *The East African Standard* (March 19, 2003); Tracy Wilkinson and Davan Maharaj, "To Israelis, Nowhere Is Safe after Attacks in 'Nice, Quiet Place,'" *Los Angeles Times* (November 29, 2002).

12. Joseph P. Farrell, "The Aga Khan Foundation Experience Compared with Emerging Alternatives to Formal Schooling," in *Improving Schools through Teacher Development: Case Studies of the Aga Khan Foundation Projects in East Africa*, edited by Stephen E. Anderson, pp. 247–70 (Lisse, The Netherlands: Swets & Zeitlinger Publishers, 2002); J. C. Ssekamwa and S. M. E. Lugumba, *A History of Education in East Africa* (Kampala, Uganda: Fountain Publishers, 2001).

13. Senegal and Uganda are the only two nations that have thus far reversed the trend of rising HIV infection rates among their adult populations.

14. Stephen E. Anderson, ed., *Improving Schools through Teacher Development: Case Studies of the Aga Khan Foundation Projects in East Africa* (Lisse, The Netherlands: Swets & Zeitlinger Publishers, 2002).

15. Timothy Reagan, *Non-Western Educational Traditions: Alternative Approaches to Educational Thought and Practice*, edited by Joel Spring, 2nd ed., 2 vols., *Sociocultural, Political, and Historical Studies in Education* (Mahwah, NJ: Lawrence Erlbaum Associates, Publishers, 2000); Abdou Moumouni, *Education in Africa* (New York: Praeger, 1968).

16. Ssekamwa and Lugumba, *A History of Education in East Africa*.

17. Marc Howard Ross, "The Political Psychology of Competing Narratives: September 11 and Beyond," in *Understanding September 11*, edited by Craig Calhoun, Paul Price, and Ashley Timmer, pp. 304–20 (New York: New Press, 2002); Peter Hudis, *The Crisis of September 11 and the Need for Conceptual Reorganization* (Chicago: News and Letters Committees, 2002), pp. 4–9.

18. "Asian Stability Fears Overhyped, Economic Problems Real: Report," *The China Post* (November 3, 2001).

19. Jimmy W. Wheeler, *Chinese Divide Evolving Relations Between Taiwan and Mainland China* (Indianapolis: Hudson Institute, 1996).

20. The China Post Staff, "Chang Aims for Peaceful Talks with Mainland," *The China Post* (April 7, 2001).
21. Richard G. Lugar, "United States, China, and Taiwan: The Policy Calculus" (paper presented at the High-level Commentary on Taiwan and China from a Hudson Institute Conference: "The USA, Taiwan, and the PRC: Security and Strategy After the Elections of 2000," Indianapolis, January 11–12, 2001).
22. Teng-hui Lee, *Special 'State-to-State' Position* (July 9, 1999), available from www.taiwanheadlines.gov.tw.
23. BBC, *Q&A: Taiwan's Relations with China* (February 21, 2001), available from news.bbc.co.uk.
24. ROC Ministry of Education, *Life.Edu.Tw* (2002), available from life.edu.tw (Chinese version); Wen-Jing Shan, Sheng Yao Cheng, and C. J. Tsao, *Hong Kong Education* (Taipei: Shang Ding Press, 2000).
25. Shui-bian Chen, *President Chen Pledges Support to the U.S. after the Terrorist Attacks of September 11* (September 12, 2001), available from www.taiwanstudies.org.
26. Ibid.
27. Hanan A. Alexander, *Reclaiming Goodness: Education and the Spiritual Quest* (Notre Dame, Indiana: University of Notre Dame Press, 2001); Elizabeth Campbell, "Let Right Be Done: Trying to Put Ethical Standards into Practice," *Journal of Education Policy* 16, No. 5 (2001); Edith Mukudi, "Gender and Education in Africa: A Review of the Issues," *Comparative Education Review* 46, No. 2 (2002); Russell T. Osguthorpe, *Education of the Heart: Rediscovering the Spiritual Roots of Learning* (American Fork, UT: Covenant Communications, 1996); Lynne Parmenter, "Internationalization in Japanese Education: Current Issues and Future Prospects," in *Globalization and Education: Integration and Contestation across Cultures*, edited by Nelly P. Stromquist and Karen Monkman, pp. 237–54 (Lanham, Maryland: Rowman & Littlefield Publishers, Inc., 2000).
28. Hanan A. Alexander, "Three Essentials of Moral Education," address given at Northridge, California (December 7, 2001).
29. Cited in Gordon B. Hinckley, *Standing for Something: 10 Neglected Virtues That Will Heal Our Hearts and Our Homes* (New York: Three Rivers Press, 1999), p. 36
30. Alexander, "Three Essentials of Moral Education".
31. Ellen W. Gorsevski, "Nonviolent Theory on Communication: The Implications for Theorizing a Nonviolent Rhetoric," *Peace and Change* 24, No. 4 (1999): 445. In his chapter, "198 Methods of Nonviolent Action," in *A Peace Reader: Essential Readings on World Order*, edited by Joseph Fahey and Richard Armstrong (Mahwah, NJ: Paulist Press, 1972), Gene Sharp outlines 198 examples of nonviolent action and groups them into six categories: (1) formal statements (2) communications with a wider audience (3) group representations (4) symbolic public acts (5) drama and music, and (6) processions.
32. Joan V. Bondurant, *Conquest of Violence: The Gandhian Philosophy of Conflict* (Princeton, NJ: Princeton University Press, 1988).
33. Alexander, *Reclaiming Goodness*; Alexander, "Three Essentials of Moral Education"; Jodie Morse, "The 9/11 Kid," *Time*, September 11, 2002.
34. Peter L. McLaren, *Life in Schools—an Introduction to Critical Pedagogy in the Foundations of Education*, 3rd ed. (New York: Longman, 1998).
35. Henry A. Giroux, "Democracy, Freedom, and Justice after September 11th: Rethinking the Role of Educators and the Politics of Schooling," *Teachers*

College Record 104, No. 6 (2002); W. James Jacob and Sheng Yao Cheng, "Toward the Future of Education: The EPAM Approach to Educational Reform," *Journal of Education*, forthcoming (2003); Douglas Kellner, *Media Culture: Cultural Studies, Identity, and Politics Between the Modern and the Postmodern* (New York: Routledge, 1995); Raymond A. Morrow and Carlos A. Torres, *Social Theory and Education: A Critique of Theories of Social and Cultural Reproduction* (Albany, NY: State University of New York Press, Albany, 1995).

36. Sandra Harding, *Is Science Multi-Cultural? Postcolonialisms, Feminisms, and Epistemologies* (Bloomington, IN: Indiana University Press, 1998).

37. Meenakshi Gigi Durham and Douglas M. Kellner, eds., *Media and Cultural Studies: Key Works* (Malden, MA: Blackwell Publishers, 2001); Stuart Hall et al., eds., *Culture, Media, Language* (London: Hutchinson, 1980); Edward Herman and Noam Chomsky, *Manufacturing Consent: The Political Economy of the Mass Media* (New York: Pantheon, 1988).

38. Cited in the U.S. Department of Education's website *No Child Left Behind*, available at www.nclb.gov. See also George W. Bush, *No Child Left Behind* (Washington, DC: U.S. Department of Education, 2001).

39. Earl H. Fry, Stanley A. Taylor, and Robert S. Wood, *America the Vincible: U.S. Foreign Policy for the 21st Century* (Englewood Cliffs, NJ: Prentice Hall, 1994).

40. Michael Duffy, "The President: Marching Alone," *Time*, September 11, 2002.

13

Multiple Perspectives on Terrorism and Islam: Challenges for Educators in Egypt and the United States before/after September 11, 2001[1]

Mark Ginsburg and Nagwa Megahed[2]

Introduction

In this chapter we examine the issues related to two separable topics (terrorism and Islam), which we believe need to be addressed as part of the content in preservice and in-service social foundations of education courses. Certainly, educators and their occupational socialization have a strong, if not always acknowledged, political dimension,[3] and thus such topics constitute a relevant focus. This is not only because of the enormity of the death and destruction that occurred within U.S. territory as a consequence of the hijacking and crashing of four commercial airliners on September 11, 2001 or because of the way many people have defined these events as a turning point in contemporary world history.[4] These topics (and others, such as capitalism, Christianity, Judaism, revolution, and socialism) are salient in any attempt to understand the global social context of education.[5]

Multiple Perspectives on Terrorism and Islam

To stimulate social foundations colleagues to consider what to discuss with educators we present here some of the issues associated with the topics of terrorism and Islam. Because we are committed to critical pedagogy,[6] we offer multiple perspectives on the issues.

Terrorism

In dictionaries the word terrorism has been defined as "threats or acts of violence, esp[ecially] as a means of intimidating or coercing"[7] that can serve as "a mode of [either] governing or opposing government."[8] However, at least in the United States "[d]uring the Reagan years [1980–1988], the simple term 'terrorism'... became short-hand for any perceived threat of violence directed at U.S. interests."[9] This bipolar, but unidirectional conception of "terrorism" was clearly enunciated by U.S. President George W. Bush in his September 20, 2001,[10] television address to a joint session of Congress when he asserted that "there are thousands of these terrorists in more than sixty countries" and then stated: "Every nation in every region now has a decision to make. Either you are with us, or you are with the terrorists. From this day forward, any nation that continues to harbor or support terrorism will be regarded by the United States as a hostile regime."[11]

We agree that the actions allegedly perpetrated by members of Osama bin Laden's Al-Qaeda network on September 11, 2001, should be considered acts of terrorism against the U.S. government, as were the bombings of the U.S. Marines barracks in Beirut, Lebanon on October 23, 1983, the World Trade Center in New York City (U.S.A) on February 26, 1993, and the U.S. embassies in Nairobi, Kenya, and Dar es Salaam, Tanzania on August 7, 1998.[12] But we cannot agree that terrorism is only directed at the United States and its allies and we join in criticizing "[s]uccessive U.S. administrations... for using an overly narrow definition of terrorism—the killing of noncombatants by individuals or small groups of irregulars— while ignoring the usually more widespread killings of equally innocent people by sanctioned organs of recognized states."[13]

Many leaders and other citizens in the United States may disagree, but Amnesty International (1998) has reported "that the United States was as responsible for extreme violations of human rights around the globe— including the promotion of torture and terrorism and the use of state violence—as any government or organization in the world."[14] McSherry[15] summarizes the historical evidence of terrorism committed by the U.S. government and its allies:

> As McClintock[16] noted, U.S. counterinsurgency doctrine and operations [initially developed and deployed after World War II in Europe] essentially legitimized the use of state terror.... Moreover, as Jeffrey A. Sluka[17] has pointed out, "the structures, tactics, and technology of state terror have been diffused, in fact aggressively marketed and exported as a form of 'military aid' to developing countries."

Thus, the appellation of a violent act as an act of "terrorism" involves a subjective interpretation.[18] Ironically, "terrorism" like "beauty" is in the eye of the beholder. It is more likely that the acts of "others"—rather than one's own or one's allies' acts—are considered to constitute "terrorism."[19]

Discussions of terrorism are complicated, moreover, because of differences in how violence is conceived,[20] especially since the "most basic pattern is for defenders of constituted authority to use more restrictive definitions of violence and for opponents of constituted authority to use broader definitions."[21] Generally, the concept of violence is associated with "acts of physical force aimed at severe injury or destruction of persons, objects or organizations."[22] In contrast or in addition to physical forms of violence, there is what some term "structural" violence,[23] that is, "nonphysical acts of 'violation'"[24] or violation of "the most fundamental natural rights of persons."[25] At a macro-level, structural violence could involve governmental or other institutional policies and practices that create or perpetuate hunger, illness, illiteracy, or environmental degradation or otherwise cause premature death and/or diminish the quality of people's life.[26] Thus, government agencies, international financial organizations, transnational corporations, and the like can be seen to engage in structural violence—even "terrorism," if such violence is used "as a means of intimidating or coercing"—when they pursue policies that deprive people of food, medical care, education, or a sustainable environment.

Especially given a conception of terrorism that is not limited to the actions of our enemies and that includes structural as well as physical violence, we agree with Zunes that "[t]here is nothing inherent in Islamic, Middle Eastern,...or any other tradition that spawns terrorism."[27] And we would add that there is nothing inherent in any religious or cultural tradition that prevents it from being used to motivate violence or terrorism. For example, while the doctrines of all major religions promote peaceful relations, groups associated with various religions have claimed that their acts of violence and "terrorism" are justified by their religious faith.[28] Therefore, although it may be dispiriting, it should not surprise us that Osama bin Laden issued an edict calling "on every Muslim...to comply with God's order to kill the Americans and plunder their money wherever and whenever they find it"[29] and that George W. Bush exclaimed on September 20, 2001, that the United States would use "every necessary weapon of war" against its enemies, adding that "'God is not neutral."[30]

Islam

"The word Islam derives from the three-consonant Arabic root SLM,"[31] "which generates words with interrelated meanings, including 'surrender,' 'submission,' 'commitment' and 'peace.'"[32] Thus, "Islam means the state of submission to the one and only God 'Allah,' and Muslim refers to a person who has submitted to the will of Allah."[33] For believers, Islam is not a new religion, but is rather the last reiteration of the primordial message of God's Oneness that God revealed through prophets associated with Judaic and Christian traditions as well as through the Prophet Muhammad.[34] Soon after Muhammad's death the records of God's revelations (via angel Gabriel) to Muhammad were collected and put in a standardized form, the Qur'an.[35]

For Muslims, Islam is both a religion and a method of life. In addition to the Qur'an, there are three other source of Islamic law (Shari'a): (a) the hadith, which contains the Sunnah or life examples of the Prophet Muhammad; (b) the Ijma or consensus of the community of Islamic scholars in a given society and era; and (c) *Qiyas* (analogy), applying an injunction that applies in one case to another similar case.[36] Because of variations in scholars' interpretations and in individuals' choices of action, there are similarities as well as differences in the practice of some Islamic rules across societies and within a given society.[37] Moreover, under the belief in the Judgment Day and individual accountability for actions, Muslims are considered responsible for their own activities and thus exercise a degree of freedom.

To illustrate the relationship between Islamic law, group differences in interpretation, freedom, and personal choice, we discuss here two Islamic rules that are viewed by some as contradicting Judeo-Christian or "Western" ideas of liberty and modernization: *hijab* (veiling of women) and *jihad* (directed struggle). These discussions provide illustrations of multiple perspectives on and within Islam.

The word *hijab* comes from the Arabic word *hajaba* meaning to hide from view or conceal. The Qur'an and the *hadith* do not present a fixed standard for the type of clothing that Muslims must wear. However, they specify that some requirements of modesty must be met: (a) women's clothing should be loose and thick enough so as not to reveal the shape of their bodies; and (b) men's clothing should not be too tight or provocative.[38] Modesty in clothing is important not only as an expression of commitment to God, but also because both men and women should be evaluated for their intelligence and skills instead of their looks and sexuality.[39] Some people (both Muslims and non-Muslims) view *hijab* as liberating for women, while other people (both Muslims and non-Muslims) view this Islamic rule as being oppressive, especially of women. Cook represents the former view in commenting, "[t]he *hijab* is important in Islamic society...as a symbol of a women's commitment to God and as a form of protection from the unwanted advances of men."[40] In contrast, the latter view is signaled by the statement that "the most visible symbol of the Taliban's oppressive regime [in Afghanistan] was the order that placed all women under the *burka*"— "the head-to-toe garment...a kind of body bag for the living."[41] It is important to point out that there are variations among Muslim societies and among individual Muslims in what, if any, head covering (e.g., a scarf, a veil, a *burka*) is required to maintain a woman's modesty. And in Afghanistan under the Taliban[42] as well as in other societies,[43] Muslim women differ regarding whether they are covering their heads (and other parts of their bodies) because of personal choice; duty to God; or coercion/oppression by family members, religious leaders, and/or government officials.

The Arabic word *jihad* is derived from the three consonants, JHD and its literal meaning is exertion of effort or directed struggle.[44] "It is a central and broad Islamic concept that includes struggle against evil inclinations within oneself, struggle to improve the quality of life in society, struggle in the battlefield for self-defense."[45] Some people (both Muslims and non-Muslims) define *jihad* as "holy war," directed either against people and governments seen to be "un-Islamic" or against the forces of "modernization."[46] However, according to Islamic teachings, it is unholy to instigate or start

war, although some wars are inevitable and justifiable.[47] Islamic law forbids
and condemns wars of extermination or territorial conquest, but the Qur'an
states that it is a religious duty for the entire Muslim community, women as
well as men, to struggle (against people who attack first) in self-defense to
protect life, property, and freedom. As with the case of *hijab*, one can see
that, in the case of *jihad*, interpretations and choices have to be made. For
example, when is an act of violence justified as self-defense and when is it an
offensive action, an initial act of violence, a form of revenge, or an action in
anger? While individuals and groups can reach their own conclusions, it may
be difficult to reach consensus on such issues. This only reminds us that there
is not a single, monolithic vision on Islam, nor is it appropriate to condemn
or applaud Islam based only on the actions of one group that identifies itself
as Muslim.[48]

Audiences in Different Contexts

In reading the foregoing discussion about the separable topics of terrorism
and Islam, presumably you considered the issues identified with at least
some vague conception of the audience and context. That is, you likely sup-
plied answers to questions such as the following. In what region of what
country am I teaching social foundations of education? Who are the preservice or in-service educators with whom I am interacting? Who are the students with whom these (future or current) educators will encounter in their
classrooms? While we are not suggesting that what one tells educators about
these issues should vary significantly in relation to differences in audience or
context, we do believe that it is important to consider audience and context
in anticipating how educators and their students will interpret and respond
to the issues raised. Here we focus on the Egypt and the United States,
exploring variations in audiences across and within societal contexts.

Egypt

Egypt is considered a Middle Eastern country located in the northeast
corner of Africa. It has a population of over 69 million people, most of whom
are Arabs with small minorities of Bedouins and Nubians. There are also
important rural/urban, age, and social class differences among Egyptians.
Islam is the official religion of Egypt, and Muslims constitute 90 percent of
the population, though other religious groups, including the next largest
group—Coptic Christians, are legally granted freedom of worship. This het-
erogeneity among Egyptians must be considered in teaching Egyptian educators about terrorism and Islam; however, perhaps more significant is the
long-term, often violent conflict involving some groups of Muslims.

Of these groups, which developed initially during the British colonialism (1882–1922) and then after Egypt's independence continued to confront the monarchies of Ahmed Fuad Pasha (1922–1936) and Farouk
(1936–1952) as well as the postrevolutionary governments of Gamal Adb

El–Nasser (1952–1970), Anwar al-Sadat (1970–1981), and Hosni Mubarak (1981-present), the most well known is *al-Ikhwan al-Muslimun* or the Muslim Brotherhood, which was founded in 1928 by a schoolteacher, Hasan al-Banna.[49] Before the 1952 revolution the Muslim Brotherhood grew rapidly and developed into a militant mass movement, viewed to have been the most powerful among radical university student and worker groups (of Muslims and non-Muslims), including those led by marxists.[50] After the 1952 revolution, "the Muslim Brotherhood issued a declaration of support for the revolution's leaders [and] ... repeatedly proclaimed the need for basing the new government on Islam." In 1954, when the Brotherhood and other radical groups challenged his government's decision to alter the Suez Canal Treaty with Britain, Nasser ordered that thousands of their members be imprisoned (without trial). Nasser also initiated a policy of secularization, for example, bringing religious courts and Al-Azhar University under secular state control[51]—actions that reinforced the Brotherhood's perception that the government of Egypt was "un-Islamic." This perception was further strengthened because of the increasing military and economic influence of the Soviet Union, especially after the 1956 war over control of the Suez Canal and the 1967 war between Israel and Egypt (as well as Jordan and Syria).

Perhaps ironically, in the 1970s when Sadat's government sought to address Egypt's pressing economic problems by encouraging Western European and North American investment, he also empowered once again the Muslim Brotherhood, particularly among university students, as a political force opposing the Nasserists and other leftists groups—a strategy that had the support of both Saudi Arabia and the United States.[52] At the same time, to make Egypt more attractive to such investment, Sadat dramatically scaled back relations with the Soviet Union and pursued peace with Israel (before and after the 1973 war). The *Jama'a al-Islamiyya*, an Islamic group that Sadat helped to create out of the Muslim Brotherhood, supported Sadat's moves to weaken the role of ("atheist/marxist") Nasserists in Egypt and to distance Egypt from the Soviet Union, which not only was an atheist empire, but also invaded the Muslim-majority nation of Afghanistan in 1979. However, *al-Jama'at al-Islamiyya* opposed Sadat's efforts to establish peace with Israel, a major factor instigating his being assassinated in 1981.[53] This initial "terrorist" act was followed by a wave of "terrorism" in the 1980s and 1990s, directed especially at Egyptian government officials. For example, one or the other of the subgroups associated with *al-Jama'at al-Islamiyya* is said to be responsible for killing the Minister of the Interior in 1984 and the Speaker of the Assembly in 1990, for injuring the Minister of Information in 1993, and for attempting to assassinate President Mubarak in Ethiopia on June 26, 1995.[54]

Mubarak, the president of Egypt since 1981, during a period of increased military and economic aid from the United States,[55] "rejected any possibility of negotiation [with *al-Jama'at al-Islamiyya*]. Instead [his government] relied on heavy security measures, including massive arrests, the death penalty, ... the use of military courts to try suspected militants...."

[and armed attacks], particularly in Upper Egypt."[56] And in 1996 the Egyptian government rejected a call for cease-fire from some leaders of *al-Jama'at al-Islamiyya* groups and continued its intensive security approach. In November 1997, members of the *Jama'at al-Islamiyya* groups killed 58 foreign tourists and some Egyptians in the city of Luxor—an attack that had a substantial negative impact on tourism, a major component of the Egyptian economy. Because President Mubarak was convinced that an international network was behind these terrorist attacks in Egypt, he called for international action against terrorism in 1997—a call that was not fully heeded until the events of September 11, 2001.

This long, complex history of conflict and violence obviously presents challenges in teaching Egyptian educators about terrorism and Islam. It is not just that "'Egyptians are victims of terrorism as well,'" as stated by an aide of Muhammad Sayed Tantawi, "the highest ranking cleric in Egypt and an influential figure across the Sunni Islamic world," in explaining the level of security for his boss, "known as Shiekh of Al-Azhar."[57] It is that while some view *al-Jama'at al-Islamiyya* as a terrorist group falsely basing its action on Islam, others perceive of the Egyptian government (and its allies, Israel, and the United States) as un-Islamic terrorist states. Moreover, although Egypt has for years been labeled as "a major enemy of the bin Laden network"[58] and "less than a month before [September 11, 2001]... al-Qaida chieftains received a report spelling out 'exceptionally good opportunities' for terrorism in...Egypt,"[59] "Egyptians are among those allegedly involved in the [September 11] attacks."[60]

United States

The United States of America, a North American society, has a population of more than 250 million people, composed of non-Hispanic whites (approximately 71 percent), Hispanics (12 percent), non-Hispanic blacks (11 percent), Asian (4 percent), American Indian, and others (2 percent).[61] The population is also varied with respect to rural/urban residence, region, age, and social class. Importantly, both race/ethnicity and social class are highly related to inequalities in wealth/income and political power[62] as well as to differential participation in "volunteer" military service. In terms of religion, as of 1990, 60 percent of the population identified themselves as members of organized religious groups and of these their affiliations were: various Protestant denominations (52 percent), Roman Catholic (37 percent), Jewish (4 percent), Mormon (3 percent), and Eastern Orthodox (3 percent), as well as less than 1 percent Muslims, Buddhists, and others.[63] Since 1990, however, the Muslim population has grown rapidly—through conversion and new migration from various regions of the world, such that by the end of the twentieth century it was estimated that there were between six and seven million Muslims in America, "making them the second largest religious group in the United States, after Christians."[64]

These characteristics are critical to consider in terms of anticipating how educators and their students in the United States might respond to efforts to teach about terrorism and Islam. For example, contemplate the task of teaching U.S. educators about these topics when they and the students in the schools in which they work are white, black, and brown Muslim and non-Muslim U.S. citizens from families representing different social classes and political ideologies. And what about classrooms with some students who are non-U.S. citizens, such as a young boy living in Pittsburgh, while his mother pursues her doctorate, who is dropped off at school by his parents, who (for some weeks after September 11, 2001) attached an American flag to their car in order to avoid being attacked or hassled?

Teaching about these topics in the United States, however, is even more challenging because of the complexity of U.S. society and the contradictory nature of the foreign and domestic policies of the U.S. government. The society and these policies might be characterized as "America's contradictions, its on-again, off-again interest in extending rights, its clumsy egalitarianism coupled with ignorant arrogance," with the United States being viewed as a "freedom-loving, brutal, tolerant, short-sighted, selfish, generous, trigger-happy, dumb, glorious, fat-headed, powerhouse."[65] This point is highlighted by Amnesty International:

> The USA was founded in the name of democracy, political and legal equality, and individual freedom. However, despite its claims to international leadership in the field of human rights, and its many institutions to protect individual civil liberties, the USA is failing to deliver the fundamental promise of rights for all.[66]

Engaging U.S. educators in a discussion about terrorism is complicated because, although the United States is currently leading a global "war against terrorism" and although (according to opinion polls) a large majority of the U.S. population has supported at least the initial military action in Afghanistan, some people (as noted earlier) might view the U.S. government, historically and today, as a perpetrator of state terrorism. "The United States has employed its military forces in other countries over seventy times since 1945, not counting innumerable instances of counterinsurgency operations by the CIA."[67] But the questions likely to be debated within Social Foundations of Education and other classrooms are as to what the purposes of these military actions were and in whose interests they were undertaken. Similarly, the U.S. government sends billions of dollars in aid, particularly to "developing" countries, but there are differences of opinion regarding whether such efforts are to improve the quality of life of impoverished people and/or to protect the investments of U.S.-based multinational corporations and strengthen U.S. hegemony.

Teaching U.S. educators about terrorism and Islam is also difficult given what happened in the United States following September 11, 2001. Certainly, we witnessed an outpouring of charitable and humanitarian actions for those who were killed or lost loved ones and for those who were injured or suffered economic losses on that "day of infamy" at "ground zero" in New York, at the Pentagon, or in Pennsylvania. However, there also were non-humanitarian actions by civilians against other people in the United States (primarily Muslims or people of Middle Eastern or South Asian country ethnic background or citizenship). For example, between September 11 and November 29, 2001, there were a total of 1,441 documented incidents against Muslims living in the United States, including eight people killed, 265 assaults on or damages to property, and 262 cases of hate mail.[68]

One such incident occurred in Pittsburgh on September 19, 2001. On that date Humair Ahmed, a University of Pittsburgh student from Pakistan, "was punched and beaten by a man who claimed to be enraged by last week's terrorist attacks."[69] According to a newspaper account published three days later:

> Police said Ahmed told them he was coming home from classes at the University of Pittsburgh . . . [when] a man charged at him repeatedly yelling, "Are you from Afghanistan?" Ahmed said he told the man he was Pakistani and tried to walk away, but the man started to kick and punch him. A woman passing by tried to intervene, but the man just pushed her out of the way and attacked again.[70]

Ahmed reported to those gathered at a rally for peace held on the campus of the University of Pittsburgh on September 20, that this young woman located someone with a cell phone and called the police. However, the attacker escaped into the nearby construction site, where he was working, and was not taken into custody until he came in to a local police station for questioning on September 21.

Actions undertaken by government officials in the United States also might be perceived to be in violation of the civil liberties (not to mention human rights) of Muslims and people of Middle Eastern and South Asian backgrounds. For instance, as of November 3, 2001, there were approximately 1,150 detainees, what some have labeled:

> "disappeared" in the U.S.—people who have been snatched off the streets by agents of the U.S. government, held incommunicado, put in solitary confinement, denied lawyers. . . . [M]ost of the detained are Saudis and Egyptians. There are also detainees from United Arab Emirates, Yemen, Jordan, Pakistan, India, Morocco, Mauritania and El Salvador.[71]

The legality of such actions has been debated as have (a) the initiative by Attorney General John Ashcroft "to have local police interview some 5,000 men and women in Arab-American and Muslim communities"; (b) the "U.S.A. Patriot Act" (signed in December, 2001); and (c) other U.S. government actions, which have altered the legal framework with respect to the detention of noncitizens, attorney–client privilege, military tribunals, and rights to privacy.[72] While opinion polls of the American public conducted within four months of the September 11 attacks have shown "strong support for...detaining legal immigrants, [conducting]...military tribunals,"[73] and "interviewing 5,000 people...within the Arab-American and Islamic communities,"[74] civil libertarians in and outside of government have criticized that "some government initiatives aimed at terrorist suspects, like military tribunals, simply go too far[;]...the new rules may reshape the legal landscape for all Americans[; and]...the Bush Administration is throwing off the delicate balance among the three branches of government."[75]

An incident that occurred in Pittsburgh on September 20, 2001, gives some indication of how civil liberties, such as freedom of speech, may be being restricted in the United States in the context of the "war on terrorism" (for other incidents in the United States, see Rothschild, 2002). On that date John Gardner was escorted by "four school police officers...from [the] gymnasium, where he was subbing for the gym teacher,...was sent home, [and]...given a formal letter...[stating that] he was 'released from [his] assignment as a day-to-day substitute teacher with the Pittsburgh Public Schools until further notice.'"[76] He was dismissed because another teacher had found some notes Gardner scribbled on the edge of a newspaper and gave the "incriminating" evidence to school authorities. The official report stated that Gardner had written the words: "Osama bin Laden did us a favor."[77] In fact, this was part of a longer quote that he heard on a television newscast, which he was watching during his break, and that he thought he might use in a book that he was writing. The quoted material continued: "He vulcanized us, awakened us and strengthened our resolve."[78] Although Gardner's dismissal was rescinded after he, with the help of the local chapter of the American Civil Liberties Union, filed an appeal, the incident raises concerns about the chilling effect on free speech in the current climate in schools, workplaces, and other settings in the United States. Such a climate presents enormous challenges for engaging U.S. educators in discussion about issues related to terrorism and Islam.

CONCLUSION

Educators need to be knowledgeable and should be encouraged to think critically about topics like "terrorism" and Islam, so that they can help their students learn about and analyze the related issues. Certainly, the many questions posed about "terrorism" and Islam when we met during fall 2001 with a group of 50+ Education doctoral students and with two groups of urban public high school students in the United States indicates the need for preparing educators to deal with the topics. However, educators also need to be exposed to—and encouraged to reflect upon—these topics so that they can make informed decisions about how, if at all, to become involved in the discussions and other actions that are taking place in local, national, and global communities. Our own participation in the Pittsburgh-based

"Mobilization for Peace" has reinforced for us the importance of being informed and making choices about what forms of political action and inaction we should pursue.

Our discussion of two national contexts (Egypt and the United States) illustrate the complex challenges that those of us who teach Social Foundations of Education face as we seek to engage preservice and in-service educators on the topics of terrorism and Islam. At the same time these comparative studies can serve as useful vehicles for facilitating dialogue and reflection among educators in any one society. Oftentimes it is easier to discuss controversial and emotionally laden issues by considering them in a "foreign" and/or a historical context rather than by only seeking to deal with them in one's own contemporary setting. Certainly, taking a comparative approach can enable instructors and students to focus on variations in experience and multiple perspectives, thus deepening and strengthening their critical thinking and action.

NOTES

1. *University of Pittsburgh (USA) and Ain Shams University (Egypt).* This is a condensed and slightly revised version of Mark Ginsburg and Nagwa Megahed, "What Should We Tell Educators about Terrorism and Islam? Some Considerations in the Global Context after September 11, 2001," *Educational Studies* 33 (3) (Fall 2002): 288–309. In the longer version we also explore the challenges for teaching about Islam and terrorism in Cuba and the Philippines.

2. Correspondence should be addressed to Mark Ginsburg and Nagwa Megahed, University of Pittsburgh, IISE-School of Education, 5KO1 Posvar Hall, Pittsburgh, PA, 15260, U.S.A; tel: 412-648-1783; E-mail: mbg@pitt.edu and nmmst19@pitt.edu.

3. Mark Ginsburg, ed., *Politics of Educators' Work and Lives* (New York: Garland, 1995); Mark Ginsburg and Beverly Lindsay, eds., *The Political Dimension in Teacher Education: Comparative Perspectives on Policy Formation, Socialization and Society* (New York: Falmer, 1995).

4. Anthony Lewis, "A Different World," *New York Times* (September 12, 2001): A27; Bill Marvel and Aline McKenzie, "Our Lives Will Divide into Before and After," *Pittsburgh Post-Gazette* (September 12, 2001): A5.

5. Nicholas Burbules and Carlos Alberto Torres, eds., *Education and Globalization: Critical Perspectives* (New York: Routledge, 2000); Gerald Gutek, *American Education in a Global Society* (Prospect Heights, IL: Waveland Press, 1997); Nelly Stromquist and Karen Monkman, eds., *Globalization and Education: Integration and Contestation Across Cultures* (Lanham, MD: Rowan and Littlefield, 2000).

6. Henry Giroux, *Pedagogy and the Politics of Hope: Theory, Culture and Schooling: A Critical Reader* (Boulder, CO: Westview Press, 1997); Barry Kanpol, *Critical Pedagogy: An Introduction, 2nd edition* (Westport, CN: Bergen & Garvey, 1999); Carmen Luke and Jennifer Gore, *Feminisms and Critical Pedagogy* (New York: Routledge, 1992).

7. Editors, *Funk and Wagnalls Standard Dictionary* (New York: Signet, 1980), p. 835.

8. Editors, *Webster's New Collegiate Dictionary* (Springfield, MA: G. & C. Merriam Company, 1961), p. 877.

9. Joann Kawell, "Terror's Latin American Profile," *NACLA Report on the Americas* 35 (3) (November/December 2001): 50–53; Edward Herman, *The Real Terror Network: Terrorism in Fact and Propoganda* (Boston: South End Press, 1982).

10. Historians may be intrigued that Bush's speech was given almost exactly three years following then U.S. President Bill Clinton address to the United Nations, on September 21, 1998, at which he "urg[ed] an international front to combat terrorists" (Gellman, 2001, p. 8), this following the bombings of U.S. embassies in Kenya and Tanzania on August 7 of that year.

11. Editors, "After the Attack...The War on Terrorism," *Monthly Review* 53 (November 2001): 1–9. Citing the cases of the Jewish underground in Palestine, the Palestine Liberation Organization, and Osama bin Laden, Ahmad (2001, p. 47) observes, "terrorists change. The terrorist of yesterday is the hero of today, and the hero of yesterday becomes the terrorist of today."

12. Joseph Kahn, "A Trend Toward Attacks that Emphasize Deaths," *New York Times* (September 12): A18.

13. Stephen Zunes, "International Terrorism," *Foreign Policy in Focus* 3 (38) (September 2001): 1.

14. Editors, "After the Attack," p. 9.

15. Patrice J. McSherry, "Tracking the Origins of a State Terror Network: Operation Condor," *Latin American Perspectives* 29 (1) (January 2002): 38–60.

16. Michael McClintock, "American Doctrine and Counterinsurgent State Terror," ed. Alexander George, *Western State Terrorism* (New York: Routledge, 1991), pp. 121, 130.

17. Jeffrey Sluka, "Introduction," in *Death Squad: The Anthropology of State Terror* (Philadelphia: University of Pennsylvania Press, 2000), p. 9.

18. Mark Juergensmeyer, "The Islamic Revolution Is Taking Root in Egypt," ed. D. Bender and B. Leone, *Islam: Opposing Viewpoints* (San Diego, CA: Greenhaven Press, 1995), pp. 259–67.

19. Herman, *The Real Terror Network*.

20. Mark Ginsburg with Thomas Clayton, Michel Rakotomanana, and Gilda Holly, "Education for All or Educating All for Peace," ed. Shen-Keng Yang, *Lifelong Education for All* (Taiwan: Chinese Comparative Education Society—Taipei, 1998), pp. 253–97.

21. Kenneth Grundy and Michael Weinstein, *The Ideologies of Violence* (Columbus, OH: Charles E. Merrill, 1974). p. 113.

22. John Spiegel, "Toward a Theory of Collective Violence," ed. Jan Fawcett, *Dynamics of Violence* (Chicago: American Medical Association, 1971), p. 20.

23. Johan Galtung, "Violence, Peace and Peace Research," *Journal of Peace Research* 6 (1969): 167–91.

24. Nevitt Sanford, "Collective Destructiveness: Sources and Remedies," ed. Gene Usdin, *Perspectives on Violence* (New York: Brunner/Mazel, 1971), p. 44.

25. Newton Garver, "What is Violence?" *The Nation* 206 (1968): 819.

26. Birgit Grock-Utne, *Geminist Perspectives on Peace and Peace Education* (New York: Pergamon, 1989).

27. Zunes, "International Terrorism," p. 1.

28. Shireen Hunter, *The Future of Islam and the West: Clash of Civilizations or Peaceful Coexistence?* (Washington D.C.: Center for Strategic and International Studies, 1998). In his book, provocatively entitled *Terror in the Mind of God: The Global Rise of Religious Violence* (Berkeley, CA: University of California Press, 2000), Mark Juergensmeyer presents case studies of the ideas and actions of groups that

have committed acts of "terrorism" and claim to have done so because they are Buddhists, Catholics, Jews, Muslims, Protestant Christians, or Sikhs. And Marc Gopin ["Forward," ed. S. Hunter, *The Future of Islam*, p. ix], adds Confucianism, Taoism, and Shintoism to this list of religions that have had "periods in which some in their midst utilized repressive religious laws or theological principles to commit unspeakable acts of brutality and terror." For discussions about how both peace and violence are promoted and justified within Christianity, Islam, and Judaism, respectively, see David Hollenbach, "The Relation of Justice and Peace," in *Nuclear Ethics: A Christian Moral Argument* (Ramsey, NJ: Paulist Press, 1983), pp. 16–24; Aviezer Ravitzky, "Peace," ed. A. Cohen and P. Mendez-Flohr, *Contemporary Jewish Religious Thought* (New York: Free Press, 1988), pp. 685–702; and Ismail Al-Faruqi, "Introduction," ed. AbdulHamid AbdulSulayman, *The Islamic Theory of International Relations* (New York: The International Institute of Islamic Thought, 1981), pp. xiii–xxiv.

29. Frontline, "Osama bin Laden v. the U.S.: Edicts and Statements," 2001 (retrieved on 01/05/02 at http://www.pbs.org/wgbh/pages/frontline/shows/binladen/who/edicts/html.

30. Editors, "After the Attack," pp. 1–9.

31. Arab World and Islamic Resources (AWIR) and Middle East Policy Council (MEPC), *The Arab World Studies Notebook* (Los Angeles, CA: AWIR and MEPC, 1998), p. 1.

32. Council on Islamic Education (CIE), *Teaching About Islam and Muslims in the Public School Classroom* (Los Angeles, CA: CIE Publications, 1998), 3rd ed., p. 1.

33. Attar Chand, *Islam and the New World Order* (New Delhi: Akashdeep Publishing House, 1992), p. 3.

34. John Voll, *Islam: Continuity and Change in the Modern World*, 2nd ed., (New York: Syracuse University Press, 1994); CIE.

35. AWIR and MEPC; Council on American-Islamic Relations (CAIR), retrieved on 01/03/02 from http://www.cair-net.org/asp/aboutislam.asp; (CIE); Islamic Institute, *Understanding Islam and the Muslims*, retrieved on 12/28/01 from http://www.islamicinstitute.org/understanding.htm.;Vol.

36. *Islam Today*, retrieved on 12/28/01 from http://www.islamtoday.net.

37. AWIR and MEPC; William Glaberson, "Interpreting Law for American Muslims," *New York Times* (October 21, 2001): A18; *Islam Today*.

38. Mary Ali, "The Question of Hijab: Suppression or Liberation?" (Chicago, IL: The Institute of Islamic Information and Education), retrieved on December 22, 2001 from http://www.usc.edu/dept/MSA/humanrelations/womeninislam/whatishijab.html.

39. Mary Ali, "The Question of Hijab,"; Sumayyah Joan, "Hijab" (*Resala*), retrieved on December 1999 from http://thetruereligion.org/hijabjoan.htm; Abdur-Rahman Doi, "Modesty," retrieved on December 29, 2001 from http://www.usc.edu/dept/MSA/humanrelations/womeninislam/womeninsociety.html.

40. Bradly Cook, "Islam and Egyptian Higher Education: Student Attitudes" *Comparative Education Review* 45 (3) (2001): 401.

41. Richard Lacayo, "About Face: An Inside Look at How Women Fared under Taliban Oppression and What the Future Holds for Them Now," *Time* (December 3, 2001): 36, 38. Note that women were prohibited from participation in formal education as well as active public roles in the economy and polity under the Taliban regime in Afghanistan. Another interpretation of Islamic law is that women have the right to be educated at high levels, to possess and dispose of

property, to undertake a trade or profession, and to vote and serve as government officials; see Mary Ali and Anjum Ali, "Women's Liberation through Islam," (Chicago, IL: Institute of Islamic Information and Education), retrieved on December 22, 2001 from http://thetruereligion.org/womenslib.htm; AWIR and MEPC; Karima Bennoune, "Islamic Fundamentalism Represses Women," ed. D. Bender and B. Leone, *Islam: Opposing Viewpoints* (San Diego, CA: Greenhaven Press, 1995), pp. 64–71; Nawal El-Saadawi, "Women Should Reject Islamic Gender Roles: An Interview by Gorge Lerner," ed. Bender and Leone, *Islam: Opposing Viewpoints*, pp. 80–88; Nesta Ramazi, "Islamic Government Need Not Repress Women," ed. Bender and Leone, *Islam: Opposing Viewpoints*, pp. 72–79.

42. Lacayo, "About Face."
43. Sherifa Zuhur, "Women Can Embrace Islamic Gender Roles," ed. Bender and Leone, *Islam: Opposing Viewpoints*, pp. 89–97; Irmgard Pinn, "From Exotic Harem Beauty to Islamic Fundamentalist: Women in Islam," ed. K. Hafez, *The Islamic World and the West: An Introduction to Political Cultures and International Relations*, trans. M. Kenny (Boston, MA: Brill, 1995), pp. 57–69.
44. AWIR and MEPC, p. 3.
45. CAIR.
46. Benjamin Barber, "Jihad vs. McWorld," *The Globalization Reader*, F. Lechner and J. Boli, eds. (London: Blackwell Publishers, 2001), pp. 21–27.
47. Amir Ali, "Jihad Explained," retrieved on December 22, 2001 from http://thetruereligion. org/jihad.htm.
48. Mohammed Arkon and Udo Steinbach, "Forward," ed. Kai Hafex, *The Islamic World and the West*, pp. xi–xvi.
49. Voll, *Islam: Continuity and change*.
50. Ibrahim Ibrahim, "Religion and Politics Under Nasser and Sadat, 1952–1981," ed. B. Stowasser, *The Islamic Impulse* (London: Croom Helm, 1987), pp. 121–34; Voll, Islam: Continuity and change.
51. Ibrahim, "Religion and Politics."
52. Ibrahim, "Religion and Politics"; Barnett Rubin, "Arab Islamist in Afghanistan," ed. J. Esposito, *Political Islam: Revolution, Radicalism, or Reform?* (London: Lynne Rienner Publishers, 1997), pp. 179–206.
53. Michael Dunn, "The Islamic Revolution Is Not Taking Root in Egypt," ed. Bender and Leone, *Islam: Opposing Viewpoints*, pp. 268–76; Ibrahim, "Religion and Politics"; Rubin, "Arab Islamist in Afganistan"; Noam Chomsky, "The United States is a Leading Terrorist State: An Interview by David Baramian," *Monthly Review* 53 (6) (November 2001): 10–19; Dan Tschirgi, "Marginalized Violent Internal Conflict in the Age of Globalization Mexico and Egypt," ed. S. Ismael, *Globalization: Polices, Challenges, and Reponses* (Calgary, Alberta, Canada: Detselig Enterprises, 1999), pp. 217–42; Federal Research Division, "Egypt—A Country Study" (Library of Congress), retrieved on January 8, 2002 from http://lcwb2.loc.gov/frd/cs/egypt/eg_appen.html.
54. Dunn, "The Islamic Revolution"; Juergensmeyer, *Islam: Opposing Viewpoints*; FORSNET, "Middle East and Terrorism: Islamic Group and War (Egypt)," retrieved on January 20, 2002 from http://www.teror.gen.tr/english/middleeast/organisations/radical/islamicgroup.html.
55. Since the 1979 peace accord, brokered by the United States during the Carter administration, was signed between Egypt and Israel, Egypt has become a major recipient of U.S. aid. During the same time Egypt has been a close ally of the

United States, including taking a leading role in securing the cooperation of other Arab states in the U.S.-led Gulf War against Iraq, after it had invaded Kuwait in 1990.

56. Tschirgi, pp. 221, 228.
57. Jeffrey Goldberg, "Behind Mubarak: Egyptian Clerics and Intellectuals Respond to Terrorism," *The New Yorker* (October 8, 2001): 53.
58. Chomsky, "The United States is a Leading Terrorist State," p. 11.
59. Alan Cullison and Andrew Higgins, "Al-Qaida File Maps Attack-Scouting Trip to Israel, Egypt," *Pittsburgh Post-Gazette* (January 17): A 5.
60. Goldberg, "Behind Mubarak," p. 48.
61. *World Book 2001 CD*: US Census, 1990.
62. Denny Braun, *The Rich Get Richer: The Rise of Income Inequality in the United States and the World* (Chicago, IL: Nelson-Hall Braun 1997; William G. Domhoff, "Power and Class in the United States," *Who Rules America: Power and Politics in the Year 2000*, 3rd edition (Mountain View, CA: Mayfield Publishing), Domhoff 1998, pp. 1–32; Martin Marger, "Ethnic Stratification: Power and Inequality." *Race and Ethnic Relations; American and Global Perspectives* (Belmont, CA: Wadsworth Publishing, 1997), pp. 37–69.
63. *World Book 2001 CD*: US Census, 1990.
64. AWIR and MPEC, p. 4; see also CAIR.
65. Todd Gitlin, "Blaming America First," *Monthly Review* (January–February, 2002): 25, 24.
66. Amnesty International, "The United States of America: Rights for All," retrieved on December 22, 2001 from http://web.amnesty.org/ai.nsf/Index/AMR510351998?OpenDocument&of = COUNTRIES\USA.
67. Editors, "After the Attack," pp. 1–2.
68. CAIR.
69. Ferguson Tinsley, "Pakistani Student Attacked Near Pitt" *Pittsburgh Post-Gazette* (September 22, 2001): B1.
70. Ibid., p. B1.
71. Editors, "Disappeared in the USA," *Revolutionary Worker* (November 11, 2001): 3.
72. Adam Cohen, "Rough Justice," *Time* (December 10, 2001): 33.
73. Ibid., p. 30.
74. Joel Stein, "Just a Few Questions," *Time* (December 10, 2001): 41.
75. Cohen, "Rough Justice," p. 32.
76. Carmen Lee, "Sub Teacher Fired Over bin Laden Note," *Pittsburgh Post-Gazette* (September 21, 2001): B1.
77. Ibid., p. B1.
78. Ibid., p. B1.

14

Systemic Higher Educational Crises, International Assistance Programs, and the Politics of Terrorism in Post-Soviet Central Asia

Mark S. Johnson

Introduction

This chapter seeks to bring together several different issues, and to offer insights into how and why one important policy arena in post-Soviet Central Asia has changed amid the "war on terrorism" since September 11, 2001.[1] This will include a brief analysis of the severe systemic crises that have convulsed educational systems throughout the region, especially in the higher educational sector, and a broad overview of various international assistance programs and educational exchanges that have sought to address the region's problems. This chapter will also examine the complex strategic rivalries that have played out since the collapse of the Soviet Union in 1991, as various powerful external actors such as the United States, the EU, the Russian Federation, Turkey, Iran, and, to a lesser degree, Saudi Arabia and others have sought economic advantage along with political and cultural influence in the newly independent states of the region. This will be followed by brief accounts of how the domestic political and social situation has been evolving in the five states, which include Kazakhstan, the Kyrgyz Republic or Kyrgyzstan, Tajikistan, Uzbekistan, and Turkmenistan, and especially of the model higher educational reform program that has been proposed in Kyrgyzstan. I will then consider how the situation has changed since September 11, and the ways in which the "politics of terrorism" have generated new external engagement in the region, in the form of direct military intervention by the United States as well as expanded international assistance programs in support of educational reform, democratization, and civil society.[2] On the one hand, this new engagement has clearly helped to stabilize the region, at least in the short term. However, on the other hand, the new security climate has also exacerbated the larger strategic rivalries in the region and has, perhaps inadvertently, encouraged the Central Asian regimes, with varying degrees of intensity, to clamp down on religious expression and virtually any manifestation of political dissidence. Thus my fundamental argument is that current international policy toward the region remains inconsistent and incoherent in ways that will ultimately undermine the educational and other reforms that provide the only true hope for poverty alleviation, social cohesion, and sustainable, long-term development.

That being said, several other key issues and perspectives must be acknowledged. First, there are undeniably warlords, Islamist insurgents, and other "violent non-state actors" active in the region who are involved in drug and weapons trafficking, who engage in kidnapping and terrorism, and some of whom are linked to and funded by powerful patrons in the Uzbek diaspora and other external interests from the Gulf states, Saudi Arabia, and Pakistan.[3] Whatever their grievances, and however valid their critiques of the authoritarian and corrupt regimes in the region, such activities obviously only further exacerbate the economic crisis, drive away vitally needed foreign investment, victimize innocent civilians and foreigners, and provide a rationale for state repression. While the U.S.-led military intervention in October 2001 that toppled the Taliban regime temporarily eased the dangers emanating from Afghanistan, the acute economic and social crises throughout the region remain unresolved. It must also be acknowledged that from the perspective of the Bush administration, all of the pieces of the current U.S. assistance program form a coherent whole. Current American policy argues that the increased security assistance to local military and police forces will support and stabilize the Central Asian regimes from their external enemies and internal unrest, provide leverage for the United States and other international actors to press for improvements on human rights and the rule of law, and the complementary focus on economic reform, the building of civil society, and educational reform will create the conditions for long-term development.[4] Yet, as Thomas Carothers and other critics have argued, there is a persistent tension between military and police assistance and support for democracy and human rights, which is often reflected in rivalries and the failure to coordinate between activities sponsored by the U.S. Department of Defense (DOD) and the Department of State (DOS), with the latter often losing such struggles.

More specifically, I will analyze broad patterns and several attempted reforms in the higher educational sector, as well as the ways in which otherwise well-intentioned assistance efforts are now threatened by the often single-minded and sometimes narrowly construed focus on military security. Finally, this chapter will also offer concrete policy proposals in an effort to suggest some more constructive solutions to the region's growing educational and other problems. These proposals draw together the latent capacity of the region's higher educational sector, and argue that international assistance programs could be expanded and more constructively targeted in particular ways, all in order to address fundamental and increasingly acute issues of human security and the necessity for more comprehensive policies focused on a broader conception of sustainable development throughout the region.[5] To summarize, my thesis is that the changing security climate in the region is increasingly shaping and distorting international assistance programs and educational exchanges, in ways that neglect a more balanced assessment of local educational needs and capacities, and that will only exacerbate the already tenuous security situation and especially the deteriorating internal stability and legitimacy of the regimes throughout the region. This essay thus follows a recent emerging argument in support of knowledge-based assistance policies.[6]

The Effects of Globalization and the Legacy of Soviet Education

Any attempt to understand higher educational development in post-Soviet Central Asia, and the deep systemic crises that have devastated both instructional quality and social equity throughout much of the region, must consider several related issues. These include the influence of broader trends in global higher educational development, and, in that sense, the effects of deeper processes of globalization. Other issues include the legacy of the Soviet period, and the ways in which Soviet institutional structures as well as professional and pedagogical practices have shaped and, in some cases, limited post-Soviet reform efforts. Perhaps most importantly, I am increasingly convinced that the key issue in understanding the educational crises that are convulsing the region derive from the interaction of these two phenomena: the ways in which global trends have unfolded, and generated unintended consequences, in the uniquely post-Soviet circumstances that characterize the higher educational sector in the region.

The most positive recent trends in global higher educational development include growing faculty and student mobility, as least at the heights of the emerging global higher educational marketplace. These complex "external" (between institutions and nations) and "internal" markets (within institutions, as students are increasingly interested in choosing their course of study) are radically reshaping higher education throughout the world.[7] Other positive elements include a dramatic expansion of new information technologies and of access to new research and instructional materials, as well as sweeping changes within the traditional disciplines as academic knowledge becomes increasingly global, with these latter issues becoming especially revolutionary in formerly closed Central Asia. Many analysts have argued that higher education will inexorably become more decentralized and partially privatized as these "market" forces spread, with traditional state institutions facing a rise in competition from private and commercial institutions. Negative aspects of these global trends include the "brain drain" of professional, faculty, and student talent out of developing nations; and especially the potential loss of equity and open access within national systems as state support for and regulation over the public sector deteriorates.[8]

While Central Asia experienced a remarkable educational and cultural efflorescence between the tenth and fifteenth centuries, education and especially higher education in the region then degraded steadily along with the region's economy over the early modern era, with a broad but shallow pattern of religiously focused literacy in Arabic, which often diverged from the Turkic vernacular languages. This artificiality in the educational system was compounded by severe gender inequities and an acute lack of funding and state support, and was largely restricted to the small urban areas and oases, with little or no formal educational provision for much of the rural and especially the nomadic populations. Indigenous Islamic religious education was then subjected to malign neglect after the arrival of Russian colonial power during the 1860s, and then more systematically repressed during waves of Soviet antireligious agitation in the twentieth century, especially in the 1930s and the 1950s.[9] There were some efforts to create new educational institutions after the 1890s, but again, these efforts were hampered by a chronic lack of investment and pervasive ethnic discrimination against the local populations. Yet this period also witnessed the first, tentative steps in the emergence of national movements in the region, led especially by the Uzbeks and the Kazakhs, which began the articulation of modern literary languages and national identities, often in opposition to Russian power. This period also witnessed the first articulations of a Tajik national movement, influenced by anticolonial and other modernizing currents in Persia. The Soviet period also witnessed the creation of the first secular higher educational institutions in the region, beginning with forced industrialization in the 1930s, which included an array of state universities, as well as more specialized technical, pedagogical, agricultural, and medical institutes.[10] While these institutions were rigidly bureaucratized and embraced very authoritarian models of teaching and learning, they nonetheless represented a qualitatively new chapter in the history of education in Central Asia and, for better or worse, provided the foundations upon which any contemporary reform program must be built. However, while impressive gains were made, especially in the postwar period, Central Asia remained tightly integrated with the Soviet educational system as a whole, both in the form of subsidies for the higher educational sector, but also dependent on exchanges with leading Russian and Ukrainian universities for advanced training and research, both of which have obviously been lost since 1991. This is vividly illustrated by the career of Kyrgyz President Askar Akayev, who spent more than 20 years in Leningrad during his academic career as a physicist.

The broader global trends noted here are clearly visible in Central Asia, and have been embodied in and promoted by the bilateral and multilateral assistance programs that have emerged in the 1990s, which have stressed decentralization and partial privatization. Yet these policies have played out in complex and often unanticipated ways because of the distinctive legacies of Soviet higher education, as local educators struggled to respond to and adapt global models.[11] During the Soviet era, the regime made concerted efforts to establish national borders and to mark off distinctive "ethno-territorial" identities (in a process known as "delimitation" or *razmezhevanie*). These efforts were accompanied by intermittent waves of "affirmative action" policies to cultivate and promote indigenous communists and specialists (a policy known as "indigenization" or *korenizatsiia*), which were especially pronounced in education. For all of the heavy-handed manipulation and waves of repression that accompanied these efforts at socialist and state-sponsored nation building, they undeniably helped to create at least the potential for modern, national identities among the Central Asian peoples, especially as indigenous cadres came to dominate the humanities and social science faculties, and professions such as journalism.[12] However, of course, Soviet policy also sharply restricted religious education and was characterized by frequent waves of repression against local cultural and intellectual elites. Soviet higher education was also rigidly bureaucratized, focused on the immediate agricultural and industrial needs of the planned economy, and was narrowly and inflexibly vocational, with much of the technical and security sector remaining in the hands of Slavic elites.

Finally, and perhaps most importantly, the weak and loosely articulated nature of professional networks in Soviet-style societies has sharply limited the efficacy of recent reform efforts. International assistance programs based on the emerging global model of decentralization, partial or gradual privatization, and autonomous professional development often simply presume strong professional capacity to drive and sustain such processes, and post-Soviet reform efforts have often foundered for this very reason. There is also a very real danger that chaotic, market-driven decentralization and localization could exacerbate ethnic tensions and undermine social cohesion.[13] Overall, the combination of acute economic crisis, the decline of state funding for the higher educational sector, and a severe loss of educational mobility and equity across the region has created a series of systemic crises, as the national higher educational systems are literally buckling under the strain. While new semiprivate and commercial higher educational institutions are springing up across the region, and nominal enrollments are ostensibly rising, there are serious questions about the quality of much of this instruction, and the entire system is plagued by pervasive corruption surrounding admissions, grading, and graduation. While there are some bright spots and several innovative new institutions, as detailed here, this should not cause us to lose sight of the acute crisis facing the vast majority of higher educational institutions throughout post-Soviet Central Asia, which is especially severe in the vitally important fields of vocational, technical, and semiprofessional education.[14] This systemic crisis is also degrading the profession, as young talent leaves the field or emigrates altogether, especially anyone with skills in information technology or foreign languages; and few young people are willing to enter either the teaching corps or careers in higher education. Fitful attempts at partial "privatization" have led to some administrators essentially appropriating their universities as virtual private businesses, and the emergence of these administrative "fiefdoms" has also degraded accountability, transparency, and faculty governance.

UNITED STATES, EUROPEAN, AND MULTILATERAL ASSISTANCE PROGRAMS IN CENTRAL ASIA

There is, of course, a complex interaction between the broader domestic policy environment, the specific administrative and policy structures in the higher educational sector, and external influences, whether in the form of general global trends or targeted assistance policies. In the aftermath of the collapse of the Soviet Union in 1991, Central Asia became the arena for intensifying regional rivalries, as the United States, Europe, Russia, Turkey, Saudi Arabia, Iran, and China all competed for access to the region's energy resources and water. These external actors also entered into a spirited and sometimes brutal competition to shape the foreign policy orientations of the new nations.[15] This competition also took the form of competing assistance programs, as all the various external actors sought to exert influence over the new nations' political, educational, intellectual, and religious development, and to draw them into their respective spheres of influence. This external engagement began with great enthusiasm in the early 1990s, and then became increasingly frustrated and flagged in the face of resistance to Western-style reform and pervasive corruption in the regimes of Islam Karimov in Uzbekistan and of Saparmurad Niyazov in Turkmenistan.[16] The Tajik civil war that raged from 1992 to 1997 also deterred foreign investment, and was resolved only with joint American, Russian, and UN action to forge a peace settlement and reconciliation process in the face of the rising power of the Taliban in neighboring Afghanistan after 1996.[17] There were initially great hopes for the relatively more democratic and pluralistic Kyrgyzstan, which in the early 1990s was leading the region in terms of gender policies and support for a vigorous and autonomous civil society. These policies resulted in Kyrgyzstan receiving a disproportionate share of international attention and assistance, yet this failed to translate into sustained economic growth, even as the Akayev regime slid toward the sort of authoritarianism and nepotism characteristic of the other states in the region.[18] While there were also initially great hopes for energy-rich Kazakhstan, these expectations have been thwarted by the increasingly repressive and, by all accounts, spectacularly corrupt regime of Nursultan Nazarbayev, which has embraced an aggressive and exclusive form of ethnic nationalism, and which has driven away or alienated key elements of the Slavic population, a policy that has proven especially damaging in the higher educational sector.[19] Sadly, even as Kazakhstan has been awash in profits from its energy resources, this has failed to translate into funding for education, with the steady erosion of state subsidies and even of places available in public higher education.

For the United States, the initial hopes for the region in the early 1990s were not fully realized, even given an initially limited focus on energy development and commercial access. In fact, this raises the issue of the multiple tensions within American foreign policy in the 1990s, which have only become more pronounced since September 11, 2001. First, a core priority for the U.S. government is supporting American commercial and trade interests abroad, even when this conflicts with encouraging local Central Asian producers and domestic production or export promotion. Second, there has long been interest in security issues, and the support provided to bolster police and military capacity, especially to interdict drug trafficking and to stem the threat of terrorism and political extremism emanating from Afghanistan and elsewhere in the region. Third, and often the most neglected and most minimally funded, are the programs in support of educational reform, the development of civil society, democratization, and the rule of law. While the rhetoric of "market democracy" simply assumes that all three elements of these assistance strategies cohere, the inconsistencies and tensions between these different priorities are rarely discussed. It should also be noted that many of the promised programs in the "soft" categories of education, civil society, and democracy assistance often fail to materialize for budgetary reasons.[20]

Nonetheless, major assistance and exchange programs have been funded by the United States, especially through the Bureau of Educational and Cultural Affairs (ECA) of the U.S. Department of State, especially for postsecondary exchanges and university partnerships; and the United States Agency for International Development (USAID), for basic educational assistance and teacher education.[21] The ECA programs have focused on support for individual students and educators, as well as targeted assistance to particular departments in state universities and especially for new, innovative, and often private programs in business, economics, and legal education. For example, since 1993, more than 1,000 students and faculty from Kazakhstan have participated in academic exchanges to the United States; more than 500 from Kyrgyzstan; at least 200 from Tajikistan; about 250 from Turkmenistan; and nearly 500 from Uzbekistan. While the vast majority of U.S. assistance has been targeted to economic reform and energy development, nonetheless at least $200 million has been spent on educational reform, exchanges, and advanced training since 1993. Overall U.S. funding to the region since 1992 has totaled more than $1.7 billion, with approximately $650 million of that channeled through the USAID. While USAID programs focus primarily on supporting civil society, addressing environmental problems, independent media, and local government reform, it has also included small programs in teacher education.

The EU prides itself on being the single largest source of funding for economic and administrative reform efforts in the former Soviet bloc, which has flowed primarily through the EU's Technical Assistance to the Commonwealth of Independent States (TACIS) program. However, it is also clear that the vast majority of this funding has gone to the higher priority regions of Central and Eastern Europe, including Ukraine and Russia, with Central Asia being a relatively peripheral region in EU policy. From 1991 to 1999 this amounted to more than 300 million Euros in overall assistance to Central Asia, although the vast majority of this funding was targeted to economic development, support for small and medium enterprises, energy development, and public sector reform.[22] The limited assistance funding that has been provided in the higher educational sector has tended to focus on improving university management and budgetary processes, and on vocational and technical education. Finally, it seems that the new framework for EU/TACIS assistance for 2000–2006 has moved away from the educational sector altogether, with a new stated focus only on institutional, legal, and administrative reform; private sector development; infrastructure needs; environmental protection; the rural economy; and nuclear safety.

In summary, while undeniably useful and important, it seems that both U.S. and European assistance efforts have often been thwarted or underfunded, and that educational reform has rarely been a high priority in the array of often competing assistance priorities. Many of the educational assistance programs have focused on support for individuals, often in the form of expensive international exchanges; while others have attempted to foster change within the state or administrative structures, with all of the predictable problems of corruption and the "capture" of such assistance funding. As useful and necessary as those efforts may be in offering support to individuals and in helping to encourage cooperation from still powerful bureaucratic actors, I would suggest that a renewed focus on the "middle ground" is urgently needed, an explicit shift away from the state sector and the often corrupt or dysfunctional ministerial structures, and toward higher educational institutions and the autonomous professional networks without which reform will surely fail.[23] The stakes for all of this are quite high: reform of the foundering higher educational sector in Central Asia is vitally necessary for any meaningful reform in the general educational sector, and if basic educational provision continues to deteriorate, then all the predictable problems of unemployment, youth alienation, cultural despair, and political extremism will only continue to worsen.[24]

There are, of course, also significant private efforts, funded most notably by the Open Society Institute network and various national foundations in the region funded by George Soros as well as multilateral educational assistance programs supported by the World Bank and the Asian Development Bank. However, these programs do not seem to have changed significantly as a result of the new politics of terrorism, although they are necessarily influenced by the broader contours of bilateral policies and the limitations and tensions that flow from strategic rivalries in the region.

Russian, Turkish, Iranian, and other Assistance Programs in Central Asia

In addition to the United States, European, and other Western assistance programs noted earlier, there have also been programs supported by the Russian Federation, Turkey, Iran, and other regional actors in Central Asia. Russia has offered targeted assistance for the reform of higher education in Central Asia, especially for Slavic ethnic students, and yet may be more influential as a potential model for systemic reform in the higher educational sector. Russia is experimenting with new higher educational reforms that would fundamentally shift the flow of funding from institutions to students, who would then use their voucher or coupons to choose institutions and courses of study more freely. This would be combined with a new national testing system at the secondary level, which would open up mobility for students across and between institutions, and hopefully lessen the prevalence of corruption in admissions and promotion at the tertiary level.[25]

After great initial expectations, assistance and exchange programs from Turkey have not been as large or as influential as was hoped, largely because of ongoing financial problems and political conflict in Turkey.[26] Nonetheless, by 2000 six major Turkish educational training centers were created in the region under the auspices of the Turkish International Cooperation Agency (TICA), which offered courses and language training to more than 2,000 students and 200 teachers annually.[27] More importantly, Turkey has hosted more than 10,000 students from the region on educational exchanges. Support was also provided to academic centers in the region such as the International Turkmen-Turkish University in Ashgabat, the Almaty Turkish Education Training Center, and the Kyrgyz-Manas Turkish University in Bishkek, which was also to include a new medical school that was to built with more than $100 million in Turkish government funding. The United States and Europe continued to hope that Turkey would provide a useful model for secular and pro-Western reform in the region, although this will undoubtedly be complicated by tensions surrounding recent American policies toward Iraq and the fallout from the recent strains in U.S.–Turkish relations.[28]

Iran has also been quite active in providing economic and educational assistance to post-Soviet Central Asia, although this has been obstructed by American hostility and the larger tensions of great power rivalries.[29] The inveterate American hostility to any larger regional role for Iran is, arguably, counterproductive given Iran's undeniable turn, however bitterly contested from within, toward political pluralism and geostrategic pragmatism.[30] Iran is clearly witnessing the emergence of a new middle class, inexorable internal pressures toward liberalization, and has successfully institutionalized a new framework for electoral democracy, again, however bitterly contested by the clerical establishment. In fact, there is clearly a complex evolution of a distinctively Islamic civil society emerging and a searching debate underway about gender roles and identities. Provided that some sort of rapprochement can be initiated in U.S.–Iranian relations, Iran could come to play a more significant and constructive presence in Central Asia.

Saudi Arabia, both in the form of official government assistance programs and private funding, has also helped to create a network of religious schools and religious publishing in post-Soviet Central Asia, but has found little following in the region for its Wahhabi form of Islam. In fact, Saudi attempts to create an Islamic university in the Fergana province of Uzbekistan were rebuffed by the Uzbek state in the mid-1990s. Less ambitious but still significant educational influences have also come from Pakistan, especially through the radical *madrasa* network, although that is relevant more for those young people from Central Asia who have left the region and ended up in Pakistan; as well as from South Korea, largely in support of Korean ethnic students in the region. Finally, China has also provided some economic and educational assistance, largely to help foster trade relations and, incidentally, to cooperate in order to suppress cross-border activities in support of Uighur separatism in China's Xinjiang Uighur Autonomous Region. These regional relationships are now being institutionalized through the Shanghai Cooperation Organization (SCO), which currently includes Russia, China, Kazakhstan, Kyrgyzstan, Tajikistan, and Uzbekistan, and is focused primarily on suppressing separatism and "terrorism" in the cross-border regions.

While this competition for educational and intellectual influence has spurred increased attention to educational reform, it has also led to some potentially unfortunate unintended consequences. For example, there seems to be a tendency for local ministerial officials and educators to play various competing programs off of one another, as well as complex and ultimately unsustainable patterns of patron–client dependency that have emerged in many international assistance programs. Exchange programs that are not well designed or that fail to assist and help reintegrate faculty and students after their return to their home institutions have arguably exacerbated brain drain out of the educational sector and out of the region. Finally, and per-haps most importantly, the frequent failure to adequately coordinate assis-tance programs arguably leads to a certain artificiality in the reform process, and might compromise the professional and regional cooperation that is so vitally necessary for effective reform.[31]

THE PROSPECTS FOR SYSTEMIC HIGHER EDUCATIONAL REFORM IN CENTRAL ASIA

However, for all of these problems, it is also clear that these international assis-tance programs have helped to shape a dynamic higher educational market that is emerging in the region, especially in the Kyrgyz Republic and to a lesser degree in Kazakhstan and Tajikistan, the former in large part as a result of the progressive policy environment under the Minister of Education Camilla Sharshekeeva from 1999 to 2002. Sharshekeeva made her reputation as one of the founders of the Kyrgyz–American Faculty at Kyrgyz State National University in Bishkek, which then became a private, autonomous university and was renamed the American University of Kyrgyzstan in 1997. Her model higher educational reform program, developed with significant assistance from the U.S. government and other international organizations, focused on shift-ing the flow of state funding from institutions to students, in order to open up more competitive pressures within the emerging higher educational mar-ketplace. Other measures sought to reduce the power of the rectors and uni-versity administrators, to create independent Western-style Boards of Trustees at Kyrgyz universities; and to establish a new national testing system at the interface between secondary and tertiary education. The reform program also sought to attack corruption in higher education, and to consolidate redundant institutions into new, modernized Western-style universities.[32] It must however be noted that Sharshekeeva faced ferocious resistance to these measures from the entrenched university administrations, and was recently ousted as minister in a general shake-up of the Akaev government following internal unrest in May 2002.

Nonetheless, in large part because of the supportive domestic policy environment established by Sharshekeeva and her patron Akaev, together with the significant amount of international assistance provided to Kyrgyzstan since the mid-1990s, a dynamic and competitive higher educational marketplace has emerged, at least in Bishkek. This competition was unfolding between at least some units of the Kyrgyz State National University; the American and OSI-funded American University of Kyrgyzstan (AUK, now renamed the American University of Central Asia or AUCA); the Turkish-funded Kyrgyz–Manas Turkish University; the Russian-funded Kyrgyz–Russian Slavonic University, and the International University of Kyrgyzstan.[33] Whether all of these institutions can remain competitive, and whether the relationships between them will be professionally and academically constructive, of course, remains to be seen.

Similarly, while Kazakhstan has suffered from problems of pervasive corruption, underinvestment, and a lack of central policy leadership, there are nonetheless some constructive competitive pressures emerging, at least in Almaty, almost despite the draconian official policies and steady reduction of state-subsidized places in higher education.[34] This emerging market seems to be bypassing the somnolent Abai Kazakh State National University, and student interest and tuition funding seems more focused on the American-funded International University of Business; the Kazakhstan Institute of Management, Economics, and Strategic Research (KIMEP), which has received significant funding from the EU, the U.S. government, and the Open Society Institute (OSI); and a number of small but innovative private institutions such as Turan University. Finally, the Aga Khan Foundation and the Aga Khan Development Network has launched the new private and secular University of Central Asia (UCA), which is intended to pioneer new models for rural and mountain development and adult education, with a main campus in Khorog, Tajikistan, and satellite campuses in Naryn, Kyrgyzstan and Tekeli, Kazakhstan.[35] Common to almost all of these efforts are English-language instruction, at least in part, and a new focus on Westernized curricula and student-centered instructional methods. Some institutions, most notably the AUCA in Bishkek, have also shifted to a credit-hour system and pioneered the provision of student services, student access to information technology, and independent student research and internships.

THE "POLITICS OF TERRORISM" AND CHANGES IN INTERNATIONAL ASSISTANCE STRATEGIES

As a result of renewed U.S. and other external interest in Central Asia in the aftermath of September 11, additional funding is flowing into the region, especially to the "frontline states" of Uzbekistan, Kyrgyzstan, and Tajikistan.

Yet the new assistance and educational exchange programs are often seemingly intended primarily to reward cooperative regimes in the "war on terrorism," to advance a particular patron's geostrategic influence, or to reward one's clients and coreligionists than to address fundamental issues of systemic educational reform. Others have argued that the hysteria about radical Islam is exaggerated, and that broader trends suggest a moderation of Islamic politics in the Middle East and Central Asia, as many Islamic activists turn toward grassroots community development and more democratic politics, provided that their domestic political arenas encourage such moderation and allow for such engagement.[36] Thus, ironically, these programs often have the effect of exacerbating or at the least failing to fundamentally address the acute systemic higher educational crises throughout the region. Much of the new funding is flowing to corrupt, often repressive, and dysfunctional ministerial and other state structures rather than to the NGOs, independent professional networks, and educators in the region who remain active in the region, however embattled they may be. These activists and struggling civil society organizations are arguably much more attuned than the regimes to finding solutions to issues of democratization, religious pluralism, gender equity, multicultural education and critical pedagogy, conflict resolution, and poverty alleviation.[37]

More specifically, it seems that the flow of new assistance funding has only encouraged the Karimov regime in Uzbekistan in its repression of any form of Islamic expression and political dissidence, even as that repression has crippled indigenous efforts in the educational sector, especially by suppressing moderate forms of religious education and private initiatives. After an alleged assassination attempt against President Niyazov, the Turkmen regime plunged even deeper into its xenophobic, insular, and virtually Stalinist policies of repression in early 2003. Similarly, the recent turn toward repression by the Akaev government in Kyrgyzstan, and the forced resignation of the reformist Minister of Education Sharshekeeva, suggests that the model higher educational reform efforts there will now fail, or at the very least be attenuated by bureaucratic resistance. In Tajikistan, there have been severe strains on the coalition government and new repressive measures by the regime, bolstered by Western security assistance; and the Nazarbayev regime in Kazakhstan no longer even pretends to mouth the rhetoric of democracy and human rights. Again, it must be emphasized that it is not my view that Western and especially U.S. policy is deliberately inconsistent or hypocritical, but simply that the various aspects of U.S. policy seem to be badly coordinated. As the Department of Defense DoD provides new support for the regimes' police and military capabilities, this seems to be poorly coordinated with DOS and USAID efforts in other "soft" sectors; and the Central Asian regimes often seem to be using that security assistance for their own repressive and authoritarian purposes quite apart from the stated intentions of their international patrons and donors.[38]

Thus despite the renewed engagement by the United States and other major international actors in the region, the specific ways in which many international assistance policies are unfolding are having the effect of sacrificing a deeper and more sustainable understanding of human security to short-term military necessity.[39] At a time when all the regional and international actors should be cooperating and more carefully coordinating their assistance programs, regional and international rivalries are growing, and those tensions are undermining efforts to address the acute internal crises throughout the region. It must be noted that there is a complex debate underway within the U.S. government about precisely such choices, yet the question remains whether the United States or any of the other major external actors will muster the will and the resources to really cooperate in pursuit of solutions to these deep internal problems, or whether the rising tensions throughout the world system as well as between states in the region will preclude such vitally necessary cooperation. Given the growing chorus of criticism that the Bush administration has failed to adequately fund its stated commitments to provide security and to support comprehensive reconstruction in post-Taliban Afghanistan, the prospects look, tragically, poor for Central Asia.

However, as undeniably useful as these assistance programs have been for individual educators, students, or even departments, it could also be argued that beyond the UCA and the AUCA there has been little sustained focus on cultivating the tools needed for broader and deeper institutional and professional development. For example, global trends suggest that specific internal and external tools are needed if universities are to successfully adapt to the competitive and financial pressures common to virtually all higher educational systems. Internally, they must develop a comprehensive ability to engage in program review and institutional research, as well as a mechanism to assess the quality of faculty teaching and the depth of student learning. Externally, they must develop the ability to recruit students, sustain research and training in the field, collaborate with potential employers and donors, and especially to collaborate with fellow educators and researchers in other regions. In other words, they must embrace a comprehensive agenda of professional development in order to establish their capacity for autonomy and competitiveness in an increasingly harsh higher educational environment, one in which state support will inexorably decline.[40]

Policy Recommendations and Conclusions

In conclusion, I would offer several policy recommendations that seek to draw together all of these issues, and I would also stress the ways in which sophisticated and collaborative international research on these problems is vitally necessary to help illuminate and inform the process of reform. Even as the United States intervenes and collaborates with its allies in the region to resolve urgent security issues, all concerned must not lose sight of the deeper issues of human security that are so directly shaped by the capacity and vitality of higher education and, beyond that, of national educational systems as a whole. We must redouble, continually rethink, and better coordinate our efforts in support of higher educational reform and professional development, precisely in order to help alleviate the acute unemployment, youth alienation, and economic hopelessness that continues to pervade the region, to threaten further destabilization, and that creates breeding grounds for extremism and terrorism.

More specifically, I would recommend a renewed focus on leveraging assistance programs to deliberately cultivate professional networks and new associational structures, including faculty and student organizations. Assistance programs should also focus on helping institutions, both public and private, to develop the internal capacity for program review, institutional research, and comprehensive assessment. Higher educational institutions could also be encouraged to revitalize their civic engagement, and to focus their own institutional missions more directly on poverty alleviation and community development, perhaps through a renewed emphasis on training in the service professions and the development of community-based and service learning programs. This illustrates the vital role that universities and their constituencies have to play in the broader revitalization of civil society, whether through policy-relevant research, support for civic initiatives, or independent publishing. Furthermore, the United States and other bilateral and multilateral actors could make a better effort to coordinate their assistance efforts with parallel efforts by the EU and Russia, and even beyond that with Turkish, Iranian, and other efforts, in the latter cases at least with those emanating from more reform-minded institutions and professional networks. This might entail a renewed emphasis on Central Asia's own indigenous *jadidist* tradition of moderate Islam in an effort to offset more radical *Wahhabi* and other currents.[41] Finally, a new focus on professional collaboration and possibly educational exchanges within the region would be enormously useful, both to help rebuild local and regional professional networks that have been degraded by the collapse of the Soviet system and the ongoing economic crisis, and also as confidence-building measures between states in the region around often contentious issues such as economic redevelopment, resource extraction, water, and national security. While external actors such as the United States, the EU, Russia, Turkey, Iran, and China will necessarily continue to play a significant role in shaping Central Asia's future, at least in the educational sector more of an effort can be made to really engage with and support indigenous educators and activists as equal partners in the cause of educational reform. Finally, as optimistic or perhaps naïve as it may be, one can also urge the various external actors to at least attempt to ameliorate their competitive hostilities, and to at least try and more closely cooperate as they all pursue the mutual goal of creating policies in the region that will foster stabilization, ethnic coexistence, and sustainable development for the peoples of Central Asia.

NOTES

1. An earlier version of this essay was presented at the 2003 Central Asia and its Neighbors Regional Policy Symposium, sponsored by the International Research

and Exchanges Board (IREX), the U.S. Department of State's Title VIII Program, The Starr Foundation, and the Woodrow Wilson International Center for Scholars, which was held in Shepherdstown, West Virginia, from March 13 to 16, 2003. This essay also draws on field research conducted by the author as part of evaluations of educational assistance and exchange programs in Kazakhstan and Kyrgyzstan for the Bureau of Educational and Cultural Affairs of the U.S. Department of State and the Open Society Institute in 2001 and 2002. The author alone is responsible for the views expressed, and please direct any comments or criticisms to msjohnson@coloradocollege.edu.

2. For a thoughtful consideration of the tensions between the two arenas in current U.S. policy, see also Thomas Carothers, "Promoting Democracy and Fighting Terror," *Foreign Affairs* Vol. 8, Issue 1 (January/February 2003): 84–97; on the broader context of such programs and their perils, see Thomas Carothers, *Aiding Democracy Abroad: The Learning Curve* (Washington, DC: Carnegie Endowment for International Peace, 1999).

3. Ahmed Rashid, *Jihad: The Rise of Militant Islam in Central Asia* (New Haven: Yale University Press, 2002); see also Troy S. Thomas and Stephen D. Kiser, *Lords of the Silk Route: Violent Non-State Actors in Central Asia. INSS Occasional Paper 43* (Colorado Springs: United States Air Force Academy Institute for National Security Studies, 2002); and Gregory Gleason, "The Politics of Counter-insurgency in Central Asia," *Problems of Post-Communism* Vol. 49, No. 2 (March–April 2002): 3–14. While Rashid blames the regimes for failing so badly as to call forth extremist responses, Gleason, in contrast, blames the revolutionary movements on "blowback" from the Afghan wars.

4. *Balancing Military Assistance and Support for Human Rights in Central Asia: Hearing Before the Subcommittee on Central Asia and the South Caucasus of the Committee on Foreign Relations, United States Senate, One Hundred Seventh Congress, second session, June 27, 2002* (Washington, DC: United States Government Printing Office, 2002); also at http://www.purl.access.gpo.gov/GPO/LPS25858.

5. As also argued by Shirin Akiner, Sander Tideman, and Jon Hay, *Sustainable Development in Central Asia* (London: Curzon Press, 1998); see also "Human Security: A Conversation," *Social Research* Vol. 69, No. 3 (Fall 2002): 657–73; and the recent World Development Report for 2003, *Sustainable Development in a Dynamic World: Transforming Institutions, Growth, and the Quality of Life* (Washington, DC and New York: The World Bank and Oxford University Press, 2003).

6. Jandhyala B. G. Tilak, "Knowledge Society, Education, and Aid," *Compare* Vol. 32, No. 3 (2002): 297–310; and *Constructing Knowledge Societies: New Challenges for Tertiary Education* (Washington, DC: The World Bank, 2001).

7. Sheila Slaughter and Larry L. Leslie, *Academic Capitalism: Politics, Policies, and the Entrepreneurial University* (Baltimore: Johns Hopkins University Press, 1997); also Task Force on Higher Education and Society, *Higher Education in Developing Countries: Peril and Promise* (Washington, DC: The World Bank, 2000).

8. Of many recent accounts, see Jan Currie and Janice Newson, eds., *Universities and Globalization: Critical Perspectives* (Thousand Oaks, CA: Sage Publications, 1998); also Peter Scott, *The Globalization of Higher Education* (Buckingham, U.K.: Society for Research into Higher Education and Open University Press, 1998).

9. For more background on these historical issues, see Mark S. Johnson, "Russian and Soviet Education and the Shaping of Ethnic, Religious, and the Shaping of National Identities in Central Asia," in Stephen P. Heyneman and Alan De Young, eds., *The Challenge of Education in Central Asia* (Greenwich, CT: Information Age Publishing, forthcoming); also K. E. Bendrikov, *Ocherki po istorii narodnogo obrazovaniia v Turkestane* (Moscow: Bezbozhnik, 1960); and Georgii M. Khrapchenkov, *Istoriia shkoly I pedagogicheskoi mysli Kazakhstana* (Almaty: Kainar, 1998).

10. Seymour M. Rosen, *Education in the U.S.S.R.: Current Status of Higher Education* (Washington, DC: U.S. Department of Health, Education, and Welfare, Office of Education, 1980); also Kabidulla D. Zhulamanov, *Vysshaia shkola respublik Srednei Azii I Kazakhstana, 1961–1975gg* (Alma-Ata: "Nauka," 1981).

11. V. K. Yantsen ed., *Sovremennye modeli vysshego obrazovaniia: opyt' adaptatsii I vnedreniia*, 2 Vols. (Bishkek: International University of Kyrgyzstan, 2000).

12. Abdulkhai K. Valiev, *Formirovanie I razvitie sovetskoi natsional'noi intelligentsii v Srednei Azii* (Tashkent: Fan, 1966); also Olivier Roy, *The New Central Asia: The Creation of Nations* (1997; New York: New York University Press, 2000).

13. Stephen P. Heyneman, "From the Party/State to Multiethnic Democracy: Education and Social Cohesion in Europe and Central Asia," *Educational Evaluation and Policy Analysis* Vol. 22, No. 2 (Summer 2002): 173–91.

14. On the broader dimensions of these systemic educational crises, see also Sue E. Berryman, *Hidden Challenges to Education Systems in Transition Economies* (Washington, DC: The World Bank, 2000); on the crisis in vocational education and training, see Bertil Oskarsson and Corinna Muscheidt, *Vocational Education and Training in Kyrgyzstan: Managing Educational Reforms in an Economy in Transition* (Turin: European Training Foundation, 1996); and Geoff Howse, "VET Under Review: The Challenges in Central Asia," *European Journal of Education* Vol. 36, Issue 1 (March 2001): 35–43; on the collapse of state funding for general education, Igor Kitaev, ed., *Educational Finance in Central Asia and Mongolia* (Paris: UNESCO, 1996).

15. Martha Brill Olcott, *Central Asia's New States: Independence, Foreign Policy, and Regional Security* (Washington, DC: United States Institute of Peace Press, 1996); also Touraj Atabaki and John O'Kane, eds., *Post-Soviet Central Asia* (London: Tauris Academic Studies in association with the International Institute for Asian Studies, Amsterdam, 1998); Hooman Peimani, *Regional Security and the Future of Central Asia: The Competition of Iran, Turkey, and Russia* (Westport, CT: Praeger, 1998); and Roy Allison and Lena Jonson, eds., *Central Asian Security: The New International Context* (Washington, DC: Brookings Institution Press in association with the Royal Institute of International Affairs and the Swedish Institute of International Affairs, 2001).

16. Neil J. Melvin, *Uzbekistan: Transition to Authoritarianism on the Silk Road* (Amsterdam: Harwood Academic Publishers, 2000); and *Turkmenistan: Education Sector Review* (Ashgabat: UNDP 1997); on the broader issue of changing Western perceptions, see Charles H. Fairbanks, Jr., "Disillusionment in the Caucasus and Central Asia," *Journal of Democracy* Vol. 12, No. 4 (October 2001): 49–56.

17. Mohammed-Reza Djalili, Frederic Grare, and Shirin Akiner, eds., *Tajikistan: The Trials of Independence* (New York: St. Martin's Press, 1997); and Shirin Akiner, *Tajikistan: Disintegration or Reconciliation?* (London: Royal Institute of International Affairs, 2001).

18. Armin Bauer, David Green, and Kathleen Kuehnast, *Women and Gender Relations: The Kyrgyz Republic in Transition* (Manila: Asian Development Bank, 1997); John Anderson, *Kyrgyzstan: Central Asia's Island of Democracy?* (Amsterdam: Harwood Academic Publishers, 1999); also Richard A. Slaughter, "Poor Kyrgyzstan," *National Interest* (Summer 2002): 55–65.

19. *Kazakstan: Forced Migration and Nation Building* (New York: Open Society Institute, 1998); Akezhan Kazhegeldin, "Shattered Image: Misconceptions of Democracy and Capitalism in Kazakstan," *Harvard International Review* Vol. 22, Issue 1 (Winter/Spring 2000): 76–79; and Martha Brill Olcott, *Kazakhstan: Unfulfilled Promise* (Washington, DC: Carnegie Endowment for International Peace, 2002).

20. Neil S. MacFarlane, *Western Engagement in the Caucasus and Central Asia* (London: Royal Institute for International Affairs, 1999).

21. On this and what follows, see *U.S. Government Assistance to and Cooperative Activities with Eurasia: Fiscal Year 2001* (Washington, DC: United States Department of State, 2002); also http://www.state.gov/documents/organization/17714.pdf; also *USAID's Assistance Strategy for Central Asia 2001–2005* (Almaty: USAID Regional Mission for Central Asia, 2000); and http://www.usaid.gov/regions/europe_eurasia/car.

22. On the larger framework of these policies, see Alan Mayhew, *Recreating Europe: The European Union's Policy Toward Central and Eastern Europe* (New York: Cambridge University Press, 1998); and the various documents and statistics available on "The European Union's Relationship With the Countries of Eastern Europe and Central Asia" (2001), http://europa.eu.int/comm/external_relations/ceeca/tacis/index.htm.

23. As also argued in Blair Ruble, Susan Bronson, and Nancy Popson, *The Humanities and Social Sciences in the Former Soviet Union: An Assessment of Need* (Washington, DC: Kennan Institute for Advanced Russian Studies, 1999); this document led to a major new grant program, "Higher Education in the Former Soviet Union" (HEFSU) by the Carnegie Corporation of New York, but this program is not yet active in Central Asia.

24. Kenneth Roberts et al., *Surviving Post-Communism: Young People in the Former Soviet Union* (Cheltenham, U.K.: Edward Elgar, 2000).

25. *Tertiary Education and Research in the Russian Federation* (Paris: Organization for Economic Cooperation and Development, 1999).

26. Gareth Winrow, *Turkey in Post-Soviet Central Asia* (London: Royal Institute of International Affairs, 1995); and Dietrich Jung and Wolfgang Piccoli, *Turkey at the Crossroads: Ottoman Legacies and a Greater Middle East* (London: Zed Books, 2001).

27. "Education Relations With Turkic Republics," Ministry of National Education of the Republic of Turkey (2001), available at http://www.meb.gov.tr; also Cennet Demir, Ayse Balci, and Fusun Akkok, "The Role of Turkish Schools in the Educational System and Social Transformation of Central Asian Countries: The Case of Turkmenistan and Kyrgyzstan," *Central Asian Survey* Vol. 19, Issue 1 (March 2000): 141–55.

28. James Kitfield, "The Turkish Model," *National Journal* Vol. 34, Issue 9 (March 2, 2002): 598–605.

29. Edmund Herzig, *Iran and the Former Soviet South* (London: Royal Institute of International Affairs, 1995); and Ertan Efegil and Leonard A. Stone, "Iran's Interests in Central Asia: A Contemporary Assessment," *Central Asian Survey* Vol. 20, Issue 3 (2001): 353–65.

30. John L. Esposito and R. K. Ramazani, *Iran at the Crossroads* (New York: Palgrave, 2001); and Nikki R. Keddie and Rudi Matthee, eds., *Iran and the Surrounding World: Interactions in Culture and Politics* (Seattle: University of Washington Press, 2002).

31. Renata Dwan and Oleksandr Pavliuk, *Building Security in the New States of Eurasia: Subregional Cooperation in the Former Soviet Space* (Armonk, NY: M. E. Sharpe and the East West Institute, 2000); also David L. Bartlett, "Economic Development in the Newly Independent States: The Case for Regionalism," *European Journal of Development Research* Vol. 13, No. 1 (June 2001): 135–53.

32. Camilla Sharshekeeva, *Kontseptsiia reformirovaniia obrazovaniia v Kyrgyzskoi Respubliki* (Bishkek: Ministry of Education and Culture of the Kyrgyz Republic, 2002); also Ronald A. Phipps and Thomas R. Wolanin, *Higher Education Reform Initiatives in Kyrgyzstan: An Overview* (Washington, DC: Institute for Higher Education Policy in association with the Eurasia Foundation and the Ministry of Education and Culture of the Kyrgyz Republic, 2001).

33. On AUK, see Mark S. Johnson and Leon Selig, *Creating a Regional Center for Excellence in Undergraduate Education: A Development Strategy for the American University of Kyrgyzstan (2002–2005)* (Washington, DC: assessment prepared for the Bureau of Educational and Cultural Affairs of the U.S. Department of State, 2002).

34. Ministry of Education of the Republic of Kazakhstan, *Zakon "ob obrazovanii" Respubliki Kazakhstana* (Astana: Dastan, 2000).

35. *An International Initiative for Education and Development in Central Asia: The University of Central Asia* (Geneva: Aga Khan Development Network, 2002); also available at http://www.akdn.org.

36. Gilles Kepel, *Jihad: The Trail of Political Islam*, trans. Anthony F. Roberts (2000; Cambridge: Belknap Press of Harvard University Press, 2002); also Anthony Shadid, *Legacy of the Prophet: Despots, Democrats, and the New Politics of Islam* (Boulder, CO: Westview Press, 2002).

37. See, e.g., the optimistic accounts in Holt Ruffin and Daniel Waugh, eds., *Civil Society in Central Asia* (Seattle: University of Washington Press in association with the Center for Civil Society International and the Central Asia-Caucasus Institute of the Nitze School of Advanced International Studies, Johns Hopkins University, 1999); and the more pessimistic or skeptical accounts in Sarah E. Mendelson and John K. Glenn, eds., *The Power and Limits of NGOs: A Critical Look at Building Democracy in Eastern Europe and Eurasia* (New York: Columbia University Press, 2002).

38. See, e.g., the discussions in *Contributions of Central Asian Nations to the Campaign Against Terrorism. Hearing Before the Subcommittee on Central Asia and the South Caucasus of the Committee on Foreign Relations of the United States Senate, One Hundred Seventh Congress, first session, December 13, 2001* (Washington, DC: U. S. Government Printing Office, 2002); also http://www.access.gpo.gov/congress/senate; and also *Escalating Violence and Rights Violations in Central Asia* (Washington, DC: Commission on Security and Cooperation in Europe, 2002).

39. UNDP, *Central Asia 2010: Prospects for Human Development* (New York and Bratislava: Regional Bureau for Europe and the CIS, 1999); Gary King and Christopher J. L. Murray, "Rethinking Human Security," *Political Science Quarterly* Vol. 116, No. 4 (2001): 585–610; also Matt McDonald, "Human

Security and the Construction of Security," *Global Society* Vol. 16, No. 3 (2002): 277–95.

40. Eliot Freidson, *Professionalism: The Third Logic* (London: Polity Press, 2001).

41. Mobin Shorish, "Back to Jadidism: Turkistani Education After the Fall of the USSR," *Islamic Studies* 33 (Summer-Autumn 1994): 161–82; as also argued in Rashid, *Jihad*.

V

CONCLUSIONS

15

CONCLUSIONS: TOWARD A NEW CRITICAL PEDAGOGY IN THE SHADOW OF PERPETUAL WAR

Wayne Nelles

No one book could fully assess the potentially vast array of interconnected international education, terrorism and human security issues. This volume offers just a small glimpse by introducing some innovative critical pedagogy theory with case studies to stimulate new research, policy and practice. More work is needed to understand how (in localized or particular instances and through broader structural or global contexts) education reproduces and can prevent domestic or international violence (from school-yard bullying and child soldiers to both "terrorism" and war) by assessing program, curricular reform, and policy implications. I now examine a few considerations for future research, mostly as a footnote to dramatic events following 9/11 that have thrust much of the world into a troubling insecurity through an American-led perpetual war.

THEORETICAL CHALLENGES AND CRITICAL PEDAGOGY IMPERATIVES

A major challenge for new theory and study concerning education, security or terrorism issues is to reconcile—through teaching, public dialogue, research and practice—competing visions for national and human security. "Soft" human security and "hard" traditional military security are not mutually exclusive, if the latter is used for legitimate national defense.[1] But the national security concept has been so distorted, through preemptive or expansionist wars, militarism and tolerance of human rights abuses, that a critical pedagogy approach must deconstruct its logical fallacies and misuses. It is especially important to assess the national security concept related to American domestic and foreign policy, including misuses of power.

Ironically, within days of 9/11, outpourings of sympathy came from around the world, some even saying "we are all Americans now." Within a year the United States had squandered most international goodwill and generated unprecedented anti-American sentiments from millions of people in scores of countries. Problematically most of the earth's denizens are indeed becoming de facto Americans (directly affected by U.S. policies) but without a vote on the country's leadership. Since 9/11 the United States has been waging an international "war on terrorism" with no clear end and little respect for democracy, public opinion, persons or even the sovereignty of other nations. Thousands have been persecuted, physically abused (even tortured) and imprisoned indefinitely with no legal protection within and outside the United States.[2] Military actions or education-training assistance to scores of countries have increased global violence and instability, neglect of human rights, and claimed far more civilian deaths than 9/11. The March 2003 invasion of Iraq action began a new phase in America's perpetual war, the first major step in consolidating a quasi-imperial "national security state,"[3] based on a unilateral global vision outlined in its September 2002 *National Security Strategy* (*NSS*).

American initiatives represent the antithesis of an alternative, global democratic, nonviolent, critical pedagogy-based, multilateral, human security vision for countering terrorist violence. American efforts have complemented a powerful "public diplomacy" strategy, often a militant "pseudo-education" designed to "persuade" others to see and believe the United States is a beneficent global actor, while justifying dubious wars and insidious counterterrorism efforts. Military action has been central to fighting its terror war, yet the strategy's effectiveness is questionable. Even some international student advisors at American colleges have told their charges overseas to say they are Canadians, while American academics working abroad have resorted to the "I am a Canadian" cover under in difficult circumstances.[4] Such anecdotal reports (requiring more thorough study) show how some Americans find personal safety, not with a strong military or their own government. They go through the reputation of a nation that has sought (not always with success amidst enormous continentalization and globalization pressures) to project "soft" power and create national defense through multilateral institutions, dialogue, mediation, peacekeeping and human security, seeing military intervention as a last resort.

Meanwhile, global poverty and environmental degradation (arguably among terrorism's contributing causes) have proceeded apace since the mid-1980s. A scholar then asked if related issues were avoided in U.S. universities, saying most of what counted for international education then was like "talking about what to cook for dinner when our house is on fire."[5] Another analyst suggested more study of alternatives to political violence war was needed.[6] Two decades later the world seems ablaze with greater hate and discord, much arising from the American 9/11 response. Yet sources of militancy and ecological destruction are still inadequately studied and poorly taught. There remains a pressing need to better examine educational violence prevention in all forms (school-based, military, family, religious, economic, social-structural, etc.) and holistically together—not just as particular, isolated political violence (i.e. terrorism) defined largely by nation-states and their elites for narrow, often dubious political purposes. Numerous theories suggest violence has various "root causes." Some commonly view it as a social–psychological or biological impulse, a "natural" part of human behavior, or gendered, driven by primeval male aggression and competition for scarce resources, while only the fittest survive. Here Social Darwinism meets a Hobbesian political worldview, with violence or war as "normal." When Darwin and Hobbes meet "God" (leaders claiming divine right or guidance) this becomes an unholy trinity with war necessary to fight "evil." Theology becomes foreign policy.

A review of the extensive research on violence in biological, psychological, social, economic, religious, ideological, political or other literatures is not possible here and more work is needed to explore education linkages comparatively. Multiple and interrelated causes of violence and insecurity clearly exist. But the human animal is unique in its ability to create social or educational institutions, that with sustained attention and crisis response interventions, can transcend biology or theology, mediate or mitigate violence, and provide social means to personal security for the weak and marginalized. Much violence (including ideological–social militarism and military training that normalizes it) is indeed socially sanctioned, institutionally constructed and *learned* behavior, while many nonformal or formal education systems are either complicit in, or directly responsible, for the reproduction or mitigation of violence, including specific forms or responses such as terrorism and war. Some theoretical discussion and case study evidence in this book illustrates this. But more systematic evaluations are needed to demonstrate historical–social contexts, local domestic and international or global linkages, and case studies that better illustrate socialization processes. Critical pedagogy frameworks could inform future studies.

Although related scholarship has typically focused on basic schooling or teacher training, the academic research enterprise itself is part of the violence reproduction and mitigation process. It has mostly supported the former. Mainstream political science and IR research has overwhelmingly been built on a realist paradigm, and focused on analyzing Great Power realpolitik dynamics, elite behavior, nation-state units of analysis and national security. This has largely legitimized such worldviews coupled with strategic military thinking and technical solutions to conflict, to protect territory (most already attained through war) and access to natural resources for "national interests." Governments have relied on sympathetic academics among national security "experts" while including military strategists as policy advisors or as nuclear scientists or biological technicians to help make bigger, better, more deadly and so-called smart weapons. Yet many political leaders or bureaucrats display an appalling lack of willingness to learn or apply diplomacy and human relations skills that might avoid threats of war or the terror of military violence to resolve problems.

There are no simple ways to counter the normalization of violence through educational processes or scientific institutions. But understanding of, or access to, different and marginalized perspectives about power and

IR, is essential. This is an individual and social learning challenge with significant tensions between mainstream public and government-supported views of military security deemed more important than other views. Peace and anti-globalization protests, or the intellectual and social movements behind them, representing millions of people around the world have been given comparatively little time or credibility in the media while it focuses more on aggression, including graphic displays of physical violence. Yet behind such movements are learning processes that include analyses of power, militarization, global governance and neocolonialism specifically, as well as education reform.[7] Some local, national and international teachers' organizations have long advocated social and educational change. Civil society groups or social movements have learning activities including teach-ins, newsletters, websites, advocacy research organizations, and the like. Many offer critical analyses of national interests sustaining detrimental global power relationships while sometimes discussing human security-oriented alternatives.

Although there may be some minor disagreements most critical pedagogues share a commitment to, or sympathy with, movements that challenge militarism, racism, sexism, religious extremism, violence and socioeconomic injustices. But it remains unclear (without adversely politicizing classrooms) what role schools, colleges or teacher training (preservice or in-service) already play, or can, in discussing or pragmatically responding to international or security issues through critical thinking. Those with vested interests may oppose alternative forms or dynamics in global power, and discourage discussion about new ways of nonviolent international human interactions with students. For some American right-wing (often overtly religious) conservatives this may even be viewed as unpatriotic, if it means accepting cooperative multilateral values or collaborating with the United Nations.[8] On university campuses the challenge is especially daunting since academic freedom, a cherished principle of scholarship, implies all pure research, scientific discovery and knowledge reproduction processes, have equal value, regardless of negative consequences. Still, I would argue that deconstructing (intellectually and institutionally) abuses is a critical pedagogy imperative.

A major challenge facing the formal system and nonformal educators is public awareness about alternatives. The average person learns little about global issues beyond media sound-bytes and visuals of protests against government actions, while the media covering these move from event to event and crisis to crisis. Moreover, because the American national security state, reinforced by its education system and scientific research establishment, has become so powerful, terrorism is often a means of last resort for retaliation by those who perceive they are not being heard, or feel abused. These are not just marginal or radical concerns, but have become even more intense and widespread as the Bush administration has scuttled important human security initiatives on curtailing the production and use of land mines, the International Criminal Court, curbing small arms proliferation, and the like. Future education research might examine how well such issues (if much at all) are taught or learned in American schools and colleges.

Education, Learning and Cultural Imperialism in Iraq's War Shadow

Post-9/11 American counterterrorism efforts, have meant a dramatic reordering of the world impacting education with implications barely studied. The military campaign against Afghanistan remains poorly assessed on many accounts. Civilian casualties, an alleged genocide cover-up, and international law violations remain largely ignored. Although some useful curricular reforms followed, outside Kabul many girls still do not attend schools, the national government is largely dysfunctional, poverty is endemic, aid workers are murdered and war continues with little real security for many people. Neighboring Pakistan's madrasa school problem remains, exacerbated by high military spending and American policies. Meanwhile, the United States has merely expanded its terror war elsewhere through international military education and training assistance or preemptive military action.[9]

As this manuscript was being finalized for the publisher (early April 2003 with a minor copy-editing update in July) major combat operations of an American-led Iraq invasion were drawing to a close, but a seriously problematic cultural-educational destruction, occupation and neocolonialization process had just begun. This illegal war (contrary to the UN Charter and not authorized by the Security Council) began in March 2003 with little evidence of immediate threat to the United States. Indeed much the American administration showed was false, misleading, dated, plagiarized or strategic "disinformation." Even if Iraq had hidden weapons, containment and disarmament through UN inspections was working, making war on these counts at least, unnecessary.[10] Nonetheless, with contempt for world opinion and international law the United States led a "coalition of the willing" to "liberate" Iraq through its (dangerously precedent-setting) policy of "regime change."

The military battle and invasion was largely "successful." But Baghdad and the rest of the country soon swept into anarchy, with no real governance save the American occupying force incompetent in providing the mere basics of law, order, civility and humanitarian services. Civilian deaths, injuries, revenge killings, vigilante justice and many thousands of casualties among Iraqis (if many military as innocent conscripts are included) were barely reported while most public infrastructure was trashed or stolen.[11] Meanwhile regular, almost daily targeted killings against the mostly American occupying forces became the norm, well beyond the toppling of Iraq's government. This was part of a guerrilla insurgency (which some American political leaders and military commanders at times labeled terrorism against Western interests rather than legitimate "war"). And various forms of resistance are likely to continue long term. Nonetheless President Bush and Prime Minister Blair claimed a partial "victory" in "regime change" and the United States began "rebuilding" much of what it destroyed. But its governance model immediately excluded the United Nations and important local stakeholders in decision-making. Moreover, the process began under the governorship of Jay Garner, a Pentagon-appointed, pro-Israeli, retired American general with strong ties to the defense industry. Garner's replacement, Paul Bremer, is ostensibly a "diplomat" but this label is an oxymoron given that he was chosen partly for his work as a conservative Reagan-era counter-terrorism expert now working for Bush and reporting to Defense Minister Rumsfeld, instead of more appropriately, the secretary of state responsible for official diplomacy. One of the Pentagon's principal leadership contenders, Ahmed Chalabi, has not lived in Iraq for decades and was convicted in Jordan for theft and bank fraud. The optics and reality of the American occupation are problematic. Some Iraqis appeared happy with "liberation" but many soon said "Yankee go home," or "No to Saddam" and "No to U.S." in the same breath, during public protests. Meanwhile, in light of a swift campaign with few American deaths the administration and right-wing commentators speculated on "lessons" for others making veiled threats to neighboring Syria and others.[12]

The broader educational implications, however, were disconcerting. The military invasion brought the looting of Baghdad's national museum and library, burning of precious books including ancient irreplaceable Islamic manuscripts and doctoral theses, the trashing of art galleries, and stolen university equipment or teaching resources for schools. Similar tragedies were repeated in Mosul, Basra and elsewhere. The manuscripts and artifacts were priceless heritage, yet worth billions of dollars on the black market giving a boost for organized crime. This was the equivalent of losing the entire Library of Congress, Washington's Smithsonian Institution and repositories in several other American cities, giving license to the Mafia to control the spoils. Iraq is more devastating because this was the de facto cradle of "civilization" where the world's first records of writing were kept with hundreds of thousands of other treasures. This was an easily avoidable tragedy in which the United States bears complete blame. American Marines in Baghdad guarded Oil Ministry offices but—despite repeated formal requests from international and Iraqi experts before and during the war—*not* important centers of culture, education and history.[13] Defense Minister Donald Rumsfeld dismissed critics saying looting was "unfortunate" and simply understandable "untidiness" of military operations. Conservative commentators even suggested the pillage was exaggerated, (and some material was later recovered) or that Iraqis rightly trashed it because it was a symbol of Saddam's misappropriated history. But failure to protect Iraq's heritage was arguably a war crime—cultural genocide against the Arab and Islamic world, as well as humanity itself.[14]

The Western media overwhelmingly focused on the toppling of one Baghdad statue of Saddam Hussein on April 9, 2003 as a symbol of regime change. However, I would argue the destruction of libraries, museums and religious centers represents a more profound and symbolic "tipping point." It marks the wantonly careless and violent consolidation of American cultural imperialism in the Arab and Islamic world. Ironically President

Bush just a few months earlier announced to the United Nations that (after 18 years of absence) as "as a symbol of our commitment to human dignity, the United States will return to UNESCO" in 2003, a speech that also included an advance war declaration on Iraq.[15] It is clear what American priorities were. There is little dignity in allowing the destruction of most of a nation's cultural and educational heritage, much less its lost contribution to world civilization. The United States has, yet again, dramatically and violently undermined global cultural diversity values that the UNESCO has long sought to protect.[16] Due to willful and malicious American neglect, UNESCO ironically, led a mostly futile effort to investigate and recover Iraq's stolen antiquities.

Now that the United States has permitted the ethno-cultural cleansing of much of Iraqi heritage, it has made way for the "new," which means American interests dominating. Education contracts were among those quickly negotiated with private American firms for work expected to begin within months. A Request for Proposals (RFP) was actually issued March 4, 2003, even before the war began. Some intentions sound worthwhile, including support for "child-centred, inquiry-based, participatory teaching...for democratic practices and attitudes." But the pretext of "peace building" by "demilitarizing" and "democratizing" the curriculum (likely obliterating any negative references to Israel, the United States or their militarism) will facilitate the American economic and cultural colonization of Iraq. The RFP refers to enhancement of "public–private partnerships" making this process easier.[17] But establishment of a privatizing, market-based education system would not have been possible without conquering the country first, by extreme force, then sustaining the new system with the threats of more American state-sanctioned violence against resisters within Iraq and beyond.

Permanent military bases to control access to Iraq's oil are now likely[18] (although Defense Minister Rumsfeld later denied insider reports suggesting this) and to help "enforce" a long-term national and regional economic, cultural and political future based on a wider privatization model allowing American companies to provide hundreds of products and services from water (an already contentious global issue) to electricity, to transportation.[19] To allay critics (but also to get others to help pay for cleaning up the mess it created) the United States has offered minor concessions to other countries. But American governance of Iraq, including the establishment of its entire economic system, new trade relationships, and even attempts to end its own previous harsh sanctions regime, are not altruistic. They will channel much of Iraq's national resources and wealth into American coffers, not just to pay for their "war of liberation," but to sustain the increasingly privatized, debt-ridden, military-driven, globally reaching economy of the United States. And senior American academics will help. Peter McPherson, a former USAID head, and treasury official who worked under Reagan and Ford, will organize the Iraqi economic system. McPherson, also now a university president on leave, may bring the U.S. dollar to Iraq as a "stabilization" currency helping rebuild Iraq's economy in the American free-market image.[20] It remains to be seen if anything resembling a critical pedagogy approach could appear in reforms to the official Iraqi curriculum, or through international education cooperation, that might deconstruct these dramatic developments. However, critiques—some virulent—may appear through informal learning and resistance among mosques, cultural centers and transnational networks opposed to the American occupation of Iraq and its broader designs. This could be a recipe for more terrorism. Future research should monitor developments.

A bigger tragedy, however, needs exposing first. Human security models could have been better applied to avert war first, address rights abuses, meet other injustices and improve the education system that suffered badly under sanctions.[21] Post–Cold War era literature on violent conflict prevention and peace building emerged, but governments except marginally, ignored implications.[22] This is despite the fact that prevention (different from what critics call "appeasement") is common sense—usually more effective and less expensive than war. Regarding Iraq there is no dispute that Saddam Hussein had long been a brutal dictator, but his regime became stronger and more dangerous as it was empowered by other countries competing for access to oil in the region, and joining with Iraq to fight the Cold War or to trounce Islamic fundamentalism in Iran and temper its role as a regional power. The West supported Hussein's regime when it suited their purposes, and ignored human rights abuses, including genocide, when convenient.

The United States bears significant responsibility for many atrocities. Donald Rumsfeld was Ronald Reagan's envoy to Iraq in the 1980s, apparently helping to negotiate an oil pipeline deal and facilitate American businesses to sell chemical and biological weapons behind the slaughter of some 5,000 Kurds. American business in Iraq even later increased with Reagan's support. President Bush Senior, through Ambassador Gillespie in 1990 also gave Saddam Hussein a diplomatic message that the United States would not interfere in any Iraqi–Kuwait dispute, then Iraq invaded Kuwait and the first Gulf War followed. The sanctions regime, contamination from Western munitions, lack of access to medical supplies and services, and ongoing bombings since 1991 in no-fly zones terrorized local populations, destroyed livelihoods and debilitated the population while maiming or killing thousands of innocent Iraqis since.[23]

An ongoing "educational" or "learning" challenge is to understand how and why the Iraq issue (linked to broader questions about terrorism's causes, protest in the Arab world and why many people despise U.S. policies) grew into a world crisis. Equally important is the issue of what role education can play in deescalating, and preventing, future violence and war elsewhere. This is no small task. Polls suggest the majority of Americans rallied behind the president and in "support for the troops" regardless of whether they believed the new Iraq war was a just cause or appropriate strategy.[24] Despite claims that the United States can and does fight ever more "smart" wars through more sophisticated technology, "accidents" continue through human error, "collateral damage" (civilian deaths) is simply deemed acceptable, and deadly weapons such as cluster bombs or depleted uranium among others continue killing and maiming civilians for decades to come. Many Americans seem to understand or care little about the way their government conducts diplomacy, wields power arrogantly, ignores international law, and how the United States adversely affects others. Or the reasons American actions create such enmity. Why is this so?

According to some scholars inaccurate and misleading American school textbooks have not offered fair or balanced analyses of the U.S. role in the world, which their fiercest (American) self-critics say largely reinforces "blind patriotism, mindless optimism, sheer information and outright lies."[25] Some research demonstrates many American students dislike history while teachers follow bad textbooks and avoid teaching controversial issues. A generation after the unpopular Vietnam War, many Americans have yet to come to terms with that history.[26] Marciano (chapter 6, in the present volume) suggests that the U.S. problem is "civic illiteracy." McAnnich (chapter 7) illustrates that conservative education values have dominated public policy debates on terrorism squashing academic dissent or critical thinking. So how will today's educators and students interpret and teach the Iraq war? New research among in schools, postsecondary institutions and professional associations is needed to evaluate classroom initiatives, resource materials, websites, reforms and debates. Some will no doubt emerge, reported in education journals. But much more systematic and collaborative study is needed to specifically address basic issues of American foreign policy, security, power and history, including scientific research or teaching dilemmas arising and American education aid that consolidates this power abroad.

On the other side, with respect to the alleged Arab and Islamic educational "problem" as the U.S. or conservative commentators characterize it, there is some legitimate concern. No one who understands the Middle East and Islamic or Arab worlds would deny that reforms, especially in the education sector, are needed. This was an important element in the analysis and recommendations of the first ever regional UNDP *Human Development Report* written largely by Arabs.[27] With respect to the new war, the Iraqi education system, textbooks and its own forms of police or military training reproduced allegiance to Saddam Hussein, but it was also more complex with competing nationalisms or tribal perspectives and different understandings of an Iraqi state. A culture of violence, hate and anti-Americanism (some for understandable reasons[28]) was also normalized through secular traditions, family socialization, religious education and textbooks.[29] Similar issues arose over Afghanistan and other conflict settings, and will be debated over postwar Iraq. But trends also need to be explained in the context of colonialism, economic globalization, and international or Arab relations, with major powers long interfering for their national interests. Chapter 11, in this volume, offers a timely case study putting some of these issues in perspective.

Beyond formal education and training systems in the Arab or Islamic world another factor emerged, not present during the first Gulf War of 1991. Then people learned about events from mostly Western television, particularly CNN. But since 1996 an Arab counterweight, the Qatar-based Al Jazeera network, has grown increasingly popular and after 9/11 was an important source of real-time news, information and debate for Arabs. It better depicted (than American networks) suffering of Palestinians, other Arabs and Muslims (often resulting from American and Israeli policies) while broadcasting interviews with Osama Bin Laden. The United States bombed Al Jazeera's Kabul station[30] to send a "message" about what news or information it would tolerate. One captured employee remains detained in America's prison for alleged terrorists, Guantánamo Bay.[31] The Americans made similar criticisms early in the 2003 Iraq war when it was first not going in its favor, then bombed both Baghdad offices of Al Jazeera and Abu Dhabi TV, and fired on journalists at the Palestine Hotel as well as marked Al Jazeera vehicles. Yet the Pentagon denied any wrongdoing.[32] The irony is that many Arab nations even before 9/11 saw Al Jazeera's novel open learning experience as a threat because it represents the same freedoms America claims it espouses. Aside from Pentagon military attacks on journalists and Arab media infrastructure America's new "public diplomacy" agenda after 9/11 has included a Voice of American style "Radio Sawa" in the region and "information warfare" to influence Arab or Islamic "hearts and minds." And in a de facto military coup of Iraqi airwaves, it launched a new British–American TV station broadcasting "liberation" messages from Bush and Blair.[33]

More research is needed to understand the educational reproduction of local violence, religious extremism, international terrorism and war through various means. But media literacy, encouraging critical analysis of corporate, ideological, national, historical, religious and cultural factors that gather, filter or project news through public diplomacy, is essential to a critical pedagogy for informed citizenship. Despite half-truths exploited by critics, Arab and Islamic education reform is also a complex issue needing careful study. American attacks simplify it often with racist, triumphialist, Judeo-Christian overtones, suggesting that the Arab world is not well enough "modernized." Many accusations (including serious scholarship) have been about the Arab and Islamic world as "medieval," or even simply "evil" but little has been done to deconstruct ethnocentric, religous, and political contexts of these assertions or connect debates to the development, security, ethnic studies, and anthropology literature to raise concerns or more nuanced and alternative views. Space does not permit a review of these debates here. But, even if there are relevant concerns, war is a poor development strategy. Iraq's postwar education reform challenges are also much more problematic due to America's desire to economically and administratively control the country as well as the region's future development. Invasions of other nations could also follow. New analyses are required concerning education for refugees, democratization, textbook reform, roles of aid organization delivery, Christian missionary groups as "crusaders" bringing the Cross after America's military sword,[34] and other issues for Iraq, the region and beyond.

TOWARD A NEW, ECOLOGICALLY SOUND CRITICAL PEDAGOGY

Beyond the Iraq crisis I close briefly reviewing five broad, overlapping, themes requiring closer analysis through a critical pedagogy lens. The first is the formal and informal education or learning systems (from schooling at all levels, to the sciences supporting military research, to the media, to information warfare, psychological operations and propaganda linked to foreign policy objectives) of the United States and other nations. All these have indirectly or strategically justified contentious wars and "counterterrorism" activities taught as heroic parts of American or world history.

There is no shortage of topics requiring more analysis, although one deserves particular attention. No doubt much international education work has had positive impact, but systematic critical or evaluations of American and other educational aid, foreign policy and intellectual cooperation are sorely lacking, especially in light of post-9/11 reforms.[35] Fulbright programs, secretary of state and other initiatives have promoted international educational and cultural cooperation with many useful activities. But they are undermined by a contradictory, pseudo-educational, indoctrinating, "public diplomacy" trend in American foreign policy. The stark realities of the "war on terrorism" (especially targeting Iraq) has also brought a serious backlash—including many suspended Fulbright linkages and denying other Americans research permits[36]—likely with long-term consequences. More work is needed to better understand and evaluate issues, impacts, trends and alternatives. Heidi Ross (chapter 3, in the present volume) offers a unique exploration of "relational thinking" among many other possible useful departures that might be explored in future research.

A second theme is how other peoples and countries—from major powers to the politically weakest smaller nation-states—are similarly militarized through their own education or training systems, partly to compete with the United States or serve as client-states, where privatization and globalization implicate reforms. There are few nations with clean hands in the global arms trade, but the United States is by far the biggest and dirtiest leader in production, training and export, followed by the United Kingdom, America's "closest ally" in the war on terrorism and the Iraq invasion.[37] In this respect critical pedagogy critiques must include more analyses of international production processes (and the intellectual or technical training required), globalization and military trade linkages that fuel wars and terrorism. Aid relationships, foreign student issues and collaborative research often complement these, while education over the past decade has been viewed more as a competitive commodity amidst American-led economic globalization. This means fewer resources and less time for ecologically and economically sustainable, local initiatives or for teaching subjects like social or international studies, the arts and doing human rights or peace research.

A third issue, is just how little work has gone toward understanding how terrorism or broader insecurity and violence may be partly a symptomatic reaction to related problems (from poverty and unemployment or forced labor to aggressive competition over scarce resources) associated with destructive environmental policies, or economic globalization, or military deployments that support these. Blunt, self-righteous remarks by influential commentators, however, suggest broader contexts and dubious American

motives for its expanded military occupation of the Middle East, with new
bases in Africa and elsewhere to diversify access and extend hegemony while
increasing alliances with non-democratic oil-rich regimes, to insure long-
term supply. Some market freedom or globalization advocates have virtually
equated Americanization with globalization, while the military is believed
to be the "hidden fist that keeps the world safe" for American economic
exploits.[38] Although many useful programs include civic education or
democratization efforts tempering adverse affects of globalization, education exports (or specifically politically charged aid such as in Iraq) often follow that military "fist," sustaining American economic and ideological
power through a neocolonial, free-market capitalism. More research is
needed to understand such linkages and impacts.

A fourth, more specific concern is the lack of ecological or social sustainability of the global oil-based economy as a mostly ignored educational
problem and learning challenge. The United States is the world leader in per
capita fossil fuel consumption negatively exacerbating climate change, and as
a matter of policy, rather than curbing oil use or strategically changing harmful behaviors or radically shifting its attitude or relationships to the world, it
has refused to cooperate on international treaties to reduce harmful emissions. Many of its political leaders and citizens seem ready to "defend the
American way of life" at all costs, regardless of how it adversely affects other
nations or peoples, or even their own personal health. Educational and scientific implications (including public awareness, research and training about
alternative energy) need more attention. More proactive initiatives including
appropriate financial incentives (instead of oil industry subsidies), might
better prevent terrorism through facilitating education and training for
ecologically sustainable development and human security.

This will be a major challenge. Sustaining unlimited and unfettered access
to oil, has increasingly been an American strategy while government-sponsored
international education programs have long viewed oil access among their
raison d'être. For example, the National Security Education Act of 1991 and
the National Security Education Program administered through the
National Defense University advocate continued American political, economic, corporate and military strength. Officials recently stated "the desire
of U.S. companies to exploit natural resources in the Caucasus and Central
Asia raises new challenges and policy dilemmas of how to reconcile economic opportunity with geopolitical strategy."[39] This was before 9/11.
Now oil partly explains American approaches to its "war on terrorism"[40] and
its recent invasion of Iraq. But similar issues arise in Latin America, Africa
and anywhere local elites, governments or paramilitaries and international
oil companies (backed by American or other governments) jointly protect
mutual interests.[41]

Oil and other resource disputes are "environmental security," problems
and remain part of the context for many new or emerging civil or international wars that jeopardize personal/human security.[42] Moreover, economic
and human resource development models underpinning the oil economy are

ecologically and socially unsustainable. Yet schools, colleges, universities and the media have poorly debated or challenged the dominant, business-led discourse (allied with government leaders they make campaign contributions to) that keeps fossil fuel industries empowered. More research is needed to document the evidence and understand both positive and problematic trends, including the role of university business administration or management programs and corporate-funded research centers.[43] But one can hypothesize that modern education and training systems (serving technical experts or professional managers in the oil industry, e.g.) may exacerbate global insecurity and increase the potential for disputes resulting in violence, including terrorism and war. "Critical Pedagogy theory and practice must better build on, and adapt to such challenges."[44]

A fifth (not necessarily final) concern is the poorly explored links between domestic and international violence. More work is needed to understand overlapping issues from youth bullying, to public beliefs in guns offering personal security, to military recruiting in schools, to problem-solving modeled through violence replicated in the American and other governments' chronic use of international military force. There is a substantial body of literature on domestic violence causes and prevention, including political economy, criminology, psychology, social work and community rehabilitation, some focused on youth and schools. Such work is important but barely covered here. Future studies might link disparate research or practice on environmental, multicultural, peace, antiracist, antibullying, civic and other specialized educations over the past few decades. That might help build a broader, stronger and more coherent human security vision. Future collaborative work among educators or practitioners in these specialties, as well as international scholars and security researchers might bear useful fruit.

CONCLUSION

No particular chapter or one book could thoroughly assess all these issues. Although some chapters in this volume have been particularly critical of the United States, further assessments of other nations (also with endemic militarism, ignorance of human security issues or in complicity to American demands) would be helpful. Some basic research (theoretical and empirical) has begun here to problematize and discuss significant trends, while documenting violent tendencies or linkages in domestic and international education policies or programs. This includes historical factors that led to these and current social, psychological, political, environmental or economic contexts that sustain or prevent violence. Some chapters examined theoretical or conceptual issues, teaching or foreign student issues, while others explore educational linkages to foreign policy and aid. Selected case studies examined some unique and particular implications for specific nation-states or regions. And still others discussed long-term curricular reform, research or policy implications, for both domestic and international settings.

This book has been about better understanding and responding creatively, nonviolently and nonmilitarily to terrorism and security concerns through education. It has sought to better understand concepts, policies and practices of critical pedagogy and human security leading to better mechanisms for violence prevention and more effective peace building, domestic and internationally. It is hoped the book will stimulate new reforms, research and pragmatic cooperation, especially through collaborative work among American and international scholars.[45]

NOTES

1. For one national case study of my own see Wayne Nelles, "Meeting Basic Needs, Embracing the World and Protecting the State: Integrating Human and Traditional Security in the New Mongolia," *Asian Perspective: A Journal of Regional and International Affairs*, Vol. 23, No. 3 (2001), pp. 207–45.

2. Peter Maass, "Dirty War: How America's Friends Really Fight Terrorism," *The New Republic* (November 11, 2002), pp. 18–21; and Human Rights Watch, "New Survey Documents Global Repression: U.S. Human Rights Leadership Faulted," *Human Rights News* (January 14, 2003), posted at: http://www.hrw.org/press/2003/01/wr2003.htm.

3. The notion of an American national security state is not new. It grew out of the Cold War while the Soviet Union provided a countercheck to American and NATO alliance power. For background see, Daniel Yergin, *Shattered Peace: The Origins of the Cold War and the National Security State* (Boston: Houghton Mifflin, 1977). What is new is that the United States is now the world's only superpower, which after 9/ll has bypassed most traditional Cold War alliance and collective security structures to act unilaterally.

4. Steve Giergerich, "American Students Abroad Advised to Pass Themselves Off as Canadians," *The Vancouver Sun/Canadian Press* (March 28, 2003), p. A5. For a story about a frightened American academic in Jordan telling a taxi driver he was a Canadian see, Michael Ignatieff, "Canada in the Age of Terror—Multilateralism Meets a Moment of Truth," *Policy Options*, Vol. 24, No. 2 (February 2003), pp. 14–18.

5. Munir Fasheh, "Talking About What to Cook for Dinner When our House is on Fire: the Poverty of Existing Forms of International Education," *Harvard Educational Review*, Vol. 55, No. 1 (February 1985), pp. 121–26.

6. Christopher Kruegler and Patricia Parkman "Identifying Alternatives to Political Violence: An Educational Imperative," *Harvard Educational Review*, Vol. 55, No. 1 (February 1985), pp. 109–17.

7. I argue we should extend our education research imperatives to address education–security–terrorism issues building on others who have already discussed globalization issues and implications of related social movements for education in particular. For general background see, Robert O'Brien, Anne Marie Goetz, Jan Aart Sholte and Marc Williams, *Contesting Global Governance: Multilateral Economic Institutions and Global Social Movements* (Cambridge: Cambridge University Press, 2000). On education (but not necessarily security) issues specifically see, e.g., Raymond A. Morrow and Carlos Alberto Torres, "The State, Social Movements and Educational Reform," in Robert F. Arnove and Carlos Alberto Torres, eds., *Comparative Education: The Dialectic of the Global and the*

Local (Lanham: Roman & Littlefield, 1999), pp. 91–113; and Douglas Kellner, "Globalization and New Social Movement: Lessons for Critical Theory and Pedagogy," in Nicolas C. Burbules and Carlos Alberto Torres, eds., *Globalization and Education: Critical Perspectives* (New York: Routledge, 2000), pp. 301–21.

8. The role of religion in American culture and education, affecting foreign policy and IR, is another important under-researched subject. President Bush's disdain for multilateralism, international agreements and the United Nations has been palpable, while he has couched the fight against terrorism in the language of a moral "crusade" and holy war to root out "evil" with millions of Americans sharing this language as a biblical belief and worldview. Bush is a conservative Christian who appointed senior officials of like mind building his foreign policy and international relations on that faith. For analyses before and after 9/11 see, Carter M. Yang, "Man of Faith: Religion Prominent in Bush Presidency," *ABCNews.com* (May 21, 2001); and Michael Lind, "Deep in the Heart of Darkness: Under George W. Bush, the Worse of two Texas Traditions is Shaping America," *The Washington Monthly*, Vol. 35, No. 1 (January/February 2003), pp. 22–27. These beliefs and values also adversely affect some of the world's most important, unresolved international security concerns such as the Israeli–Palestinian conflict. Note Donald Neff, "Special Report: In His Second Press Conference as President, Bush Sides With Israel, Defends Security Council Veto," *Washington Report on Middle East Affairs* (May–June 2001). On Conservative, militant Christian–Jewish alliances influences see Doug Saunders, "Evangelicals at Rally 'Zealous for Zion,'" *The Globe and Mail* (October 12, 2002), p. A18. The perception and reality of American support for Israel, has remained a source of regional instability, anti-Americanism and terrorism.

9. More work is needed to better evaluate implications in specific countries. But for some recent background in Afghanistan note Marc Kaufman, "U.S. Role Shifts as Afghanistan Founders," *The Washington Post* (April 14, 2003), p. A10. For poorly reported civilian casualties and broader implications of the American bombing campaign see Marc W Herold, "Dead Afghan Civilians: Disrobing the Non-Counters," (August 20, 2002), posted at http://www.cursor.org/stories/noncounters.htm. And (more positively) see Habib-u-Rahman Ibrahimi, "Schools Look to the Future *IWPR Afghan Recovery Report*, No. 56 (April 15, 2003) available at www.iwpr.net. For concerns about Pakistan see International Crisis Group, *Pakistan: Madrasas, Extremism and the Military*, ICG Asia Report # 36 (Islamabad/Brussels: International Crisis Group, July 29, 2002), posted at http:// www.intl-crisis-group.org.

10. For a summary of the case against an invasion see John M. Mearsheimer and Stephen M. Walt, "An Unnecessary War," *Foreign Policy* (January–February 2003), pp. 50–59.

11. Much reporting was through "embedded journalists," some networks offering gushing "support for the troops," stories of heroism, parades for returning POW's, brilliant success of the military campaign, the "evils" of the Hussein regime (with little of how the United States long supported it or made life more desperate for average Iraqis), "liberation" and concern for American casualties more than any others. At least three major issues deserve more detailed research treatment here. One is the orientation of mainstream American and other Western media to follow and identify with Americans and legitimize government policies or military actions. A second is lack of attention to alternative voices and perspectives.

A third is the "media literacy" needed to interpret and deconstruct bias. Among many sources with links to different stories or issues see, e.g., FAIR, "Iraq and the Media," *Fairness & Accuracy In Reporting*, posted at http://www.fair. org/international/iraq.html. The media also have tremendous power in shaping public "learning" about international affairs generally and pose a significant challenge for measuring "success" of the Iraq war through human security perspectives (e.g. www.iraqbodycount.net) as well as for how educators might learn and teach this war from a critical pedagogy perspective or more broadly as history.

12. James Schlesinger, "Now It's Political Shock and Awe," *The Wall Street Journal*, (April 17, 2003), p. A12; and David E. Sanger, "Viewing the War as a Lesson to the World," *The New York Times* (April 6, 2003).

13. Having spent some of my early career doing anthropology and working as a professional archaeologist (M.A. 1984) I take personal umbrage to Rumsfeld's comments and the maliciously incompetent neglect of the American administration. On the catastrophe see Rajiv Chandrasekaran, "'Our Heritage Is Finished': Looters Destroyed What War Did Not," *The Washington Post* (April 13, 2003), p. A01; Guy Gugliotta, "Pentagon Was Told of Risk to Museums: U.S. Urged to Save Iraq's Historic Artifacts," *The Washington Post* (April 14, 2003), p. A19; and Charles J. Hanley "Looters Erase Iraq's Intellectual Legacy," and *Associated Press* and "Looters Ransack Iraq's National Library," *The New York Times* (April 15, 2003).

14. Eric Gibson, "Steal This Vase? Iraqis Get Some of Their Own Back," *The Wall Street Journal* (April 18, 2003), p. W13. There was not even an apology from the administration. See Reuters, "Rumsfeld Denies U.S. Blame for Iraq Museum Plunder," *Reuters* (April 15, 2003). The United States and United Kingdom could both be spared war crimes prosecution since neither has signed the 1954 *Convention for the Protection of Cultural Property in the Event of Armed Conflict*. Some critics, however, still argue they were obligated. Beyond this specific tragedy, a group of 317 American law professors from 87 law schools before the war also issued a statement on its illegality in American and international law (posted at: www.the-rule-of-law.com/index.html). Elsewhere, former attorney-general, Ramsey Clark, has led a bid to impeach President Bush and his administration for war crimes and violating the Constitution in not adhering to international treaties (including the UN Charter) the United States signed. For draft articles see www.VotetoImpeach.org. This issue would be a useful case study for educators teaching civics, social studies, history and IR.

15. George Bush, "President's Remarks at the United Nations, General Assembly," *White House, Office of the Press Secretary* (September 12, 2002).

16. Since the United States left UNESCO in 1984 it has consistently undermined most of what it stood for. More recently, even amidst its pledge to rejoin in 2003, there were already that indications that the United States was attempting to scuttle a new Universal Declaration on Cultural Diversity led by UNESCO. I discuss related issues in Wayne Nelles, "American Public Diplomacy as Pseudo-Education: A Problematic National Security and Counter-terrorism Instrument," *International Politics: A Journal of Transnational Issues and Global Problems*, (In Press/forth coming).

17. USAID, *Request for Proposals (RFP) M/OP-03-EDU2 Revitalization of Iraqi Schools and Stabilization of Education (Rise)*, Issue Date: (March 4, 2003), posted at http://www. usaid.gov/iraq/pdf/web_education.pdf; David B. Ottaway and Joe Stephens, "In Bid to Shape a Postwar Iraq, U.S. Goes by the Schoolbook,"

The Washington Post (April 6, 2003), p. A32; and USAID, "USAID Awards Contract to Revitalize Education in Iraq," *The United States Agency for International Development, Press Release* (April 17, 2003), posted at http://www. usaid.gov/press/releases/2003/pr030411_2.html.

18. Thom Shanker and Eric Schmitt, "Pentagon Expects Long-Term Access to Four Key Bases in Iraq," *The New York Times* (April 20, 2003).

19. For broader context see Naomi Klein, "Privatization in Disguise," *The Nation* (April 28, 2003) posted at www.thenation.com.

20. Bob Davis and Mirela Vlad, "University Leader will Oversee Iraq's Finances," *The Wall Street Journal* (April 18, 2003), p. A3.

21. For related discussion see Peter Ackerman and Jack DuVall, "With Weapons of the Will: How 22 million Iraqis can Overturn Saddam and Bring Democracy to Iraq," *Sojourners Magazine* (September–October 2002), pp. 21–23; Lloyd Axworthy, "On Terrorism and Iraq: The Human Security Solution," *Peace Magazine*, Vol. 18, No. 4 (October–December 2002), pp. 14–15; Raid Fahmi, "Regime Change in Iraq through Non-military Intervention," and Metta Spencer, "Ushering Democracy into Iraq Nonviolently," *Peace Magazine*, Vol. 19, No. 1 (January–March 2003), pp. 7–13.

22. Norms have been discussed, e.g. in OECD, Development Assistance Committee, "Conflict, Peace and Development Cooperation on the Threshold of the 21st Century" (Paris: OECD, 1997), p. 1. The OECD also recently issued an updated, full length report: OECD, Development Assistance Committee, *The DAC Guidelines: Helping Prevent Violent Conflict* (Paris: OECD, 2001). For a sampling of literature that continues to grow, also see, e.g., Michael Lund, *Preventing Violent Conflicts: A Strategy for Preventive Diplomacy* (Washington: United States Institute of Peace Press, 1996); and David Hamburg, Chair, *Preventing Deadly Conflict: Final Report* (New York: Carnegie Commission on Preventing Deadly Conflict, Carnegie Corporation of New York, 1997), posted at www.ccpdc.org.

23. Evidence of early American–Iraqi connections and ongoing American atrocities are now available public knowledge, even the subject of recent television documentaries, while alternative press has begun investigating Donald Rumsfeld and the Reagan administration. On Canadian public television see *The Fifth Estate* program, "The Forgotten People," discussing the American–Iraqi relations and use of chemical weapons against the Kurds with details posted at http://www. cbc.ca/fifth/kurds/index.html, especially the section "A Convenient Alliance," on American–Iraqi history at http://www.cbc.ca/fifth/kurds/alliance.html. On American public television see *Frontline* and "The Long Road to War," with a handy chronology giving broader context at http://www.pbs.org/wgbh/pages/frontline/shows/longroad/etc/cron.html. In the alternative press see James Ridgeway, "Rumsfeld's Dealings with Saddam: Were Trips to Iraq Meant to Secure Pipeline Deal?" *The Village Voice* (March 28, 2003), on-line at http://www.villagevoice.com/issues/0314/ridgewar3.php. For early commentary see Kenneth R. Timmerman, *The Death Lobby: How the West Armed Iraq* (Boston: Houghton Mifflin Company, 1991). Aside from many scholarly works not discussed here there are other easily accessible and sources through Internet search.

24. For a snapshot as the war began see Marjorie Connelly, "Most Americans Support Iraq Action, Poll Finds," *The New York Times* (March 21, 2003). This suggested that 65% supported the war while 35% believed arms inspections should have had more time. Another indicated 70% supported the president's

handling of the Iraq crisis, but among politicians 93% of Republicans and 50% Democrats. See Adam Nagourney and Janet Elder, "Support for Bush Surges at Home, but Split Remains, Poll Shows" *The New York Times* (March 21, 2003).

25. A conclusion based on a survey of 12 textbooks commonly used in American schools. The quote was from the back cover of James W. Loewen, *Lies My Teacher Told Me: Everything Your American History Book Got Wrong* (New York: Touchstone, 1995).

26. James W. Loewen, "The Vietnam War in High School History," and David Hunt, "War Crimes and the Vietnamese People," in Laura Hein and Mark Selden, eds., *Censoring History: Citizenship and Memory in Japan, Germany and the United States* (Armonk, NY: M. E. Sharpe, 2000), pp. 150–72; 173–200.

27. UNDP, *Arab Human Development Report 2002* (New York: UNDP, Regional Bureau for Arab States, 2002). I have also touched on related issues in my own chapter (chapter 2) noting education debates and reform issues concerning Saudi Arabia, Afghanistan and Pakistan.

28. An estimated 500,000 Iraqi children alone died through the American imposed and insidiously manipulated UN sanctions regime by prohibiting badly needed medicines, heath equipment, water purification systems, etc. Former secretary of state, Madeline Albright, has been widely reported as saying child deaths arising from these problems were "worth it." Yet their plight did little to weaken Saddam Hussein, only making the average Iraqi suffering greater and (beyond regime propaganda) many know the United States had a significant role. Thousands had direct personal experiences with maiming, killing or health defects from depleted uranium and munitions left from the first Gulf War and errant American bombs in "no-fly zones" over a decade. For a critique of sanctions see Joy Gordon, "Cool War: Economic sanctions as a Weapon of Mass Destruction," *Harpers Magazine* (November 2002), pp. 43–49. For a field assessment and analytical report on the adverse effects of sanctions on Iraqi children, and lack of a coherent development framework for schooling, health and social services before the 2003 war, see UNICEF, "Iraq Situation Analysis" (February 2002), posted at http://www.unicef.org/media/publications/iraqsitan2002index.htm. For a suggestive table on child death rates before and after the 1991 Gulf War see UNICEF, "Child mortality Iraq," posted at http://www.childinfo.org/cmr/cmrirq.html.

29. On challenges for U.S.-led democratization in textbooks see Phebe Marr, "Civics 101, Taught by Saddam Hussein," *The New York Times* (April 20, 2003).

30. BBC News. "US Urges Curb on Arab TV channel," *BBC News*, (October 4, 2001), posted at http://news.bbc.co.uk/1/hi/world/americas/1578619.stm; and Matt Wells, "Al-Jazeera Accuses US of Bombing its Kabul Office Targeting of Building Denied by Pentagon," *The Guardian* (November 17, 2001).

31. CBC News, "Al-Jazeera Junkies," *The Current, Canadian Broadcasting Corporation Radio* (March 12, 2003).

32. Reporters san frontiers, "Bombing of Journalists 'May be War Crime' Report," *Reporters san frontiers* (April 10, 2003), posted at http://electroniciraq.net/news/617.shtml.

33. Ciar Byrne, "Blair Launches New Iraqi TV," *The Guardian* (April 10, 2003).

34. This is another extremely problematic, and poorly researched international and religious "education" issue. Aside from humanitarian aid many Christians bring "learning" resource materials from pamphlets to "Jesus videos" to convert

Muslims while offering material aid. This raises the credibility of accusations from the Osama Bin Ladens of the world, exacerbates a "clash of civilizations" and encourages more terrorism. For recent developments and controversy see Jan Cienski, "Evangelical Christians Ready to Aid, Invade Iraq," *The Vancouver Sun* (April 17, 2003), p. A6; Mark O'Keefe, "Mixing Iraq Aid and the Gospel Stirs Debate," *Christianity Today*, (April 4, 2003), posted at http://www.christianitytoday.com/ct/2003/113/52.0.html; and Editorial, "Evangelize Elsewhere," *The Washington Post* (April 15, 2003), p. A24. On broader trends and similar issues raised over Afghanistan see Barry Yeoman, "The Stealth Crusade," *Mother Jones* (June 2002), pp. 43–49.

35. For some general studies from the early Cold War era see Phillip Coombs, *The Fourth Dimension of Foreign Policy: Educational and Cultural Affairs* (New York: Harper and Row, 1964); and Howard Wilson "Education, Foreign Policy, and International Relations," in Robert Blum, ed., *Cultural Affairs and Foreign Relations* (Englewood Cliffs: Prentice Hall, 1963), pp. 80–111. For later commentary see Beverly Lindsay, "Integrating International Education and Public Diplomacy: Creative Partnerships or Indigenous Propaganda," in *Comparative Education Review*, Vol. 33, No. 4 (November 1989), pp. 423–36. For my own recent critique see Wayne Nelles, "UNESCO Reflections on Educational Aid, Rights and Development: A Review Essay," *Canadian Journal of Development Studies*, Vol. 23, No. 2 (2002), pp. 368–72. Mark Johnson (chapter 14, in the present volume) also begins to assess post-9/11 activities.

36. Sam Dillon, "Islamic World Less Welcoming to American Scholars," *The New York Times* (April 18, 2003), p. B10.

37. The United States ranks first among global suppliers with the United Kingdom next highest at just one-third of U.S. trade. France, which was actually the principal opponent of the American-led Iraq war, and which had also early dealings with Saddam Hussein, is the world's third largest arms trader. See Gideon Burrows, *The No-Nonsense Guide to the Arms Trade* (Toronto: New Internationalist Publications, 2002), p. 68.

38. Thomas L. Friedman, *The Lexus and the Olive Tree* (New York: Anchor Books, 2000), p. 464.

39. National Defense University, *NESP News*, Vol. 2, No. 2 (October 2000), posted at http://www.ndu.edu/nsep/NSEPnews/nsep10001.htm.

40. Jean-Charles Brisard and Guillanne Dasquie, *Forbidden Truth, U.S.-Taliban Secret Oil Diplomacy and the Failed Hunt for Bin Laden* (New York: Thunder's Mouth Press, 2002).

41. For example, note the more explicit deployment of American troops to protect the economic interests of the U.S. multinational company, Occidental Petroleum, working with the Columbian government to prevent "terrorism" that targets oil pipelines. See T. Christian Miller, "Chaos in Colombia: Blood Spills to Keep Oil Wealth Flowing" *The Los Angeles Times* (September 15, 2002).

42. Michael T. Klare, *Resource Wars: The New Landscape for Global Conflict* (New York: Henry Holt and Company, 2002), paperback edition with December 2001 Introduction; and Thomas F. Homer-Dixon, *Environment, Scarcity, and Violence* (Princeton: Princeton University Press, 1999).

43. Some of my own research has examined the challenges and policy implications of Canadian youth training and internship programs aimed at furthering careers in ecologically sustainable development. But analyses are also needed for other countries and regions. See Wayne Nelles, "Globalization, Sustainable

Development and Canada's International Internship Initiative" in *Special Issue—Labour and Employment under Globalization—Canadian Journal of Development Studies*, Vol. 20 (1999), pp. 800–28. For a broader, historical and international perspective on ecological sustainability concerns for human resource development and training also see Wayne Nelles, "Consequences of Market Change for Human Development and Global Life Support Systems," in *UNESCO Encyclopedia of Life Support Systems* (Oxford, UK: EOLSS Publishers, Inc., 2002), forthcoming as contribution 1.10.5.1 at www.eolss.net.

44. This is a complex issue hardly addressed in critical pedogogy literature but for a useful entry point for discussion see, e.g., C. A. Bowers, "Can Critical Pedegogy be Greened," *Educational Studies: A Journal of the American Educational Studies Association*, Vol. 34, No. 1 (Spring 2003), pp. 11–21.

45. Anticipating critics, much could not be covered given space limitations. Nonetheless this book has sampled some critical, policy-oriented and forward-looking scholarship. Graduate students and others might take up new topics for more in-depth study. Subject to discussion with the publisher, future volumes might further explore theoretical, national, regional or comparative case studies on education, terrorism, violence and security issues. Scholars or practitioners interested in offering thematic suggestions for future books or submitting a related chapter should contact me by-Email <wnelles@sdri.ubc.ca> through the Sustainable Development Research Initiative (SDRI) at the University of British Columbia (UBC).

INDEX